Helen Nicholson is Reader in History at Cardiff University. She has published extensively on the Templars and the other Military Orders.

THE KNIGHTS TEMPLAR

A Brief History of the Warrior Order

Helen Nicholson

RUNNING PRESS
PHILADELPHIA · LONDON

Constable & Robinson Ltd
3 The Lanchesters
162 Fulham Palace Road
London W6 9ER
www.constablerobinson.com

First published in the UK as *The Knights Templar*
by Sutton Publishing Limited in 2001.
This updated edition published by Robinson,
an imprint of Constable & Robinson Ltd, 2010

A copy of the British Library Cataloguing in
Publication data is available from the British Library

UK ISBN 978-1-84901-100-6

1 3 5 7 9 10 8 6 4 2

First published in the United States in 2010 by Running Press Book Publishers

US Library of Congress Control Number: 2009935108
US ISBN 978-0-7624-3848-8

Running Press Book Publishers
2300 Chestnut Street
Philadelphia, PA 19103-4371

Visit us on the web!
www.runningpress.com

Printed and bound in the EU

CONTENTS

LIST OF PLATES

The Holy Land
1. The Church of the Holy Sepulchre in Jerusalem.
2. The interior of the Aqsa mosque ('Temple of Solomon').
3. Baghras Castle.
4. Ruad (Arwad) island.
5. The Templars in battle against the Muslims: mid-twelfth-century fresco from the Templars' former church at Cressac-Saint-Génis, Poitou-Charente, France.

The Iberian Peninsula
6. The Templars' castle of Pombal, Portugal.
7. The Templars' castle of Miravet, Tarragona, in the kingdom of Aragon.
8. The Templars' castle of Monzón, Huesca, in the kingdom of Aragon.
9. The Templars' castle of Peñíscola, Valencia, in the kingdom of Aragon.

Templar images and imagery
10. Templars in battle, showing the Order's banner; from the fresco in the Order's church of San Bevignate, Perugia.
11. Matthew Paris's sketch of the Templars' seal with the banner, from his *Historia Anglorum*.
12. Two Templar knights playing chess; from a manuscript of Alfonso X of Castile's *Libro de Ajedrez, dados y tables*.
13. A group of Templar knights on the tomb of the infante Don Felipe in the Templar church of Santa María la Blanca de Villasirga, at Villalcázar de Sirga (Palencia, Castile, Spain).

Religious life

Economic activities

After the Templars

LIST OF FIGURES

A key to the symbols used on the maps appears on figure 6.

LIST OF ABBREVIATIONS

AOL	*Archives de l'Orient Latin*, publiés sous le patronage de la Société de l'orient latin, 2 vols (Paris, 1881–4)
BEFAR	Bibliothèque des écoles françaises d'Athènes et de Rome
BLVS	Bibliothek des litterarischen Vereins in Stuttgart
CDRI	*Calendar of Documents Relating to Ireland, preserved in Her Majesty's Public Record Office, London*, ed. H. S. Sweetman, 5 vols (London: HMSO, 1875–86)
CH	*Cartulaire général de l'Ordre des Hospitaliers de Saint-Jean de Jérusalem, 1100–1310*, ed. Joseph Delaville le Roulx, 4 vols (Paris, 1894–1906)
CT	*Cartulaire général de l'Ordre du Temple 1119?–1150. Recueil des chartes et des bulles relatives . . . l'ordre du Temple*, ed. le marquis d'Albon (Paris: Librairie ancienne Honoré Champion, 1913)
'Eracles'	'L'Estoire de Eracles Empereur et la Conqueste de la Terre d'Outremer', in *RHC Occidentaux*, vol. 1.2 (Paris: Imprimerie royale, 1859)
MGH	*Monumenta Germaniae Historica*, ed. G. H. Pertz *et al.* (Hanover, Weimar, Stuttgart and Cologne, 19265ff.)
MGH SS	*Monumenta Germaniae Historica Scriptores*, ed.

24 vols (Paris: Imprimerie royale, 1878)

ROL *Revue de l'Orient Latin*, 12 vols (Paris, 1893–1911; repr. Brussels: Culture et Civilisation, 1964)

RRH *Regesta Regni Hierosolymitani* and *Additamentum*, ed. Reinhold Röhricht (Innsbruck, 1893–1904; repr. New York: B. Franklin, 1960)

RS Rolls Series

Règle *La Règle du Temple*, ed. H. de Curzon (Paris: Librairie Renouard, 1886)

SATF Société des anciens textes français

SHF Société de l'histoire de France

WT Guillaume de Tyr, *Chronique*, ed. R. B. C. Huygens, Corpus Christianorum, Continuatio Mediaevalis, 63, 63A (Turnholt: Brepols, 1986)

PREFACE

This is a revised edition of my book *The Knights Templar: A New History*, which was first published in 2001 as a 'book on the Templars for a general audience'. It is based upon a final-year undergraduate course on the Military Orders that I teach in the School of History and Archaeology at Cardiff University, and on my own current research. My own views have been amended over the years of teaching by input from my students. There have been too many to name them all, but I thank them.

I began work on this new edition in 2009, while I was completing my new edition of the documents recording the trial of the Templars in the British Isles, 1308–11. My research into these documents was carried out with the assistance of a British Academy/Leverhulme Trust Senior Research Fellowship in 2003–4, and some of the results are included in this book.

I am grateful to the help of many other colleagues who generously contributed to the original book. For this new edition, I repeat my thanks to my 'crusading' colleagues at Cardiff University, Professors Peter Edbury and Denys Pringle. For the original book, Professor Alain Demurger of the University of the Sorbonne, Paris, Dr Edward Coleman of University College, Dublin, Prof. Luis García-Guijarro Ramos of the University of Zaragoza, Huesca, Dr Anthony Luttrell, now retired, Zsolt Hunyadi of the Central European University, Budapest, and Dr Vít Jesenský of Prague also supplied me with essential advice and contacts. Dr Alan Forey, now retired, Dr Jochen Burgtorf, now at California State University, Fullerton, Dr Simonetta Cerrini of Genoa and Dr Paul Crawford of the California University of Pennsylvania patiently answered detailed questions on particular points. Other colleagues at Cardiff also gave advice and information.

I am again indebted to Professor Denys Pringle for allowing me to reproduce some of his photographs and slides in this book, and to John Morgan of the Cardiff School of History and Archaeology, who reproduced some of the photographs. I owe particular thanks to other scholars who have generously supplied me with pictures and/or allowed me to reproduce them here: Professor Juan Fuguet Sans; Dr Jochen Burgtorf; Dr Paul Crawford; Dr Francesco Tommasi and Dr Judi Upton-Ward.

I most grateful to the following institutions which have provided me with pictures and allowed me to reproduce them here: the British Library, London, the Patrimonio Nacional, Madrid and the Staatsarchiv Amberg.

In 1999 the Academic Study Group on Israel and the Middle East gave me a grant towards travel costs of a visit to Israel during which I was able to meet fellow crusade historians and visit crusader sites, which contributed significantly towards the writing of the original edition of this book. My husband Nigel Nicholson drew the original maps and figures, and took many of the photographs.

I have incurred many other debts to scholars working in the field of crusading history and the history of the Military Orders. These are too many to list here, but I should mention the guidance and support of Professor Norman Housley,

Leicester University, who supervised my PhD thesis (1986–90) on attitudes towards the Military Orders in the twelfth and thirteenth centuries. My thanks are also particularly due to Professor Malcolm Barber for advice and support over the years. The Society for the Study of the Crusades and the Latin East has provided a goldmine of information. I am particularly grateful to Jochen Burgtorf and Paul Crawford who worked with me in 2007 to organize sessions at two international conferences on 'the Trial of the Templars, 1307–2007', and to all the scholars who took part in those sessions. Their influence will be clear in the chapter in this book on the trial of the Templars. The quadrennial international conferences on the Military Orders at Clerkenwell, organized by the London Centre for the Study of the Crusades under the auspices of Professor Jonathan Riley-Smith, have also been an invaluable opportunity for meeting fellow scholars in this area and for exchanging information and ideas. At the time of writing, four conferences have taken place and their proceedings have been published; the next conference takes place in September 2009 at Cardiff University.

Since the publication of the first edition of this book in 2001, I have met and talked with many scholars of the Military Orders from around the world, and many enthusiastic amateur historians on the subject. This new edition of this book reflects some of this discussion. The quantity of scholarship on the historical Military Orders has grown immensely since the first edition of this book appeared in 2001, and I cannot claim that this new edition fully reflects all the developments since that date. I have, however, taken the opportunity to expand the references to this book, so that readers who wish to do so can find a way into this new scholarship.

As in the first edition of this book, all translations, unless otherwise stated in the text, are my own, and should not be used elsewhere for any purpose without acknowledgement. Because this book is primarily intended for a general readership I have not referenced every sentence, but there is a reference at

the end of each paragraph or section, which readers who want
to know where I have found information can check.

Helen J. Nicholson
June 2009

INTRODUCTION: AN OVERVIEW

This account of the Templars is based on what the surviving historical evidence tells us about the Order of the Temple and what professional historians have deduced about the Order from this evidence. This means that it also includes myths about the Templars that were written during the existence of the Order – during the twelfth, thirteenth and early fourteenth centuries – but not the modern myths about the Order. It has been a convention of European historical writing since classical times that history should be based on written sources, preferably eyewitness sources but, if not, then written as soon after the actual events as possible. This history of the Knights Templar follows this ancient convention, and so modern oral myths of the Templars – supposed 'tradition' which was not actually written down until recently – will not be considered as historical evidence.

This brief history of the Knights Templar is based on recent academic work on the Order of the Temple, both my own research and the work of other professional scholars who study the history of the Order. Not only are modern scholars finding new evidence about the Templars, such as charters in archives and archaeological material, but they are also reassessing old evidence such as chronicles and other writings, asking new questions and coming to new conclusions. I have tried to include the latest findings and theories so far as I can, and I apologise to colleagues if I have overlooked anything significant. I have given extensive references in the notes, so that readers can see where I have found my material. Unlike most histories of the Templars, this is not a chronological account. It gives an outline history of the Order, but my intention is to analyse events rather than simply retelling them in the order that they happened. A narrative history of the Templars is misleading because it implies that the Templars rose and then declined, that criticism increased steadily, and that events that happened first caused events which happened later. In fact the Order did not rise and decline, criticism fell abruptly after 1250, and events which happened later often had no connection with events that happened earlier!

It has been said that the Templars were nothing special, and that in most respects they were really very ordinary.[1] This is true, but this is one of the facts which makes the Templars very interesting. We know very little about ordinary people of the twelfth, thirteenth and early fourteenth centuries. Most of the Brothers of the Order of the Temple came either from the lower ranks of knights or were not of knightly descent at all; many were craftsmen, or people who performed ordinary agricultural tasks such as herding sheep and cattle. People of these social groups left very few records, but through the surviving evidence from the Templars we can catch some glimpses of their beliefs, what mattered to them, and their everyday lives. We find people who did not travel far to join a religious house; who stayed in the same area all their lives, near to their families.[2] They were loyal to their families, to their old lords and to their king, even when they had joined the Order of the Temple and were supposed to have left all their old ties behind them. These were devout people, with an simple faith based on Christ as king (with God the Father the omnipotent ruler in the background) and Christ's mother and bride, the Blessed Virgin

Mary, as patroness and lady of the Order who protected it as a medieval queen would protect her favourite religious Orders and knights. Their dearest desire was to lay down their lives on the battlefield in the war against evil, defending Christendom against its enemies, in the service of their divine king and queen, and so to win the reward of eternal life in Heaven, wearing the martyr's crown. As I will describe in Chapter 5, 'Religious Life', for the most part the Templars were not educated; the knights and squires could read their own language, but not Latin. In England suitable religious texts and a part of the Old Testament were translated into colloquial French (the language of the warrior classes) so that the Templars could understand when these texts were read to them – reading aloud was normal at this period, so they probably listened rather than reading for themselves. In other parts of the Order education was discouraged: the Brothers were supposed to be serving God and His Lady in battle, not as scholars! We may guess that this distrust of book learning was one of the factors that helped bring about the Order's downfall.

Away from the frontiers, the Order in Europe concentrated on raising money for the war against the Muslims, so much that contemporaries saw the Templars as more concerned about money than anything else. The Templars had no interest in women, these contemporaries said: money was their only love. Nowadays it is easy to sympathize with the Templars and see them as the persecuted underdogs, the pure idealists who were destroyed by an autocratic government for its own self-interested ends. But in the early fourteenth century the Templars in Europe were not regarded as outsiders but were at the centre of the establishment. They were best known in everyday life for their financial activities: looking after the treasure of the crowns of Europe, and financial services for nobles, knights, merchants and squires. As finance managers they were respected, but they also aroused some anger when they made mistakes. If we think of the Templars as bank managers and bank clerks we probably get a far better idea of how people in cities such as London and Paris in the early fourteenth century would have regarded the Templars. I will consider their role in economics and commerce further in Chapter 7.

It is difficult to study the Templars without always having at the back of one's mind the eventual fate of the Brothers: arrested on trumped-up charges, some burned at the stake for going back on the confessions which they had made under pressure of interrogation, including torture; others serving out the rest of their days in other monastic houses, their original vocation as knights of Christ lost to them; still others returning to secular life, and the Order's possessions given to its rival Order, the Hospital of St John. Thirty-odd years later, Pope Clement VI was complaining that the Hospital had done so little good in the war against the Muslims with the Templars' lands that he would take them back and use them to form a new Military Order – as had already been done in Valencia and Portugal. The Hospital's lack of grand achievement was not its own fault: it was still recovering from the financial crisis resulting from the expenses of its conquest of Rhodes (1306–9), reimbursing King Philip IV of France for his 'expenses' in arresting and trying the Templars, and the legal costs of trying to recover the Templars' lands, many of which had been taken back by the families of the original donors or confiscated by secular rulers. The Hospital survived, but it was a close thing. In 1312 it did not have public opinion in its favour; but Pope Clement V wanted to maintain it to carry on the defence of Christendom against the Muslims, and its wily Master Fulk de Villaret managed the Order's affairs with sufficient skill to give the King of France little opportunity of attacking the Order as he had the Templars.[3]

Yet for almost two hundred years before the arrests of 1307 the Order of the Temple had operated in the Holy Land and throughout Europe as a respected religious Order. The shock and indignation with which most secular rulers outside France greeted the papal instruction to arrest the Templars at the end of 1307 indicates that the arrest of the Order came as a complete surprise to almost everyone. Until 1307, the Templars were a familiar and accepted part of Latin Christendom, with their small houses and commanderies with little chapels and big barns scattered across Europe, and fine castles in dangerous frontier areas: frontiers with the Muslims in the Holy Land and Spain, frontiers with non-Catholic Christians and non-Christians in Poland, Bohemia and Croatia, and also with fortified houses and castles in areas where there was no strong central authority to ensure law and order, such as southern France and Ireland. Their knights, with their beards and in their long dark tunics and white mantles, with the red cross on the left side, and a dark cap on their heads, were a familiar sight in every royal court in Catholic Europe and the crusader states in the Holy Land (or the 'Latin East'). Their sergeants or serving Brothers, far more common than the knights and dressed all in black, were often confused with the Brothers of the Hospital of St John, who also wore black but with a white cross on the mantle rather than the Templars' red cross. In Germany and the East from the end of the twelfth century the Templar knight-Brothers were confused with the Teutonic Order, whose knight-Brothers wore a black tunic with a white mantle and a black cross. If in doubt, contemporaries referred to all these groups as 'Templars'.

The Templars, one satirist joked, were too fond of money – unlike the Hospitallers, who were too fond of horses – but they were doughty men who were all too ready to die in Christ's name on the battlefield. In time of defeat in the East, some such as Matthew Paris, monk and chronicler of St Albans abbey, would complain that the Templars and Hospitallers must be deceiving Christendom, because such fine warriors would otherwise have defeated the Muslims long ago. Clearly they weren't trying; they must be in alliance with the Muslims; all the money which the West sent to them must be going to waste – perhaps they simply poured it into the ground![4] Such comments show how little even educated people in western

Europe appreciated the political realities of the Latin East, even though the Christian rulers of the crusader states and the Military Orders in the East went to enormous lengths to keep kings, nobles and Church leaders informed of developments through the regular despatch of newsletters. Yet at a day-to-day level in Catholic Europe and in the Holy Land, the Templars were well-respected religious men, landowners, bankers, farmers, traders, sheep farmers and so on. We can best understand them if we remember this and evaluate the Order on the basis of the whole of its history and not simply the last five disastrous years.

There are many popularly believed myths about the Order of the Temple. The first is that there is very little evidence surviving about the Order. In fact a great deal of evidence survives. It is true that the central archive of the Order is lost: this was originally held at the Order's headquarters, at first in Jerusalem, then at Acre, then (after 1291) on Cyprus. After the dissolution of the Order by Pope Clement V in 1312 the archive passed into the possession of the Hospital of St John. Presumably it remained on Cyprus and was destroyed when the Ottoman Turks captured Cyprus in 1571, along with the Hospital's documents relating to Cyprus. This archive would have held all the Templars' charters granting them land and privileges in the crusader states and in Cyprus, and general papal privileges, the proceedings of their general chapters and some of the more important correspondence and donation charters from Europe – much of this sort of material for the Hospital of St John during the twelfth to early fourteenth centuries is still in the Hospital's archive in the National Library of Malta. The loss of the Templars' central archive means that we do not know exactly what property and privileges the Templars held in the crusader states and in Cyprus. However, anything that concerned both them and the Hospital is preserved in the Hospital's archives, while papal bulls for the Templars are preserved in the papal registers in the Vatican. In other words, the loss of the central archive has meant the loss of certain valuable documents, but not all of them.

For the Order's European possessions, much remains in archives and museums across Europe. *Charters* relating to the Order's English possessions, for example, are preserved in the Hospital's cartulary in the British Library. The cartulary of the commandery of Sandford survives and has been published. Other charters relating to the Order in England survive in other monastic cartularies. Documents issued by the English royal chancery relating to the Templars after around 1200 are preserved in the registers in the Public Record Office, and many have been published, for the most part in calendar form. The English *government records* are particularly well preserved, but there is also a good deal of documentation surviving in the Iberian Peninsula, for example in the archives in Madrid and Barcelona. Many of the French government records for this period were destroyed in the eighteenth century, but royal letters and charters and some financial records have survived. In addition much material survives in French local archives; many cartularies of individual French commanderies have been published.

Yet charters cannot tell us everything we want to know about the Templars. They show us patterns of patronage: who gave what to the Order, how patrons were related to each other and sometimes what they expected in return. They seldom give much indication of why patrons gave to the Templars, except that they regarded the Order as being of high spiritual value, and believed the Brothers' prayers on their behalf were worth having. Occasionally a donor's charter refers to the Templars' defence of Christendom, but this is unusual. Charters tell us what land and rights the Order had in a particular area, although we do not always know whether they were actually able to use that land or those rights or whether someone else had a claim on them. These are problems historians face in studying all religious Orders in the Middle Ages. Charters also usually include witness lists, which tell us (among other things) who was living in the Templars' commandery at that time and their order of precedence, as the most important usually comes first in the list. It may tell us if they held any office. But charters are not always dated, although they usually tell us where they were written. In short, charters give us some evidence, but not all we want to know.

Other evidence of the Order's actual activities comes from *chronicles*. Those written in the twelfth to fourteenth centuries recorded recent events and provided a commentary on them. They vary in quality. Chroniclers tended to moralize on the terrible state of the world, and had a rather pessimistic view of the situation in the Holy Land and the Military Orders' activities. *Annals* gave a year-by-year account of events, but with little commentary. From the twelfth century we also have *histories*, which differ from the chronicle in that they focus on one event (such as a crusade) or one theme (such as William of Tyre's history of the kingdom of Jerusalem). These can be contemporary or near-contemporary. Their joy and their difficulty is that they give a very personal view. The writer always had a message, and all evidence was interpreted to underline this message.

None of these sources are 'objective' in the modern sense of the word, nor were they intended to be. Their accuracy in recording actual events depended on the quality of their sources: whether they were eyewitness or relying on information from other people. Chapter 2 will show that William of Tyre is an unreliable witness for the activities of the Military Orders in the period before 1165. As he was at university in Europe from around 1146–65, his information for the siege of Ascalon (1153) must have been taken from second-hand information given to him by people who wanted to exonerate their ancestors for failing to assist the Templars when they broke into the city. William was writing around twenty years or more after events at Ascalon; if we use contemporary European sources for the siege, we receive a completely different picture of what happened.

Histories are of most interest when they include the writer's own experience of the Templars. Further material about the Templars can be found in satirical and moralizing works, which show how the writer saw the Order and how the audience of the work was expected to relate to the Order. As the writer often intended to amuse or shock, these images of the Templars are exaggerated; but they enable modern readers to see how medieval people expected to find the Templars depicted. The most positive views of the Templars appear in pilgrim accounts, where pilgrims to the Holy Land described what they had seen and what future pilgrims should expect; and in fictional literature, epic and romances, where the Templars help the hero in his battles against the Muslims, and sometimes help hero and heroine in their love affairs.

We also have some evidence referring only to the Templars. The Rule of the Order survives, which includes many 'customs' and 'judgements' that claim to record actual incidents within the Order. The 1185 Inquest of the Templar possessions in England is not complete, but it tells us much of what the Order owned and what income it expected to have at that date. The trial proceedings of 1307–12 are far more difficult to use because in regions of France under the control of the French king and in regions ruled by his relatives (such as the kingdom of Naples) evidence was extracted by use of torture or the fear of torture. This was normal for the time, as it was believed that torture would force people to tell the truth. In fact, as recent miscarriages of justice in the UK have made clear, torture and the threat of violence lead the victim to say what he or she believes that the interrogator wants to hear.[5] It is clear that Templars were imprisoned together and agreed together on what they would tell the interrogator, and that individual interrogators differed on what they wanted the Brothers to tell them, so that confessions come in 'batches' of similar material.[6] The Brothers' evidence is most reliable where they were contradicting the charge and telling their interrogator something different from what he wanted to hear. This evidence must be reliable because contradicting the charge would result in their receiving still worse treatment, and who would lie when a lie brings more torture? The Brothers' evidence is potentially more reliable for regions where we know that no torture was used (such as Cyprus, Aragon, England, and parts of France outside the control of the king of France), but even here the Brothers were under pressure to confess, and so their testimonies would have been distorted in some way. Some modern scholars, reading the Templars' 'confessions' from France, have wondered whether there was some truth behind some of the charges against the Order – for instance, that the charge that the Templars denied Christ might refer to some test of obedience during the admission ceremony – but the records of the trial from outside France tell a completely different story.[7] Where no torture was used, the Templars emphatically denied all the charges, and when told that the Brothers in France had confessed, retorted that they were lying. Third-party evidence was only occasionally brought in, and this varies in quality: in Cyprus it appears to be objective, in France it was usually objective, but in England much of it was popular gossip, the sort of material now known as 'urban myths'.[8] So the evidence from the trial has to be used with great care.

Archaeological evidence survives in quantity, as the Order had houses scattered across Europe as well as in the East. Some work has been done on the Order's archaeological remains, but much remains to be done. Seven centuries of war and 'improvements' have, obviously, left their mark. Some Templar churches are still in use as churches and the excavation work that can be done is therefore limited. But in some places – such as Larzac in the Languedoc, France, and Cressing in Essex, England – our knowledge of the Order of the Temple is increasing through archaeological investigation.[9]

In short, a good deal of material about the Templars survives. The Order is far from being a mystery. Far more could be made of the surviving evidence, but this problem will be overcome as the cartularies are published and as historians become more confident in using different forms of evidence.

Other myths about the Templars abound. It is not true, for example, that the Templars were found guilty as charged in 1312; Pope Clement V declared the charges not proven, but dissolved the Order because it had been brought into so much disrepute that it could not continue to operate. The Templars were not monks, although they took the three monastic vows of poverty, chastity and obedience; they were religious people who followed a religious Rule of life and wore a distinctive habit, but who unlike monks did not live in an enclosed house and whose purpose was not to pray and fight spiritual battles but to fight physical battles in defence of Christendom. Their houses in Europe did not have large outer walls to keep outsiders out, except in dangerous areas where there was no strong central government to enforce law and order – they were more like manor houses than monasteries. The Templars did not introduce playing cards to Europe – these did not come to Europe until the late fourteenth century, and are first mentioned in the sources in the 1370s, half a century after the demise of the Order of the Temple.[10] There is no evidence at all that the Templars had any knowledge of science, and certainly they had no knowledge of magic: medieval magic was a supremely literate science, recorded and performed in Latin, whereas the Templars in general were remarkably illiterate, apparently through deliberate policy, since educated Brothers were likely to be troublemakers.

The Templars did have ships to carry personnel, pilgrims, and supplies across the Mediterranean between the West and the East and back, but if the Hospital after 1312 is any guide they did not have more than four galleys (warships) and few other ships, and if they needed more they hired them. They certainly could not spare ships to indulge in world exploration – in any case, their ships were not strong enough to cross an ocean and could not carry enough water for more than a few days. The Order had vast resources in land, but was always very short of liquid capital, which was needed to invest in fortifications and personnel in the East. Hence their houses in the West were always very small in comparison to the houses of other religious Orders (except when they performed an important political role, as at Paris, where the Temple was the royal treasury office). No Templar house in the West could compare in size or wealth with the great monastic houses such as Cîteaux or Clairvaux in what is now France, or Fountains Abbey or Bury St Edmunds Abbey in England – to cite but a few. This was because these monasteries existed as powerhouses of prayer on a single site, whereas the houses of the Temple in the West existed to raise funds and other supplies for the war in the East, and all their resources were concentrated in the East. The Templars did not contribute towards the building costs of cathedrals or castles in the West, as they had barely enough money to finance the building of their own castles in the East.

The Templars were not particularly secretive – no more so than other religious Orders of their period, and certainly no more so than the other leading Military Orders, the Hospital of St John and the Teutonic Order. During the trial of the Order, some Brothers admitted that no outsiders were supposed to be present at their admission ceremonies, but others stated that in fact outsiders were sometimes present. Again, chapter meetings of all religious Orders were supposed to be secret, because outsiders should not know about the internal problems of the Order. Which modern international corporation would allow outsiders to come uninvited to its board meetings? Perhaps the Templars were particularly insistent about evicting non-members of the Order from chapter meetings, but there is no evidence for this.

There is no evidence before October 1307 that the Templars were especially unpopular: if it were possible to conduct a poll of the population of Europe at that period to discover the most unpopular religious Order, the Cistercians and the Friars would probably have been rivals for first position, with the Teutonic Order the most unpopular in Poland. At that time the Templars were still receiving pious donations, and contemporaries saw their Order as one of the best religious Orders. Certainly its financial operations irritated some; equally, certainly its failure to defend the Holy Land was a great disappointment to Christendom. The Order was vulnerable to attack because it had had a single, specific vocation in which it could be seen to succeed or fail. Most modern scholars, like most contemporaries of the trial outside France, consider that Philip IV of France attacked the Order of the Temple because he needed its money, and to demonstrate that he was the most Christian king of Europe. He also had Pope Boniface VIII arrested, persecuted the Jews and Lombard bankers of France, burned a religious woman, Marguerite Porete, at the stake in 1310 for writing a book which three respected religious men had approved as non-heretical, and prosecuted Bishop Guichard of Troyes and the lovers of his own daughters-in-law. Those he attacked were accused of heresy or sorcery and 'unnatural' vices. These actions point towards a deliberate policy against anyone whose demise could assist his financial situation or raise his prestige.[11]

In considering the Templars' downfall, we must ask whether the Order could have continued to exist after 1310 even if there had never been any trial. After 1291 the central headquarters of the Order (the 'convent') was on Cyprus. In 1306 the Brothers were involved in a coup against the king, Henry II. When the king returned to power in 1310 he had the leading Templars arrested and imprisoned. Along with the other leaders of the coup, they died in prison in around 1316.[12] Although the trial in the West made Henry's actions against the Templars more straightforward and ensured that the pope would not interfere to rescue the Order, events on Cyprus could have brought about the end of the Order even if Philip IV had not begun the trial. The Templar officials on Cyprus led the Order. Without its leading officials, the Order could not continue to operate, trial or no trial. Henry was also able to destroy many of the nobles of Cyprus, members of the powerful Ibelin family, and their relatives were unable to save them. It is hard to see how the papacy which was unable to save the Templars in France could have intervened to save them in faraway Cyprus; while the kings of the West would have been happy to take over the Templars' property in the West, as they actually did in 1307–8. If any of these Christian powers had objected to his punishment of the Templars, Henry could simply have resorted to the same methods as Philip IV of France and accused the Brothers of being heretics.

Finally, the Order of the Temple was dissolved in 1312 and then ceased to exist. It is true that the new religious Military Orders in the Iberian Peninsula, the Orders of Christ and of Montesa, were successors to the Order and inherited its property, but their scope was far more limited than the original Order, their operations limited to a single area, and they were very closely linked to the king, in contrast to the Order of the Temple's at least theoretical independence. The Order of the Temple could not continue after the pope had removed ecclesiastical recognition of the Order and taken away its property. Its organizational structure had been destroyed; it could no longer raise money or operate as an institution. And, as noted, it no longer had any of its chief officials to lead it.

It is true that certain Templar houses 'held on' in areas where the secular lords were sympathetic towards the Order and hostile to outside interference. For example, in Brunswick in what is now north-western Germany, Otto of Brunswick, commander of the Templars' house at Supplingenberg and a member of the high nobility, remained as secular lord of Supplingenberg after the dissolution of the Order; only on his death did the commandery pass to the Hospital.[13] At Mühlen, a nunnery near Frankfurt which belonged to the Order of the Temple, the nuns resented being transferred to the Order of the Hospital and wanted to remain as Templars.[14] Some individual Templars fled: in 1313 King James II of Aragon wrote to Bishop Pons of Lérida (Lleida) that the former Templar Brother Bernard des Fons, now ambassador for the alcalde of Tunis, had come to Aragon on an embassy.[15] Bernard had obviously found a new career among those whom he had originally sworn to fight if they attacked the Christians, and was now pursuing by a rather different route his former vocation of ensuring the safety of Christendom. James does not state that Bernard had become a Muslim, and as the Muslim rulers were perfectly happy to employ Christians, Bernard had probably remained a Christian. Yet he was now a *former* Templar; he could not be a Templar any more, because the Order no longer existed.

Some writers have speculated that in remote areas such as Scotland Templars could have survived as an Order. Yet there had never been many Templars in Scotland even during the heyday of the Order, and the Anglo–Scottish wars had reduced them still further. By 1338 the Hospitallers were complaining that they had no possessions at all in Scotland; all had been destroyed in the war.[16] The same would have applied to the Templars. The English connections of the Scottish Templars would have made Scotland the last place for them to take refuge in 1312, following Robert Bruce's rebellion and coronation in 1306 and the resumption of the anti-English war. The modern 'Templar' orders date back no further than the romantic revivals of the eighteenth and nineteenth centuries.

As this book is not aimed at academic scholars I have tried to use accessible language: for instance, 'Europe' rather than 'Citramer' or 'Christendom on this side of the sea'. I have tried to use the form of place names that will be most familiar to English-speaking readers, or at least most pronounceable, although I have also given alternative forms to assist readers in locating them on a map. This book does not attempt to replace the great scholarly works on the Order, by Marie Luise Bulst-Thiele, Alain Demurger, Alan Forey and Malcolm Barber.[17] Those seeking more information on the Order should refer to these works.

I

THE ORIGINS OF THE ORDER OF THE TEMPLE

After the forces of the First Crusade had captured the city of Jerusalem on Friday 16 July 1099, and had defeated the Egyptian relief force which had arrived too late to prevent the fall of the city, most of the crusaders returned to Europe bearing tales of deprivation and danger, miracle and victory, some with holy relics acquired on their travels, but few with any wealth. Only a small proportion of the army remained in the newly conquered territory, not enough to dominate the land. The priest Fulcher of Chartres, writing as one of the first generation of settlers, recorded that only 300 knights and 300 foot soldiers remained in the vicinity of Jerusalem by 1100. This was not enough to protect the country.[1]

The crusaders saw their conquests as a part of a Christendom that had been temporarily captured by Islam but was now restored to its rightful owners. Jerusalem, a walled city on a low hill surrounded by deep valleys and overlooked by higher hills all around, was and is the focus of the three great religions 'of the book': Judaism, Christianity and Islam. For Jews it covers the hill where the father of the nation, Abraham, nearly sacrificed his son Isaac – Isaac was saved when God sent a ram to be sacrificed in his place (Genesis 22). It is also the city first captured by King David, where David's son Solomon built a great temple to the only God; in the temple's inner Holy of Holies was housed the Ark of the covenant – the portable wooden casket enclosing the stone tablets on which were carved the laws which God gave to Moses on Sinai. Under the Roman Empire, Jerusalem remained a symbol of Jewish nationhood: Jews continued to live there, and it was a place of pilgrimage.

As the city where Christ had debated in the Temple, preached, was condemned to death and rose from the dead, Jerusalem also became a place of Christian pilgrimage. In 326 the Empress Helena, mother of Constantine the Great (sole emperor 324–37), came to Jerusalem on pilgrimage and discovered the remains of the 'True Cross'. The Roman Empire was now ruled by a Christian dynasty; Constantine had been converted to Christianity in 312. In Jerusalem, impressive Christian shrines were built over the significant places of Christ's passion, death, burial and resurrection, with a great rotunda, the *anastasis*, over the supposed site of the empty tomb, the Church of the Holy Sepulchre (plate 1). These sites originally stood outside the old city but in AD 70, after the Jewish revolt against Rome in AD 66, Jerusalem was destroyed by the Roman conquerors. When the city was rebuilt, these sites formed the focus of the new city. Christian pilgrims travelled to Jerusalem to visit the holy places or to settle there permanently. This was relatively straightforward while Jerusalem remained a part of the Roman Empire.

The Roman Empire had been divided into West and East under the Emperor Diocletian (284–305), for more efficient administration. After Constantine the Great won control of the whole empire in 324, he made the city of Byzantium his capital and renamed it Constantinople. From that time the empire was sometimes governed by a single emperor but more usually by co-emperors, one in the West and one in the East. In the West, the administration fragmented, and by the second half of the fifth century the Western Empire was no longer a political reality. In 476 the last Western Emperor, Romulus Augustulus, was pensioned off by the Ostrogoth ruler of Italy, Odoacer. The Eastern Empire survived, ruled from Constantinople. In 614 the city of Jerusalem fell to the Persians under the Sassanid ruler Chosroes or Khusro II (591–628) who carried off the True Cross. Both city and cross were recovered by the Byzantine Emperor Heraclius (610–41), but the city fell to the expanding forces of Islam in 638.

When the Muslim Caliph 'Umar I ibn al-Khattab (634–44) arrived in Jerusalem in 638, he was shocked by the state of the Temple Mount (figure 1). To the Muslims, this is the place from which the Prophet Mohammad ascended to Heaven in his 'Night Journey', and is the third most holy site in the Islamic world after Mecca and Mdina in Arabia. The site was cleared, and between 688 and 692 the tenth Caliph, 'Abd al-Malik ibn Maruan, built the Dome of the Rock in the centre of the site. This has an octagonal plan, with a golden dome. In or after 709, al-Walid (705–15) built at the southern end of the site a small rectangular mosque (plate 2). This mosque came to symbolize the farthest point from Mecca and Mdina that the Prophet reached on his Night Journey, and was called 'the Aqsa', 'the furthest away'.

Christian pilgrimage to Jerusalem continued under Islamic rule, and for the most part the Islamic rulers, in accordance with the Prophet's instructions, were happy to allow their subject races to practise their religions without interference. There were some problems: in 1009 the Caliph al-Hakim Bi-amr Allah (996–1021) destroyed the Church of the Holy Sepulchre and persecuted non-Muslims. The church was rebuilt and pilgrimages continued throughout the eleventh century, but the journey to the East became more difficult as the Seljuq Turks advanced westwards from Central Asia. Previously, most of the

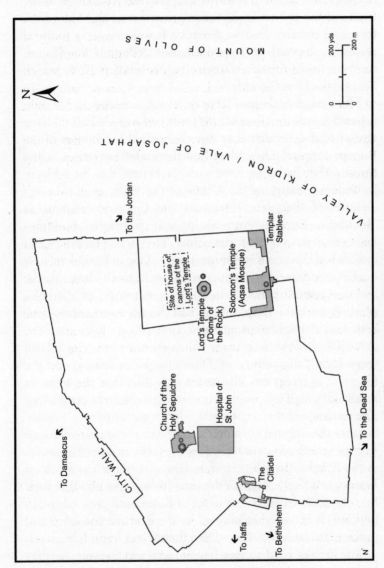

Figure 1 The old city of Jerusalem during the crusader period

journey to Jerusalem could be made by land through Christian territory, but as the Byzantine Empire suffered defeats at the hands of the Seljuq Turks the pilgrims found that they were travelling through frontier territory. It was necessary to travel armed. Such problems were one factor in Pope Urban II's call to western European warriors in November 1095, which became the First Crusade.

The crusaders claimed Jerusalem for Christendom not only because it was the place where Jesus had lived, died and risen again but also because they saw themselves as the heirs of the Roman Empire. They identified the many holy sites in the country they had conquered with places named in the Bible, in Jerusalem identifying the Dome of the Rock as the 'Lord's Temple' of the New Testament and the Aqsa mosque as 'Solomon's Temple', not realizing that the original buildings had been destroyed centuries before. They set up lordships and established their own administrations; a king in Jerusalem, new Catholic patriarchs in Jerusalem and in Antioch alongside the Syrian Orthodox patriarchs, and a network of Catholic archbishops and bishops throughout their new territories. Four major secular lordships emerged, centred on major cites: the principality of Antioch (now Antakya), the county of Edessa (now Urfa), the county of Tripoli (now Tarābulus) and the kingdom of Jerusalem. Historians now call these 'the crusader states', although the people who lived there were not crusaders. The settlers and the original crusaders were known as 'Franks' because the original crusaders came from the areas of western Europe inhabited or controlled by the Germanic people known as the Franks: the Rhineland, northern, southern and central France, and Sicily. Because the chief bishop (the pope) of their branch of Christianity was based at Rome, and their Christian faith was based on that adopted by the Romans and expressed in the Latin language, they called themselves Latin Christians.

The Franks' hold on their 'reconquest' was insecure, for they had come to an unsettled part of the world. One of the reasons for their relatively easy victories in Syria and Palestine was that the region was going through a political crisis. To the south, in 1094 the Fatimid caliph of Egypt, al-Mustansir, had died and was succeeded by his younger son, Ahmed, who took the title al-Musta'li (1094–1101). The succession was disputed and not all the Shi'ites recognized the new caliph. In the north, the grand vizier (the equivalent of a prime minister) of the Seljuq Empire had been murdered in 1092, followed soon after by the death of the Seljuq sultan Malikshāh. The result was the break up of his great empire which had stretched from Asia Minor to Persia and south into Arabia. The upheaval and confusion that followed these deaths was made worse by the religious divisions in Islam, between the Sunnite caliphs of Baghdad and the Shi'ites of Egypt. The caliph of Baghdad (the religious leader of the Sunnis) had also died in 1094.

The political and religious differences in the region worked in the crusaders' favour. The Sunnis had for centuries waged religious war against the Shi'ites, whom they regarded as heretics. Both the Sunnis and the Shi'ites sometimes viewed the Christians as useful allies against their Islamic religious rivals. One fanatical Shi'ite sect in Syria was to become notorious as the 'Assassins' who eliminated any political figure, of whatever religious belief, who threatened them. There were also various Christian communities within the area, who followed different versions of the Christian faith and did not recognize each other's faiths as valid: Syrian Orthodox, Armenian, Maronite and Nestorian.

By allying with these various groups and playing them off against each other, the leaders of the First Crusade had been able to advance their campaign far more effectively than by military force alone. Yet, once they had achieved their goal and captured the holy city of Jerusalem, these various political and religious divisions meant that peace was difficult to achieve. Even if the crusaders could negotiate peace with one group, or defeat another group in battle, other opponents remained ready to attack the new allies or to assist the defeated to fight again. Over the next two centuries, the Catholic Christian settlers in the East would strive by arms and negotiation to maintain a balance of power, with themselves in a favourable position. Sometimes they were successful, and sometimes they were not. But it was obvious from the first that the newly won territory needed more personnel, both to settle the land and to defend it against all the other interests that claimed it.[2]

After the disastrous campaign of 1101, which was annihilated by the Turks in Asia Minor, there were no major international military expeditions from western Europe to the East until the Second Crusade set out in 1147. However, groups of pilgrims continued to come out each year by land or by ship. As shipping became more reliable, more and more pilgrims preferred to travel by sea rather than overland through Turkish-occupied Asia Minor. Typically, pilgrims would come out on a spring voyage from Italy or southern France, sailing via Sicily, Crete, Rhodes and Cyprus to pick up water and supplies (ships of this period could not carry enough water for more than a few days), 'island-hopping' across the Mediterranean as ships had done for centuries before them, and never far out of reach of land. Their final stage was to sail from Cyprus due east until they were in view of the Syrian coast, then to turn south and sail down the coast until they reached a convenient landfall. This could be Jaffa (also known as Joppa, now Tel Aviv Yafo), which was the nearest port to Jerusalem but which lacked a secure harbour; Acre (captured from its Muslim ruler in 1104: now Akko), a safe port further north; Beirut (captured 1110); or the isthmus port of Tyre, attached to the mainland by only a narrow peninsula (Sūr, captured 1124). Wherever the pilgrims landed, they would travel down the coast road to Jaffa, and then across country to Jerusalem. Their first view of the holy city would be a glimpse of the golden Dome of the Rock from the hill of the monastery of Saint Samuel, known as 'Montjoie' – 'Mount Joy' – because it offered the joyful sight of their journey's end.[3] They first arrived in the Holy Land in time to reach Jerusalem for the Easter services in the Church of the Holy Sepulchre. They then visited the other holy places, joined any military campaigns which were in progress, and sailed home at the end of the summer before the autumn storms began at the end of September.

Among the pilgrims arriving in the East during the first decade of the existence of the new crusader states was Hugh, count of Champagne in north-eastern France. Hugh set out for the East in 1104. He went back to Champagne in 1105, but returned to the East again in 1114. Ivo, bishop of Chartres, wrote to him, rebuking him for abandoning his wife and vowing himself to the 'knighthood of Christ' (*militiae Christi*) in order to take up 'that gospel knighthood' (*evangelicam militiam*) 'by which two thousand may fight securely against him who rushes to attack us with two hundred thousand'.[4] This biblical allusion was used two decades later by Bernard, abbot of Clairvaux, writing in support of the new Order of the Temple; but Ivo did not mention any Templars. Perhaps he simply meant that Hugh had taken crusaders' vows to go to Jerusalem and defend it against the Muslims. Although there was no 'official' crusade in 1114, called by the pope, Hugh could have taken crusading vows as part of his vow of pilgrimage. Alternatively, possibly Hugh had vowed to join a confraternity of knights who had formed up to protect the holy places in the East.

Knightly confraternities were becoming common in western Europe during the eleventh century (that is, the century before the First Crusade). These were groups of warriors of a certain social status – not necessarily nobles, but wealthy enough to provide themselves with full military equipment: chainmail armour and helmet, a horse, sword and shield, and a lance. 'Confraternity' (Latin: *confraternitas*) literally means 'a brotherhood together'; that is, a group of people working closely together as equals towards a common aim. For the eleventh-century knightly confraternity, the aim was both military and religious. Groups of knights formed to defend churches or monasteries against bandits. Some knights on the First Crusade formed confraternities, promising to share their resources to help each other on the journey. These groups might seek the formal blessing of a priest, or might have no formal religious recognition. They believed, as many knights did, that a knight should use his sword in God's service to fight evil and promote God's will, and that God would reward him.[5]

Hugh of Champagne did not remain in the East in 1114. However, in 1125 he left his wife for good, went back to the East and joined the Order of the Temple. This group of knights, formed for a pious military purpose, had been given Church recognition at the Council of Nablūs in January 1120.[6] According to the prologue of the new Order's Rule, drawn up in 1129 at the Council of Troyes (in Champagne), the Order was called 'the Poor Knights of Christ of the Temple which is in Jerusalem', and one of the founders was Hugh of Payns.[7] Scholars have deduced that Hugh had been one of the knights employed by Count Hugh of Champagne. Possibly Hugh had accompanied the count to the East in 1114 and remained behind when the count returned home.

What became of the 'knighthood of Christ' and 'gospel knighthood' that Ivo of Chartres had referred to in 1114? Perhaps Ivo was referring only to crusader vows. If Hugh of Champagne had formed a knightly confraternity to go out to the East, it would have broken up as soon as his expedition was over. It is tempting to see it as the first beginnings of the Order of the Temple, but before leaping to such a conclusion it is necessary to consider the evidence for the beginning of the Order.

The beginnings of the Order of the Temple

The Order of the Temple was the first military religious Order founded in the Catholic Church, but twelfth-century writers did not agree on how it began. The Templars themselves did not write any histories. This lack of historical activity was unusual for religious Orders, but not surprising in one which emphasized warfare over all other pursuits and actively discouraged learning among its members.

Archbishop William of Tyre, composing his history of the crusader states between 1165 and 1184, wrote that the first Templars were a group of noble knights, 'devoted to God, religious and God-fearing', who entrusted themselves into the hands of the patriarch (Warmund of Picquigny, 1118–28) to serve Christ. They had intended to become regular canons – that is, priests following a religious rule and living a communal lifestyle in a religious house – and they took the three monastic vows of chastity (that is, no sexual relations with anyone), poverty (no private property) and obedience (to their leader, under God). Their leaders were Hugh de Pagens, or Payns, and Godrey of St Omer. There was nowhere for them to live, so King Baldwin II of Jerusalem (1118–31) gave them his palace which was on the south side of the 'Lord's Temple' or Dome of the Rock (this palace was the Aqsa mosque, which the crusaders called 'Solomon's Temple'), while the canons of the Lord's Temple gave them an area around the palace. The king and his nobles and the patriarch and his prelates gave them some income which they could use to buy food and clothing. The patriarch and prelates told them that their duty as men under religious vows was to keep the pilgrim routes safe for pilgrims. For the first nine years they wore ordinary clothes like secular knights, but at a Church Council at Troyes in Champagne in the ninth year they were given a religious rule and a white habit (simply a light cloak or mantle): distinctive clothing that marked them out as people who had taken monastic vows. White symbolized purity. Later, Pope Eugenius III (1145–53) allowed them to wear a red cross on their white mantles, as a symbol that they were Christ's knights.[8] The red cross on white was also a symbol of martyrdom. William of Tyre stressed the Brothers' initial poverty and the fact that recruitment was slow: he wrote that after nine years there were still only nine Brothers. He regarded the Brothers as religious, as the equivalent of regular canons or priests in a religious community, and he stated that their military vocation was the creation of the patriarch and prelates – in other words, that the concept of the first Military Order sprang from the Church.

Was William's interpretation correct? Earlier writers, writing closer to the original foundation of the Order, told a different story. One Simon, a monk of the abbey of St Bertin (near St Omer, in what is now north-east France) wrote in around 1135–7 that the first Templars were crusaders who had decided to stay in the Holy Land after the First Crusade instead of returning home.

> On the advice of the princes of God's army they vowed them-
> selves to God's Temple under this rule: they would renounce
> the world, give up personal goods, free themselves to pursue
> chastity, and lead a communal life wearing a poor habit, only
> using weapons to defend the land against the attacks of the
> insurgent pagans when necessity demanded.[9]

Simon was writing within a generation of the beginnings of the Order. His view of the Order stressed its religious nature: although the first members had been warriors, they had given up their previous lifestyle and taken vows that involved chastity and poverty. He believed that the secular nobles in the kingdom of Jerusalem advised this move, and did not refer to any involvement by the patriarch of Jerusalem.

The Anglo-Norman monk Orderic Vitalis (1075–c.1141), writing in the Norman monastery of St Évroul, recorded in the 1120s or 1130s that Count Fulk V of Anjou (d. 1143) had joined the 'knights of the Temple' for a while when he was on pilgrimage to Jerusalem in 1120. After returning to the West he continued to pay them an annual sum of money, thirty pounds of Anjou, to support them. Orderic called the Templars *venerandi milites*, knights who should be held in great respect or admiration, and wrote that they devoted their lives to physical and spiritual service of God, despised all worldly things and faced martyrdom daily.[10] He certainly admired them, but regarded them as very pious knights rather than as the equivalent of monks.

Orderic said nothing about how the Order began, but showed that it was in operation by 1120. Later writers' views of the Order were influenced by a short exposition composed by Bernard, abbot of the Cistercian abbey of Clairvaux, later St Bernard (d. 1153). Written before 1136 and addressed to 'my dearest Hugh, knight of Christ and Master of the knighthood of Christ', this claims to be a letter of encouragement to the Brothers of the Order of the Temple written on the request of Hugh de Payns. The letter was written in Latin, which most Templars could not understand, but Bernard probably intended it to be read to them in translation. During the later trial of the Order one Brother stated that he used to own a copy of this letter. Entitled 'In Praise of the New Knighthood', Bernard's letter also circulated among other religious Orders, and was copied into manuscripts owned by other religious houses – along with copies of the Latin version of the Templars' religious rule.[11]

Bernard set out the spiritual basis of the new religious Order. It was, he said, a new type of knighthood, which had arisen in the lands where Christ had walked on earth. Unlike secular knights, who took a pride in their appearance and were stimulated to fight by pride, irrationality, anger, a wish for honour and glory or greed for power, the new knighthood dressed austerely, with short hair and dirty skin darkened by their mailshirts and the sun, and fought for pure motives to defend Christendom against its relentless enemies and to destroy evil. Bernard delighted in elaborate word-play: the secular knighthood was not a *militia* (knighthood) but a *malicia* (evil); the member of the new knighthood preserves himself (that is, his soul) when he is killed and preserves Christ (that is, Christendom) when he kills. The death he inflicts is Christ's gain; the death he receives is his own gain. Bernard painted a picture of the Brothers of the new Order living together in peace and tranquillity, gentle lambs at home and fiercer than lions in the field. 'I am almost in doubt whether they ought to be called monks or knights; except that perhaps it would be more appropriate for me to call them both.' The Brothers possessed both the mildness of monks and the fortitude of knights.

Bernard's word-play and style, piling stanza upon stanza, combines to create a powerful effect: the new Order of the Temple is an exciting new development – knights who live like monks, knights who dedicate themselves to die as martyrs for Christ's sake. The religious intention of his letter is expanded in the second part when he expounds the spiritual significance of the holy places where the knights lived and worked and which they defended. The letter was intended to educate the Brothers as well as to encourage them.[12]

This letter inspired a number of religious writers on the new Order in the 1140s and 1150s: Otto, bishop of Freising (d. 1158), writing in 1143–7, Anselm, bishop of Havelberg (a Premonstratensian canon) writing in 1150, and Richard of Poitou, a monk of the great abbey of Cluny, writing in 1153, all borrowed either directly or indirectly from Bernard's work as they described the new Order. They were not sure when it began: Anselm dated it to around the time of the First Crusade, referring to Pope Urban II (d. 1099) as giving approval to the new Order. Richard of Poitou dated it to the year Abbot Hugh of Cluny died, 1109, and the year Louis VI succeeded to the throne of France, 1108. Otto of Freising linked it to the Investiture Contest, which ended in 1122. Their uncertainty over how the Order was founded indicates that westerners did not notice the foundation of the new Order in 1120. It was only a generation later, after the publicity efforts of Abbot Bernard and the events of the Second Crusade (1147–9), that writers in the West began to take an interest in the Order. Richard of Poitou, writing after the Second Crusade, noted: 'There are some who say that, had it not been for them, the Franks would have lost Jerusalem and Palestine long ago.'[13]

Abbot Bernard had been present at the Council of Troyes in January 1129 when the Council established the Rule of the Order of the Temple and gave the Brothers a habit. The clerk

Jean Michel, who recorded the Latin Rule of the Order of the Temple, wrote that it was Bernard and the Council who ordered him to do this. He also noted that Bernard's words were much praised by the others present at the Council.[14] This suggests that Bernard played an important role in drawing up the Latin version of the Order's Rule. Jean Michel recorded that Hugh de Payns set out before the Council how the Order of the Temple began and its way of life, and the Council delegates praised what they thought was good and beneficial and set aside any practices which they did not approve.

The Rule itself was far from secret. The Latin manuscripts of the Rule which survived into modern times did not belong to the Templars, but were copied for other religious people outside the Order. Pope Clement V also owned two copies of the Templars' Rule in French translation. The Templars' Rule formed the basis of later Military Orders, such as the Teutonic Order and the Swordbrothers of Livonia. During the trial of the Order on Cyprus, 1310–11, one of the lay witnesses said that he had read the Rule and was very impressed by it.[15] In short, it was a public document and had the approval of other members of society.

Who was Abbot Bernard of Clairvaux, and why was he interested in the Order of the Temple? Bernard was a highly influential figure in the Catholic Church in the first half of the twelfth century. He was born from a noble Burgundian family, on the eastern frontier of France. As a young man he joined a new monastic Order based at Cîteaux in Burgundy, on the central eastern French frontier. The Cistercians, named after their mother-house, were radical religious men in tune with the radical religious reform of their day. They lived very simply and austerely, wearing simple white habits of undyed wool; they tried to cut themselves off entirely from the outside world. Unlike traditional monasteries, Cistercian monasteries were not independent units; they were linked together by a system of affiliation (mother and daughter houses) and every year each abbot was expected to travel to the general chapter at Cîteaux –

a sort of international board meeting of executives. Unlike traditional monasteries, the Cistercians would not accept children, and would not allow women's houses in their Order; but non-noblemen were allowed to enter as 'lay brothers' and earn their salvation by physical work. This was revolutionary, as traditional monastic Orders only accepted nobles who earned their salvation by prayer and meditation. The Cistercians claimed to be more spiritually pure than the other Orders, which upset many religious people, but others respected the Brothers' piety and gave them generous donations.

The Cistercians' austerity and white habits were mirrored in the lifestyle and habits of the new Order of the Temple that Abbot Bernard of Clairvaux wrote to support. The Templars also had plain, austere buildings; they were organized on a supranational basis with one central base and regular general chapter meetings which all provincial commanders were to attend; their Rule stated that they did not admit children or women to their Order; the great majority of the Brothers were 'lay brothers', as there were only a small number of priest-Brothers; and they earned their salvation by physical activity, fighting. These parallels between the two Orders point to a close relationship between the two and suggest that Bernard exerted a considerable influence on the original form of the Order.

The Templars' later tradition gave Abbot Bernard and the Cistercians an important role in the foundation of the Order. In July 1202 Brother Philip de Plessis, Master of the Order from 1201 to 1209, wrote to Arnold I, Abbot of Cîteaux, about the Muslim attacks, sandstorms, plagues and earthquake which had struck the crusader states in the East. He asked for the Cistercians' prayers and added: 'And since our House took its institution from yours and your predecessors, it seems to us that we are especially bound to love you and you similarly ought to love us.'[16] During the trial of the Templars some Brothers stated that they wore woollen cords around their waists, over their shirts, because this had been ordained by the blessed Bernard (that is, Abbot Bernard of Clairvaux).[17] At Poitiers one Brother Giraud Beraud, knight, believed that the blessed Bernard had founded the Order; at Lincoln, Brother John of Whaddon thought that he had composed the Order's Rule.[18]

Why was Bernard interested in the new Order? This is not clear. Certainly he was a friend of Count Hugh of Champagne, who was Hugh de Payns' lord. Count Hugh joined the Order of the Temple in 1125, although Bernard had hoped that he would join the Cistercian Order. A letter survives from King Baldwin II of Jerusalem (1118–31) to Abbot Bernard, asking him for his support for the new Order, and naming two Templars whom King Baldwin was sending to Bernard: Brothers Andrew and Gundemar. Andrew was presumably Bernard's uncle Andrew, a Templar; a letter sent by Bernard to his uncle in around 1152 survives.[19] It is possible that Baldwin II's letter to Bernard is a forgery, drawn up to explain why Bernard supported the Order. It refers to the Brothers as *Fratres Templarii*, but the term 'Templar' does not appear elsewhere until the 1140s (the Brothers were initially known as *milites Templi Salomonis*, knights of Solomon's Temple). In short, Bernard may have favoured the Order because his uncle was a Brother, or because of his friendship for Count Hugh, or because of other personal connections now unknown.

However, Bernard's role was played only after the Order had come into existence. The survey so far has shown that contemporaries and near-contemporaries were not sure when the Order of the Temple began, or why it began, or who was responsible for its beginning. The general view was that it began on the initiative of a group of knights who were in the Holy Land, either on crusade or on a peaceful pilgrimage, and that the Order was approved by the patriarch and/or the king and/or the secular lords of the land.

Later writers had heard other stories. Walter Map (d. 1209/10), a secular clerk at the court of King Henry II of England (1154–89), told a number of anecdotes about the early

days of the Templars. He probably heard these from William of
Tyre or his fellow-delegates from the kingdom of Jerusalem at
the Third Lateran Council of 1179. According to Walter,
'Paganus', a knight of Burgundy, went on pilgrimage to
Jerusalem and undertook the defence of a horse pool (that is, a
pool used for watering horses) which was being attacked by the
Saracens, not far from Jerusalem. He set up the Order of the
Temple to carry on the work. Content with austere clothing
and simple food, he spent all he had on his weapons and his
horse, and recruited warriors to his cause by preaching and his
personal approach, and in any other way that he could.[20]

Walter saw the Order as the initiative of one pious man; and
approved heartily of this. But no other account agrees with him.
Walter's account was written late, no earlier than the 1180s. An
even later version of the Templars' beginnings survives in the
chronicle attributed to Ernoul and Bernard the Treasurer of
Corbie Abbey in France. Ernoul, one version of this chronicle
tells us, was a squire in the entourage of Baldwin of Ibelin – the
Ibelins being one of the greatest noble families in the kingdom
of Jerusalem. According to this chronicle, the first Templars
were a group of knights who had dedicated themselves to the
Holy Sepulchre after the First Crusade. They realized that the
country needed warriors, and criticized themselves for living
an idle and comfortable life when they should be working. So
they decided, with the permission of the prior of the Sepulchre,
to elect a Master who could lead them in battle as necessary.
King Baldwin II gave his approval for the scheme, and called
the patriarch of Jerusalem, the archbishops and the bishops, and
the barons of the country together. After discussion the new
Order was approved. King Baldwin gave them land, castles and
towns and persuaded the prior of the Sepulchre to release them
from their obedience to him. The Brothers still carry a part of
the badge of the Sepulchre, a scarlet cross, whereas the sign of
the Sepulchre is a cross with two scarlet arms. The chronicler
adds: 'And so the Hospital threw out the Temple, and gave it its
Rule and the standard which is called the *Bauçaut* [piebald]

standard.' He then explains that the Brothers asked the king to give them his palace in front of the Lord's Temple as a dwelling until they could have one built. He did so, and the Order used to entertain him there when he had a crown-wearing ceremony in Jerusalem. 'Later they built a beautiful and luxurious dwelling next to it, which the Saracens demolished when they took the city . . . Thus the Templars were from then on called "Templars".'[21]

Although this account was written after 1187, when the Saracens captured Jerusalem, it does give a convincing account of the Order's beginnings. It combines the suggestions of the earlier accounts: the Order of the Temple was set up on the initiative of the knights themselves, and that these knights were pilgrims who had come to the kingdom of Jerusalem but who had settled in the city, and who saw that the country needed warriors. The new Order was approved both by the king and by the patriarch. In addition, this account would help to explain why writers in the West were sometimes confused about the relationship between the Hospital of St John, set up in the 1060s or 1070s to care for poor sick pilgrims to Jerusalem, the Order of the Temple, and the canons of the Holy Sepulchre – the priests who lived and worked in the Church of the Holy Sepulchre. It also explains why the Hospitallers and the Templars in the Holy Land followed the liturgy of the Holy Sepulchre in their church services, and why the seal of the Master of the Temple bore the image of the dome of the Holy Sepulchre. According to 'Ernoul', all three groups were originally together. The Hospitallers and Templars had begun life as part of the religious community based in the Church of the Holy Sepulchre.[22]

The role 'Ernoul' gave to King Baldwin II is particularly interesting. While William of Tyre gave the patriarch the credit for creating the new Order, 'Ernoul' insisted that it was the king who first supported the Order. The Templars had very close connections with the kings of Jerusalem during the twelfth century, as they did with kings in western Europe, much closer than their connections with the patriarch. This suggests that William exaggerated the Templars' dependence on the patriarch, perhaps in order to heighten the contrast between the early Order (which he regarded as humble and useful to the kingdom of Jerusalem) and the Order of his own day (which he regarded as too independent and a danger to the kingdom).

In short, contemporaries disagreed over how the Order of the Temple began. They agreed that it was set up with the approval of the highest religious and/or secular authorities in the kingdom of Jerusalem, and that it was given approval quickly: since this happened in 1120, the Brothers probably formed the original group no earlier than 1119. Contemporaries also disagreed over the Order's original purpose: defending pilgrims visiting the Christian holy sites, or defending the territory of the new crusader states against Muslim raids. The first function was far more obviously 'religious' than the second. While defensive warfare could be justifiable holy warfare (more on this below), there was always a danger that it would become aggressive warfare, which could not be justified.

Reactions to the new Order

Contemporaries disagreed in their reaction to the new Order. The leaders of the Church at the Council of Troyes in January 1129 welcomed it, and when Hugh de Payns and his companions travelled around western Europe in 1127–9 before the Council of Troyes, secular and religious leaders welcomed them and gave them many donations.[23] People making donations drew up a charter, which was witnessed by the donor, the recipient (Hugh de Payns and/or his Brothers in the Order) and the notable men present. At this period such charters often included a statement of why the donor was giving the gift. So a donation charter issued by Simon, bishop of Noyon, and the canons of his cathedral in 1130–1 states that they were giving thanks to God for restoring the lost order of society, the warriors.

For we know that three orders have been instituted by God in the Church, the order of prayers, of defenders and of workers. The other orders were in decline while the order of defenders had almost completely perished. But God the Father and our Lord Jesus Christ, God's Son, had mercy on the Church. Through the infusion of the Holy Spirit in our hearts, in these most recent times he deigned to repair the lost order. So in the holy city where once the Church originated, the lost order of the Church began to be repaired. . . .[24]

Bishop Simon was referring to the 'three orders', which some churchmen depicted as the natural divisions of society.[25] The bishop and his canons were declaring that they regarded the new religious Order as God's method of revitalizing a whole order of society: the warriors, those who fight. This echoed the words of the Rule of the Order of the Temple: 'in this religious Order, the order of knighthood bursts into flower and is restored to life'.[26] Other donors saw it in more mundane terms. Baldwin Brochet of Hénin-Liétard declared simply:

How the knights of the Temple of Jerusalem abound in the heights of charity and the grace of laudable renown! They care for those who out of pious devotion assiduously visit the holy Jerusalem and the Lord's Sepulchre through the various dangers of sea and land. The aforesaid knights are ready to lead them there and back, so that they can proceed more safely to the aforementioned places which are consecrated by the bodily presence of our Lord Jesus Christ. Their glorious fame has become known to many people and has spread openly through every land, arousing many people to offer benefits generously to them, as is appropriate.[27]

Baldwin gave all his property at Planques in Flanders to the Templars.[28] His donation charter shows that even early in its history the Order was famous for defending pilgrims.

The papacy gave donations of a different kind to the new Order: exemptions from the authority of the secular clergy, and certain rights which would enable the Order to use its resources exclusively towards the defence of the Holy Land. Pope Innocent II (1130–43), issuing a large bull or papal charter of privileges to Robert de Craon (Master of the Order of the Temple 1136–48), declared:

> We praise the all-powerful Lord about you and for you, since your religious Order and your venerable institution is proclaimed throughout the whole world. For although you were naturally a son of anger given to the pleasures of the world, through the inbreathing grace of the Gospel, to which you have not turned a deaf ear, you have left the pomp of the world and your own possessions. Having left the wide road which leads to death, you have humbly chosen the narrow way which leads to life; and so that you might be regarded especially as part of God's knighthood you carry about constantly and laudably the sign of the life-bringing cross on your breast. It amounts to this: like true Israelites and warriors most equipped for divine battles, truly aflame with the flame of charity, your actions fulfil the Gospel saying that 'Greater love has no man than this, that a man should lay down his life for his friend'.[29]

This was the great bull *Omne Datum Optimum*, which established the new Order as an exempt Order of the Church, answerable only to the papacy.

Not all writers were so forthright in their approval of the new Order. Some were positive, but uncertain as to how to approach this military religious Order. Guigo, prior of La Grande Chartreuse, the mother-house of the Carthusian Order (whose members had individual houses within the monastic complex, and lived an almost completely solitary life of prayer and reading), wrote to Hugh de Payns, 'prior of the holy knighthood', shortly after Hugh's return to the East in 1129. He regretted that he had not been able to meet Hugh and talk with him while he was in France, and went on, 'It seemed to me . . . that I could at least talk with you in a letter.' He continued:

> I have no idea how to encourage you, dear friend, in physical battles and combats, but I desire at least to give you advice about spiritual battles, in which I am involved on a daily basis, although I am no better equipped to encourage you in this sort of battle either.[30]

He argued that in order to win physical battles, a person must first win the spiritual battle against their own bodily desires.

> Therefore, my dearest friends, let us get control over ourselves first, so that we may attack our external enemies safely; let us purge our minds from vice first, and then we may purge lands of barbarians.

It was good spiritual advice, but of a general nature. Guigo clearly wanted to express his support for the new Order, but was uncertain as to what would be of most use to the Brothers. He went on to a problem that was particularly associated with knights and warriors in general: the problem of pride.

> In this battle, a person will be tougher and have more glorious triumphs and throw down more numerous enemies under the direction and protection of God the more this person strives to be more humble in everything. For the more someone wishes to be proud, the weaker they become and less able to do anything . . .
> Let us follow the road of great humility, so that we may reach the glory of God the Father.

But there is no sign that Guigo had any personal knowledge of the Order and its problems. His advice was positive and favourable, but general.

Guigo's letter depicts the Brothers as fellow-fighters with monks against evil, and he asks for their prayers: 'Dearest and most outstanding and most renowned Brothers, we wish you good health, and remember us in the holy places which you guard, in your prayers.' A Cistercian monk named Gauchier or Galtier (English: Walter) at Clairvaux Abbey composed a letter to an anonymous Brother of the Temple which expressed similar views, but more intensely.[31]

Yet other religious writers were not so sure that a religious Order that used violence was a proper religious Order. In around 1150 Peter the Venerable (d. 1156), abbot of the monastery of Cluny, wrote with many expressions of affection and praise to Brother Evrard des Barres (Master of the Temple 1149–52):

> I have had respect for your Order since it was first instituted, and I marvelled and rejoiced that it began during my lifetime, illuminating the whole world like the golden rays of a new star.[32]

He went on to state that all Christians should rejoice that 'a knighthood for the eternal King, an army for the lord of hosts' had been set up to attack the devil and the enemies of Christ, and that the Brothers of the new Order fought both spiritual battles against forces of evil and physical battles against physical foes. In the first, they performed the role of hermits and monks; in the second, they went beyond what was expected of religious people.

> You are monks in your virtues, but knights in the methods you use . . . You lay down your lives for your Brothers . . . you are true participants in that supreme and excellent love of which the Saviour spoke: 'Greater love has no one than this, laying down their life for their friends.'

He then urged the Master to release from his vows a nobleman, Humbert III de Beaujeu (d. c.1192), who had joined the Order of the Temple some time ago but had now returned to the Cluny region and was playing an important role in keeping the peace by force of arms. Yet the Templars were trying to force him to return to the Order. Peter argued that it is more important to attack Christians who act contrary to their faith than it is to attack pagans who do not know God. Cluny was as much in need of defence from evil as the Holy Land. Humbert should be released to fulfil God's real calling for him – to keep the peace in his home locality.

Writing to Pope Eugenius III, Peter expressed himself somewhat differently. He pointed out that Humbert had left his wife illegally when he joined the Templars. What was more, the Order of the Temple was only another group of knights. If Humbert had left a monastic Order and abandoned monastic vows, that would have been a serious matter, but he had only changed one sort of knighthood for another.

> If I might say what many of us think: if he had left an Order of canons, a monastic Order or an Order of hermits, or any ancient Order, it would be right for the censure of the Church to compel him to return to what he illicitly left; but since his only change was from one knighthood to another, since he only transferred the sword he had taken up against Saracens, to fighting against false Christians, who are even worse than Saracens – and since, what is more, as I have heard from many and ought to be believed, he left his wife illegally – I ask that your Wisdom may consider whether he should be forced to return or allowed to remain here until the truth of the matter is made clear, and this great investigation into this great man should be ended by papal judgement.[33]

Peter made two accusations against the spiritual validity of the Order of the Temple: first, that it was modern innovation; the second, that it was only an Order of knights, not a valid religious Order. Considering what he had written to Master Evrard des Barres, he may not have meant his statements to be taken literally; he was arguing a case, and overstating it so as to make the maximum impact on the pope. But he was not alone in doubting the spiritual validity of a military religious Order.

Isaac of Étoile (d. *c*.1159), a Cistercian philosopher and theologian who became abbot of the monastery of Étoile near Poitiers in 1147, composed a sermon in which he chided his audience for running enthusiastically after anything new. On the one hand, there are dangerous new doctrines. On the other,

> There has sprung up a new monster, a certain new knighthood, whose Order – as a certain man says neatly – is from the fifth Gospel [because it does not come from the other four!] because it is set up to force unbelievers into the Christian faith by lances and cudgels, and may freely despoil those who are not Christians, and butcher them religiously; but if any of them fall in such ravaging, they are called martyrs of Christ.[34]

Isaac went on to point out that these warriors had forgotten that we should do to others as we would like them to do to us, and that their violence was a bad example to others. He did not condemn them, but he clearly harboured serious doubts about their vocation. The Templars were not set up to convert non-Christians. Yet the reference to 'a certain new knighthood' and the fact that they were regarded as martyrs if they died in battle indicates that Isaac was talking about Templars.

John of Salisbury (d. 1180), friend of Thomas Becket and later bishop of Chartres, wrote his *Policraticus* in 1159. This, a commentary on contemporary society, included a section on religious Orders. John praised the Templars for following in the footsteps of the Maccabees, the Jewish warriors led by Judas Maccabeus (d. 161 BC) who had defended the Temple against pagans before the time of Christ. The Templars laid down their lives for their brothers; they were almost alone in waging war for the right reasons. Yet this did not allow them to usurp the rights of ordained priests.[35] Being holy warriors gave them some status, but not as much as priests.

After 1187 the secular cleric Walter Map made a few remarks on the Templars' vocation. Christ taught St Peter to pursue peace, but the Templars used force; and whereas the apostles won Damascus, Alexandria and much of the world by preaching, the Templars had lost these territories by fighting. Map had heard stories that showed that the Templars did not want peace or to convert Muslims; they wanted only to fight.[36]

Such views show that there was some debate among theologians as to whether Christians could validly fight, or whether the shedding of blood made a Christian less worthy in God's eyes than one who did not shed blood. Although Christians had fought from the early years of Christianity, the New Testament was ambiguous on the question of whether or not Christians could fight. On the one hand, Jesus told Simon Peter to put away his sword: 'all who draw the sword will die by the sword' (Matthew 26: 52). Yet, on another occasion, Jesus declared that a Roman centurion had more faith in God than anyone He had met, even in Israel (Matthew 8: 10 and Luke 7: 9). Clearly, being a soldier and using violence did not prevent a man from being pious and pleasing God. The great Christian writer Augustine (d. 430), bishop of Hippo Regius in North Africa (now Annaba or Bône in Tunisia) condemned war in his immensely influential work *City of God*, but saw that violence had to be met by violence in order to keep the peace. He believed that war is justifiable provided it is waged to enforce the peace.[37] According to Abbot Bernard of Clairvaux, this was the sort of war which the Templars were fighting, and therefore it was justified war.

Augustine, however, saw war in the context of the emperor's divinely imposed duty to protect the people who had been entrusted to him by God. As supreme military commander of the empire, the Roman emperors were responsible for initiating and carrying on warfare; the soldiers need only obey their commands. From the conversion of Constantine I in AD 312, the emperor, as God's representative, fought in God's name. Even after the disintegration of the Western Empire, the protection of the people and leading the army in battle remained the Christian responsibility of western European secular rulers.

This was a sort of holy war, warfare on God's behalf, in that the ruler was performing the duty to which God had appointed him. After the creation of the papal states in central Italy in the eighth century the papacy also depicted its wars against its neighbours, be they Christian or Muslim, as holy wars. In the second half of the eleventh century the papacy became more proactive in war, promising warriors forgiveness of sins if they fought in papal wars; and the crusade itself was a development of this concept.[38]

By the twelfth century, the concept of warfare being a religious activity that could be a service for God was well established. Yet clearly some ecclesiastics were anxious about this concept, and this would have affected the fortunes of the new Order of the Temple.

A letter survives, written by a writer calling himself 'Hugh Peccator', that is, 'Hugh the Sinner', to the 'knights of Christ in the Temple at Jerusalem'. It has no date, and the identity of 'Hugh' is unclear. Originally identified as the theologian Hugh of St Victor, many scholars now believe that 'Hugh' was Hugh de Payns himself, first Master and founder of the Order of the Temple.[39] He writes in simple Latin, too simple for a great theologian; and although scholars believe that many knights from the lesser nobility could not read Latin, Hugh de Payns might have received some training in Latin and in the Bible if his family originally intended him to have a career in the Church. Alternatively, 'Hugh' might have dictated his letter in French to a professional clerk who wrote it down in Latin.

The picture he painted was a sad one: outsiders were telling the Templars that their vocation was very humble in spiritual terms, that fighting was not allowed for Christians and that Christians should not hate their enemies or take plunder. Outsiders said that if the Templars wanted to serve God and win His approval they ought to leave their humble little Order and join a more spiritual Order where the members spent time praying and meditating, the 'contemplative life' traditionally followed by monks. These opponents of the Order were telling the commanders of the Order that because they held positions of authority they could not win salvation, since worldly authority is the enemy of spiritual progress. At the same time, those who were under the command of others resented being in a lowly position in the Order. Yet again, the Brothers were depressed because they were, they thought, forgotten by Christendom. They were not receiving many gifts of money or land; Christians were not praying for them. They encountered a great deal of physical labour and danger in defending Christendom, and received no thanks for it.

Hugh replied that even though the Order was humble, it was essential. If it were not for the Brothers of the Temple, Christendom would be damaged by the storms that assail it. The Brothers lived a spiritual life when they were not fighting; they fasted and prayed. They had a fair reason to hate because they hated wickedness, not humans; they had a fair reason to take plunder because it was their just payment for their fighting. Their Order was as good a place to serve God as any Order; although they had to work rather than resting in prayer, their work was essential for the survival and expansion of Christendom. They should be content with their lot, and commanding or being commanded was all part of humility and obedience, which would win them a reward from God. Finally, although Christendom seemed to have forgotten them, God had not, and the fact that their work was done in secret would win them a greater reward from God.

Hugh valued the active religious life much higher than the contemplative religious life. This attitude was very unusual among clerics in this period, when the contemplative life was the Christian ideal.

Look, Brothers (Hugh writes): if you were supposed to seek rest and quiet like this, as you say, there would be no religious Orders left in God's Church. Even the desert hermits were not able to escape work altogether; they had to work for food, clothing, and the other necessities of this mortal life. If there was no one ploughing and sowing, harvesting and preparing food, what would the contemplatives do? If the Apostles had said to Christ: 'We want to be free and contemplate, not run about or work; we want to be far from people's objections and disputes,' if the Apostles had said this to Christ, where would the Christians be now?

This attitude reflects the views of the secular warriors of the twelfth century, most famously expressed in the epic poem *La Chanson de Roland*, 'The Song of Roland':

The archbishop said [watching Roland cut the Muslims to pieces]: 'You're doing well. A knight who bears arms and sits a horse ought to act like this. He should be fierce and strong in battle, otherwise he's not worth four pence and should be a monk in one of those churches and pray all day for our sins.'[40]

The attitude is also expressed in the epic poems about William 'Shortnose', lord of Orange in the south of France, historically Duke William of Toulouse (d. 812), in particular *Le moniage Guillaume* or 'How William became a monk'. According to this humorous story, written down in the late twelfth century, this noble warrior and scourge of the Muslims decides that he must do penance for his many sins and so becomes a monk. His abbot decides to send him to buy fish and warns him that if he is attacked by bandits he may not defend himself because monks must not use violence.

When William heard this, he was enraged. 'Master,' he said, 'the rules of your Order are too harsh. Such an Order could come to a bad end; may God burden the person who set it up! The order of knighthood is much more worthwhile: they fight against Turks and pagans, and allow themselves to be martyred for love of God. They are often baptized in their own blood, in order to conquer the Kingdom of Right. Monks only want to drink and eat, read and sing and sleep and snore. They are cooped up like hens, fattening up, daydreaming in their psalters.'

... William said: 'May God bring shame on this Order, and Jesus curse whoever set it up, because he was a bad man and full of cowardice. The order of knighthood is more worthwhile because they fight the Saracen race, take their lands and conquer their towns, and convert the pagans to our law. Monks only want to stay in the abbey, and eat and drink wine to the dregs, and go to sleep when they've said compline.'[41]

William represents the hero of the twelfth century: a huge, muscular warrior, generous to his servants and followers, extravagant in his dress and with an enormous appetite. None of these characteristics endears him to the austere, penny-pinching and peace-loving monks. The author sees the monks' love of peace as cowardice, while knights serve God better than monks, because God needs men who are prepared to fight for Him more than He needs people who can pray.

As the writer 'Hugh the sinner' shared these knightly views, he was probably a knight, and it is reasonable to conclude that he was Hugh de Payns himself. His letter did not circulate widely, as only one copy is extant; but this one copy survives in a manuscript that did not belong to the Templars, showing that the letter was also known outside the Order. It reveals that the early Brothers had to face some fierce criticism for their interpretation of God's service. The picture it gives of the early Order supports William of Tyre's account of the Order's humble early years. In the 1250s, Matthew Paris (d. 1259), chronicler of St Albans Abbey in England, expressed the Order's early financial problems in visual terms:

At first although they were active in arms they were so poor that they only had one war horse between two. As a result, and as a record of their early poverty and as an encouragement to be humble, there are inscribed upon their seal two men riding one horse.[42]

The memory of their Order's early poverty remained a powerful image for the Templars throughout the Order's history. Certainly it reminded them of the need for humility, but it also encouraged them to believe that the Order could easily slip back into poverty, and that there was a constant need to gather and guard wealth and to economize in small matters wherever possible. This fear of poverty and need for careful use of resources pervades the pages of the Order's customs and statutes, and brought the Order a reputation for greed – and thus ultimately contributed towards its downfall.

2

THE LATIN EAST: DEFENDERS OF HOLY CHURCH

In 1289, the Flemish satirical poet Jacquemart Giélée composed *Renart le Nouvel* ('The new Renart') in which he described how the amoral, unscrupulous fox Renart takes over the whole of society, including the Church. At last Renart's fame reaches even the kingdom of Jerusalem, where the patriarch of Jerusalem and the masters of the Temple and Hospital want Renart to rule over them so that they may triumph over their enemies. Summoned to the papal court to plead their respective cases, the advocates of the two Orders are soon in bitter debate. The Templar declares:

> We demand Renart by right. For it is common knowledge that we are defenders of and fighters for the Holy Church. We have sergeants and knights, we must employ many mercenaries and spend much gold and silver, all to defend the Holy Church. Throughout the towns we have many houses, estates and garrisons, under the authority of many powerful lords who

often do us great wrong, so we have a great need for someone to maintain us and uphold our rights against everyone. For if we do not increase in wealth we will have little power to sustain the Holy Church; and instead we will all have to flee and abandon the land of Syria. Then the sultan of Cairo will come over here with a fleet. Holy Father, you must realize that our men defend the Holy Church and Christendom against the unbelievers.[1]

This is a fair description of the situation of the Order of the Temple in 1289, just before the final loss of the kingdom of Jerusalem to the Mamluks of Egypt. The Brother's warning that the Order would have to abandon the Holy Land if help were not forthcoming was a threat actually made many times by the Order during the twelfth and thirteenth centuries.[2] The fact that Giélée included it indicates that it was familiar to his audience; so familiar that it had become almost a joke. Yet this did not mean that what Giélée's Templar said was not true. The Order regarded itself, and was regarded by others, as the defender of Christendom; if not the sole defender, then certainly the most important. It was so prominent in this role that the author Wolfram von Eschenbach identified the Grail Castle in his verse romance *Parzival* as Jerusalem by making 'Templars' its guardians.[3] Although the Order of the Temple was criticized by a number of commentators for various aspects of its activities in the Holy Land, it was regarded as the major military force of Christendom and the group most responsible for the defence of the Holy Land, even after the final loss of the crusader states in 1291.

The history of the crusader states

The history of the crusader states can be conveniently considered in three stages. In the first stage, 1100–1193, the Muslim powers that surrounded the crusader states recovered their unity. Under outstanding leaders such as Zangī of Mosul (d. 1146), his son Nūr al-Dīn (d. 1174), and Saladin (d. 1193),

Muslim armies won lasting gains in territory from the crusader states. By 1193 the city of Jerusalem had been lost and the kingdom of Jerusalem had been reduced to a narrow strip of coastal territory with its capital at the port of Acre. In the second stage, 1193–1260, Saladin's empire was divided between his brother and sons. The Ayyubids (so-called because they were descendants of Saladin's father, Ayyūb) were often at war with each other and allied with Christian leaders against other Muslim leaders. The 'Latin' or Roman Catholic Christians in the Middle East took advantage of this situation to gain territory: for instance, the city of Jerusalem was recovered by a treaty with the Ayyubid Egyptian sultan al-Kāmil in 1229 and held until 1244. This period saw a series of five- to ten-year truces between Muslims and Latin Christians, each followed by a crusading campaign and then followed by another truce (see figure 2). During a truce, all raiding and sieges stopped.

In the final stage, 1260–1300, the Muslims were unified under the Mamluks following the Mamluk victory over the Mongols (nomadic mounted warriors from eastern Asia) at 'Ayn Jālūt in Galilee in September 1260. The Mamluks had initially come to power in Egypt in 1250 as the result of a palace coup. Under the Mamluk sultan Rukn al-Dīn Baibars Bunduqdārī (d. 1277) and his successors, the Mamluks continued to advance. The Mongols were a constant threat to Mamluk dominance in the Middle East and the Latin Christians hoped to take advantage of this rivalry to regain territory, but without significant military aid from the West they could do nothing. As they were unable to equal the Mamluks in the field, they had to fall back on negotiating truces. This period saw the progressive retreat of the Latin Christians. Finally, the city and port of Acre, capital of the kingdom of Jerusalem, fell to the Mamluk sultan of Egypt al-Ashraf Khalil in May 1291.

The strength and unity of the Muslim powers was the most important factor in determining the eventual fate of the crusader states. The states' internal history was less important, although it did affect the political influence of the Order of the

Figure 2   The crusades to the Holy Land, 1095–1291

1096–99	First Crusade: captures Jerusalem. Latin Kingdom of Jerusalem founded.
1100–01	Follow-up expedition: defeated by Turks.
1107–10	King Sigurd of Norway brings army to Holy Land.
1122–24	Venetian expedition to Holy Land.
1144	Zangī, ruler of Mosul and Aleppo, captures Edessa.
1146	Death of Zangī.
1147–49	Second Crusade: attacks Damascus. Failure.
1154	Nūr al-Dīn (Zangī's son) captures Damascus.
1158	Pilgrimage of Count Thierry of Flanders.
1169	Saladin becomes vizier of Egypt.
1172	Pilgrimage of Duke Henry the Lion of Saxony.
1174	Death of Nūr al-Dīn. Saladin seizes Damascus.
1177	Pilgrimage of Count Philip of Flanders.
1187	Saladin captures Jerusalem.
1189–92	Third Crusade: to recover Jerusalem. Fails but recovers some territory.
1197–98	German Crusade. Recovers some territory.
1201–04	Fourth Crusade: to assist Christians in Holy Land. Captures Constantinople.
1217–21	Fifth Crusade: attacks Egypt. Initially successful but army cut off when Muslims open sluice gates of Nile.
1228–29	Crusade of the Emperor Frederick II. Jerusalem recovered by treaty.
1239–40	Crusade of Theobald, count of Champagne and king of Navarre.
1240–41	Crusade of Earl Richard of Cornwall. Recovers territory by negotiation.
1244	Jerusalem finally lost to Muslims.
1249–54	First Crusade of King Louis IX of France: to Egypt. Initially successful but defeated at Mansurah, February 1250. Louis then goes to the Holy Land and strengthens its defences.
1269	Crusade of the princes of Aragon.
1269–70	Frisian Crusade.
1270	Second Crusade of King Louis IX of France: to Tunis. Failure.
1271–72	Crusade of the Lord Edward of England.
1274	Second Council of Lyons discusses plans for recovering the Holy Land. No decision reached.
1291	Acre captured by al-Ashraf Khalil, sultan of Egypt. The remaining Latin Christian territories in the Holy Land fall to the Muslims soon afterwards.

There are no more crusades to the Holy Land but Jerusalem remains the long-term goal of crusades.

Temple, and was marked by succession crises caused by the ruler's death without a suitable heir, through accidents or illness.

Figure 3 illustrates how often succession problems occurred in the monarchy of the kingdom of Jerusalem. The problems were already becoming crises during the long-term illness of King Baldwin IV (1174–85), who suffered from childhood from a debilitating skin disease identified as leprosy. After his death he was succeeded by his nephew, the child Baldwin V, who died in 1186 and was succeeded by his mother, Sibyl, and her spouse, Guy of Lusignan. Guy came from the county of Poitou in western France and was thoroughly disliked by some of the Latin Christian nobility in the crusader states. After the death of Sibyl and her daughters in 1190, Guy was deposed. Sibyl's half-sister Isabel was made ruler of the kingdom. But first Isabel was forced to divorce her husband, Humphrey of Toron, whom many of the leading nobles did not want as king, and she was then married to a succession of eligible men, all of whom died in unpleasant accidents: her second husband, Marquis Conrad of Montferrat, was assassinated in spring 1192; her third husband, Henry of Champagne, fell to his death from a first-floor window in 1197; while her fourth died of food poisoning in 1205, shortly before Isabel's own death. Those who believed in divine judgement would have declared that this was God's punishment on them for marrying a woman forcibly separated from her first lawful spouse, whom (a witness said) she had loved dearly.

Isabel's eldest daughter, Maria, married the French nobleman John of Brienne. In 1225 their daughter, Isabel II of Jerusalem, was married to the emperor Frederick II of Germany (king of Germany, 1212–50). Frederick then insisted that John of Brienne surrender the throne of Jerusalem to him, as John had only been king of Jerusalem by right of his wife Maria, and she had died in 1212. Isabel II herself died in childbirth in 1228, leaving a baby son, Conrad. Frederick claimed the right to act as regent for his son, but the custom of the kingdom of

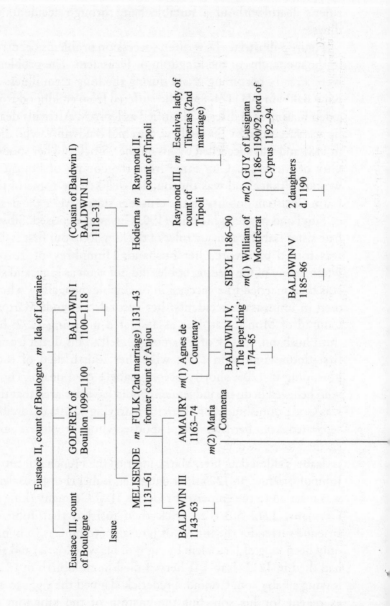

Eustace II, count of Boulogne

Eustace III, count of Boulogne — GODFREY of Bouillon 1099–1100 — BALDWIN I 1100–1118 *m* Ida of Lorraine — (Cousin of Baldwin I) BALDWIN II 1118–31

Issue

MELISENDE *m* FULK (2nd marriage) 1131–43 former count of Anjou
1131–61

Hodierna *m* Raymond II, count of Tripoli

Eschiva, lady of Tiberias (2nd marriage)

BALDWIN III 1143–63

AMAURY *m*(1) Agnes de Courtenay
1163–74
m(2) Maria Comnena

Raymond III, count of Tripoli

BALDWIN IV, 'The leper king', 1174–85

SIBYL 1186–90 *m*(1) William of Montferrat *m*(2) GUY of Lusignan 1186–1190/92, lord of Cyprus 1192–94

BALDWIN V 1185–86

2 daughters d. 1190

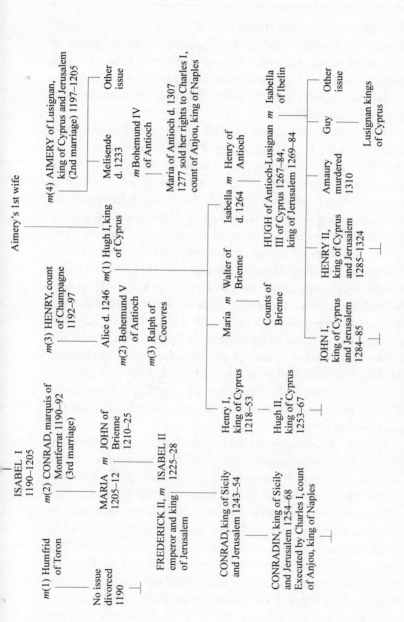

Figure 3 The rulers of the kingdom of Jerusalem

Jerusalem was that the regent should be the next in line to the throne: in this case Alice of Champagne, dowager queen of Cyprus (d. 1246). As neither Conrad nor his son Conradin ever came to the East, those with political influence in the kingdom of Jerusalem were divided over who had the best claim to govern on their behalf.

After Conradin's death in 1268, the king of Cyprus, now Hugh of Antioch-Lusignan (king 1267–84), expected to inherit the throne of Jerusalem, but Maria of Antioch was one generation closer. Yet neither Hugh nor Maria could win control of the kingdom. In 1277 Maria sold her claim to Charles, count of Anjou and king of Naples, who hoped to acquire authority in the eastern Mediterranean. Charles's claim to the kingdom of Jerusalem was supported by his relative William de Beaujeu, Master of the Temple (1273–91). William would not recognize any king of Cyprus as king of Jerusalem while Charles lived. Only after Charles's death in 1285 was the king of Cyprus, now Henry II (d. 1324), able to gain full recognition as 'king of Jerusalem' and unite behind him the nobles and political powers in the crusader states. By the time of Henry's coronation as king of Jerusalem in 1286, the kingdom was severely threatened by the Mamluk sultans of Egypt, and the new king could not prevent the final loss of the kingdom in 1291.

During the succession crises to the kingdom of Jerusalem, various factions struggled to control the kingdom, either by acting as regents or by supporting one or more of the claimants to the kingdom. The nobility made up the first and most influential of these factions. The lords of the kingdom were very rich, mainly from trade and rents from the towns. By the late twelfth century the most important family were the Ibelins. They opposed King Guy before the Third Crusade and the Emperor Frederick II during his crusade of 1228–29 and during the 1230s. Without their support, no one could rule the kingdom.

In contrast, the Church in the crusader states was not particularly powerful. It had few outstanding leaders:

Archbishop William of Tyre in the twelfth century and James Pantaleon, patriarch of Jerusalem and later Pope Urban IV (1261–64), were notable exceptions. However, the Church did produce some new religious Orders, such as the Order of the Holy Sepulchre, the Carmelite friars and the Military Orders. The Church in the crusader states did not control large ecclesiastical lordships as it did in Europe, although as in Europe Church leaders had to provide troops to help defend the kingdom. It was usual for Church properties in the crusader states to be fortified, in defence against Muslim raiders.

Because of the military needs of the crusader states, the military religious Orders became highly influential in political affairs. In addition to the Order of the Temple, officially established in 1120, other Military Orders developed. Soon after 1120 the Order of the Hospital of St John of Jerusalem, which had been set up in the 1060s or 1070s to care for sick poor pilgrims to the city, began to employ mercenaries to defend pilgrims, and in 1136 King Fulk gave the Hospital the castle of Beit Jibrin near Ascalon (see figure 4) specifically to guard the Latin Christian territory against Muslim raids.[4] As these two religious Orders developed they worked alongside each other in raids on the Muslims, in campaigns and in the royal council. Further Military Orders were founded, most developed from pilgrim hospitals: the most important of these was the Order of St Mary of the Teutons (or the Teutonic Order), which began as a field hospital at the siege of Acre in 1189–91, and became a Military Order in 1198.[5] However, the similarity of these religious Orders' activity meant that they came into conflict over policy and territory. When the Holy Land was lost some commentators in the West blamed the Military Orders for quarrelling between themselves when they should have been fighting the Muslims.

The Italian communes were at least as influential in the crusader states as the Military Orders. These were made up of merchants from the Italian trading cities, most importantly Genoa, Venice and Pisa. While some of the Italians would have

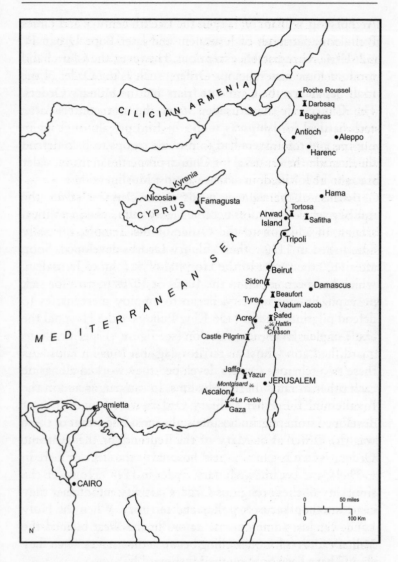

Figure 4   The Holy Land during the crusader period,
showing Templar fortresses and other locations
mentioned in the text

lived in the East for several years at a time, many others came to the crusader states each year in spring and autumn to buy and sell merchandise; they had their own quarters in the major ports such as Acre and Tyre, where they enjoyed various privileges such as being able to hold their own courts to deal with their own legal business. They were vital to the crusader states because they provided the link with Europe that brought pilgrims and colonists and supplies, and they carried the trade, which made the crusader states so wealthy. In addition, they brought the kingdom sea power, which gave the Latin Christians an advantage over the Muslims. Yet the Italian city republics were rivals, often at war with each other, and they brought their wars to the Holy Land. Venice and Pisa usually sided against Genoa, and made such disputes worse. In addition, as they traded with the Muslims, some European commentators complained that they were strengthening the enemy at the expense of Christians.

The Templars in the crusader states

It is difficult to say how many Templars there were in the Latin East (as historians call the crusader states and kingdom of Cyprus) but it has been suggested that the Orders of the Temple and the Hospital could each put an army of 300 Brothers in the field, knights and armed sergeants (non-knights), as well as mercenaries or hired soldiers.[6] The Orders had houses of Brothers in the major towns of the Latin East and held manors, villages and fortresses which they had been given in pious donation or had bought, including a few fortresses they themselves constructed.

The Templars' impact on their Muslim adversaries indicates their effectiveness as warriors. Muslim commentators regarded the Military Orders in general as a terrible menace to Islam. Saladin's secretary 'Imād al-Dīn described the Templars as rebels, demons, evil men, with their castles built on inaccessible crags which were the lairs of wild beasts. Every victory over the Templars and their comrades in evil the Hospitallers gave grounds for rejoicing. After the battle of Hattin on 4 July 1187, when Saladin's army destroyed the army of the kingdom of Jerusalem and captured King Guy and the leading nobles, Saladin paid the Muslims who had captured the Templars and Hospitallers, and then had the prisoners killed. Muslim holy men and theologians lined up to have the honour of executing one of these outstanding enemies of their faith. 'Imād al-Dīn claimed that Saladin declared: 'I will cleanse the land of these two impure Orders.'[7]

Castles. The Templars received their first fortresses in East in the 1130s, not in the kingdom of Jerusalem but in the north of the crusader states, beyond Antioch in the Amanus Mountains which divided Antioch from the Christian state of Cilician Armenia. These castles included Baghras (called Gaston by the Franks – see plate 3), Darbsaq, Roche Roussel and Port Bonnel, and the mysterious Roche Guillaume whose site is not identified and which may have been identical with Roche Roussel. These castles guarded the mountain passes not so much against Muslims as against the Cilician Armenians and the Byzantine Greeks. The Templars held Baghras by 1142, when the Byzantine emperor John Comnenos invaded the area and attacked Antioch. All these castles fell to Saladin in 1188. Baghras was occupied by the Cilician Armenians after Saladin's withdrawal, and the Templars had a great deal of trouble in recovering it with the support of Bohemond IV, Prince of Antioch.[8] Their problems will be described in more detail below. Other castles were not recovered.

In the kingdom of Jerusalem the Templars received the castle of Latrūn, otherwise known as Toron des Chevaliers, which according to a Castilian chronicle was built by Count Rodrigo Gonzalez of Toledo between 1137 and 1141 while he was in the Holy Land fighting the Saracens. After garrisoning and equipping the castle, he gave it to the Templars.[9] After the Second Crusade, in 1149, the Brothers received the fortress of Gaza. This was on the main north–south coastal road and was constructed by King Baldwin III and the nobles of the kingdom of Jerusalem as part of a strategy of surrounding the Muslim-held city of Ascalon, which was on the coast ten miles to the north of Gaza. The castle was entrusted to the Templars, who guarded it and used it as a base not only for raids against Ascalon but also for protecting the southern frontier of the kingdom of Jerusalem against Egypt. A generation later William of Tyre recorded in his history of the crusader states that the Templars discharged their responsibilities well, but Gaza was only the latest in a series of castles constructed around Ascalon by the kings of Jerusalem.[10] Apparently it was not until 1149 that the king believed that the Order of the Temple was capable of guarding the castle and defending the frontier – an interesting contrast with the situation in the Iberian Peninsula.

In 1152 Bishop William I of Tortosa asked the Templars to take over responsibility for the castle at Tortosa to protect the town against the threat from Nūr al-Dīn, who had captured Tortosa in spring 1152, sacked it and withdrawn. The bishop gave the Templars extensive rights in the town: their chapels were exempt from his authority and their payments of tithes (the tenth of all produce which should be paid to the Church) were reduced. The Templars were to build a new castle to protect the bishop and people of the town.[11] In 1188 the Templars, commanded by the Master Gerard de Ridefort (1185–9), successfully defended their fortress against Saladin, who retired without capturing it.

In the 1160s the castle of Safed in Galilee was entrusted to the Order, but was lost to Saladin in December 1188 after a bitterly fought siege. The Order recovered the castle in the summer of 1240 as a result of a treaty between the Ayyubid lord of Damascus, al-Sālih Ismā'īl, and the crusaders led by Theobald, king of Navarre and count of Champagne, supported by the Templars. Urged on by the bishop of Marseilles, who had been involved in the crusade, the Templars undertook the restoration of the castle. To publicize the rebuilding and raise funds for the work, a cleric wrote a tract,

De constructione castri Saphet, 'the construction of Safed Castle'. The castle finally fell to Baibars in the summer of 1266, and the whole Templar garrison was massacred.[12]

From the 1250s the Templars, Hospitallers and Teutonic Knights were given or sold many castles by the secular nobility of the crusader states, who could no longer afford to maintain and garrison them. After the Mongols sacked Sidon in 1260, the lord of Sidon gave the Templars his lordship, which included the castle of Beaufort.[13] The Templars lost Beaufort to Baibars in 1268, but held Sidon until 1291. Sidon was evacuated without a fight after the final loss of Acre. These gifts and sales made the Military Orders powerful and influential within the crusader states, but at the same time loaded them with a financial burden which their resources could not meet.

The Templars also constructed new castles. In 1178–79 they were involved in the construction of a new fortress at Jacob's Ford or Vadum Jacob on the Jordan river, called the *chastellet* or little castle. According to William of Tyre, here writing as a contemporary of events, King Baldwin IV was responsible for the construction of the castle and then entrusted it to the Templars. In the 1220s the author of the first part of the chronicle attributed to Ernoul and Bernard the treasurer of Corbie Abbey wrote that it was the Templars who had decided that a castle was needed at this site. The king could not build it himself because he had a peace treaty with Saladin which prohibited the construction of castles on the frontier, whereas the Templars were not constrained by any such treaty. In any case, its first enclosure was complete but the outer enclosures had not yet been built when in 1179 Saladin attacked the castle, captured it, executed the Templar garrison and demolished it.[14]

During the Fifth Crusade (1217–21) the Templars replaced their small watchtower, called Le Destroit ('the Pass'), at 'Atlīt on the coast road south from Haifa to Caesarea with a major fortress constructed on the nearby headland. This was named Castle Pilgrim in honour of the crusaders (pilgrims) who had assisted the construction. The builders reused stones from a previous Phoenician wall and in the course of their work they found a hoard of ancient coins, which were put towards the cost of the building. Many springs of sweet water were also discovered, to provide a water supply for the castle. In 1219 Duke Leopold VI of Austria and Earl Ranulf of Chester (d. 1232) made additional generous donations of money towards the construction. Oliver the schoolmaster of Cologne Cathedral, later bishop of Paderborn (d. 1227), described the building of the castle in detail in a letter to his colleagues in Cologne; his letter was copied into the Great Annals of Cologne and thence found its way into the chronicle of Roger of Wendover, chronicler of St Albans Abbey in England. The new bishop of Acre, Jacques de Vitry (1216–c.1228), reported on the new castle to Pope Honorius III (1216–27): he was amazed at the Templars' readiness to invest all their wealth in the construction, and declared 'it is a wonder where they get it all from'. Perhaps he had not heard about the discovery of the hoard of coins. In fact, the large donations given by leading crusaders indicates that the bulk of the expenses were met by the crusaders themselves, as was appropriate for 'their' castle.[15]

Castles had various functions. They were administrative centres, from which estates were governed. For the Military Orders, they were a centre of religious life. Some scholars have noted that the concentric castle-plan which developed from the mid-twelfth century was particularly well suited to the Military Orders, as the central enclosure could house the Brothers and their chapel, cut off from the rest of the world, while outer enclosures housed mercenaries and other lay people. It has even been suggested that the Military Orders developed the concentric castle deliberately to meet their religious need for enclosure. Other scholars, however, believe that the concentric castle developed primarily to meet the danger from the new Muslim siege machinery.[16] This does seem more likely, for castles were first and foremost military centres. They varied in size from simple towers to large and complex fortresses.

Military Order castles were garrisoned by a small number of Brothers and a large garrison of hired mercenaries. At the Templars' castle of Safed in Galilee in the 1260s there were fifty knight-Brothers, thirty armed sergeant-Brothers, fifty turco-poles (native lightly armed mercenaries) and also 300 hired archers.[17] Garrisons were called on to fight in the field when necessary. For instance, according to the chronicle attributed to Ernoul, on 1 May 1187 Gerard de Ridefort, Master of the Temple 1185–89, took nearly the whole of the garrison of the small castle of La Fève ('the Bean') to enlarge his small force of Templars and Hospitallers for an engagement with Saladin's forces at the Spring of the Cresson, near Nazareth. When Balian of Ibelin, who was following behind, arrived at La Fève a few hours later he was amazed to find no one around and sent his squire Ernoul ('this was he who had this tale written down') to search; Ernoul found only two invalids, who knew nothing of what was going on. As Balian and Ernoul left, a Brother of the Temple rode out of the castle behind them and hailed them – although Ernoul had not seen him while searching the castle. The Brother told them of the disaster at the Spring of the Cresson: the Master of the Hospital and all the Templars dead except for three Brothers and the Master of the Temple, who had escaped. The whole account has the atmosphere of romance: the mysteriously empty castle, and a knight appearing from nowhere. Perhaps Ernoul exaggerated the situation to emphasize the strategic foolishness of taking the whole garrison of a castle to fight a battle, leaving the castle completely indefensible.[18]

Yet even a well-defended castle could not hold out for ever against a determined besieger. Saladin's secretary 'Imād al-Dīn described at length the magnificent fortifications of Baghras: 'erect on an unshakeable summit, rising on an impregnable hill top, its floor touching the sky' – and went on to describe how Saladin set up his siege machines and bombarded the fortress until at last the commander came out and surrendered. According to the custom of war the commander was correct to surrender if he knew that he had no hope of relief. In military terms, if there was no hope of being relieved it was better to surrender and save the lives of the Brothers and mercenaries to fight another day, rather than to lose everything without any gain to the Order and Christendom except the honour of dying a martyr.[19] But opinions differed as to when a commander should decide that there was no hope of being relieved. William of Tyre records the fury of King Amaury of Jerusalem (1163–74) when twelve Templars surrendered a royal castle which they had been defending against a Muslim siege and which he had intended to relieve. He hanged the Templars responsible. In 1268 the Templar garrison of Baghras surrendered the castle to Sultan Baibars because there was no hope of relief; they were later in trouble with their Order because they had surrendered the castle before receiving instructions to do so and they had not destroyed everything inside it, making it indefensible, before withdrawing.[20]

From their castles the Templars performed various military functions: they conducted raids (*chevauchees* – that is, 'rides') against Muslim territory, property or people; they escorted pilgrims on the pilgrim routes from the coastal ports to Jerusalem and the Jordan valley and back again; they played a military role in major military campaigns led by the king or his representative and gave military advice. Although the Templars had extensive rights and territories in the county of Tripoli, in other areas they were not autonomous. Even their castles in the Amanus march between Antioch and Cilician Armenia were in territory subject to the prince of Antioch. Instead, in the twelfth and early thirteenth centuries, the Templars worked in cooperation with the king of Jerusalem – or, in the north of the crusader states, the prince of Antioch or count of Tripoli. Although in theory they were subject only to the pope on earth, in practice they operated more like a special sort of royal or seigneurial militia.

The Templars' raids on the Muslims were as much offensive as they were defensive. The object was not to conquer land but to capture animals and humans and other booty, which could be used or turned into wealth (for instance, by ransoming the humans back to their families). This raiding and counter-raiding was, and is, typical of frontier societies. The castle of Gaza was deliberately constructed to enable the Templars to launch raids on the city of Ascalon and on the caravans which the caliph of Egypt sent regularly to supply the city. It was in such a raid in 1154 that the Templars ambushed a party of wealthy Muslims coming from Egypt, including Rukn al-Dīn 'Abbās and his son Nāsr al-Dīn, who had just murdered the caliph al-Zāfir and plundered his goods. 'Abbās was killed and Nāsr was captured. A Premonstratensian monk from the diocese of Reims or Laon recorded this event in around 1155, depicting the Templars as God's instruments of justice. Guy of Bazoches, who wrote a chronicle in the 1190s, recorded these events similarly (although under the wrong date) and emphasized the image of the Templars as God's instruments of justice by adding that the Templars handed Nāsr al-Dīn over to his enemies to be punished for his involvement in the murder of the caliph. A similar account was given by Baldwin of Ninove in the second half of the thirteenth century. The Muslim historians supported this version of events, adding that when Nāsr was returned to Egypt he was executed and his body was hung on a cross on the city gate – the standard punishment for traitors.[21]

The fact that Nāsr's body was hung on a cross led some Christian contemporaries to believe that he was a Christian when he died. Thirty years after his death both William of Tyre in the East and Walter Map in the West recorded that Nāsr had converted to Christianity while he was in the Templars' prison, but that the Templars had sold him back to the Egyptians for a large ransom, because they preferred money to converts. There is no evidence for this conversion in the contemporary Christian or Muslim accounts.[22]

In 1157 the Templars reported a successful raid on a Muslim wedding party, in which around 230 Muslims were either captured or killed.[23] This was a small-scale raid; some were much larger, involving royal, noble, and/or other Military Orders' forces. Raids were also risky. William of Tyre noted a raid against an invading Turkish force near Hebron in 1139, led by the Templar Master, Robert de Craon, at which one Bernard Vacher carried the king's banner. This attack was a disaster, and many nobles were killed.[24] The St Albans chronicler Matthew Paris recorded in his *Chronica majora* ('Great Chronicle') and in his *Historia Anglorum* ('History of the English') how in 1237 the Templars and Hospitallers set off from Baghras to attack Darbsak, but rode into an ambush and were cut to pieces.[25] In 1261 the Templars of Acre, Safed, Beaufort and Castle Pilgrim set out under their Marshal, Stephen de Sissy or Cissey, with the marshal of the kingdom of Jerusalem, John of Gibelet, and the Ibelins, and attacked the Turcomans. John of Ibelin, lord of Beirut, John of Gibelet, Matthew le Sauvage the Commander of the Temple and many other knights and men at arms were captured and the Templars lost all their equipment.[26]

Castles were not only aggressive, but also defensive. They could be a refuge for the Brothers and their tenants when a Muslim raid swept over the countryside; after the raiders had gone, the people could emerge and go back to their homes. William of Tyre complained that in 1180 when Saladin's forces ravaged the land the Templars and Hospitallers sat tight in their fortresses and did not go out to engage him; but the Brothers clearly considered that in this case it was better to keep their forces safe rather than risk them in attack against overwhelming odds.[27]

A castle could also be a point of refuge for the Order's allies and for those fleeing from the Muslims. Some time before 1179 a renegade Christian knight engineered the capture of Saladin's great-nephew, Shāhanshāh, son of Saladin's nephew Taqī al-Dīn. He took him to the Templars at Safed where he was held prisoner for many years, until Saladin ransomed him for a large sum and many Christian prisoners.[28]

For pilgrims to the Holy Land, the Order's most important role was the protection of pilgrims. Their castles guarded the pilgrim routes, while their warriors provided a military escort for pilgrims as they travelled around the holy places. Theodoric, a pilgrim to the Holy Land in around 1162, describes the Templars and Hospitallers escorting bands of pilgrims down to the Jordan to bathe in the holy river, watching over them while they stayed the night there, and protecting pilgrims on the Jordan plains.[29] In 1172 Duke Henry the Lion of Saxony (d. 1195) came East on pilgrimage; he was entertained in Jerusalem by King Amaury, visited the Jordan with a military escort of Templar knights to guard against Muslim attack, and then proceeded to Antioch, again with an escort of Templars.[30] He gave generous gifts to the Church of the Holy Sepulchre, the Templars and the Hospitallers.

Sometimes pilgrims and their Templar escorts were involved in battles with the Muslims. In around 1163 Geoffrey Martel, brother of the count of Angoulême in western France, and Hugh le Brun of Lusignan (in Poitou, western France) were on pilgrimage in the Holy Land. Having visited the holy places they were on their way north to Antioch when they were attacked by Nūr al-Dīn. The pilgrims and their escort of Templars, led by the English nobleman Gilbert de Lacy (who had joined the Order of the Temple some years previously), defeated their attackers and put them to flight.[31]

The Order also assisted in various military expeditions and gave military advice. In 1177 Philip of Alsace, count of Flanders (d. 1191) came out to the Holy Land. He had been anxiously awaited by the barons and Church, as the king, Baldwin IV (1174–85), was seriously ill. The nobles of the kingdom hoped that the count, who was Baldwin's first cousin, would take over the regency. But Philip refused, and set off north with an army including a large number of Templars, to besiege the Muslim town of Hama in northern Syria. Failing to capture Hama, he went on to besiege Harenc (now Harim, in Syria). When the city was on the point of falling, the Muslim garrison paid Philip to withdraw.[32] The contemporary sources for this siege do not mention that the Templars were involved in the negotiations, but thirty years later Roger, former royal clerk and parson of Howden in Yorkshire (d. 1204), claimed that the Templars had urged Philip to accept the Muslims' peace terms. He went on to claim that when Philip and the earl of Mandeville (who had accompanied him) looked at the money which the Muslims had paid they found it was nothing but copper and brass.

In telling this story Roger was echoing an ancient story of greedy men who are fooled by supernatural beings or non-Christians into accepting gold which later turns out to be false: there are versions of this story in the writing of Gregory of Tours (c.539–94) and in the Welsh *Mabinogion*. But Roger did not mention miraculous divine retribution or magic. His story suggests that the Muslims were trying to pass off bad coin, a practice that both Muslims and Christians were often guilty of. Yet the Muslim sources make no reference to bad coin being used at the siege of Harenc. Philip certainly was paid to abandon the siege, but as one of the principal purposes of military activity in the East at this period was to acquire booty and prisoners rather than to acquire castles which could not be held, he had achieved one of his main aims by forcing the Muslims to pay him a large sum of money.[33]

Battles. Meanwhile, Saladin had taken advantage of Philip's expedition in the north to attack the kingdom of Jerusalem. Led by Reynald de Châtillon, lord of Transjordan, and King Baldwin, the Franks won a decisive victory at Montgisard, notable for an impressive use of the Templars' cavalry charge. Ralph of Diss (in Latin, *Diceto*), dean of London, recorded an eyewitness account of the battle, presumably given to him by a pilgrim returning from the Holy Land.

Odo the Master of the Knighthood of the Temple, like another Judas Maccabaeus, had eighty-four knights of his Order with him in his personal company. He took himself into battle with his men, strengthened by the sign of the cross. Spurring all together, as one man, they made a charge, turning neither to the left nor to the right. Recognizing the battalion in which Saladin commanded many knights, they manfully approached it, immediately penetrated it, incessantly knocked down, scattered, struck and crushed. Saladin was smitten with admiration, seeing his men dispersed everywhere, everywhere turned in flight, everywhere given to the mouth of the sword. He took thought for his own safety and fled, throwing off his mailshirt for speed, mounted a racing camel and barely escaped with a few of his men.[34]

The cavalry charge was the most high-profile military manoeuvre in warfare in this period. Although pitched battles were very much the exception rather than the rule – warfare usually consisted of ravaging enemy territory and besieging castles – when battle was engaged there was a set system of manoeuvres to follow. These had been described in Vegetius' famous treatise *De re militari* ('on military matters') written in the late fourth century AD, which was the standard written work on warfare in the West during the Middle Ages. Vegetius had suggested various ways in which battle could be joined, but by the twelfth century commanders generally used only one. First the artillery would fire (the artillery were the archers; stonethrowers were usually only used in sieges), with the aim of breaking up the enemy lines. Then, when the artillery had run out of ammunition, the cavalry would charge and break the enemy lines. They would be followed by the footsoldiers, who would kill the soldiers knocked down by the mounted knights. Knights also fought on foot, but in a battle situation being on horseback gave an advantage of height and speed. Mounted warfare required more skill, more training and more financial investment in horse and weapons. It was therefore more prestigious.

The Military Orders excelled at mounted warfare. They were highly trained professional soldiers whose rules demanded that they keep formation and fight as a group on behalf of Christendom, not seeking their own individual glory. The accounts of the crusader army just before the battle of Arsūf on

7 September 1191 describe the rearguard, which was commanded by the Hospitallers, as riding 'so close together that an apple thrown into their midst would not fall to the ground without touching people or horses'.[35] Such a tightly grouped squadron, if it kept its close formation when charging, would have a devastating impact on the enemy lines. A pilgrim account of the Holy Land written during the period 1167–87 and known as the *Tractatus de locis et statu sanctae terrae* ('Tract on the places and state of the Holy Land') includes a stirring account of the Templars' military role and discipline:

There are two religious houses in that Jerusalem region, the Temple and Hospital, who have a great deal of wealth from revenue collected from the whole of Europe, and have very large revenues and possessions in the Land of Promise. When the Lord's Cross [the standard of the kingdom of Jerusalem] proceeds to battle these two escort it, one on each side: the Templars on the right and the Hospitallers on the left. The Templars are excellent knights, wearing white mantles with a red cross. Their bicoloured standard which is called the 'baucant' goes before them into battle. They go into battle in order and without making a noise, they are first to desire engagement and more vigorous than others; they are the first to go and the last to return, and they wait for their Master's command before acting. When they make the decision that it would be profitable to fight and the trumpet sounds to give the order to advance, they piously sing this psalm of David: 'Not to us, Lord, not to us but to your name give the glory' [Psalm 115: 1], couch their lances and charge into the enemy. As one person, they strongly seek out the units and wings of the battle, they never dare to give way, they either completely break up the enemy or they die. In returning from the battle they are the last and they go behind the rest of the crowd, looking after all the rest and protecting them. But if any of them turns their back on the enemy or does not act with sufficient courage, or bears weapons against Christians, he is severely disciplined. The white mantle with the cross which is the sign of knighthood is ignominiously taken away and he is thrown out of the community and eats for a year on the floor without a napkin, and if the dogs trouble him he is not allowed to complain. After the year, if the Master and Brothers judge that he has paid for his crime, his original knighthood is returned to him with all honour. Those Templars carry on a harsh religious observance, obeying humbly, doing without personal property, eating and dressing moderately, living all the time out of doors in tents.[36]

Likewise, Oliver, the schoolmaster of Cologne Cathedral, described a charge by the Templars at the siege of Damietta, in July 1219, during the Fifth Crusade:

After a long assault [the Muslims] crossed the ditch at the point where the knighthood of the Temple were, burst violently through the barriers and turned our footsoldiers in flight, so that the whole Christian army was endangered. The knights and horsemen of France tried three times to drive them back outside the ditch, but they could not. The Saracens within our ramparts broke the entrenched lines of horsemen and footsoldiers and drew up their army. Their voices rose in derision, all their multitude prepared the pursuit, and timidity grew in the Christians; but the spirit which clothed Gideon [Judges 6: 11–8: 35] aroused the Templars. The Master of the Temple, with the Marshal and the rest of the Brothers who were there then, made a charge through a narrow exit and manfully put the unbelievers to flight. The Teutonic Order and counts and knights of various nations, seeing that the knighthood of the Temple was in danger, hastily brought them aid through the gates near them. Thus the Saracens' footsoldiers were destroyed and their shields thrown down, except for those whose headlong flight snatched them from their attackers . . . Thus the Lord saved those who hoped in Him, through the courage of the Templars and of those who worked with them and committed themselves to danger.[37]

These accounts by Ralph of Diss, the anonymous pilgrim, and Oliver the schoolmaster of Cologne indicate the value of the Templar cavalry in the field. In a battle situation, a small, well-disciplined force hitting the enemy ranks at just the right time and place could have a decisive impact. At Montgisard and at Damietta the Christians were heavily outnumbered, but quick, decisive action by the Templar Master won victory for the Christians. Such accounts illustrate why the Muslim generals regarded the Military Orders with such respect.

The hierarchical statutes of the Order of the Temple laid down the procedures for military action. There are sections on 'How the Brothers should make camp', 'How the Brothers should form the Line of March', 'How the Brothers should go in a Squadron', and 'How the Brothers should charge'. The chief military official of the Order was the Marshal. Contemporary accounts depict the Master as taking military command, but the Order's own statutes indicate that the Marshal was in military command over the army. In practice, the Master would normally be in command if he were present, but the written procedures allowed the Marshal to take command if the Master were not present.

What happened if the two disagreed? A later adaptation of the chronicle attributed to Ernoul gives a description of a quarrel between the Master (Gerard de Ridefort) and the Marshal before the battle of the Spring of the Cresson on 1 May 1187. According to this writer, the Marshal advised the Master not to attack, at which the Master accused the Marshal of being a coward; the Marshal retorted that he was no coward but he would see the Master flee from the field while he himself went down fighting – which was in fact what happened. However, as almost every witness to this supposed dispute died in the engagement that followed, this account is dubious. The more contemporary accounts of the battle do not mention the quarrel. Yet this story does indicate that sometimes the Master and Marshal disagreed in the field, and that when they did the Master's decision was final.[38] On this particular occasion, the charge did not win the battle for the Christians, just as it did not at Hattin on 4 July. But, as Vegetius himself had pointed out, in a battle situation, a great deal must always be left to chance.

The statutes indicate that the cavalry charge was the sole feature of the Order's military tactics, and everything else was centred upon it. There is no indication of the role of the footsoldiers or archers the Order might employ, except to note that the unarmed sergeants could act as they thought best and retire when they felt it appropriate. The squires employed by the Order were there to assist the knights, not to fight on foot.[39] Clearly, in raids across Muslim territory a mounted force was advantageous, as speed and manoeuvrability were the keys to success. But a cavalry charge would not always be the most suitable tactic, and the Templars could and did dismount to fight when necessary.[40] So why this emphasis upon the cavalry charge? Simply, the cavalry charge was a most problematic military manoeuvre, which needed to be employed with care, organized correctly and well disciplined for maximum impact. The activities of footsoldiers and archers were far less problematic and did not need to be set down in writing.

Royal expeditions and crusades. It was in royal service that the Order made its largest military impact during the twelfth and early thirteenth century. At least three Masters of the Temple were royal ministers before they joined the Order, to become Master: Philip de Milly (1169–71), Odo de St Amand (1171–79) and Gerard de Ridefort (1185–89). Odo had been royal butler in 1171, while Gerard was royal marshal in 1179.[41] The Order was involved in a royal expedition against Damascus in 1129; the expedition of 1139 was under the royal banner; the Order was present at King Baldwin III's siege of Ascalon in 1153, and was involved in Amaury's invasions of Egypt in the 1160s. Even though William of Tyre recorded that the Templars opposed the Egyptian expedition of 1168, the contemporary *Annals of Cambrai* of Lambert Wattrelos show that they accompanied the expedition nevertheless.[42] In early July 1187 Master Gerard de Ridefort led a Templar contingent when King

Guy took the forces of the kingdom of Jerusalem to relieve the town of Tiberias, then under siege by Saladin. The chronicle attributed to Ernoul blamed Gerard for giving Guy bad advice, leading directly to the disastrous defeat at Hattin. Yet Ernoul, as a squire of Balian of Ibelin, would have wanted to acquit the Ibelin's ally Count Raymond III of Tripoli (d. 1187) from accusations of treachery and being in alliance with Saladin. Other contemporary and near-contemporary sources blamed Count Raymond for the defeat at Hattin and did not mention Gerard de Ridefort's advice to King Guy.[43]

The Order worked alongside King John of Brienne during the Fifth Crusade (1217–21).[44] After 1225 there was no king present in the kingdom of Jerusalem until 1286. The Order also worked alongside and in cooperation with royal leaders of crusading expeditions throughout the history of the crusader states.

The Templars played a significant role in all the crusading expeditions to the Holy Land. They guarded the vanguard or the rearguard while the crusading army was on the march. This was a prominent role during the Third Crusade, during the march from Acre to Jaffa in the autumn of 1191, when the crusaders had shown that they lacked the discipline to keep the army together. The Templars covered the crusaders' retreat when they were trapped by the flooding Nile at the end of the Fifth Crusade in August 1221. Even during the crusade of the Emperor Frederick II, the Templars and Hospitallers accompanied the crusader army, although they were not supposed to associate with the emperor because he was excommunicate.[45] They also offered to help him refortify Jerusalem, although he declined the offer.

During crusades the Military Orders would take responsibility for the defence of part of the crusader camp and guard it if it were attacked, as in the description given by Oliver the schoolmaster of Cologne, above. The Templars and Hospitallers gave military advice, notoriously during the Third Crusade (1189–92) in June 1192, when they advised Richard I of England not to advance to attack Jerusalem as the city could not be held if it were captured.[46] At Mansurah in February 1250, during the first crusade of King Louis IX of France, the Templars and Hospitallers advised against a cavalry charge, but were overruled by Count Robert of Artois, the king's younger brother, who (according to some accounts) accused them of cowardice. The result was a disaster for the crusade. Hardly anyone escaped alive, and the count himself was killed; but the Military Orders were vindicated.[47]

The Military Orders supplied artillery, stone-throwers and other siege machinery: at the siege of Acre during the Third Crusade the Templars had a large stone-thrower which 'wreaked impressive devastation' on the walls of the city, while at the siege of Damietta during the Fifth Crusade the Templars placed fortifications on one of their ships and used it to attack the city walls from the water. They also owned one of three powerful trebuchets – huge stone-throwers – that bombarded the city walls; they were given this by Duke Leopold VI of Austria. The other two were owned by the Romans and by the Hospital of St John.[48] The Templars lent money to crusading leaders, supplying King Louis IX with his ransom money after he was captured by the Muslims during his crusade to Damietta in 1250.[49] They also led negotiations with the Muslims, as Muslim leaders trusted them.[50] During the Third Crusade, they purchased the island of Cyprus from Richard I, providing him with much-needed cash.[51]

Criticism. Because the Military Orders were so prominent in the military forces of the crusader states, any failure was likely to be blamed on them by western commentators. An early example of this was the failure of the Second Crusade.

Odo of Deuil, who wrote an account of King Louis VII of France's journey to Jerusalem during the crusade, was full of praise for the Templars' discipline and the military aid which the Templars gave the crusader army as it passed through Asia Minor. Not only did the Templars excel in the field (again, employing the cavalry charge against the Turks) but they also introduced discipline and order to the crusading army.[52] When the expedition reached the Holy Land a decision was taken to besiege the city of Damascus, in order to prevent Nūr al-Dīn capturing it. As the siege proceeded slowly, the leaders decided to move the besieging army to a new position – which turned out to be disastrous as there was no water supply. The siege was abandoned.[53]

The failure of the siege of Damascus led to great controversy. A generation later Archbishop William of Tyre wrote that he had spoken with many people who remembered the siege and found that there was no agreement over what had gone wrong. Some blamed Count Thierry of Flanders; others said that the enemy bribed certain people, but that by a miracle afterwards the money that they had been given turned out to be worthless – another version of the story of the false gold. William himself was uncertain as to what had actually gone wrong.[54]

In the West, blame was initially placed on the 'men of Jerusalem', that is, the Franks who had settled in the crusader states.[55] The author of 'Casus monasterii Petrihusensis' blamed certain 'knights of God.'[56] This could have meant any of the crusaders, but may have meant the Templars and Hospitallers. The English cleric John of Salisbury, writing in around 1163, recorded that some blamed the crusaders and some the Templars for the failure to capture Damascus, but the king of France always tried to exonerate the Templars. John of Würzburg, travelling to Jerusalem in the early 1160s, was convinced that the Templars were to blame for the failure. The most vehement condemnation of the Templars' actions at Damascus came from John's fellow-countryman, the annalist of Würzburg, who claimed that the Templars had betrayed the crusade for money, and he accused the Brothers of greed, fraud, jealousy (presumably jealousy of the western crusaders) and pride.[57] These accusations sound like the complaints brought against the Order by the clergy at the Third Lateran Council of 1179. The date of the Würzburg annalist's work is not known, so he may have been writing nearer to 1179 than 1148.

A number of accounts claimed that 'men of Jerusalem' had received money from the Muslims for lifting the siege, money which later turned out to be false coin – either by a miracle or as a deliberate ploy by the Muslims.[58] The English Cistercian chronicler Ralph of Coggeshall (d. 1216) recorded that the siege had failed because the Templars were bribed by Nūr al-Dīn to persuade the crusader army to withdraw.[59] He did not mention false coin, simply implying that the Templars put money before Christian victory. His contemporary Gervase of Canterbury (d. 1210) wrote that Templars had treacherously negotiated with the Damascenes under pretence of leading the attack, and had accepted three jars of gold besants (the currency of the Middle East) in exchange for ending the siege. But when the crusaders had withdrawn and the Templars received the money, they found that the jars contained only copper, which they ascribed to a miracle.[60] Gervase did not explain why this should be a miracle rather than Muslim treachery; but he clearly preferred to give the credit to God as this made a better moral point and fitted neatly into his scheme of history. The chronicle ascribed to Ernoul and Bernard the Treasurer, which reached its present form in the 1220s, has the Templars and Hospitallers receiving packhorse loads of false coin in return for making the crusaders lift the siege. The author did not explain when or how the Brothers discovered that the money was false. Albert Milioli, notary of Reggio, included a version of the story in his chronicle of the emperors, written between 1281 and 1286: here the Templars, the Hospitallers and King Baldwin III of Jerusalem, 'stimulated by jealousy or corrupted by money', withdrew from the siege; Albert remarked that it served them right that the money was false.[61]

When all the stories are put together, it is striking that the most discerning of these historians, and the historian often most critical of the Templars and Hospitallers, on this occasion made no mention at all of the Military Orders being to blame for the failure. This historian was William of Tyre. William's version of events can never be lightly dismissed, and on this occasion he himself hesitated to ascribe blame. As he omitted the Military Orders from his list of culprits, it is safe to assume that they were not principally responsible for the failure of the siege. John of Salisbury also notes that King Louis VII of France was adamant that the Templars were not to blame. Perhaps they supported whoever gave the disastrous advice that led to the failure of the siege; but they were not the main wrongdoers. In 1148 the Templars and the Hospitallers were still too lacking in personnel and influence in the East to have had the disastrous impact on the siege that later historians credited to them. The fact that writers after the event considered the Templars or the Templars and Hospitallers to be the principal culprits does not reflect the Templars' actions in 1148 but their actions later, when they had become two of the most powerful groups in the crusader states.

William, however, did blame the Templars for their actions during the siege of Ascalon in 1153. According to him, after the Christian army under King Baldwin III had besieged Ascalon for many months, the Templars broke in through a breach in the wall. They would not allow any other Christians to follow them, even holding them back with their swords, because they wanted all the booty from the captured city, which they would win if they were able to capture the city by themselves. As a result they were all killed and their bodies hung by the Muslims from the walls of the city. So the city was not taken, because of the Templars' greed. However, the Christians rallied, and the city fell shortly afterwards.

William was not in the Holy Land when these events occurred, and, as in his account of the Second Crusade, he must have made enquiries of those who were there and their descendants. Ascalon was a large city; later accounts state that it had fifty-three large towers, as well as smaller ones.[62] During a general assault, people who were not immediately next to the Templars would not have realized that they had broken into the city. Their accounts would have been based on what was said later, after the Templars had been killed. As the king was greatly distressed by what had happened, the rest of the military leaders would have been extremely anxious to clear themselves of blame for the massacre. Their descendants, recounting events to William of Tyre, would have been equally anxious to clear their ancestors of blame.

Contemporary accounts of the siege give a different picture. The Muslim sources do not mention the Templars' deaths, but two contemporary accounts from the Low Countries do: one written at the abbey of Anchin at Pecquencourt near Waziers in what is now north-eastern France, and the other at Affligem in the duchy of Brabant. The second of these notes that the account came from a person who was present at the siege. Both accounts state that after the wall of Ascalon was breached, the Master of the Templars, Bernard de Trémblay (1152–3), and his troop broke into the city and reached the centre, where they made a stand. However, the streets were narrow, the walls were high and they received no support from the rest of the Christian forces, who did not follow them into the breach. They were surrounded and crushed by the enemy. Their beheaded bodies were hung from the city walls. Three days later the Christians made another assault and captured the city.[63]

These accounts are stronger evidence than William of Tyre's version, as they were written soon after the event and rely on an eyewitness who had no interest in distorting events; William was writing at least twenty years later and was relying on sources that had ample motives for misrepresenting the facts. Apparently, what really happened at Ascalon was that the Templars succeeded in breaking into the city through the breach in the wall, but the other Christian attackers did not realize that they had done so, or were reluctant to follow them in to probable death. The Templars were killed, and the king was angry. His generals excused themselves by saying that the Templars had prevented them from following them into the city – and this was the account that they and their children gave to William of Tyre.

Still, the Templars were rather rash in bursting into the city without making sure that the rest of the Christian army was following them. In 1179 the Master of the Temple, Odo de St Amand, made a rash charge during a battle at Marj 'Uyūn and was captured; he died in prison. In 1187 Saladin defeated the Military Orders at the Spring of the Cresson near Nazareth after the Master of the Temple, Gerard de Ridefort, had led a charge of a small force of Templars and Hospitallers against Saladin's army; almost the entire Christian force was killed. On 4 October 1189 Gerard was killed in a battle against Saladin's forces outside the city of Acre, when the Templars had gone on too far ahead of the rest of the crusader forces. This raises the question of whether the Templars were unreasonably rash in their military tactics.[64]

Some contemporaries certainly thought that they were. After the defeat at Marj 'Uyūn a Benedictine monk, Nigel Wireker, wrote that he (or, rather, his anti-hero Burnel the Donkey) would not join the Templars because the Order had petty and silly rules and Saladin would have his guts for shoelaces. In the first decade of the thirteenth century the knight-turned-Cluniac monk Guiot de Provins wrote that he admired the Templars' courage, but they could fight without him. But these writers were religious, not soldiers; and not even all religious writers agreed with them. Bernard of Clairvaux and a whole succession of popes praised the Order's self-sacrificing courage, declaring that it showed Christian love in action. The Brothers, they wrote, were prepared to lay down their lives for their fellow-Christians. Jacques de Vitry, bishop of Acre, praised the Order's devotion, telling the story of the Templar who rode into battle declaring to his horse Morel ('Blackie') that today he would carry him to paradise.[65]

In laying down their lives for Christendom, the Templars were following in Christ's steps, and emulating the great Christian warriors of the past such as Roland, half-legendary nephew of the Emperor Charlemagne (d. 814), who (according to legend) had refused to call on the emperor's assistance when the rearguard which he was commanding was treacherously attacked by the Muslims, preferring to die in arms with honour rather than to live knowing that his courage and steadfastness could be called into question. As Roland says in the oldest surviving version of the epic poem telling of his death:

> In his lord's service a man must suffer harsh straits and endure great heat and great cold, and even lose hair and hide. Now everyone take care to give strong blows, so that no one may ever sing a derogatory song about us! The Pagans [Muslims] are in the wrong and the Christians have the right; I will never give a bad example of how a warrior should act. (Lines 1010–16)
>
> May it not please our Lord God or His angels that France ever lose her strength because of me! I would rather die than be dishonoured; the emperor will love us more for our good blows. (Lines 1089–92)

The stories of Roland and other such Christian heroes of the Carolingian age were very popular among the warrior class of the twelfth and thirteenth century. With such examples to follow, how could the Templars, as Christ's knights, do other than to throw themselves fearlessly into seemingly impossible situations, trusting in God to give them the victory? For very often their apparently rash charges did win the day.

The Franks in the crusader states, and the Military Orders in particular, were dependent for their survival on support from the West. They had plenty of financial resources, but were lacking in personnel. As a result, they had always to bear in mind how their actions would look to their well-wishers and potential donors in the West. They could not afford to seem unenthusiastic about attacking the Muslims; and when, for example, in June 1192 they advised Richard I against advancing on Jerusalem, they were criticized for their approach by western commentators. During the German Crusade of 1197–8 the Templars were involved in some sort of disagreement with the German leaders that led to the abandonment of the siege of

Tībnīn, for which the Templars later were blamed by the German commentator Otto of St Blasien (writing between 1209 and 1222).[66]

Yet western commentators often did not appreciate the subtle power-politics of the Middle East, strategic considerations, the need for truces, or the cost of keeping so many warriors ready and able to fight and so many fortresses in a defensible condition. During the two centuries of the crusader states' existence the Military Orders, the Church and the secular authorities in the East tried to keep westerners informed by sending a steady stream of information to the West, in the form of letters addressed to the pope, leading officials of the Church, kings and leading nobles. Most of these letters are now lost, although some remain in administrative registers, while others were copied into chronicles. The Annals of Burton (upon Trent, England) contain a letter written in March 1260 by Thomas Bérard, Master of the Temple 1256–73, to Brother Amadeus, commander of the houses of the Temple in England, setting out the danger from the Mongols. The Order was desperately in need of aid because it had seven castles to keep garrisoned and defensible, and was also responsible for the defence of the city of Acre. Following the war of St Sabas (see below) and because of the danger in the kingdom, there were no merchants in Acre at present and it was therefore impossible to raise loans, but at the same time the Order had to quadruple its expenses to meet its military obligations, and the mercenaries wanted 'danger money' on top of their usual pay. The Order was prepared to pawn its Church plate to meet its financial needs, if only someone could be found to lend: the Master asked Amadeus to press King Henry III of England (1216–72) to lend the Order 10,000 silver marks (6,667 pounds sterling).[67] Thomas Bérard obviously did not know that Henry's own crusading ambitions in Sicily had brought him into financial crisis, that Henry's barons had taken over his financial affairs and he was certainly in no position to lend anything. The danger from the Mongols was ended by the Mamluk victory at 'Ayn Jālūt in September 1260, but was replaced by an even greater danger from the now all-powerful Mamluks.

Such letters did not always achieve their purpose. Events could change quickly in the East, and it too often happened that by the time the West had received one report, the situation had completely altered. In 1243 Hermann de Périgord, Master of the Temple 1232–44, reported to the West that the whole of Jerusalem had been recovered by treaty with the sultan of Damascus, along with other territory, and that the Christians were making great progress. The Templars hoped to build a castle near Jerusalem to help protect the newly recovered territory, but they needed aid from the West. However, Matthew Paris, who copied this letter into his *Chronica majora*, remarked sourly that this good news was not believed in the West because the Templars and Hospitallers were not trusted: it was believed that they had no interest in conquering the Muslims and wanted to prolong the war as a pretext for extorting money. In addition, they fought each other. The Templars had 9,000 manors in the West, the Hospitallers 19,000 (exaggerated figures!), and they could perfectly well support their war by themselves; but they were fooling Christendom.

Matthew's sourness was expressed after the event; shortly after the Master's letter was received in the West, terrible news followed. Al-Sālih Ayyūb, sultan of Egypt, reacted defensively to the Latin Christian truce with Damascus and called on a troop of Khwarismian Turks, originally led by the Uzbek warlord Jalal al-Dīn Menguberdi or Mingburnu, for military assistance. On 23 August 1244 the Khwarismians took Jerusalem, and on 17 October 1244 the combined Latin Christian–Damascene forces were heavily defeated at La Forbie, near Gaza, by the combined forces of the Khwarismians and Egyptians. Matthew included in his chronicle various letters from the East reporting these disasters, including a letter from the Emperor Frederick II to his brother-in-law, Earl Richard of Cornwall, crusader and King Henry III's younger brother, in which Frederick condemned the Templars' truce with the

Damascenes which, he said, had brought about the disaster. The Templars had received Muslims within their own house and allowed them to carry on their superstitious rites under their roof. Their defeat was God's judgement on them. Frederick had started a policy of alliance with Egypt while he was in the Holy Land in 1228–9, and he resented the change in policy that had followed the defeat of his regent in the East in the spring of 1242. Against later events, Hermann de Périgord's letter could certainly have appeared misleading, but it had been written in good faith.[68]

Complaints against the Templars' alliances with Muslims had some basis in fact. It was true that the Military Orders did keep up diplomatic relations with Muslim leaders and dignitaries in the East. The Templars' friendship with the Arab-Syrian gentleman and warrior Usāmah ibn Munqidh is well known: the Brothers allowed him to pray in a side chapel in the Aqsa mosque when he came to Jerusalem. But this friendship did not stop the Templars of Gaza almost killing Usāmah when they ambushed Rukn al-Dīn 'Abbās and his son Nāsr al-Dīn in 1154: Usāmah was part of 'Abbās's party, and barely escaped with his life.[69] Such diplomatic contacts and a healthy respect for a formidable enemy were essential for the Templars as part of their battle to defend Christendom in the East. Truces and alliances with Muslims enabled the crusader states to live to fight another day. The fact that Muslim writers always rejoiced over the Templars when they were defeated and depicted them as evil enemies of Islam shows that, despite alliances and friendships, in reality the Templars always remained what they claimed to be – fanatical warriors of Christ.

William of Tyre and Walter Map believed that the Templars were too fanatical: they refused to make peace with the Muslims even when it would help Christendom. They cited the case of Nāsr al-Dīn as one example of this; another was that of the Assassins. William recorded that in 1173 the Templars thwarted the conversion of the Shi'ite Assassins. One of the terms of the conversion was that the Assassins would no longer pay the Templars an annual tribute, and William blamed the Templars for preferring money to converts. In 1911 the historian Friedrich Lundgreen suggested that William himself had been involved in the negotiation of the treaty with the Assassins and was incensed when it fell through.[70] William's story of the Templars' murder of the Assassins' envoy was widely reported by later European chroniclers, but was not mentioned by any other contemporary or near-contemporary eastern source. Jacques de Vitry, bishop of Acre, repeated the story but did not blame the Templars for the murder, simply saying that one of the Christians responsible for escorting the Assassins' envoy back to his country murdered him on the way.[71] What actually happened on this occasion is not clear.

Disputes. Matthew Paris's complaint that the Military Orders fought between themselves had a good basis. Modern historians have pointed out that the Orders often cooperated: this was indeed the case, but their contemporaries expected them to work together and so did not comment when they did. But Orders that were vowed to the service of Christ should not disagree with each other or with other leaders on political policy, and this (contemporaries believed) they did too often, and for petty reasons.[72] For instance, three historical accounts written in the early thirteenth century accused Master Gerard de Ridefort of opposing Count Raymond of Tripoli and bringing about the catastrophic Christian defeat at Hattin on 4 July 1187 simply because of a broken promise. When Gerard was a knight in Raymond's service (the story went) Raymond had promised him the hand in marriage of the next heiress who became available, but when the heiress of Botron was due to marry he sold her to an Italian merchant rather than bestowing her on Gerard.[73] However, Guy of Bazoches and the Anglo-Norman historical writers, such as William of Newburgh, Roger of Howden, Ambroise the trouvère and the author of the second version of the *Itinerarium Peregrinorum*, blamed the count of Tripoli and his treaty with Saladin for the disasters of 1187.[74]

In the first decade of the thirteenth century the Templars and Hospitallers were in conflict over the succession to the

principality of Antioch. Following the death of Prince
Bohemond III in 1201, the Templars supported the claim of
Bohemond's second son, Bohemond of Tripoli, while the
Hospitallers supported Raymond-Rupen, Bohemond III's
grandson by his eldest son Raymond. Raymond had married
Alice, niece of King Leon of Cilician Armenia, but had died in
1197. Cilician Armenia was an independent Christian state in
southern Asia Minor; its people were Armenian Christians, not
Roman Catholics like the western Europeans. Its prince, Leon,
had won recognition as king in 1198 from the chancellor of the
western emperor, Henry VI (ruled 1190–97), and the papal
legate, and was now planning to unite Cilician Armenia and the
principality of Antioch under the person of Raymond-Rupen,
who was his own heir. Raymond-Rupen had been recognized
as heir to Antioch by the papal legate, but in 1201 he was not
yet five years old, and therefore an Armenian regent would be
appointed. Yet the population of the city of Antioch was not
prepared to submit to Armenian domination, and supported
Bohemond of Tripoli as prince.

The Templars supported Bohemond of Tripoli against the
Cilician Armenians because Leon had seized some of their
castles in the Amanus Mountains after Saladin's withdrawal
from the area and was refusing to give them up. The
Hospitallers supported Raymond-Rupen, who, with Leon of
Armenia, granted them territories and privileges in Cilician
Armenia. Leon of Armenia complained to Pope Innocent III
about the Templars using arms against him, but the pope
pointed out that their behaviour was understandable, as he was
holding their castles illegally. In 1211 open war broke out
between the Templars and Leon. Eventually, in spring 1213, a
peace was negotiated by which the Templars got back some of
their castles, but they did not get Baghras until 1216, when
Raymond-Rupen won control of the principality of Antioch.

His success was short-lived. He quarrelled with Leon and
alienated many of his supporters. In 1219 Bohemond of Tripoli
recovered Antioch by conspiracy. Following Leon's death in
the same year, the Hospitallers supported Raymond-Rupen's

attempt to claim the Cilician throne, but he was defeated, captured, and died in prison. The Hospitallers continued to support the Cilician Armenians, while the Templars continued to support the princes of Antioch.[75]

Such disputes, which involved fighting Christians and sometimes forming alliances with the Muslim enemies, did not do the Military Orders' reputation any good, but were not well known in the West. The political disputes which marked the crusade of Emperor Frederick II and its aftermath were far more damaging. In 1228–9 both the Hospital and the Temple had tried to cooperate with Frederick (so far as they could cooperate with an excommunicate crusade leader). Relations between the Templars and Frederick broke down apparently because the latter, as father of the infant King Conrad of Jerusalem, tried to enforce royal authority by taking over the Templars' strong fortress of Castle Pilgrim. When the Templars refused to surrender the fortress, Frederick besieged their house in Acre, but failed to capture it.[76] Despite Frederick's attack, the Templars tried to preserve the truce which he had made. The emperor had also confiscated the Templars' and Hospitallers' properties in Sicily under his mortmain regulations (which tried to stop property falling into the hands of religious institutions, which would pay no taxes or dues on it). Pope Gregory IX (1227–41) tried to negotiate: the Orders would do all they could to protect Christendom and uphold the truce, but Frederick must return their Sicilian properties, which were essential to them. In fact it is not clear when or whether Frederick returned the properties of the Hospital and Temple in Sicily, but by 1239 diplomatic relations between the Hospital and Frederick had been restored. The Templars in Frederick's own domains worked with him, but in the Holy Land relations were less cordial.

During the crusades of Theobald, count of Champagne and king of Navarre, and Earl Richard of Cornwall in 1239–42, the Hospitallers supported the emperor's policy of making peace with Egypt and maintaining war against Damascus. The Templars, the Italian communes and many of the barons of the kingdom of Jerusalem preferred to make peace with Damascus and maintain war against Egypt. In 1243 the leaders of the kingdom abandoned the truce with Egypt and made a treaty with Damascus by which Jerusalem and other properties were handed over to the Franks. Al-Sālih Ayyūb, sultan of Egypt, reacted by calling in the Khwarismian Turks, who captured Jerusalem and defeated the Latin Christians and Damascenes at La Forbie in 1244; and Emperor Frederick II blamed the Templars for abandoning his policies.

Between 1256 and 1258 civil war broke out in Acre. This was the so-called war of St Sabas, which began between the Italian communes of Genoa and Venice over the property of the abbey of St Sabas in Acre. The Hospital supported Genoa; the Templars supported Venice. There is no evidence that the two Military Orders were actually involved in the fighting, but the episode added to their reputation for rivalry. The Genoese were defeated and driven out of Acre, leaving Thomas Bérard to complain in 1260 that he could not raise loans because of the absence of the Genoese merchants.[77]

In 1276 Hugh of Antioch-Lusignan, king of Jerusalem and Cyprus, left Acre and went to Tyre, leaving no regent or representative behind him, because he had so many disputes with the religious orders and communes and fraternities in the kingdom that he could not govern. The immediate cause of his departure, according to the writer of the *Estoire de Eracles*, a continuation of William of Tyre's chronicle, was that the Master of the Temple, William de Beaujeu, had bought a village or 'casal' called La Fauconerie from a knight of Acre without informing the king of the transaction. No military service or homage was due to the king in rent for the casal, but the king still considered that he should have been informed and allowed to give or withhold his consent. The king's problem was that for many years there had been no active monarch in the kingdom of Jerusalem to take a role in its government and enforce royal authority, and that therefore government structures had not developed in the kingdom in the thirteenth century as they had in western European kingdoms. As a result when a king did take office he lacked the structures and procedures through which to impose his authority. What was more, William de Beaujeu and the commune of Venice did not recognize Hugh as king, preferring the hereditary claim of Maria of Antioch to the realm. Maria sold her claim to Charles I of Anjou in 1277. When Hugh left Acre, the Templars and Venetians would not support attempts to persuade him to return, and William de Beaujeu worked on behalf of Charles of Anjou, hoping that he would come east to claim the throne.[78]

It is easy to blame William de Beaujeu for opposing the king of Cyprus's authority and so prolonging the governmental problems of the kingdom of Jerusalem. His actions could be interpreted as purely selfish, promoting his relative Charles of Anjou against the interests of the kingdom. Yet it is clear that William cared deeply about the kingdom of Jerusalem. On his first arrival in Acre as Master of the Temple in October 1275, he wrote to King Edward I of England, who had been in the Holy Land on crusade a few years previously and was much interested in the state of the country. William observed that there was nothing good to say about the situation: the land and its inhabitants were destitute; the sultan of Egypt was in Damascus waiting for the Mongols to return – but the Christians believed he was planning another attack on them. The Order of the Temple was in a weaker state than it had ever been, with many expenses and almost no revenues, as its possessions had all been plundered by the sultan. The Order's revenues from Europe were not enough to support it, and it had enormous expenses in the upkeep of castles and defending the Holy Land; William feared that the Order would not be able to continue its work. He asked Edward to send aid to enable the Order to keep going until the crusade planned by Pope Gregory X (1271–6) arrived.[79]

In the event, the pope's planned crusade was abandoned on his premature death, and the Holy Land was left to cope alone. In these circumstances, it was for each of the political leaders in the crusader states to judge the best policy to follow. William de Beaujeu believed that his cousin Charles of Anjou had the initiative, vision and drive to succeed in the eastern Mediterranean: as uncle of the king of France he had immense influence at the French court; the pope supported him; he was already king of Naples and Sicily and had ambitions to become emperor of Constantinople. As king of Jerusalem, he would be able to raise the supplies of money and warriors needed not only to defend what remained but to win back what had been lost. In contrast, the king of Cyprus lacked the resources and influence of Charles of Anjou and his family. For William, the choice of Charles of Anjou as king of Jerusalem must have seemed like simple common sense.

Yet some of William de Beaujeu's other policies seem less reasonable in view of the poor state of the country. While he was defending the rights of the Order, he was weakening the country as a whole. Between 1275 and 1282 the Templars were involved in the succession dispute in the county of Tripoli. Bohemond VI died in 1275; the regent was his widow Sibyl, daughter of King Hetoum I of Cilician Armenia and mother of the young Prince Bohemond VII. Sibyl appointed as her chief minister Bishop Bartholomew of Tortosa, vicar of Patriarch Opizo of Antioch, but the Latin Catholic clergy in Tripoli resented Bartholomew being brought in over their heads. The opposition was led by young Bohemond's great-uncle, Paul of Segni, bishop of Tripoli, who was a Dominican friar and a *confrère*, or associate, of the Templars. Another player in the conflict was one of the young prince's vassals, Guy II of Gibelet. After a dispute with the prince, Guy left Tripoli, went to Acre and became a Templar *confrère*. The Master of the Temple, William de Beaujeu, took up Guy's case.

When open war broke out between the two factions in the county of Tripoli the Templars were in the centre of the conflict. The Templars' house in Tripoli was destroyed. The Master besieged Tripoli, had the castle of Botron destroyed, and tried to take Nephim, where twelve Brothers were captured. The Master then returned to Acre, while the men of Gibelet and thirty Templars defeated their opponents at Tripoli. A truce was made.

Early in 1278 the Templars tried to attack Tripoli by sea but were driven back by a storm; Bohemond VII occupied the Templars' island fortress near Sidon. In 1279 Guy of Gibelet attempted to attack the town of Tripoli in cooperation with the Templars, but because of various mishaps – such as Guy failing to see the signal that it was safe for his ships to come to shore, his sailors mistaking a bright star for the morning star and retreating because they thought that dawn was coming, and simple mistiming – three attempts at attack failed. Guy was captured, tried, blinded and imprisoned.

In 1287 Bohemond VII died and his mother tried to make Bartholomew of Tortosa regent for her daughter Lucia. The people of Tripoli opposed Bartholomew, elected one of the Gibelet family as their leader and called on Genoese aid. The disputes were ended by the loss of Tripoli to the Mamluk Sultan Qalawūn in March 1289.[80]

The end of the crusader states

Yet, even if the crusader states had had strong leadership and unity and avoided factional infighting, could they have survived? From 1240 western Christendom was distracted by the war between the Emperor Frederick II and the papacy, and the papacy's attempts to prevent Frederick's relations from holding any power in Sicily because they were threatening papal territory in Italy. In England the king and his barons were at loggerheads from 1258, and peace was not fully restored until after 1267. After the death of Emperor Frederick II in 1250 (and even beforehand) there was no single generally recognized authority in Germany. In short, Europe had its own problems. The papacy was anxious that heresy and his political enemies should be crushed in Europe before a new crusade was launched, for God would not support the crusaders if they were tainted by sin. During the 1260s the people of the Holy Land watched with indignation as European crusaders were diverted to fight papal wars in Sicily at the same time as their castles were falling one by one before Baibars's inexorable advance. The Templar poet Ricaut Bonomel complained:

> The pope is very generous with his indulgences
> Against Italians, to Charles and the French;
> But he makes great profits out of us,
> For he pardons for money people who have taken our cross;
> And if anyone wishes to swap the Holy Land
> For the war in Italy
> Our legate lets them do so
> For he sells God and indulgences for cash.
> O French lords! Alexandria
> Has done you more harm than Italy,
> For here the Turks are overrunning us,
> Capturing and conquering and giving us away for cash.[81]

Other factors combined to weaken the Latin Christian states in the East. The wars between the Italian communes damaged trade. The Mongol conquests in central Asia and incursions into Mesopotamia caused the trade routes to move north during the 1250s, so that the important entrepôts, which had been such an important source of income to the crusader states, now received far less trade, and the lords of the kingdom grew poorer. But the all-important change was the unification of the Muslims under the Mamluks. Faced by a united, militarily efficient enemy, the Franks were too few to hold out for long. They survived by a series of truces, but in the end any pretext would serve to give the sultan an excuse to wipe out the infidel on his doorstep.

On 6 April 1291, Acre, the last major European Christian stronghold in the Holy Land, came under attack from the troops of Sultan al-Ashraf Khalil. The siege lasted over a month. The Muslims began their final assault on 18 May. Contemporary writers described the final battle in the city streets. The Military Orders were generally praised: the Teutonic Order fought to the last man, the Templar Master William de Beaujeu was killed in action. Several commentators on the last battle judged that his death was the last blow, sealing the fate of the crusader kingdom of Jerusalem; if only he had not died, the city could still have been saved.[82] Those of the population of the city who could escape fled to the port to seek ships. The Military Orders assisted with the evacuation. Those who escaped capture fled to Cyprus, which continued to resist the Mamluks.

In late summer 1291, the chronicler of St Peter's, Erfurt (in Germany), wrote an account of the last defence of Acre:

> Also, it is said that a good 7,000 people fled to the house of the Templars [in Acre]. Because it was located in a strong part of the city, overlooking the sea shore, and was surrounded by good walls, they defended it for perhaps twelve days after the capture of the city [by the Muslims]. But when the Templars and the others who had fled there realised that they had no supplies and no hope of being supplied by human help, they made a virtue of necessity. With devoted prayer, and after confession, they committed their souls to Jesus Christ, rushed out strenuously on the Saracens and strongly threw down many of their adversaries. But at last they were all killed by the Saracens.[83]

This was a fitting end to the great Military Order; its last Brothers dying in the defence of the capital of the kingdom. In fact, the chronicler knew that the Templar fortresses of Sidon and Castle Pilgrim still held out after the fall of Acre, as well as the cities of Tyre, Beirut and Tortosa. He hoped that the Christians would be able to rally their forces again and recover their kingdom in the East, as they had done after Saladin's victories in 1187, when only Tyre had held out under the command of Marquis Conrad of Montferrat. But in 1187 Saladin had had his own problems with his commanders and his troops, and western Christendom had been ready and able to send aid under powerful leaders: the emperor of Germany, the kings of France and England, as well as important lesser nobles such as the duke of Austria and the landgrave of Thuringia. In 1291 England and France were on the verge of war, there was no emperor in Germany, and the pope was preoccupied with the situation in Sicily, where his favoured regime had been thrown out by revolt in 1282 and replaced by a regime supported by the royal dynasty of Aragon. Without hope of being relieved, the remaining Latin Christian fortresses in the East rapidly surrendered: Tyre in May, Sidon and Beirut in July, Tortosa and Castle Pilgrim in August. Their garrisons retreated to Cyprus, there to plan their next move and initiate negotiations for a new crusade.

Meanwhile, when Pope Nicholas IV (1288–92) heard the news, he summoned provincial Church Councils to meet in 1292 to discuss how the Holy Land could be recovered. High on the agenda was the question of whether the Military Orders should be unified – thus neatly throwing the blame for the loss of the Holy Land on to the Military Orders.[84]

Were the Templars an asset to the crusader states?

Writing between his return to the kingdom of Jerusalem from a university career in Italy in 1165 and his death in around 1184, William, archbishop of Tyre, had regarded the Templars and Hospitallers as a force for disintegration and lawlessness in the kingdom. Although their beginnings had been propitious, he saw that by his day they had become too rich and proud, refusing to obey the authorities set over them by God: the patriarch of Jerusalem and the king. Describing their deeds after 1150, he brushed over their successes, minimized their positive role and emphasized their failures. The disastrous campaign against Egypt in 1168 was all the fault of the Hospitallers; the failure of the negotiations with the Assassins was all the fault of

the Templars.) Yet examination of William's account and
comparison with other, often more contemporary, sources
indicates that his picture of the Military Orders was not
accurate. If twelve Templars had defied their king by sur-
rendering a castle too quickly, the king had been able to hang
them, thereby restoring his authority; and the pope and the
Order not been able to do anything to stop him. His account of
the Templars' rash greed at Ascalon was based at best on
misinformation; even his account of the death of the Assassins'
envoy was not entirely accurate, to judge from the later account
of Jacques de Vitry. The Templars may have refused to
accompany the Egyptian campaign of 1168, but Lambert
Wattrelos's account makes it clear that they had to go whether
they liked it or not, because the king commanded it. William
certainly disliked Odo de Saint-Amand, Master of the Temple,
but this appears to have been for personal reasons: at
Montgisard Odo proved his worth to the king of Jerusalem.
Certainly the Masters of the Temple had their own military
strategies, but at least three of them had previously been royal
servants, and they would hardly openly oppose their old
master.

William's attitude to the Templars, and also the Hospitallers,
was part of the message of his *History*. He was writing for the
people of the kingdom of Jerusalem to encourage them to be
proud of their homeland, to show them what had gone wrong
and how the kingdom could be saved. After he attended the
Third Lateran Council of 1179 he was also writing for
the people of western Christendom, to show them, too,
how the kingdom of Jerusalem could be saved. He repeatedly
demonstrated that Christians from the West – such as Thierry
of Flanders and his son Philip of Alsace – did not understand
the kingdom and did not act in its best interests. Describing the
childhood and reign of King Baldwin IV, whose tutor he had
been and whose chancellor he was, he was aware that he was
writing against a background of papal anxiety that the king's
leprosy indicated God's anger, that God had abandoned the

kingdom of Jerusalem to the Muslims, and that only western Christendom could save it. Popes were telling western Christians to give their aid to the Templars and Hospitallers and to crusaders rather than to the natives of the kingdom. William's message was that this attitude was completely misconceived. The crusaders and the Military Orders were the greatest danger to the kingdom. The natives of the kingdom knew how the kingdom could best be saved and they deserved the support of western Christendom.[85]

To judge from a perspective of over 700 years later, the Military Orders in general and the Templars in particular appear to have been generally beneficial to the crusader states. They were a vital military force: they kept up military pressure on the Muslim neighbours of the crusader states in raids, they formed part of the military forces of the crusader states when the secular rulers led their armies in the field; they protected pilgrims, who brought money and personnel to the kingdom. Their fine buildings in Jerusalem and later in Acre greatly impressed pilgrims with the Orders' piety and power. The Templars played an important political role, advising the king of Jerusalem (until 1225), or initiating policy in the absence of a monarch.

Yet the Masters of the Temple and of the other Military Orders had their own views on the best policies to follow, and this certainly caused problems within the crusader states. As the secular nobles and the Church lost resources after 1250 and were unable to maintain fortresses and protect their territory, the Military Orders took over almost all the fortresses and became not only the most effective military unit in the crusader states but almost the *only* military unit there. This had never been intended, and they became – as William of Tyre had foreseen – a force for disintegration rather than for unity. Nevertheless, they united in the face of common danger, in 1260 against the Mongols and in 1291 at Acre. They fought bravely and died honourably during the final battle for Acre, fulfilling what Latin Christendom expected of them. And even after the loss of the crusader states in the Holy Land they were expected to lead the army that would recapture the Holy Land, once a few necessary reforms had made them more efficient.

3

HOLY WAR IN THE IBERIAN PENINSULA AND IN EASTERN EUROPE

While the Order of the Temple was defending pilgrims and waging war against the enemies of Catholic Christendom in the Middle East, it was also becoming involved in holy war on other European frontiers. In the Iberian peninsula and in eastern Europe it was involved in holy war against non-Christians and in economic expansion. In these areas it can be asked whether the Order of the Temple was acting as an exempt religious Order of the Catholic Church, answerable to no one on earth except the papacy, or whether it was acting more like a royal or episcopal militia, employed to meet the secular or religious prince's purposes – which might be religious or territorial. The fact that the Templars often operated alongside local Military Orders created by the local prince does suggest that they were being used for personal purposes; but as a supranational religious Order they offered certain advantages over local Military Orders, although they also created certain disadvantages.

The Order was used extensively in the Iberian Peninsula from early in the Order's history; it was used in a far more limited way in eastern Europe, and not until the thirteenth century.

The Iberian Peninsula and the 'reconquista'[1]

The Iberian Peninsula had been part of the Roman Empire and was converted to Christianity in the fourth century. It was conquered in the early fifth century by the Visigoths, who were Arian Christians. After the battle of Guadalete in 711 the Muslims overran most of the peninsula, although the north was never conquered. The Christian rulers there and the Muslims further south evolved means of co-existing: for instance, Christian rulers allied themselves with the Muslim rulers and charged them tribute, called *parias*, in exchange for their alliance and in return for not attacking them. The historian Angus Mackay has aptly termed this system a 'protection racket'. The situation was similar to that in Holy Land in the twelfth and thirteenth centuries where the Latin Christian lords allied with Muslim lords for mutual advantage. As in the Holy Land, Christian rulers in Spain would also ally with Muslim rulers against other Christians.

There was a good deal of cooperation within each society between Christians and Muslims. In Muslim Spain lived Christians who had adopted Muslim customs but not converted to Islam; these Christians were known as Mosarabs. When Christian conquerers defeated Muslims in Christian Spain they often allowed them to follow their religion and mosques remained open. They did this because, just as in the crusader states, there were not enough Christians to populate the newly conquered land.

Despite protection rackets, toleration and alliances the Christian rulers of the north were still determined to push south into the lands the Muslims had never colonized thoroughly. Although they presented this to their subjects and to other Christians as religious expansion into lands that were rightfully Christian (hence the term *reconquista*, 'reconquest', used to describe it), they also intended to win new territory and wealth. Various factors enabled the Christian rulers to expand their territories more quickly.

As in the East, the most important of these was divisions among the Muslims themselves. From 756 the Iberian Peninsula was independent from the rest of Islam and from 929 it had its own caliph, or religious leader. But by the early eleventh century the caliph's power was breaking down; the last caliph was deposed in 1031. The Muslim territories here split into *Taifa* states, or 'party states' identified with different ethnic groups, such as the Berbers on the south coast. The *Taifa* states were rivals, and there was no united front against the Christian attack.

This power vacuum drew in the Christian rulers from the north. In the eleventh century the main Christian kingdoms were León, Castile and Aragon; in addition, there were the counties of Portugal and Barcelona. In 1085 Alfonso VI of León-Castile (d. 1109) captured Toledo, which had been the Visigothic capital before the Muslim invasion. This was a major propaganda coup, since Alfonso could claim to be restoring the Visigothic empire and to be the rightful ruler of the whole of the Iberian Peninsula, as the Visigothic king had been. The conquest also raised the prestige of Castile because Toledo possessed a large library, and kings of Castile became famed as patrons of learning.

The support of the papacy also speeded up the 'reconquest' because this helped recruit warriors for campaigns in Spain. A letter of Pope Alexander II (1061–73) survives, which states that those who were intending to journey to Spain were to confess their sins but would not have to do any penance because the expedition would be penance enough.[2] Alexander was offering incentives to warriors who went to Spain similar to those offered later to crusaders – although not a complete remission of all sins. Warriors came to Spain from Normandy, Aquitaine, Burgundy and elsewhere in France.

After the First Crusade the pope recognized the war against the Muslims in the Iberian Peninsula as a crusade. The Iberian kings had complained to the pope that their warriors wanted to go on crusade to the Holy Land, yet they needed them on the Iberian frontier to fight the Moors (the Iberian Muslims). In 1100 and 1101 Pope Paschal II (1099–1118) banned Spanish knights from going on crusade while the Moors were a danger in the Iberian Peninsula. He also declared that anyone going on crusade against the Moors would have the same remission of sins as if they had gone to Jerusalem. During the first few decades of the twelfth century the Iberian frontier came to be generally recognized both within the Iberian Peninsula and in the rest of western Europe as a crusading arena.

Yet the Moors were not a dying force. After the loss of Toledo in 1085 the Muslim ruler of Seville called in help from the Almoravids of North Africa who took over Muslim Iberia, defeated the Christians and temporarily halted the expansion south. The Almoravids also succeeded in imposing some unity on the Muslims in the peninsula. But by the 1140s they were losing control and Muslim Iberia was fragmenting again. During the Second Crusade, expeditions were launched in the Iberian Peninsula against the Muslims, which were reinforced by crusaders from outside the peninsula. These won territory from the Muslims, notably Lisbon in the west and Tortosa in the east. In the 1150s the Almohads moved in from North Africa and again imposed unity on Muslim Iberia, forcing the Christians on to the defensive.

The turning point came in 1212, when the Muslim forces were defeated by a Christian force made up from the various Iberian kingdoms at Las Navas de Tolosa. Muslim control of the Iberian Peninsula was destroyed, and the Christian rulers advanced south rapidly. By 1300 they had conquered the whole of the peninsula except Granada: the Muslim kingdom of Granada remained independent until it was captured by Ferdinand and Isabella of Aragon-Castile in 1492.

The Military Orders

As in the crusader states, the concept of the Military Order was attractive to monarchs in the Iberian Peninsula, who were short of fighting power to defend frontiers and yet needed to keep up continual skirmishing along the frontier, as the Franks did in the East. There were two options: either to give territory to the Military Orders that had been set up in the East, and ask them to give assistance in the Iberian Peninsula, or to set up local Military Orders.

The Templars received their first land in the Iberian Peninsula in the 1120s and 1130s. The earliest donations were in Portugal. In 1128, Countess Teresa, countess of Portugal (1097–1128), gave the Order the castle of Soure (see figure 5), which had been recovered from the Muslims and repopulated a few years previously. As in the East, the Order provided only part of the defences of the area around the city of Coimbra, while Countess Teresa's son and successor Afonso Henriques, count of Portugal (1114–85), also built the castle of Leirena, which was garrisoned by his own forces. Until the early 1140s there is no evidence that the Templars actually undertook military operations in Portugal; the first record of the Templars of Soure being involved in military action is in 1144. In 1147 they sent troops to assist Count Afonso Henriques in an assault on the Muslim-held town of Santarém, which was successful. As a reward for their assistance the Templars were given the churches of Santarém. When, after the capture of Lisbon in 1147, a bishop of Lisbon was established and the churches of Santarém given to him, the Templars were compensated with the castle of Cera on the River Tomar. In 1160 the Master of the Temple in Portugal, Gualdim Pais, founded a town here which he called Tomar (see plate 30); this became the Order's centre in Portugal, and was one of the most defensible castles in the kingdom. He had already constructed a castle further to the north, at Pombal (see plate 6).

The Order had also been given 'reconquered' land to recolonize and cultivate. In 1145 the Brothers were given the castle of Longroiva. The archbishop of Braga gave them a pilgrim hospital at Braga, which had been originally established by an earlier archbishop; they were responsible for maintaining the hospital and keeping up pilgrim care. In 1170 Afonso Henriques gave the Order land beyond the River Tagus (Tejo), recently recovered from the Muslims. In addition to this, the Order could keep a third of all the land it could acquire and settle.

The Order became well established in Portugal, and relations with the rulers of Portugal were close. In the Templars' early days in the country Count Afonso Henriques referred to himself as a 'brother in your fraternity', indicating that he had become an associate or *confrater* of the Order. This meant that he had undertaken to give the Order regular gifts and to support and protect it, while in return the Brothers would pray for him and he would receive spiritual benefit from their good works. Afonso Henriques's son, Sancho I (1185–1211), gave the Templars extensive lands, and used their castle at Tomar as a safe depository for his treasure. In 1216 Pope Innocent III (1198–1216) decided that the castles of Montémor-o-Velho and Alenquer, which were being disputed between King Afonso II (1211–23) and two of his sisters, Teresa and Sancha, should be entrusted to the Templars as reliable neutral parties; this was done in 1223. The Templars supported Sancho II (1223–45) during the rebellion against him led by his brother Afonso, count of Boulogne; the Master in Portugal, Martim Martins, was a childhood friend of Sancho. But the rebellion was successful, Sancho lost his throne, and the Templars later lost territory because of their support for the deposed king.[3]

Donations on the eastern side of the peninsula were slower than those in the west, but followed a similar pattern. The Templars may have had land in Aragon as early as 1130. In 1131 Ramon Berenguer III, count of Barcelona and marquis of Provence, joined the Order of the Temple as an associate or *confrater*, and also gave the castle of Granyena (Grañena) 'for the defence of Christendom, which is the purpose for which

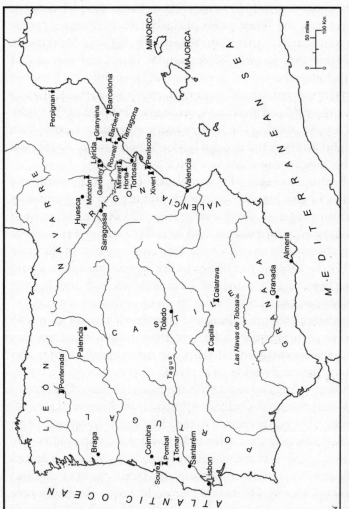

Figure 5 The Iberian Peninsula during the twelfth and thirteenth centuries, showing Templar fortresses and other locations mentioned in the text

their Order of knighthood was set up'. On his death, he gave the Order his horse, named Danc, and all his armour. Other rulers in the frontier zone, notably the counts of Urgel, also gave donations. In 1132 Armengold or Ermengaud VI, count of Urgel, gave the Templars his castle of Barberà (Barbará) 'in the Saracen March' – that is, on the frontier with the Muslims. In 1134 his lord Ramon Berenguer IV, count and marquis of Barcelona, repeated the donation; but apparently the Templars had not yet garrisoned either Granyena or Barberà. Ramon Berenguer IV also undertook to become a member of the Order for a year, obeying the Master and giving equipment for ten knight-Brothers and enough land to support them. Twenty-six of his knights also made vows to aid the Order.

Ramon Berenguer IV was clearly trying to persuade the Order to give him active military support, but the Order was slow to cooperate. At this stage it did not even own castles in the kingdom of Jerusalem, and lacked the manpower to begin operations from castles in the Iberian peninsula. In the early 1130s the Order's properties in the Iberian peninsula would have been its only source of income. It was not until Ramon Berenguer had become ruler of Aragon that he was able to bring more pressure to bear, and even then it was not until 1143 that he persuaded the Order to commit itself to military action in the peninsula, around the same time that the Order also became militarily active in Portugal.[4]

Other rulers endowed both their own Military Orders and the supranational Orders. Alfonso I of Aragon (1104–34) dreamt of going on crusade to the Holy Land himself and he set up his own military Order at Monréal del Campo (1126–30). However, this was not successful, apparently because it lacked resources to be able to operate effectively. In 1131 Alfonso drew up his will. He had no heir, so he bequeathed his whole kingdom to the Holy Sepulchre in Jerusalem, the Order of St John of Jerusalem (the Hospital) and the Order of the Temple. Perhaps he thought that only these three Orders could defend the kingdom. Although at this time the Order of the Holy

Sepulchre was not a military Order as such, knights and the Orders of the Temple and Hospital were associated with it in the early years of their development.[5] Alternatively, perhaps he did not intend these Orders to fight – perhaps he was using them as a political tool.

The historian Elena Lourie has argued that Alfonso gave his kingdom to the Military Orders, who were under the direct protection of the pope, because he was worried that his stepson Alfonso VII of Castile (1126–57) would take over Aragon. He knew that the pope would protect the Military Orders' interests and prevent Alfonso VII from invading Aragon. This was what happened. While the pope kept Alfonso VII out of Aragon, Alfonso I's brother Ramiro, a monk, came out of his monastery, married, and fathered a daughter, Petronilla. She was quickly engaged to the adult count of Barcelona, Ramon Berenguer IV, who took over the government of Aragon – and Ramiro went back to his monastery.[6]

Lourie's theory has not been widely accepted, and most historians believe that Alfonso's will should be taken at face value. But whatever Alfonso I intended, Ramon Berenguer IV became ruler of Aragon, and had to compensate the Orders of the Temple, Hospital and Holy Sepulchre.

His first charter for the Templars tried to combine compensation with persuading the Order to become militarily active in Barcelona-Aragon. He asked the Master, Robert de Craon, to send him ten Templar Brothers who could act as the core of a Templar force in Aragon. He would support them; and he promised property, people and a tenth of everything he should acquire in the Iberian Peninsula. This was not accepted by the Master, and so negotiations continued. In 1143 Ramon Berenguer issued a charter that set out the final terms. He conceded the castles of Monzón (plate 8), Montjoy, Barberà and others, with other property, a tenth of all his rents and a hundred *sous* a year income from Saragossa (Zaragoza); a fifth of the booty from every expedition that the Templars made; a tenth of everything he could 'justly acquire with God's help'; and a fifth of the land recovered from the Muslims. He would help them build castles and fortresses against the Moors, and he would not make treaties and truces without their advice. In addition, they were exempted from various dues.[7]

This agreement marked the beginning of the Templars' military involvement in Aragon, and corresponded with the beginnings of the Templars' recorded military involvement in Portugal. Clearly, by the early 1140s the Order of the Temple had acquired sufficient properties both in the West and in the East and had recruited sufficient members to be able to carry out military operations on two fronts, in the East and in the Iberian Peninsula. The Brothers often formed part of the military force on all the king of Aragon's campaigns against the Muslims. They were also prominent in an advisory role. Yet their importance lay not their numbers, which were never large, but in the fact that they could mobilize quickly and could stay in the field for a long time – unlike the secular nobles and their forces, who went home after their forty days' service, or went to get in the harvest.

Ramon Berenguer IV continued to favour the Templars. In 1153 he gave them the castle of Miravet (plate 7) because he reckoned that they were trustworthy guardians; he also kept his promise to give them a fifth of conquests. His successor Alfonso II (1162–96) was not so conscientious in sticking to the 1143 agreement; instead of giving the Order conquered lands, he gave it the equivalent in lands away from the frontier. Presumably he considered that the Templars were getting rather powerful in Aragon and did not want them to build up large areas of potentially independent power. The Templars could still, however, conquer lands on their own initiative, so they continued to build up their territories. Alfonso II's successor, Peter II (Pedro or Pere II, 1196–1213) was even more cautious in giving the Order newly conquered territory, but he did make some grants in return for military aid.[8] The change in patronage was not entirely because of royal concern about making the

Templars too powerful; there was also competition from other Military Orders.

The Hospitallers had also become involved in military operations in the Iberian Peninsula during the 1140s; they and the Templars contributed troops to Ramon Berenguer's attack on Tortosa in 1148. By the 1180s the Hospitallers had become the favoured religious Order of the royal family of Aragon.

The Templars and Hospitallers played a significant role in the campaigns of King James I of Aragon (Jaume or Jaime I, 1213–76), assisting in his capture of the Balearic islands (Majorca and Minorca) from the Almohad ruler Abu Yahya in 1229–30, and his conquest of the kingdom of Valencia, completed in 1238. However, the Templars did not do so well out of their assistance as they might have hoped. In 1228 and 1229, before the attack on Majorca, the Cortes (parliament) met and decided that the land conquered during the proposed expedition should be divided according to the contingents that each group brought. Yet, according to James himself, the Hospitallers received as much as the Templars even though they arrived late and missed the fighting.[9]

In James's autobiography the Templars performed the same sort of functions as they did in the Latin East and in Portugal: providing military forces which could be quickly mobilized and were reliable in the field, and providing military advice. It was on the advice of the Templar commander of Majorca (the nephew of the commander of Monzón) that James attacked Minorca.[10] The Masters of the Hospital and Temple in Aragon also gave security for a loan James wished to take out, and the Templars and Hospitallers accompanied him when he set out on crusade in 1269 – although he had to turn back because of poor weather conditions at sea. During the voyage the Templars' ship lost its rudder and James sent over his own ship's spare rudder, although one of his advisers opposed this action, saying that the Templars should have brought their own spare. The Masters of the Temple and Hospital in Aragon were members of the council that advised James to turn back to Aragon.[11] Yet throughout James's autobiography the Hospitallers received more favour than the Templars. The Prior of the Hospital in Aragon was Hugh of Forcalquier, James's personal friend – James had asked the Master of the Hospital in the East to appoint Hugh as prior in Aragon.[12] The Master of the Temple was not so close to James. When James wanted to persuade the Templars to act as security for him, he plotted with Hugh of Forcalquier over how they could best be persuaded.[13] While the Masters of both Orders in Aragon were members of his private council, Hugh could speak to James privately as a friend, whereas the Templar Master could not.

James did make many grants to the Templars, but he was apparently determined not to give them a leading role in the defence of the kingdom, and he did not adhere to the agreement of 1143. After 1244 Aragon no longer had a frontier with the Muslims, and possibilities of gaining wealth from conquest and booty were severely reduced. It can only be speculated whether James's determination not to let the Templars become too powerful in Aragon was a result of his having been brought up by the Templars at Monzón from the age of six to the age of nine. His account of this episode from his childhood does not indicate that he enjoyed being under Templar tutelage.

As the thirteenth century progressed the kings of Aragon complained more and more that the Military Orders were not meeting their military obligations. The Orders were genuinely short of money because of losses in the Holy Land and a fall in pious donations to all religious Orders in western Europe, and were therefore less able to undertake military responsibilities. The resources in their houses were not impressive: Alan Forey has noted that in 1289 the Templars' house at Huesca, on the order of the provincial Master of Aragon, had lent three hauberks, or mailshirts, and three other coats of mail to their house at Novillas, leaving only four hauberks and seven-and-a-half pairs of chausses (chainmail leggings).[14] This major Templar house with military obligations apparently had expected to have to arm only seven knights and three sergeants; but it is interesting that they kept one spare chausse handy.

Not only were the Military Orders short of military resources in Spain, but the kings were also asking more of them; they wanted the Military Orders to help defend the realm against Christian enemies as well as Muslims. In 1285 a French army invaded Aragon in a crusade that had been declared against Peter III of Aragon (1276–85) for his support of the rebels in Sicily in 1282. The Military Orders were theoretically only answerable to the pope (who had called the crusade) and one of their most important patrons was the king of France (who led it), but Peter III still expected them to support him against the crusaders. The crusade failed and the French retreated, but Peter died shortly afterwards. His successor Alfonso III (1285–91) attacked the Hospitallers for giving support to the king of France, after his own predecessors had given them so much support. James II of Aragon (1291–1327) made a request of the pope that the Templars should use their resources in the Iberian Peninsula for fighting the Moors of Granada, and should not send any forces to the East.[15]

Elsewhere in the Iberian Peninsula the Templars were less prominent than in Portugal and Aragon-Catalonia. In Castile they were made responsible for the frontier fortress of Calatrava, but gave it up in 1158. In 1236 Fernando III of León and Castile (king of Castile 1217–52; king of León from 1230) gave the Templars the castle of Capilla in south-central Castile. An illustration in the book of chess produced for King Alfonso X of Castile and León (1252–84) shows two Templars playing chess, an indication that they were a common sight at the Castilian court (plate 12).[16] The Order held some property on the pilgrimage route to Santiago de Compostella, including a fortress at Ponferrada. Yet the kings of Castile preferred to use locally founded Military Orders for military purposes rather than the supranational Orders, notably the Order of Calatrava, which was formed in 1158 from a knightly confraternity that took over the defence of the frontier fortress of Calatrava when the Templars gave it up; the Order of St James of Santiago, which was formed in 1170; and the Order of San Julián de Pereiro or Alcántara, which was founded in León in around 1176.

These localized Military Orders could give the same assistance to the king as the supranational Orders: they were quickly mobilized and could remain a long time on campaign. They could garrison castles and give military advice in council. Because they were based in the Iberian Peninsula there was no danger of them withdrawing valuable forces to go to the aid of Christians in the East and abandoning their responsibilities in the peninsula (as the Templars abandoned Calatrava in 1158) or suffering such losses in the East that they were unable to help the Spanish cause. The king could control the election of Master of a local Military Order. In theory he could also do this for the Hospitallers and Templars, but because these Spanish Orders were dependent on the king they would not defy his authority, and they would not ally with his enemies. Their allegiances were not divided, as the allegiances of the Hospitallers and Templars were in 1285 in Aragon.

But the localized Military Orders suffered from two drawbacks: they had only a small resource base and they were unable to act independently. Orders had to be dissolved or amalgamated into other Orders because they lacked the resources to continue their operations, and the king could use them for his own purposes even if this damaged their ability to fight the Muslims. This meant that they were distracted from their original purpose. In the sixteenth century the Iberian Military Orders were amalgamated to their respective royal families.

The Military Orders did more than provide supplementary military forces for the use of rulers in the Iberian Peninsula. As in the East, the Templars also assisted crusaders who arrived from elsewhere in Europe en route by sea to the Holy Land. Their assistance for Afonso Henriques of Portugal in 1147 in the capture of Santarém was followed by the attack on Lisbon, which was completed with the assistance of English, German,

Flemish and Boulogne crusaders on their way to the East. They assisted in the attacks on Almeria by Alfonso VII of Castile and on Tortosa by Ramon Berenguer IV, ruler of Aragon, in 1147–8. In Portugal, the arrival of crusaders from the Rhineland going to join the Fifth Crusade in 1217 gave King Afonso II the means to attack the city of Alcácer do Sal; the Templars and Hospitallers also contributed troops. The attack was eventually successful.[17]

The Military Orders also played an important economic role in encouraging recolonization and exploitation of newly conquered land. In addition, as in the East and elsewhere in Europe, they were used as depositaries for valuables as well as being trusted neutral parties who could guard castles or people of importance. For this reason the Templars were entrusted with the upbringing of the child King James I of Aragon, and with the defence of the disputed castles of Montémor-o-Velho and Alenquer in Portugal. In 1285 Peter III of Aragon found that his brother James, king of Majorca, had been in treasonable correspondence with King Philip III of France (1270–85); the incriminating evidence was in James's treasure chest in the Templars' house at Perpignan.[18]

The military and political importance of the Military Orders to the rulers of the Iberian Peninsula was demonstrated by events in 1274 at the Second Church Council of Lyons. Proposals were made to unify all the Military Orders into one, but the proposals were dropped because the Iberian rulers objected so strongly, arguing that one Order would be too powerful and if the local Iberian Military Orders were included in the new unified Military Order the crusade against the Moors in the Iberian Peninsula would be overlooked in favour of the Holy Land. The same objections were made again after the arrest of the Templars in France in 1307; James II of Aragon suspected that Philip IV of France (1285–1314) wanted control of the Templars' possessions as a 'back-door' method of getting control of the most important strongholds in Aragon. He hotly opposed every proposal that the Hospital should receive the Templars' lands. His objections were echoed by the other rulers of the Iberian Peninsula. When the Order was dissolved in 1312 its property in Portugal and Valencia was exempted from the settlement, and was later used to set up new Military Orders.[19]

The Military Orders in eastern Europe

In eastern Europe, the Templars' role was somewhat different from that in the Iberian Peninsula, although eastern Europe (figure 6) was also a frontier region. In the south-east of Europe, the Catholic kingdom of Hungary bordered the territory of the Greek Orthodox Serbs and Bulgarians to the south and the pagan Cumans to the east. In the east, although Bohemia was a part of the 'empire', it was not German but Czech, and from 1198 had its own kings – who were eager to acquire territory to their east if possible. The Catholic kingdom of Poland, Christian since the tenth century, had divided into dukedoms at the beginning of the thirteenth century, each duke anxious to increase his own power, authority and territory over the others. The kingdom of Poland as a single entity was not revived until 1295, and did not have a stable kingship again until 1320.

The whole of this area was underpopulated and under-cultivated in comparison with the rest of Europe. Unlike, for instance, England, where the primeval forest had been cleared by 1000 BC and even apparently untouched 'wilderness' was carefully managed by the local inhabitants, eastern Europe contained vast areas of forest, mountain and marsh that had never been subject to human cultivation. The economic revolution of the eleventh and twelfth centuries, with its associated population growth, had led to great pressure on land in western and central Europe, and there were many poorer farmers from Germany in particular who were eager to acquire new landholdings in the east. The rulers of eastern Europe were for the most part anxious to have them, for cultivated land produces wealth. The German settlers were given the same tenancy rights as they enjoyed in Germany, which were generally better than those enjoyed by the local inhabitants.

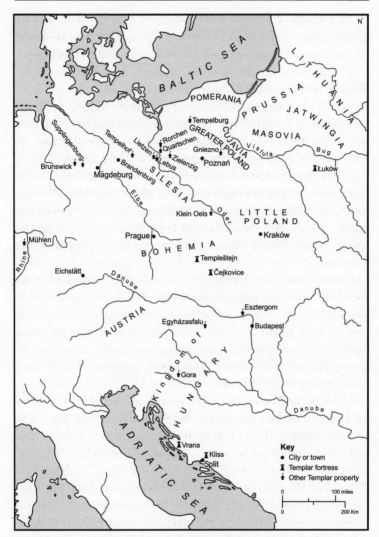

Figure 6   Eastern Europe, showing Templar houses and other places mentioned in the text

The rulers of eastern Europe found that the best way of getting their empty land populated was to give it to religious Orders – traditional monastic Orders such as the Benedictines and Cistercians, and the more radical and adaptable 'new-style' Orders such as the Augustinian canons and the Military Orders. These religious Orders had the capital to found villages and towns and could bring in tenants from their lands further west. Tenants would be encouraged to move by promises of large landholdings and attractive terms of lease. Once the land became productive, the original donor could claim some benefit through an annual payment or a share of the produce. Whether or not the donation charter specified some sort of return to the donor, the donor would benefit from increased trade in the region, which would help to generate wealth throughout their territories.

Donors also hoped, through donation and colonization, to establish their ownership of frontier land. Whoever gave land to a religious Order was effectively demonstrating that it was their land to give in the first place, and henceforth the religious Order that held it would owe thanks and rent to the donor. In short, colonization meant increased prestige, wealth and territory for the landowner.

Colonization was the major reason for bringing religious Orders into this region during the Middle Ages, but there was another reason. The Orders could also play a role in the conversion of non-Christians. The whole of eastern Europe formed a frontier zone against pagans and Greek and Russian Orthodox Christians. The region was worth bringing into Catholic Christian Europe not only for its land but also because it was important for trade: the rivers of north-eastern Europe are effectively highways into the Euro-Asian interior.

The pagan frontier was managed in different ways in different parts of eastern Europe. In Hungary, an attempt to settle the Teutonic knights in south-eastern Hungary ended in the early 1220s when the Brothers were viewed as a threat to Hungarian dominance of the area.[20] The pagan Cumans seemed less of a threat than the Germans; and the Cumans came to be regarded as allies to be assimilated rather than fought. In the north-east of Europe, the Russian Orthodox rulers preferred to exact tribute, while the Catholic Christians wanted to convert and/or conquer.

The Military Orders could play an important role in missionary campaigns. They could work alongside missionaries (typically Cistercian monks or Dominican or Franciscan friars), protecting them as they went preaching through the pagan lands. They also protected the new converts from attack by those who were still pagan, and could raid into pagan lands, taking prisoners and other booty, 'softening up' the pagans as a preliminary to the peaceful missionary work. Churchmen thought that demonstrating Christian military superiority would persuade the pagans to convert more readily. In the early thirteenth century Bishop Albrecht of Riga, a new trading post at the mouth of the River Düna in Livonia (now Latvia), founded the Order of Knights of Christ, or Swordbrothers, to support his mission to the pagan Livs, Letts and Ests. The Order certainly made an impact on the local pagans and established widespread territorial authority before it was heavily defeated at Saule by the Lithuanians in 1236. In the following year it was amalgamated into the Teutonic Order. Likewise, in Prussia, Bishop Christian, who was leading the mission to the Prussians, set up a local military Order, the Order of Christ of Dobrin (the Polish town where it had its headquarters), which worked alongside his missionaries. This Order, too, was amalgamated into the Teutonic Order in the 1230s. Both of these Orders followed religious rules based on the Rule of the Templars.

The Templars' role in this area was far less significant than that of the Teutonic Order, or even the Hospital. They came into the north-east of Europe quite late, not acquiring significant properties until the 1220s. As this corresponds with the beginning of active crusading against the pagan Prussians, it appears that rulers began to favour the Templars because of their connection with holy war – even though the Templars were not being asked to fight the Prussians. Donations of frontier land to the Templars were given with declarations that the donor wished to help the Brothers' war against the infidel in the Holy Land, but in fact the donors believed that if they favoured the religious Order that was most connected with holy war, God would help them with their own causes.

Yet it was also the case that the Templars were not well known in north-eastern Europe before the 1220s. In fact they were not well known in central and eastern Germany before the late twelfth century. But the more German magnates from central and eastern Germany became involved in the crusade to the Holy Land and the more they saw the Order in action in the field, the more they liked what they saw. German magnates from Thuringia and Austria played a significant role in the Third Crusade of 1189–92, the landgrave of Thuringia joined the German Crusade of 1197–8, while the duke of Austria and the king of Hungary were prominent in the Fifth Crusade of 1217–21. From the late twelfth century the Templars began to receive generous donations in the German Empire. These donations continued throughout the thirteenth and into the fourteenth century, after all donations to religious Orders had fallen off in western Europe. So it appears that the decisive factor in donations to the Templars in German-speaking lands was the crusade, and widespread German involvement in the crusades.[21]

The Templars never held much property in Bohemia and Moravia, where the Hospitallers and the Teutonic Order received far more donations. The first donations to the Templars in this area were in around 1230. They had a house in the city of Prague, founded shortly after 1230; this had a chapel with a round nave, deliberately reminiscent of the Church of the Holy Sepulchre in Jerusalem. In southern Moravia there was a fortified commandery at Čejkovice – now a baroque castle, with the Templar wall and tower built into it – and a castle at Templštejn, constructed between 1281 and 1298. Presumably the castle was built to provide local security in response to dangerous neighbours. The Templars were not brought into Bohemia to fight. They were given lands partly in recognition of their piety and defence of Christendom in the East but also so that they would encourage colonizers to come into barren areas and make the land productive.[22]

Again, the Templars did not hold wide properties in Hungary, although they were receiving gifts of land and buildings in Hungary from at least the 1160s. The monastery of St Gregory of Vrána in Dalmatia (Croatia), which was part of the kingdom of Hungary, was confirmed as theirs by Pope Alexander III (1159–81) in 1169, and by the 1170s the Order had so many properties in the area that it established an administrative 'province' of Hungary. King Béla III (1172–96) and his sons Imre I (1196–1204) and Andrew II (1205–35) gave territory and privileges to the Order within their domains. The generosity of these kings to the Templars stemmed from their interest in crusading: Andrew himself joined the Fifth Crusade in 1217. These kings also endowed the Hospital of St John, and Andrew was a generous patron to the Teutonic Order.[23]

Templar properties in central Hungary have not survived: two houses are known, at Kereszteny (now Egyházasfalu) and Esztergom. More houses are known in Croatia, where some churches and chapels that belonged to the Templars survive, and the remains of a fortress at Vrána. The Templars' activities at Vrána received some attention from contemporary writers. The 'History of the bishops of Salonika and Split' by Thomas of Split or Spalato (1200–68) mentions that in 1203 the king had deposited a quantity of silver with the Templars of Vrána. He also notes that in 1217 King Andrew of Hungary came to Split and entrusted the castle of Klis to Pons, Master of the Temple in Hungary, because none of his own nobles were prepared to garrison it.

Thomas also mentions the Templars in Croatia in April 1241, when Hungary was attacked by the Mongols. The Hungarian nobles, he states, were slow to make preparations to fight, and King Béla IV (1235–70) of Hungary was negligent. But at Sajó in Croatia, King Koloman (Béla's brother), his Archbishop Hugrin and 'a certain Master of the knighthood of the Temple' (James of Montreal) took action.

> As befitted active men, they did not give themselves over to quiet slumber like the rest but kept watch the whole night under arms. As soon as they heard the shout, they at once burst out of the camp. Then, girded in military arms and grouped in one wedge they rushed boldly into the enemy army and fought with them for some time with much fortitude. But, since they were very few in number in comparison with the infinite multitude of Mongols, who bubbled from the ground everywhere like locusts, they returned to their camp, after killing more than they had lost themselves.

Having aroused the Hungarians to action, our heroes then launched a second attack on the Mongol army. Thomas described the sequel:

> Archbishop Hugrin was borne between the most closely packed troops of the enemy with such great fortitude that they fled from him with a great noise as if they were fleeing from a bolt of lightning. In the same way, King Koloman and the Templar with his fellow Latin knights inflicted great slaughter on the enemy. But at last, unable to bear the blows of the multitude, Koloman and the archbishop barely escaped, bitterly wounded, with their men; while the Templar Master and the whole army of Latins fell.

As in the East, the Latin Christians could be accused of having acted rashly in engaging the enemy. The Mongols' retreat later in the year was nothing to do with the Christians' resistance. Yet Thomas's disgust at the cowardice of the Hungarian nobles and the inadequacy of King Béla as a general demonstrates why it was essential for them to act. Those who fled the enemy or who failed to meet the enemy in the field were accused of cowardice and lost their military reputation for ever – and a warrior who lost his reputation was better off dead. It was far better to attempt something against the enemy, even if it was hopeless, than to do nothing at all.[24]

The Mongols also attacked Poland in April 1241. The Templars in Poland sent a letter to their Brothers in France asking for help, and the Master in France, Pons d'Aubon, wrote to King Louis IX of France, describing the disaster.

> They have ransacked the land which belonged to Duke Henry of Poland [Silesia] and killed him and many of his barons . . . and they have laid waste all the land of Hungary and Bohemia. They have three armies, which have divided up; one army is in Hungary, one in Bohemia and one in Austria . . . and we fear that the same will happen in Germany . . . And you should be aware that they spare no one; they kill everyone, poor and rich and small and great . . . and if any messenger is sent to them, the leaders of the army blindfold him and lead him to their lord, who should be, they say, lord of the world. They do not besiege castles or strong towns, but they destroy everything . . . And you should be aware that their army is so large, as we have been informed by our Brothers who have escaped from their army, that it is a good eighteen leagues long and twelve wide and they ride as far in a day as it is from Paris to the city of Chartres.[25]

The Mongols devastated the Templars' possessions in the area, destroying two of their 'best towers' and three unprotected villages. The Templars and Hospitallers in Poland were among the army of Duke Henry II of Lower Silesia, which fought the Mongols at Liegnitz on 9 April 1241 and was heavily defeated. The duke was killed, and the Order lost knights and sergeant-Brothers and 500 other people in its service.[26] In these battles against the Mongols the Order was not fighting a holy war but was fighting as a landowner. The ruler expected all landowners to help him defend his land – and theirs – if it were attacked.

The Templars' territories in eastern Germany and Poland formed part of the province of Alemannia and Sclavonia (Germany and Slavland), which was established in the 1220s. The Templars received their first lands before 1220 at what is now Tempelhof, south of modern Berlin by the River Oder, and nearby. This was land belonging to the margraves of Brandenburg, the Ascanier family, who continued to support the Templars into the second half of the thirteenth century.[27]

In the 1220s the Ascaniers' neighbour and rival, Henry I of Breslau, a member of the Piast family and duke of Lower Silesia (d. 1238), was a generous donor to the Benedictine monks, Cistercians, Augustinian canons and the Templars. In 1226 or 1227 Henry gave the Templars Klein Oels (now Mała Oleśnica) near Olava in Lower Silesia.[28] In 1225 his neighbour and rival Władysław Odonicz of Greater Poland had given the Templars some lands in his estates and in 1232 he gave them Quartschen, now Chwarszczany, with 1,000 *hufen* (an area of land: a *huf* = a hoof) and permission to found a city. The Templars founded a house there, which became an important commandery. Odonicz also gave further large areas of land within Greater Poland, and the neighbouring bishops of Lebus and Kammin were also enthusiastic donors to the Templars.[29]

In 1290 another large barren area of land in the same region was given to the Order by Duke Przemysl of Greater Poland. The Templars moved their commandery at Kron (now Walcz), founded in 1249, to this new site, which was called Tempelburg (now Czaplinek). The Templars set about colonizing this area with gusto: in 1933 the German historian Helmut Lüpke estimated that before 1312 the Templars founded half the settlements that now exist in this region.[30]

The Templars were also on friendly terms with Duke Henry I's wife Hedwige, who was recognized by the Catholic Church as a saint after her death. In her official 'Life' it is recorded that a Templar gave charitable assistance to her at a time of need: she had been wearing a tightly knotted belt of horsehair next to her skin as a penance, but when this wore out she had no means of obtaining another. However, a Templar came to court and presented the pious woman with a small bag containing a new horsehair belt. The gift was received by the duchess' companion Lady Anna, who opened the bag and rebuked the Templar for giving a lady such a gift; but the saint asked her to desist, for the Templar, she said, was doing God's will, and his action was well pleasing to God.[31]

The Templars also received other lands in this area, nearly all of them on frontiers within Christian territory (between Brandenberg, Silesia, Pomerania and Greater Poland), and on underdeveloped land within this region. None of the donors considered above actually expected the Templars to fight pagans nor even to fight their expansionist Christian neighbours. The Templars were given a territorial and symbolic rather than a military presence.

The Templars were not the only Military Order on the north-eastern European frontier. The Hospitallers had been in the east German and Polish lands since the mid-twelfth century.[32] The Teutonic Order became established in the land of Culm (Chelmno), on the Polish/Prussian frontier, from 1230: this was the year Pope Gregory IX approved the charter by which Duke Conrad of Masovia-Cujavia had invited the Order to help him fight the pagan Prussians in return for Culm. While the Teutonic Order was invited specifically to help protect Polish territory against the pagan Prussians, the Hospitallers, like the Templars, were given land to assist their war against the Muslims in the East. These donations tailed off after 1250, when many of the lords of the area apparently decided that the religious Orders had been given enough land. The monasteries and the Templars and Hospitallers had to renew many of the agreements by which they held their land, and give up some of their territory. The Orders suffered because of their success in settling the area and setting down frontiers; in effect, their presence was no longer needed. Donations continued to be given in areas where the land remained unsettled and frontiers were disputed.[33] However, in one area the Templars were invited to do more than colonize and settle frontiers. This was the town of Łuków in Poland.[34]

The Templars first entered the area east of the River Vistula, well beyond 'German' frontier territory, in 1239. Duke Boleslaw of Kraków-Sandomir gave them three villages in the area, for the help of the Holy Land. Nothing more definite is heard of them in eastern Poland until 1257, when Pope Alexander IV (1254–61) commissioned the archbishop of Gniezno (Gnesen) to organize the establishment of a bishopric in the town of Łuków, and instal one Bartholomew as Bishop. This was done on the request of the duke of Kraków, his sister Salomea and the 'Master of the house of the knighthood of the Temple in Alamannia and Sclavonia', since the duke had given the castle of Łuków to the Master and his Brothers.

The duke and Bartholomew, a Franciscan friar, had been operating in the area for a while. Łuków was on the frontier with the pagan Jatwingians, a Lithuanian tribe. By 1249 the Teutonic Order had subjugated the pagan Prussians, imposed Christianity in Prussia, and quashed a rebellion. The Order then made an alliance with Mindaugas, a Lithuanian prince, who received baptism in 1251. The Teutonic Order hoped that Lithuania would soon follow Prussia into Christendom. Some of the Polish and Russian princes allied with the Teutonic Order, hoping to gain land or glory: for instance, in 1253 the Russian Prince Daniel of Galich-Volyn' was crowned king at Drohiczyn (on the eastern Polish frontier) by the papal legate Otto of Mezzano in return for his support of the Teutonic Order. Others hoped to get a slice of Jatwingian territory when it was conquered.

Other princes saw the Teutonic Order as a rival rather than an ally, perhaps because they were at war with the Teutonic Order's other allies. They hoped to get part of the Jatwingian lands for themselves through their own mission to the pagans. At the beginning of 1253, Duke Kasimir of Cujavia and Duke Boleslaw of Kraków-Sandomir informed Pope Innocent IV (1243–54) that the pagans whose lands bordered their own wished to convert to Christianity, if their freedom were guaranteed (whereas, if the Teutonic Order converted them, they would be enslaved) and wanted to come under the lordship and protection of the dukes. The pope was delighted at the prospect of a peaceful mission of conversion, and gave his agreement.

Walter Kuhn, examining these events in detail, noted that the pope obviously did not have a map. If he had looked at one he would have realized that the mission of the two dukes covered exactly the area in which he had just given the Teutonic Order and its allies permission to wage a crusade. The Teutonic Order was furious at this intrusion on their 'territory' and complained to the pope. The pope, quite oblivious of the contradiction, agreed that only the Teutonic Order had the right to operate in that area. For its war against the Jatwingians the Teutonic Order won powerful allies, Daniel of Galich-Volyn' and Duke Semovit of Masovia, promising them a third of the pagan lands captured. King Ottokar II of Bohemia came to the Order's support in 1254. At this point Duke Kasimir abandoned his project of conversion.

Duke Boleslaw, however, pressed on. If he could not operate within Jatwingian territory he could still set up a new bishopric within his own territories and convert the Jatwingians from there. A Franciscan master from Prague, Bartholomew, came to lead his mission. But in 1255 the Lithuanians under Mindaugas attacked and devastated the area. The peaceful conversion now became a crusade. The Teutonic Order would normally have taken control, but Duke Boleslaw asked the pope for a Polish crusade, to operate alongside the German one, with all lands conquered to fall to the Poles rather than the Germans. In August 1255 Pope Alexander IV approved his request.

The Teutonic Order saw the danger to their ambitions in the area, but Alexander – who, like Innocent IV, did not have a map of the Polish frontier – did not realize that again he had approved two rival crusades in one area. The Polish missionaries complained that the Teutonic Order was preventing free conversions. The Teutonic Order complained that dangerous rivals were invading their rights. It was at this point, in February 1257, that the pope approved the setting up of the bishopric at Łuków, and we learn that the Templars were responsible for guarding the castle. The Templars may have been there in 1255–6 as they made an appeal for help after the Lithuanians sacked Łuków. Presumably Bartholomew intended that the Templars would protect the new converts from attacks by the pagans and give military support to his missionaries in the field.

In June 1257 the Vice-Master of the Teutonic Order in Prussia made a special appeal to the pope. The pope gave his full support to the Order: no other group could preach the cross in the area and no one else could wage holy war. This was the end of the peaceful mission and the crusade at Łuków, and the Templars were not heard of again in the area.

In the Iberian peninsula and in eastern Europe, the Templars played a role in colonizing newly acquired or underpopulated land. By giving the Templars land and enabling them to set up a base, rulers effectively established their own presence in the area: the Templars would be their representatives, looking after their interests and ensuring that no one else took over the land. The colonizers also generated wealth, which was to everyone's benefit. In addition, the Templars played a military role in the Iberian Peninsula and, briefly, in eastern Poland. As landowners and vassals of the duke of Silesia and the king of Hungary they joined the armies that went out to face the Mongols in 1241 and, true to their calling, died in battle against the infidel. They did not, however – except under pressure from the king of Aragon – fight other Christians. Their vocation remained the defence of Christendom against non-Christians, and all their activities were focused upon that end. Yet their presence at the courts of the kings of Portugal, Castile and Aragon and that of the duke of Silesia demonstrates their political importance in the courts of Europe. This will be considered at greater length in Chapter 6.

4

THE ORGANIZATION AND GOVERNMENT OF THE ORDER

The Order of the Temple was organized on similar lines to the Hospital of St John and the Teutonic Order. Like those Orders, it was governed by a Master who was based at the Order's headquarters in the East, with a number of great officials who were also based at the Order's headquarters and who dealt with specific matters of government. Subordinate officials assisted them. The Order's lands in Europe were divided into provinces, each administered by a provincial commander, who in turn had subordinate officials under him who were responsible for the running of individual houses. A system of general chapter meetings kept the officials of the Order in the East in touch with the Brothers in the West. But as the Order of the Temple existed for less than two centuries, its organization and government never became as sophisticated as those of the other two supranational Military Orders.

For instance, by the mid-fourteenth century the Brothers at the central convent of the Hospital of St John were divided into 'tongues' – linguistic divisions – for administrative purposes, and the great officials of the Order were each taken from one of these tongues. The same linguistic differences existed among the Templars, but such 'tongues' never became official divisions within the Order. Whereas for the Order of the Hospital the Order's general chapter proceedings meetings show such practices in operation, no proceedings of the Templars' general chapter meetings survive. Any such records would have been kept at the central convent, so would have been lost with the rest of the Templars' central archive. In any case, the Order of the Temple was dissolved before such records began to be systematically kept, for the Hospitallers' oldest record of general chapter proceedings dates only from 1330.[1]

The Master of the Order of the Temple was elected for life. The election was made in an assembly of the officials of the Order in the East and the whole convent, that is, the Brothers living in the headquarters of the Order: in Jerusalem before 1187, in Acre from 1191 to 1291, or in Cyprus from 1291. Scholars differ over the best definition of the personnel of 'the convent', but the most recent study describes it as 'a community . . . those who lived and worked at the headquarters, specifically the high officials'.[2]

The hierarchical statutes, composed before 1186, laid down the procedure for election.[3] The day was set by an official called 'the Grand Commander', in consultation with the Marshal, the commanders of the land of Jerusalem, of Antioch and of Tripoli and other officials. The statutes give the impression that it was more important to ensure that the right person was elected than to elect quickly. All the Brothers in the West who could not attend the election were to fast and pray that God would advise the electors, and the Brothers also asked other religious Orders for their prayers. At the assembly where the election took place, thirteen electors – eight knight-Brothers, four sergeant-Brothers and one chaplain-Brother – were chosen by a complex procedure which was intended to allow God maximum intervention in the electoral process. These thirteen represented

Christ (represented by the chaplain-Brother) and His twelve disciples. They should be chosen from various nations, but no specific division of nations was laid down. The choice should be a majority decision, and a Brother who was already in the East was preferred over Brothers in Europe. Although the Master was chosen for life, a few Masters eventually resigned the office, such as Evrard des Barres, who later joined the Cistercian Order, and Philip de Milly, who returned to secular life after his resignation.

The Master was chief executive of the Order, led the Brothers in battle when he was present, and represented the Order to the outside world. He was also the spiritual head of the Order, effectively chosen by God. The Order of the Temple did not experience the vicious quarrels over the constitution of the Order and the role and authority of the Master that beset the Hospital of St John, either because in the Temple the Master always took the great officials' advice and ruled according to custom and precedent as a ruler should, or because the Templars preferred a Master who led from the front, as expected of a military leader.[4]

Officials of religious Orders had their own seals to validate documents approved by the Order. The Master of the Temple's great seal was double sided and showed the circular dome of the Church of the Holy Sepulchre on one side, and the Order's symbol of two knights on one horse on the other (see plates 14–15). There was also a smaller, single-sided seal which showed the circular dome of the Holy Sepulchre. The images on the seal reminded anyone who looked at it that the Templars defended the Holy Sepulchre, and were the poor knights of Christ.

The Master did not rule the Order alone. The hierarchical statutes refer to general chapters being held in the Order's headquarters or in one of its leading houses in the East. General chapters could also be held in the West.[5] They were meetings of the Master and central convent and leading officials of the Order from Europe, rather like the courts held by secular rulers, at which business was discussed and legal cases heard. The Templars' general chapter appointed leading officials of the Order, dealt with disciplinary cases and other problems that had been referred to it by the Master and convent or by the provincial chapters, and decided which Brothers were no longer fit for active service in the East and should be retired to western Europe.[6] The only extensive records of the decisions taken at these meetings are the references to them in the collection of 'retrais' or legal decisions that accompanies the Rule of the Order. There are also some references to the general chapters in the proceedings of the trial of 1307–12.

Scholars have not agreed over how frequently Templar general chapters were held. Other religious Orders that held general chapters had different regulations on how often they should meet: the Cistercians held them every year. Jochen Burgtorf has argued that the Hospitallers and Templars held a general chapter meeting in the East every year, but the western officials attended only every five years (for the Hospital) or every four years (for the Temple) when their terms of office expired. No written procedure for the Templars' general chapters survives. To judge from the procedures laid down in the Rule for ordinary weekly chapter meetings and from the practices in the Order of the Hospital, general chapters probably began and ended with prayers led by the chaplain and were presided over by the Master. The provincial officials would surrender the symbols of their office (their seals) and render their accounts. This would be a verbal report, which those present heard (auditum) – in short, their accounts were 'audited'. General regulations were made.[7]

The day-to-day running of the Order was under the government of various administrative officials. Their posts were called bailies (things entrusted to someone), and the officer in charge was the baili (the one to whom things have been entrusted, or the one responsible for them; in English, 'bailiff'). None of these posts was given for life, and there was no clear career structure in the Order. Brothers did not have to complete a set period of service before holding office: both Philip de Milly, lord of Nablūs, and Robert de Sablé or Sabloel (1191–3) became Master of the Order a very short time after joining the Order.[8] The titles of the great officials of the Order are set out in the hierarchical statutes, but only their roles and relative status before 1187 are recorded; these would have changed as the Order developed. To complicate the picture further, some prominent figures in the Order held offices that do not fit into the pattern laid down by the statutes: the most obvious example is Brother Geoffrey Fulcher, who appears as 'procurator' and 'preceptor' or commander in the 1160s and 'commander of the Order overseas' in the 1170s. None of these offices is listed in the statutes, yet Geoffrey Fulcher was clearly an official of great importance.[9]

In the mid-twelfth century the major officials in the East were, in order of precedence: the Seneschal (*dapifer* in Latin), the Marshal – the chief military officer, the Draper – in charge of clothing and other household equipment, and the Commander of the Land of Jerusalem – who also acted as Treasurer. At the end of the twelfth century the office of Seneschal was dropped and an officer called the Grand Commander took over some of his functions. This is a confusing title, because the Order also had a 'Grand Commander' who was appointed on a Master's death to govern the Order during the vacancy and organize the election of the new Master. The Order's preference for calling any official 'commander' (Latin: *preceptor*) causes problems for modern historians trying to work out the Order's leadership structures.[10]

The great officers of the Order at the Central Convent at the end of the Order's history were the Marshal, the Commander of Apulia (southern Italy), the Grand Commander, the Commander of the Land, the Draper and the Turcopolier: these were the officials arrested in Cyprus in 1310. The Turcopolier was originally a subordinate official, under the authority of the Marshal. He was in command of the turcopoles – mercenary cavalry recruited in the East – and the Brother-sergeants.[11]

Another subordinate military official was the *Gonfanier* (Banner-bearer) who was responsible for carrying the Order's standard in battle. The standard was *baucant* (piebald), with a black and a white section. Contemporary illustrations differ over which part of the banner was white and which was black. Matthew Paris, the chronicler of St Albans Abbey, shows it with the upper section black and the lower section white (plate 11); the Order's own frescoes at the church of San Bevignate, Perugia, show it with a white upper section (with cross superimposed) and a black lower section (plate 10). Possibly the banner shown at San Bevignate was the Master's standard while Matthew Paris drew the smaller 'piebald banner' carried by the Marshal and other commanders in the field. The standard itself played an essential role in the field: it represented the centre of the Order's troops, a place to which the Brothers could withdraw to regroup and charge again; it represented the Order itself. Its loss was a terrible disaster, and the Brothers should die rather than allow it to be captured.

The Order had an Infirmerer, who was responsible for running the infirmary of the central convent, where old Brothers were cared for. Unlike the Hospital of St John and the Teutonic Order, the Order of the Temple did not have a hospital at its central convent for poor pilgrims and the needy, although the Brothers had to give alms (charity to the poor), and in Europe the Order was responsible for the maintenance and administration of some hospices.[12]

It is not clear whether there was a chief chaplain in the Order. In the Hospital of St John, the chief chaplain at the Order's headquarters – the 'conventual prior' – held spiritual authority over all the Order's priests. Within the central convent he was responsible for the Brothers' spiritual health and for the care of the conventual church of St John. The Order of the Temple also had chaplain-Brothers, but the statutes do not mention any prior in charge of them. Yet during the trial of the Order on Cyprus an official with the title 'prior of the Order of the Temple', *prior de ordine Templi*, was interrogated.

This was Brother Hugh de Bensano. On Cyprus the title 'prior' indicated a priest in charge of a parish, but Brother Hugh was not given a parish location. In contrast, the other prior who appears in the trial records for Cyprus, Brother Stephen de Safed, was 'priest, prior of the house of the Temple at Limossol'. Possibly Brother Hugh's 'parish' was the whole Order, and he was the equivalent of the conventual prior in the Hospital of St John.[13]

The Order's properties in the West, in Europe, were divided into provinces. An officer called the 'Master on this side of the sea' or the 'visitor' could be appointed by the general chapter to oversee the overseas provinces, but each province also had its own hierarchy of officials. The exact organization of the provinces in the West was fluid and changed during the course of the Order's history. In the Temple, the official in charge of a province was called a 'master', a 'procurator', or a 'commander'. The provinces developed as the Order acquired territory in the West. By 1143 the Templars had a province covering 'Provence and parts of Spain', but there was no province for Germany until the 1220s.[14] One house in the province would be used as the centre of the provincial administration, where records were kept and where the treasury was based. In England this was at London, in northern France it was Paris, in Aragon by the late thirteenth century it was at Miravet.[15] The provincial Master had his own seal for validating legal documents. The provincial seal generally had a standard design: the seal of the French province showed a domed circular building – the Church of the Holy Sepulchre; the seal of the English province showed the *agnus Dei*, the lamb of God – a symbol of Christ, the head of the Order. The seal of the German provincial Master varied: at the end of the thirteenth century Bertram von Esbeck's seal showed an eagle, but in the 1270s and 1280s the Master of Germany had Christ's head on his seal, just as the head of the king or queen appears on modern British coins. In the same way the provincial prior of the Hospital of St John in England had the head of St John

the Baptist on his seal. If the seal were double-sided, the back
could show the provincial Master's own symbol, typically his
own family coat of arms.[16]

The principal house of a Templar province was also a
collection point for all the dues or 'responsions' which were
payable by the individual houses within the province, for
dispatching to the Order's headquarters in the East. The
provincial commander was responsible for ensuring that the
responsions, which in theory should amount to a third of
annual income, were properly assessed and collected. As the
Order had wide possessions in land and much of its income
came from rents it could be difficult to establish exactly what its
income should be. In England in 1185 the Master of England,
Geoffrey fitz Stephen, initiated an investigation into all the
Order's incomes in England: these were recorded in a bound
volume which would have been kept at the 'New Temple'– the
Templars' headquarters just outside the city of London (see
plate 19). Confiscated by the king when the Order was
dissolved, this volume is now in the UK National Archives, at
the Public Record Office at Kew, London. It should have been
given to the Hospitallers' provincial prior, but the Hospitallers
in England never managed to acquire all the Templars' English
documents.

The provincial Master did not necessarily live at the provincial headquarters; in a large province he needed to travel
about to visit the individual houses, or he might be resident at
the royal court.

Once a year, a provincial chapter meeting was held at a
central location, presided over by the provincial Master, for all
the heads of individual houses to attend. This was sometimes
called a 'general chapter' to distinguish it from the weekly
chapter meetings in each individual commandery. King John of
England (1199–1216) gave the Order in England ten bucks
(male deer) each year for their provincial chapter meeting at
Pentecost, to which his son Henry III added a barrel of wine,
until the financial crisis of the late 1250s cut his expenditure.[17]

Edward I (1272–1307), a crusader with a keen sense of money's worth, ended the donation of venison. As well as enjoying a good meal, the provincial chapter discussed legal cases, problems of discipline, the collection of monies and other business relating to the province. Difficult cases were referred from the provincial chapter to the general chapter in the East.

At a local level, the basic administrative unit of the Templars in the West was the commandery or preceptory. 'Preceptory' is the Latin term; 'commandery' meant exactly the same thing in French. The commandery was the equivalent of the secular manor, and the commandery buildings looked very like secular manors except that they usually included a chapel. By the papal privilege *Omne Datum Optimum* of 1139 the Templars were allowed to have their own chapels, provided that they were only for the use of their Brothers. In practice, associate members of the Order and donors also used these chapels, and many became parish churches. Smaller houses, too small to have their own chapel and sometimes let out to tenants, were called *camerae*, which literally means 'rooms', or *membra*, 'limbs'.

The commander of the commandery was effectively lord of the manor. He had to look after his tenants, keep law and order and see that justice was done, and ensure that rent was paid (in money, kind or work). He was responsible for collecting the money and other produce and sending the requisite amount to the provincial headquarters.

The commander would also receive gifts made to the Order. Each commandery contained a strong chest holding charters of donation and records of legal cases to prove the Order's ownership of its properties in the commandery; or, if not the originals, copies bound into a single volume. Many of these local collections of charters, called cartularies, survive in local, provincial and national archives in Europe, although centuries of war, fire and accident have taken their toll. Such charters rarely offer any great insights into the Order. Here is a typical charter from the Order's principal house in Champagne, at Provins:

Concerning how Adam, marshal of the church of the Blessed
Stephen of Meaus, gave in alms to the Brothers of the Knights
Templar Mathelina, the daughter of Theobald, his female serf.

I, Adam, marshal of the church of the Blessed Stephen of
Meaux and canon of the church of the Blessed, Quiriace of
Provins give notice to all who inspect the present document that
out of piety I have given and conceded Mathelina, the daughter
of Theobald of Boissac, my bondswoman, in perpetuity to the
Brothers of the Knights Templar, so that she might henceforth
be their bondswoman. So that this may remain fixed, I have had
the present document confirmed by my seal. Done at Meaux,
the year of Our Lord 1221, the month of May.[18]

Adam did not explain exactly why he was giving Mathelina
to the Templars. 'Out of piety' could mean that it was a pious
deed to give something to a religious Order, or could mean that
he was acting out of pity for Mathelina – perhaps her husband
or boyfriend already belonged to the Templars. Nor does he
explain what he expected Mathelina to do for the Templars. As
religious houses usually employed women as dairymaids and
laundresses, it is likely that Mathelina would take on that sort
of essential work.[19] The 'serf' or 'bondswoman' was a person
without full legal rights, effectively in permanent unpaid
employment. In practice, as their owner was responsible for
meeting all their needs, they might have a better quality of life
than free, paid workers.

Donors expected a spiritual reward from God for themselves
and their family in return for supporting His knights. Their
charters often said nothing about the Order's work defending
Christendom, and referred to the Templars as if they were
simply a group of religious people following a religious Rule
like any other monastic Order. Yet donors were clearly
impressed by the Templars' spiritual standards, for otherwise
they would not have given their land to this Order. After all,
there were plenty of religious Orders around, and one would
not want to 'waste' a donation by giving it to a second-rate

Order. Only first-rate religious Orders would attract the best rewards from God for their donors.

Many charters included a list of witnesses who were present when the donation was made and could later testify that it had taken place as set out in the charter. These included both members of the Order of the Temple and outsiders. In a larger house, the charter would list only the names of the principal Templars present, and then lump the lesser members together as 'others'. For example, on 11 August 1198, at the commandery of Rourell in Catalonia, one Berengier Duran gave himself to be an associate of the Order of the Temple, and gave a piece of partly cultivated land at Robarroja. This was given to Lady Ermengard de Oluja, sister of the Order of the Temple and at that time preceptrix (female commander) of the House at Rourell, and Brother Raymon de Solson, and Brother John, and Brother William Escansset, Titborgs (a woman's name) and other Brothers and Sisters present and future.[20] Apparently Rourell was too large to list all the members present, but there were at least nine members.

The quality of life at a commandery would have varied according to its location and importance. Except in lawless areas such as Ireland and the south of France, it would not be enclosed by a tall outer wall as a monastery would be. Houses at a distance from the frontiers of Christendom did not have stores of weapons, which meant that the Brothers were open to attack from their lawless neighbours. The commandery was not a wealthy place; most commanderies were small, and all possible resources were sent to the East.[21]

When the Templars were arrested from October 1307 onwards, royal officials made a record of what was found at each house. Chapels were well stocked with valuable plate and the necessary books for services and the maintenance of religious life: the Masters of the Temple were rightly proud of the quality of their Order's religious observance.[22] But the houses themselves were not generally well supplied with the comforts of life, even at this period when furnishing was generally minimal. The Templars lived at the same sort of level as the farmers who were their tenants. At the small house of Llanmadoc on the Gower Peninsula in south Wales no furnishings of any sort were listed; there were a few utensils in the kitchen, and a few animals in the barns, including two dead oxen.[23] Broken equipment was left lying around. The commander was expected to send any surplus income to the provincial Master for despatch to the East rather than spend it on making the Templars' lives more comfortable.

The commandery was the basic unit of life for the members of the Order in Europe. The people living in a commandery would be of different status: some were fully professed members of the Order; others were associates or pensioners of the Order; while others were servants – both free, employed servants and unfree serfs or slaves. The fully professed members of the Order were the chaplains, knight-Brothers, Sergeant or serving Brothers (armed or non-armed) and Sisters. They had taken the three monastic vows of poverty (no personal property), chastity (no sexual relations with anyone) and obedience (obeying God through the Master of the Order, their immediate commander and the Rule of the Order). Associates of the Order had taken only a vow of obedience.

Some modern writers have been uncertain what Templars actually looked like. Bernard of Clairvaux indicates that they wore their hair short, but their beards long, and this is supported by other contemporary accounts: an anecdote in Jacques de Vitry's sermon 37 indicates that they shaved their heads completely. I have not been able to trace any medieval pictures of Templars without their armour from before the mid-thirteenth century. The picture of Templars in Alfonso X of Castile's book of chess, and a contemporary sculpture on the tomb of the infante Don Felipe in the church of the Templars' commandary at Villasirga, Palencia, show the Templars as bearded, with their hair short but neatly curled in the current fashion, and wearing the caps usually worn by religious men (plates 12–13). They wear ankle-length, dark-coloured tunics, with a white mantle which has a red cross on the left breast. A Templar illustrated in a manuscript of Jacquemart Giélée's *Renart le Nouvel* wears a red tunic with a white mantle. He wears a white cross on the chest of his tunic, and the characteristic soft cap on his head. Another manuscript of the same work shows both the Masters of the Hospital and Temple. The Templar mantle here appears more grey-blue than white, but perhaps it has become tarnished through association with Renart the Fox. The red cross appears on the left breast of the mantle. Under the mantle is a dark tunic.[24]

These pictures show that the knight-Brothers of the Temple were not dressed wholly in white but wore a long tunic of a darker shade with a white mantle over it. None of these pictures shows other members of the Order, only knights.

Most of the people living in a commandery in the West would never have fought the Muslims and were not expected to do so. The chaplains' role was to provide spiritual services to the members of the Order, to celebrate mass and to pray. Priests were not to shed blood, so the chaplains were not supposed to fight. The non-military sergeants or serving Brothers did manual work, such as carpentry, looking after animals, acting as smiths or stone masons. The Sisters' and associates' role was to pray; their warfare was spiritual warfare – the warfare of all religious people.

The papal bull *Omne Datum Optimum* of 1139 allowed the Brothers to have priest-Brothers, who were not subject to their local bishop. The priests were of high status within the Order, and the Order's statutes and '*retrais*' frequently refer to them. They did not have to be of knightly birth to become chaplains.

The other members of the Order were laity – unlike traditional monastic Orders where the majority of the fully professed Brothers would be priests. The knight-Brothers were the most prominent, although there were far fewer knight-Brothers than sergeant-Brothers in the Order. In theory, only the knight-Brothers could hold the highest offices in the Order, but in fact some sergeant-Brothers also obtained high offices. For instance, Jochen Burgtorf has noted that Peter de Castellón, who was treasurer of the Order in the early fourteenth century, was a sergeant-Brother, not a knight-Brother.[25]

In the early twelfth century, when the Order was founded, the status of 'knight' was not well defined. Knights were trained professional warriors who typically fought on horseback, fully armed, with their preferred weapons the sword and the lance. Yet they also often fought on foot, and using battleaxes or bows and arrows. They were sometimes, but not necessarily, of noble birth: the Latin word used to mean 'knight' in the Middle Ages was 'miles', which meant simply 'soldier' in classical Latin and even 'servant' in early medieval times.[26]

But during the twelfth century knights rose in social status. This was partly because becoming a professional, fully armed warrior became more difficult: new fighting techniques, particularly the cavalry charge with couched lance, required long hours of training which were possible only for those with the time and money to spare – either professional warriors or the nobility. As chainmail armour became more specialized and swords improved in quality they became more expensive. Knights also grew to be more important in government, particularly in local government: King Henry II of England (1154–89) gave knights important responsibilities in the running of the shires. At the same time, knightly culture began to develop. Warriors were under pressure from hostile forces: the Church attacked them as mindless bloodthirsty murderers (as in Bernard of Clairvaux's letter 'The new Knighthood') and merchants sneered at them for being impractical, without business sense, and having no idea of the value of money.[27]

In response – although not consciously so – the warriors developed their own culture: 'knighthood', *chevalerie* in the common language of French, now called 'chivalry' in English. Already by the mid-twelfth century a warrior went through a special ceremony in order to become 'a knight', which involved his laying his sword in the altar and then taking it up again, showing that he was God's knight. Those who regarded themselves as knights had their own invented tradition, the stories of the emperor Charlemagne and Roland, of William 'Shortnose' of Orange and of King Arthur. In these stories a knightly culture was developed, often contradictory and inconsistent, but with certain common features. The most important thing for a warrior was to preserve his honour. He should be active and he should die fighting, not in his bed. Knights should be wise, but sometimes it was more honourable to take risks.

It was shown in Chapter 1 that when the Order of the Temple was founded some commentators regarded the Templars as representing what knighthood should really be: they were the most perfect form of knighthood. Whether this was ever true or not, knightly ideals did not stop developing after the Templars were founded, and by the early thirteenth century knights were claiming that they could serve God as individuals, simply by being knights, and they did not need to join a religious Order. The Templars' ideal of working as a community for God was still accepted as one way for a knight to serve God, but it certainly was not the only way.[28]

Rather than the Templars affecting the development of knighthood, developments in knighthood affected the Templars. One area of obvious influence was in the Brothers' self-image. Knightly culture demanded that a knight should have a strong sense of self-esteem. Outsiders saw this as pride. All the supranational Military Orders were accused of being proud, a particularly knightly sin.[29] Another obvious area of influence was in the Order's policy on admitting knights. In the thirteenth century, as becoming a knight became more expensive and more onerous, fewer men were prepared to take up knighthood. If only nobles could afford to be knights, then knighthood must be a sign of nobility. Not all knights were from the high nobility, but all regarded themselves as being of higher social status than merchants, who had to lie and cheat in order to make money, and clerics, who never got their hands dirty. During the thirteenth century the Military Orders started to insist that only the sons of knights or of knights' daughters could enter their Orders as knight-Brothers, and the judgements recorded with the Rule of the Temple note a case of a knight-Brother who was demoted because he was not from a knightly family.[30]

Men of lesser social status joined the Military Orders as a way of rising in the world. The Brothers were often employed as royal and papal officials, and individual commanders and officers could hold considerable power and authority. These Orders provided a route for a young warrior from a non-noble knightly family or a family of just below knightly status to win high office by hard work and dedication.[31]

A sermon of Jacques de Vitry, bishop of Acre, pointed out some of the problems that arose when Brothers from poorer backgrounds came into the relative prosperity of the Order of the Temple. He had heard of a Brother who never in his whole life in the outside world had laid his head on a pillow, but when he entered the Order he got so used to having a pillow that one night when it was taken away, because the pillow case was being washed, he kept the whole house awake with his muttering and complaining. Other Brothers who used to be poor and needy became so proud when they entered the Order and were given some minor office that they became rude and abusive to secular knights.[32]

The problems could also work the other way: Brothers from higher social groups despised those of lesser birth, and those with power despised those without. Jacques told his listeners not to despise Brothers who were the children of humble parents. In November 1309 Brother Ponzard de Gizy, commander of Payns (Aube) in France, put forward as part of his evidence against his Order that the lesser Brothers were victimized by the officials of the Order.[33] Such attitudes reflected the conflicts in the society from which the Brothers came.

When the Order was founded, its squires and servants were not members of the Order. This policy soon changed and auxiliaries were admitted to full membership. It was also possible to join the Order for a fixed period only, as did Count Fulk V of Anjou and Ramon Berenguer IV.

Sergeant-Brothers or serving-Brothers could act as warriors or unarmed servants. Although the Rule restricted their access to high office, many acted as commanders and held subordinate offices. The vast bulk of the Brothers were sergeants. The Rule stated that only knight-Brothers could wear white mantles (symbolizing purity) while sergeants and associates of the Order should wear black (the traditional colour of monastic habits, symbolizing human sin).[34] If this ruling was enforced, it is not surprising that contemporaries so often muddled the Hospitallers' black mantles with the Templar sergeants' black mantles and could not tell the two Orders apart. The non-fighting sergeants were essential to the running of the Order, but whereas warriors would be sent to the Holy Land, where fighting men were always needed, servants such as shepherds would probably stay in their homeland, in the house which they originally joined. They were not expected to attend provincial chapter meetings, and if they were running a *camera* where there was no chapel and there were fewer than four Brothers they might never even attend a Sunday chapter meeting. Such Brothers lived lives hardly different from those of their farming neighbours.

The Rule of the Order forbad the reception of Sisters.[35] This made good sense for a military force, because women in the army would distract the men and disrupt discipline. But in the West, away from the battle lines, military considerations were not important. The reason given in the Rule for excluding women from the Order was that they would lead the Brothers astray from their spiritual path. Other religious Orders of the twelfth century had the same ruling for the same reason. The Cistercian Order would not accept women, while the Premonstratensian Order at first accepted women and then forbad their admission. The Rule of the Teutonic Order stated that women should not be admitted because they would make the Brothers 'go soft'; women could only be accepted as 'half-Sisters' and had to live separately from the Brothers.

Yet in practice both the Cistercians and the Premonstratensians continued to admit women on a regular basis, while the Teutonic Order accepted women as full Sisters and their houses were sometimes attached to the Brothers' houses.[36] In fact, it was not possible for a religious Order to keep women out if they wanted to join, because they brought with them money, influence and other valuable gifts such as the favour and support of their families. Any Order that refused to accept all women would lose much more than it would gain, and no religious Order would want to refuse entry to pious women who could improve the spirituality of the Order.

The Templars had at least one nunnery. In 1272 Bishop Eberhard of Worms gave the Order of the Temple ownership and responsibility for the administration of the nunnery of Mühlen (between Osthofen and Westhofen in the diocese of Worms), and the duty of supporting the women there. After the dissolution of the Order of the Temple the nuns of Mühlen, *quondam ordinis Templi*, 'formerly of the Order of the Temple', were transferred to the Order of the Hospital, although the Sisters did not want to be transferred.[37] There were also a number of women living in commanderies of men. Presumably there was some form of segregation within the house, although we have no information about this. Sister Adelheide of Wellheim is recorded at the Templar house of Mosbrunnen (now Moritzbrunn) in the diocese of Eichstätt in the early fourteenth century. She was the former wife of Templar Rudiger of Wellheim, and had chosen 'continual habitation' in the house of the Temple of Moritzbrunn for the rest of her life in order to serve God better. However, because of her physical weakness she could not bear living under the Rule, and she was moved out of the house to a separate dwelling.[38] The charter setting out her situation indicates that she had been living in the commandery before the decision was taken to move her elsewhere, and that she had been following the complete Rule, as a Sister of the Order.

Adelheide entered the Order as the wife of a Brother of the Order. The Rule did permit married couples to become associate members, but stated that wives could not become full Sisters and could not live in a house of the Order.[39] Yet the Brothers stretched the Rule to meet the needs of the Order and its donors. While scholars have identified some couples whose association with the Order fitted the requirements of the Rule, other arrangements expected either the man or the woman to enter the Order eventually, whichever outlived the other.[40]

The papal commissioners' examinations of the French Templars during the trial of the Order suggest how one man and wife could have entered the Order together. On 23 February 1310 Raynand Bergeron, a serving-Brother, told the papal commissioners that he had been invited to join the Order by the local commander and had refused unless his wife was allowed to enter with him. The commander agreed, because (said Raynand) he wanted to gain Raynand's property for the Order. Raynand did not say whether his wife went through the same admission ceremony as he did, nor did he explain what her standing was in the Order.[41]

However, because torture was used during the initial interrogations in France, and because once a person had confessed to heresy they could not go back on their confession without being condemned as an obdurate heretic, the evidence from the French trial is, to use the modern phrase, 'unsafe'. This applies even where the accused produced evidence that contradicted the charges, as modern scientific psychological research has demonstrated that those under interrogation may invent information in order to distract the interrogator.[42] Brother Raynand seems to have wanted to convince the commissioners that the Order had tricked him into joining for the wrong motives, and so his membership of the Order was invalid. Hence his story is probably untrue.

More certain examples of men and women joining the Order together are known from the donations they gave the Order when they joined. Gombau and Ermengarda d'Oluja joined the Order as donats, a type of association with the Order. Gombau was lord of the castle of Vallfogona and held other properties in the area of Tarragona. On 31 December 1196 the couple gave their property and themselves to the house of the Temple at Barberà, and entered the house as resident donats. Gombau disappears from the record: presumably he died. We next encounter Ermengarda as commander of the nearby house of Rourell, where there were also other Sisters.[43] We do not know whether Ermengarda carried out all the duties of a commander herself, such as attending provincial chapters, or whether she sent a male representative in her place, but her title of *preceptrix* – commander – is beyond doubt.

In 1288 Geoffrey de Vichier, Visitor of the Order of the Temple in France, England and Germany, noted that Adelisa, widow of Henry Morsels, 'our associate sister' (*consoror*), who was living (*manens*) in the Order's house at Ghent, had asked him to receive lord Arnulph of Assche, priest, to serve in the second chapel in the house at Ghent, which Adelisa had founded.[44] As Geoffrey specifically stated that Adelisa was living in the house it is possible that she had paid for a second chapel so that she would have somewhere to worship separately from the Brothers.

Although Adelisa was living in the commandery, she was not a fully professed Sister but an associate. There was a wide range of possible levels of association. Various terms were used for associates: these include *familiars* (friends), *conversi* and *conversae* (literally 'converts'), *confratres* and *consorores* (fellow-Brothers and Sisters), *donati* and *donatae* (men and women who had 'given' themselves to the Order). At one end of the spectrum were those who had promised to take the Order's habit if they decided to enter a religious Order. They gave the Order their possessions but retained the income from them for their lifetime, and chose to be buried in the Order's cemetery. In return the Order promised them a share in its spiritual and worldly benefits, and gave them economic assistance if required.

Then there were those who had made a firmer commitment with a vow of obedience, but not the full profession of the three monastic vows. They would be associated with their local house (for example, making a small annual donation in return for the Brothers' prayers and a share in their good works), but remained in their own home. If they later joined a religious Order, they would join the Order to which they were associated – but they need not actually join any Order and they need not wear a habit. The Order would undertake to take care of them in their old age, and bury them on their death. In effect they had made an arrangement to give a regular donation to a worthwhile charity, with pension and burial insurance benefits in return. The most committed had made a vow of obedience to the Master, had the definite intention of entering the Order, and might actually be living within a house of the Order, waiting for the opportunity to make their final vows. They wore a special habit, different from the habit of fully professed members of the Order: perhaps the cross on their mantle would be a different design from that worn by full members.[45]

The Templars had many male and female associates, some so closely associated that they are all but indistinguishable from fully professed members of the Order. It is possible that the Brothers and Sisters at Rourell were actually associate members of the Order and not fully professed, but if they were living a religious life, following the Rule and attending Church services, there was no difference in practice between them and the fully professed members of the Order. Berengaria of Lorach, whom Alan Forey found cited in a number of thirteenth-century documents relating to the Templars' house of Barberà, was described as both *donata* (associate) and *soror* (full Sister), her name appears in the witness-lists of Brothers of the Order (as if she, too, were a 'Brother') and she gave counsel to the commander of the house.[46] The fact that she was acting as a witness does suggest that she was living within the precinct of the commandery, but it is not clear what her status was within the Order.

It is noticeable that many of the women recorded as being Sisters or associates of the Order of the Temple were in houses in Catalonia. This may be because extensive records survive from Catalonia and scholars have studied them in detail; but the same could be said of England, where only one female associate of the Order is known, and no full Sisters.[47] In contrast, in Germany, where the records of the Templars are scanty, one nunnery and a Sister are known to have been members of the Order. Women in the Iberian Peninsula had more extensive property rights than those in most of western Europe, and so were better placed to endow religious houses, and were able to take their property with them when they entered a religious Order; likewise, in much of Germany women were able to inherit property and dispose of it as they wished. This made them more attractive recruits to a religious house, and more difficult to turn away. In England, in contrast, married women did not control their own property, so they were less attractive recruits.

Religious Orders and religious houses usually had lay people associated with them in a 'confraternity', an organized association of spiritual brothers and sisters, something similar to the modern supporters' club.[48] A charter of the Templars' confraternity at Metz in Lorraine (or Lotharingia) has survived. Dated to January 1288, this is an agreement between Martin, commander of the Templars' *bailie* of Lorraine, and a number of men and women representing the confraternity of the Temple at Metz. The confraternity ceded an area of vineyard to the Templars at Metz. In exchange, the Templars of Metz had to keep a lamp burning before the statue of Our Lady in the chapel of the house of the Temple at Metz (plate 22). This lamp represented the people's prayers to God through Our Lady. The confraternity had also given the Templars sixty *sous* ('shillings' in English) to buy property which would give them rents and dues. The Templars should use this income to buy three sesters (a large measure) of middling good wine each year for the 'mayor' and associates of the confraternity.[49] Presumably the confraternity had an annual religious service and meal, at which the wine would be consumed.

All the people listed above were members of the Order to a greater or lesser degree, and were admitted to the Order in an special ceremony. Although the Rule of the Order indicates that there would be a period of training before an applicant was admitted to full membership the Order – the novitiate – in fact this training period was dropped because the Order needed to be able to recruit military personnel quickly to replace losses in the East. The same happened in other Military Orders.[50]

The admission ceremony for Brothers was laid down as part of the Rule and Statutes of the Order.[51] Although the Brothers were accused in 1307 of conducting admissions in secret and at night, the evidence given during the trial indicates that admission procedures varied according to local practice. Relatives and other outsiders might be present at the ceremony, which usually took place at dawn. In the outside world by the late thirteenth century, the ceremony for making a new knight consisted of an all-night vigil, followed by a service starting at dawn. Presumably the Templars were following common practice.[52]

Those entering as full members of the Order should not have any commitments outside the Order – they should not belong to anyone as a serf, or as a husband, or owe money they could not repay. The new member was warned that life in the Order would be harsh; he would have to do what he was told, and he might find his work demeaning or consider it beneath him. He had to promise, as all religious did, to live chastely, without any personal property, and to obey the Master and the Rule of the Order. In addition, he promised to work to help to conquer the Holy Land. His promises were made to God and 'Our Lady St Mary'. He was given the white mantle, and told that he should always wear a cord tied over his shirt, under his tunic, as a sign of chastity. During the trial proceedings many

Brothers explained that they had to supply their own cord. A few said that their own families supplied them, although one noted that his girlfriend supplied his.[53]

Commanderies also contained people who were not members of the Order. These could be religious persons, such as hermits or anchoresses living holy lives in separate cells cut off from humanity. Such persons were often attached to religious houses. There were also servants, who could be men or women. The Rule of the Temple forbad the employment of women, but nevertheless there are records that dairymaids were employed at some houses, although they might never actually have entered the precinct of the house. At the Templars' estate at Rockley in Wiltshire, England, a woman was employed to milk the cows, but it was the duty of the tenants to employ her. In 1307 there were three dairymaids working in the dairy at the Templar house at Baugy in France. There were also two women servants living in the hostel at the commandery of Corval, in Normandy, perhaps to care for the sick.[54] Another job routinely done by women in the Middle Ages was the laundry, and women were generally employed by religious houses for this purpose.

A final group who might be living at a Templar commandery comprised those who held pensions from the Order; either because they were elderly servants of the Order, now too old to work, or because they had given the Order a gift in return for support in their old age. This support came in the form of food, clothes and money, and was called a corrody. Men, women and married couples could be recipients of corrodies. Such people seldom appear in day-to-day records, but are mentioned in the documentation surrounding the trial and dissolution of the Order of the Temple. They were still entitled to receive their corrodies even though the Order was under investigation, and when the Order's property passed to the Hospital of St John in 1312 the Hospital had to support them. Some lived in the Order's houses, while others lived in their own houses but were supported by the Order.[55]

Such people could be enthusiastic supporters and donors to the Order. In the 1320s the Franciscan friar Nicholas Bozon recorded a story about a Templar pensioner, a parish priest who had been a 'procurator' for the Templars at Bow in London. He was entitled to receive from the Order food, a servant, a horse, clothes and an annual pension, but he spent nothing on himself, instead saving all his income and handing it over to the Templars whenever he was able to go up to London. He died in poverty, but after his death 8,000 pounds was found hidden in his house, which he had intended to hand over to the Order during his next visit to London. Nicholas Bozon told the story as an example of miserliness, but it also illustrates how dedicated the Templars' supporters could be to helping the Order.[56]

5

RELIGIOUS LIFE

A Templar commandery was a busy place, a mixture of a secular farm and/or industrial site and/or business centre, which saw the daily round of religious observance. Once a week members of the Temple met in their individual houses in chapter. In traditional monasteries the monks met daily in a specially built chapter house, but the Templars' houses did not run to such expense and the members would meet in the most suitable building available, such as the chapel. The weekly chapter meeting began and ended with prayers led by the chaplain (if the house had a chaplain), and dealt with house business and the correction of faults, that is, things that had been done which were against the Rule. The chapter discussed and decided punishments; Templar discipline was strict, but errors might be forgiven if there were mitigating circumstances.

The chapter meeting was for members of the Order only, and outsiders were not supposed to attend. This was normal practice for religious Orders. It was a reasonable procedure, as the meeting would deal with private business of the house, problems and misdeeds which could cause scandal for the Order if they became known outside the House, and other matters that concerned no one but the Order. As the chapter was effectively a management meeting, there was no reason why outsiders should be admitted or even why they should want to attend. Just as modern-day managers should not discuss the proceedings of management meetings with anyone not at the meeting, those present at a chapter meeting were not to discuss its proceedings with anyone who was not present. The Hospital of St John had a similar ruling, which was apparently introduced after rumours of various misdeeds and scandals in the Order reached the ears of Pope Gregory IX. Religious Orders in general were aware of the need to protect their reputations and tried to prevent outsiders finding out about scandals and problems in their houses, but it was very difficult to prevent rumours.[1]

To judge from the Rule, even associate members of the Order living in the house could not attend weekly chapter meetings. In practice, if they formed a major part of the community it would be odd if they did not attend, but presumably if they did they could not vote.

Not only did the Templars follow monastic tradition in holding chapter meetings, but their whole day was structured around the traditional monastic day, as laid down in the sixth-century Rule of St Benedict (see figures 7–8). Provided that the house had a chapel where services could be heard, the Brothers were to hear the whole divine office each day ('the hours', so called because they took place at the first, third, sixth and ninth hours), as well as additional services. In the East or in the Iberian Peninsula, if they were out on campaign or in a place where they could not hear the hours, they were to say the Lord's prayer a set number of times instead.

The statutes of the Order laid down the details of the Templars' day, starting with the religious services they had to attend every day (sections 279–312, 340–65), and going on to

Figure 7 The monastic day according to the Rule of St Benedict

> So, whoever you are, hastening to your heavenly home, you should first carry out with Christ's help this little rule for beginners.
> *The Rule of St Benedict (6th century)*

The monks or nuns were to live a life of obedience, silence, humility and poverty. Their day was made up of services in church with private study and work for the religious community e.g. in the fields or in the kitchen. The times of the services were calculated by dividing the hours of daylight into twelve, and the hours of dark into twelve. So in summer each daylight hour was longer than each night hour, and vice versa in the winter.

Time	Service in Church	
c.2am winter; just before Lauds in summer	Vigils/Matins	Shorter service in summer, longer in winter
	'Night Office'	Takes around 2 hours on Sundays and feast days
		After night office in winter, read quietly until Lauds
First light	Lauds	
c.6am	Prime (1st hour)	
c.9am	Tierce (3rd hour)	
12 noon	Sext (6th hour)	In summer, followed by a meal and then sleep.
c.3pm	Nones (9th hour)	Followed by a meal in winter. Then reading in cloister.
Before dark	Vespers	Followed by supper in summer. Then reading in cloister
Sundown (8pm summer)		Compline Silence after Compline. Followed by bed in dormitory

At services, the hymns are sung, psalms are recited and lessons read from the Bible and the works of the Fathers of the Church (early authoritative Christian writers), as well as verses for meditation related to the lessons.

Meals: two a day from Easter to 14 September, except on fast days. One a day from 14 September to Easter. The single meal is taken after Vespers during Lent.

Sleep: They sleep from sundown to the 8th hour of the night. In summer they also sleep after their noon meal until the service of Nones.

Figure 8 The Templars' day according to the Rule of the Temple

Time	Service in chapel (if house has one, otherwise half)	
At night	Matins in chapel	Brothers to join in prayers Brothers then go and check horses and equipment and speak to their squires Sleep until dawn
c.6am	Prime Mass (or after Sext)	
c.9am	Terce	
c.12 noon	Sext Mass (if not heard earlier	Afterwards repair armour and equipment, make tent pegs, tent posts, or anything necessary Followed by lunch: knights eat at first sitting; sergeants at second sitting; clerk to read aloud while they eat Go to chapel and give thanks: 'Go to their posts and do the best that God instructs them'
c.3pm	Nones Vespers for the dead Vigils for the dead	
Dusk	Vespers	Followed by supper
	Compline	Followed by a drink Check horses and equipment, speak to squire if necessary
Dark		Bed

During periods of fasting there was only one meal a day at 3pm or 4pm. Orders were handed out to Brothers before the 'Hours' services in chapel.

Chapter meetings were held on Sundays and at Christmas, Easter and Pentecost. In Europe, away from the frontier, attention to horses and equipment would be replaced by whatever work was needed in the House.

other regulations regarding everyday life. The tone of the statutes is monastic, with the emphasis on silence, humble obedience – orders were to be carried out with the words *de par Dieu*, literally 'on God's behalf', or as it could be rendered in English 'as God wills' (section 313). Brothers should speak quietly and politely to each other (sections 321, 325). There was to be no swearing (section 321), no gambling (section 317), no drunkenness: a Brother who was habitually drunk could be required to leave the Order.[2] Brothers were to avoid the company of women; a Brother who was found with a woman could lose his habit, that is, be thrown out of the Order, or would at least be barred from holding responsible office within the Order.[3] Sex of any kind was completely out of the question.

Without swearing, gambling, drinking or women, the Templars would have been hardly recognizable as knights, for these were all normal parts of the knightly life. Clearly the strict rules were a shock for some Brothers: during the trial proceedings in France one ex-Brother explained that he had left the Order because 'he was young and could not bear to abstain from women'.[4] Others declared that the Templars could have women whenever they wanted them, despite the Rule.[5] Yet the history of the Order produced no public sexual scandals, unlike other religious Orders. During the trial of the Templars on Cyprus, one of the lay witnesses made a joke implying that the Templars were womanizers, but he was the only lay witness to make such a remark.[6] In fictional literature the Templars were depicted as helping lovers, but this image was based more on Templars' love for God than their love for women. There were no scandals in the Order of the Temple to compare to events in the Dominican friary and nunnery at Zamora, for instance, where the friars apparently regarded the Sisters' house as a source of women for their pleasure. No one wrote stories about the Templars like the French poet Rutebuef's scandalous story about the Franciscan friars, 'Brother Denise', where a friar seduces a young girl by telling her she will save her soul by doing everything he tells her. The Templars were never accused of systematically raping women, as were the Teutonic knights. There were no complaints such as Pope Gregory IX's about the Hospital of St John in the East in 1238, stating that he had heard rumours that the Hospitallers were keeping harlots in their villages. Nor were there any individuals like Brother Ramon d'Ampurias, prior of the Hospital of St John in Catalonia, who was accused in around 1314 of having impeded two of his squires from giving their confessions when they were dying at Rhodes, so that his homosexual relations with them would not become public. He was also accused of raping many ladies and having many illegitimate children. Ramon d'Ampurias was eventually deprived of office after a long armed resistance and a papal excommunication.[7] It does appear that the Templars were more chaste than many other religious men.

Sexual relations with a man would result in automatic expulsion from the Order of the Temple. The only case of sodomy ever recorded within the Order resulted in the imprisonment of two of those involved, while the third escaped and went over to the Muslims.[8] Even during the trial of the Templars, when Brothers were being actively encouraged to confess to the practice of sodomy, very few were prepared to do so. Malcolm Barber has noted that in the depositions made in Paris in October and November 1307 only three Templars out of a total of 138 were named as having been involved in acts of sodomy; Anne Gilmour-Bryson has noted a few Templars who accused others of the practice; an Irish Templar priest stated that a Templar in Ireland had died as a result of practising sodomy. Of all these testimonies, I have identified only three that I would consider as possibly genuine.[9] This is remarkably few for a large international organization, given that contemporaries regarded the traditional monastic Orders such as the Benedictines and Cistercians as being rife with active homosexual practices.[10]

In short, for the most part the Templars kept their Rule. Many contemporaries considered them to be pious. It was the practice for dying nobles to 'give' themselves to a religious

Order. In their last few days of life they could do penance for their sins and the Order would then be responsible for their burial, receive some or all of their possessions and be honoured with having the tomb of a noble person in the Order's church, ensuring continual financial support from that person's family. Many elderly or dying noble warriors gave themselves to the Order of the Temple, including illustrious knights such as William Marshal, earl of Pembroke (d. 1219). In the East, the leading nobleman John of Ibelin, lord of Beirut, joined the Order in 1236 when he was dying, while Garnier l'Aleman (Werner of Egisheim) joined towards the end of his life in 1233.[11] Many donors gave to the Templars' chapels, so that their priests would say mass for the donor's soul and the souls of their families, or so that a lamp would be kept burning in the Order's chapel, such as the lamp paid for by the confraternity at Metz to burn in front of the Templars' statue of Mary, mother of Jesus, or the lamps that donors paid for to burn in the chapel of St Mary at the Templars' house at Sandford and at Cowley in Oxfordshire, England. Although the Order's commanderies in the West were generally small and unimpressive, their chapels were well equipped.[12] Donors would have made these donations because they believed the Order to be pious and its prayers and service to be pleasing to God.

During the trial of the Order in Cyprus, the non-Templar witnesses agreed that the Templars were devout, never missing mass, hearing the divine services as good Christians should, and taking part in vigils and processions on holy days.[13] During the trial in France, the Brothers presented to the papal commissioners a copy of the prayers which the Brothers said each day: these included prayers to Mary, Star of the Sea (the Blessed Virgin Mary, mother of Jesus), Christ, St John the Evangelist and St George. The papal commissioners complained about the bad quality of the Latin in these prayers and instructed the notaries to correct it, but the Brothers' piety was not questioned.[14]

The Brothers had a reputation for being steadfast in prayer. The Cistercian monk Caesar of Heisterbach, a contemporary of

Jacques de Vitry, and Oliver, schoolmaster of Cologne, recorded an anecdote of a group of Templars who were praying in their chapel when the Muslims launched a surprise attack. The Master ordered them to continue praying, which they did. When they emerged to meet the Muslims, they found that they had already been defeated. It transpired that angels had defeated the enemy while the Templars prayed.[15] There were various other stories of the Templars' piety circulating within the Order, and among those close to the Order. Jacques de Vitry recounted several as examples of pious Brothers of the past, to guide or inspire the Brothers of his own day: the tale of the Brother who fasted so much that he kept falling off his horse; the tale of the Brother who urged his horse 'Morel' (Blackie) to carry him to Heaven through martyrdom in battle against the Muslims; the tale of a Brother who made a miraculous leap on his horse right down a cliff in order to escape Muslim bandits, and lived to tell the tale – although the horse died.[16]

Walter Map, who knew plenty of derogatory stories about the Templars, the Hospitallers, the papacy and the Cistercians, also told some stories that implied the Templars were outstanding Christians. He recorded that one Salius, son of a Muslim emir, had converted to Christianity and joined the Templars. He also told the story of Aimery, a knight who had been on his way to a tournament but had turned aside to hear mass in a chapel of Our Lady (the Blessed Virgin Mary). He missed the tournament, but the Virgin attended in his place and won the prize on his behalf. Aimery was so struck by this miracle that he joined the Order of the Temple.[17]

Aimery's choice of the Order of the Temple made sense in that he was a knight, the miracle involved military activity, and the Blessed Virgin Mary was the patron of the Order of the Temple (for example, see plate 16). Many donation charters to the Order were given 'to God, the Blessed Virgin Mary and the Order of the Temple',[18] and many of the Order's houses and churches were dedicated to her, including the house at Richerenches and the church at Silva in the diocese of Rodez, where many miracles were reported.[19] The standard admission ceremony set out promises to be made 'to God and Our Lady St Mary', and candidates for admission to the Order were told that 'we were established in honour of Our Lady'.[20] An anonymous sympathizer who wrote in defence of the Order during the trial in France stated that the Brothers had 'dedicated themselves to the service of the glorious Virgin'.[21]

Ancient legend, preserved in the *Legenda Aurea* of Jacobus de Voragine (1267), connected Mary, mother of Jesus, with the Temple of Jerusalem and thus indirectly with the Order of the Temple. According to this, Mary was brought up in the Temple in Jerusalem; in one version of the legend not preserved by Voragine, while she was living in the Temple she received prior warning from an angel that in three years' time he would return to inform her that she would conceive God's son (the Annunciation). The Templars in the East may have taken up and developed these traditions, as the late twelfth-century epic poem *La chanson de Jérusalem* claims that the Annunciation took place in the Temple of Solomon.[22] The Templars interrogated in the West during the trial of the Order did not know of this legend, but still saw themselves as connected with Jesus' mother, Mary. Giving testimony to the papal commissioners, one Brother Guy Delphini stated that the woollen cord that he wore around his waist as a sign of chastity had touched the pillar at Nazareth where the Annunciation had taken place, while Brother Gerald de Marcial, giving evidence at Poitiers, said that his cord had been wound around the door posts of the church of the Blessed Mary at Nazareth; some of the English Brothers claimed the same for their cords.[23] These Brothers certainly thought that their cords were of much greater value because they had been in contact with the place where Mary had stood on that momentous occasion. A pilgrim's guide of the thirteenth century states that there was a stone on which Mary had rested outside the Templars' fortress of Castle Pilgrim.[24] The Templars also publicized the miracle of the icon of Our Lady of Saïdnaia, which exuded milk from its 'breasts': the Templars collected and distributed the milk.[25]

The Templars' veneration for the Virgin Mary won them respect from other Christians, for Roman Catholics in general venerated her. Mary was also the patroness of the Cistercian Order and the Teutonic Order, many churches were dedicated to her and many miracles were attributed to her intervention. During the twelfth and thirteenth centuries, Roman Catholic devotion to the Virgin and to female saints was increasing dramatically.[26] Modern people who are not Catholics and who are not familiar with Catholic beliefs often find the medieval veneration for the Virgin and for saints difficult to understand. They cannot distinguish between 'veneration' and 'worship', and assume that medieval Catholics actually worshipped the Virgin Mary and the saints. Some then take another step of misunderstanding and assume that because they were supposedly worshipping women they must have been pagans.

Medieval Catholics would have been very upset and indignant to have been labelled as 'pagans'. They would have retorted that their veneration of the Virgin Mary and the saints was respect, not worship. They did not pray to Mary and the saints asking them to give help from their own power, but expecting them to intercede for them with God, or to act as a conduit for God's power. They also venerated the Virgin Mary and the saints because these people, who had once been ordinary humans living on earth, were an example to them of how humans should live and acted as an inspiration to them in their everyday lives. In the twelfth and thirteenth centuries religious men and women were concentrating more and more on the importance of humility and of human frailty and sin in comparison with God's power, and also on the importance of Christ's physical body, remembering that Christ had been a physical person living on earth. Traditionally, women were associated with humility, frailty and physical things, an association that went back to ancient Greek philosophy. Therefore veneration for female saints and the Virgin increased during the twelfth and thirteenth centuries.[27]

The basis of the Order of the Temple was the warrior, but the warrior of the twelfth and thirteenth century was not a good subject for a religious Order. He had a strong sense of self-esteem and cared more about his personal honour and glory than about the success of the community. The example of female saints would be very valuable to him, reminding him of the need to be humble, and to remember human frailty and sin. It is true that he might also find the female saint more interesting than the male saint, but this was true of all religious men of this period and not only the Templars.

Ordinary knights in the secular world were also looking to women as an example of how knights should act. By the late twelfth century, writers of romance literature were depicting noble women educating knights in the function of knighthood and knightly behaviour. Famous examples include Ninianne, the lady of the Lake, educating the young *Lancelot*, and Perceval's sister educating Galaad, Perceval and Bors in the *Queste del Saint Graal*. The author of the immensely influential prose romance *Perceforest* wrote between 1335 and 1344:

> Knights and clerics should be like maidens, for the maiden should be straightforward and coy and say little, courteous, chaste and honourable in word and deed, gentle, easy-going and sympathetic towards all good people, fierce, righteous and harsh towards all those who ask them to do what is wrong. And she must also have sufficient beauty and worldly goods, and desire to acquire virtue and to do works which please the Sovereign God. My lords, the knight and the cleric must be like the young girl in all these things, if they wish to come to perfection in whatever they have committed themselves.[28]

The Templars also venerated other female saints, apart from the Virgin Mary.[29] These were saints who had been martyred by pagans after refusing to deny the Christian faith, and therefore were a good example to the Templars. During the Middle Ages, as in modern times, many devout Catholics

The Holy Land

1. The Church of the Holy Sepulchre in Jerusalem.
(© Denys Pringle)

2. The interior of the Aqsa mosque ('Temple of Solomon').
(© Denys Pringle)

3. Baghras Castle. *(© Denys Pringle)*

4. Ruad (Arwad) island. *(© Paul Crawford)*

5. The Templars in battle against the Muslims: mid-twelfth-century fresco from the Templars' former church at Cressac-Saint-Génis, Poitou-Charente, France. *(© M. Debès)*

The Iberian Peninsula

6. The Templars' castle of Pombal, Portugal. *(© Juan Fuguet Sans)*

7. The Templars' castle of Miravet, Tarragona, in the kingdom of Aragon. *(© Juan Fuguet Sans)*

8. The Templars' castle of Monzón, Huesca, in the kingdom of Aragon. (© *Juan Fuguet Sans*)

9. The Templars' castle of Peníscola, Valencia, in the kingdom of Aragon. (© *Juan Fuguet Sans*)

Templar images and imagery

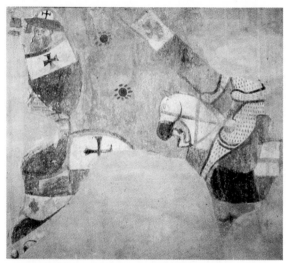

10. Templars in battle, showing the Order's banner; from the fresco in the Order's church of San Bevignate, Perugia. *(© Francesco Tommasi)*

11. Matthew Paris's sketch of the Templars' seal with the banner, from his *Historia Anglorum*. *(© The British Library)*

12. Two Templar knights playing chess; from a manuscript of Alfonso X of Castile's *Libro de Ajedrez, dados y tables*. (© Patrimonio Nacional, Spain)

13. A group of Templar knights on the tomb of the infante Don Felipe in the Templar church of Santa María la Blanca de Villasirga, at Villalcázar de Sirga (Palencia, Castile, Spain). (© Juan Fuguet Sans)

14. Lead seal of Brother Bertrand de Blancafort, Master of the Temple, showing two knights on one horse.
(© Staatsarchiv Amberg)

15. Reverse side of the lead seal of Brother Bertrand de Blancafort, Master of the Temple, showing the cupola of the Church of the Holy Sepulchre.
(© Staatsarchiv Amberg)

Religious life

(*left*) 16. The statue of the 'White Virgin Mary' and Christ child in the Templars' church of Santa María la Blanca de Villasirga.
(© *Juan Fuguet Sans*)

(*right*) 17. The 'Templars' Head': the modern icon of St Euphemia in the Patriarchal Church of St George, Constantinople (Istanbul).
(© *J.M. Upton-Ward*)

18. The interior of the Templars' church at Shipley, Sussex.
(© *Nigel Nicholson*)

(*left*) 19. The exterior of the twelfth-century circular nave of the church of the New Temple in London.
(© *Nigel Nicholson*)

(*right*) 20. The interior of the twelfth-century circular nave of the church of the New Temple in London.
(© *Nigel Nicholson*)

21. The interior of the thirteenth-century extension to the church of the New Temple, London. *(© Nigel Nicholson)*

22. The polygonal chapel of the Templars' reputed commandery at Metz. *(© Jochen Burgtorf)*

Economic activities

23. The Templars' mill at Da'uk, to the south of Acre.
(© Denys Pringle)

24. The wheat barn at Temple Cressing. *(© Nigel Nicholson)*

(*top*) 25. Garway church.
(© *Nigel Nicholson*)

(*above*) 26. Temple Bruer.
(© *Nigel Nicholson*)

(*left*) 27. A ship from the
frescos on the west wall of
the Templars' church of San
Bevignate, Perugia.
(© *Francesco Tommasi*)

28. Acorn Bank, formerly Temple Sowerby, in Cumbria, England. *(© Nigel Nicholson)*

29. The Hospitaller fortifications of the Templar village of La Cavalerie, Aveyron, France. *(© Helen Nicholson)*

30. Tomar, a former Templar castle. *(© Juan Fuguet Sans)*

31. The Good Templars: a nineteenth-century ornament, 28cm high, depicting the temperance movement's ideal of partnership in marriage. *(© Nigel Nicholson)*

32. The modern monument to the Templars outside Temple church, London.
(© Nigel Nicholson)

placed great importance on physical items connected with the saint, left from the time which the saint actually lived on earth. They believed that the saint was still physically present in these objects that had once been connected with them. These could include clothes, objects that had been used by the saint, or the saint's actual body. Because these were things left behind by the saint on earth they were called 'relics', which means 'left behind'.

Christians believed that saints were able to act on earth through their relics. If a saint's relics were well looked after, the saint would be pleased and would help the owners of the relics, so that all would go well for them. But if the relics were not well treated the saint would be angry and would punish the relics' owners.[30] The Templars took pride in looking after their relics with great care.

The Order of the Temple claimed to possess the relics of St Euphemia at Castle Pilgrim. These were stated to be the relics of the illustrious St Euphemia of Chalcedon, martyred in 303, which had been miraculously translated to Palestine from Constantinople[31] – presumably obtained during the sack of Constantinople in 1204, or donated to the Order subsequently by the victors. During the trial of the Order in France, a group of Templars submitted a defence of the Order to the papal commissioners stating that the body of St Euphemia had come to Castle Pilgrim by the grace of God, God had done many miracles through it there, and it would not have lodged itself with the Templars if they were criminals, nor would any of the other relics which were in the possession of the Order.[32] The Teutonic Order had used a similar justification for its acquisition of the head of St Barbara, carried off from the Pomeranians in a raid on the castle of Sartowitz in the 1240s: the saint, it was claimed, had deliberately abandoned her former resting place to be with the Order, witnessing to the Brothers' great spirituality.[33]

It is not clear whether the Order of the Temple claimed to possess the whole body of St Euphemia or simply the head:

witnesses differ. Witnesses described the head as being kept in a silver reliquary, which by 1307 was kept in the church of the house of the Temple at Nicosia on Cyprus.[34] After the dissolution of the Order, it passed to the Hospital of St John with the Templars' other possessions, and was recorded in 1395 as being in the conventual church of St John on Rhodes; by the seventeenth century it was on Malta with the other relics of the Hospital.[35] As such, the reliquary would have been among those which were stolen by Napoleon's plundering troops in June 1798 and were blown up with Napoleon's flagship in Nelson's victory at the Battle of the Nile, 1 August 1798. Yet the real relics of St Euphemia are still in Constantinople, now Istanbul, at the Patriarchal Church of St George (see plate 17). It is not clear what the Templars' relics actually were, but the important point is that the Templars believed that they were genuinely the remains of St Euphemia.

The so-called 'Templars' head' was probably the head of St Euphemia. The Draper of the Order and two knights stated during the trial of the Order on Cyprus that they had never heard of any idols in the Order, but the Order had the head of St Euphemia. Some French Brothers of the Order stated that they had heard that the Order had a head in Cyprus which was possibly the idol that the Order was accused of venerating.[36] Brother Guy Delphini declared proudly to the papal commissioners that the cord he wore around his waist had touched the relics of both St Policarp and St Euphemia – the Order was looking after the relics of St Policarp on behalf of the abbot of the Lord's Temple in Jerusalem, who had entrusted them to the Templars for safe keeping.[37] But St Policarp's relics did not belong to the Order, and no other Templar mentioned them. It was St Euphemia's head that the Order was so proud of possessing. Yet St Euphemia was a young woman, and the Templars were accused in 1307 of venerating a bearded male head. This curious discrepancy between Templar devotion and the charges will be considered in Chapter 8 with the trial of the Order.

Other Brothers during the trial of the Temple in France stated that there was a head kept in the chapel of the Templars' house in Paris, and thought that perhaps this was the idol in question.[38] Investigation by the papal commissioners, however, revealed this too to be the head of a woman.[39]

Brother William of Arreblay, who had been almoner to King Philip IV of France, testified that he had often seen on the altar in the Temple of Paris a silver head, and the leading officials of the Order adoring it. He had understood that this was the head of one of the 11,000 virgins who had been martyred with St Ursula at Cologne at the beginning of the fourth century, but since his arrest, he had realized that he had been mistaken. He had thought it looked like a woman's head, but now he realized that it had had two faces and a beard – a strange mistake to make! The papal commissioners asked him if he would recognize the head if he saw it, and he assured them that he would; so the relevant officials were instructed to search for this head.[40]

When the head arrived, it fitted the original description perfectly. There was a large silver reliquary containing the skull of a young woman, wrapped and stitched into a white linen cloth covered in a piece of red muslin: the red and white symbolizing martyrdom. To clinch the matter, a small piece of parchment was sewn on to the cloth, on which was written: 'Head no. 58'.[41] This female martyr's head was certified genuine.

After the dissolution of the Order, the Templars' Parisian head seems to have passed to the Hospital of St John. Apparently the Teutonic Order also possessed a head of one of the 11,000 virgins in their commandery of the Holy Trinity in Venice.[42] The cult of St Ursula and her maidens was widespread during the Middle Ages, and it is not surprising that the Templars, like every religious Order, wanted to acquire such relics to demonstrate its piety and holiness.

The Templars also had a devotion to St George. George, like the Templars, had been an active warrior; he had patiently died a horrible martyrdom at the hands of pagans because of his Christian faith. His life was an obvious model for the Templars to follow. St George appears on some seals of the Order; his statue was in the chapel of the Order's castle of Safed, and the Order reportedly believed that he protected the castle; his image appears in a fresco in the Order's chapel at Cressac (Charente) in France. A few anecdotes regarding the Templars' military activity mention St George, as does one of the prayers recorded by the Order during the trial of the Order.[43]

So far, the Templars appear to have been typical examples of pious Catholics of the twelfth and thirteenth centuries. They venerated the saints, they attended services in church piously, and they were steadfast in prayer. Yet they were not typical of religious people in monastic Orders, because they were not enclosed and they were not educated in theology. Enclosure meant that all members of the Order lived within a walled religious house, and were not allowed to go out of it except in exceptional circumstances. The Military Orders could not be enclosed, because their members had to go out of their houses to fight; in the same way, the new Orders of canons and later of friars were not enclosed as they also went out to work in the secular world. Jocelin of Brakelond's account of everyday life in the Benedictine abbey of Bury St Edmunds (Suffolk, England) in the late twelfth century reveals the drawbacks of enclosure, with backbiting, gossip and jealousies, and chapter meetings breaking up in uproar.[44] In an unenclosed house, where members could come and go, they were less likely to get on one another's nerves and relations were less likely to become strained. Set against the example of Bury, it is easy to understand why many pious donors of the twelfth century should have preferred to give to the new, unenclosed religious Orders.

The lack of education was more of a drawback. Religious Orders were centres of Christian learning; in fact it was the religious Orders that had kept learning alive from the fifth to the eleventh centuries, when secular schools were scarce and most of the laity could not read or write. However, the function of the Order of the Temple was to fight in defence of Christendom, and its leaders did not see education as a high priority. The Brothers were mainly drawn from the lesser warrior classes, and could read and write in their own language but not in Latin, the language of education. In fact it appears that education was discouraged in the Order, because it encouraged Brothers to think too much for themselves and argue with their superiors, undermining discipline.[45]

Nevertheless, there were some attempts to educate the Brothers. The English province took the initiative here in producing translations of Latin religious works into Anglo-Norman French, which the Brothers could understand. These translations were made during the second half of the twelfth century, at the same period as the English priory of the Hospital of St John had the Hospitallers' Rule and legends translated into Anglo-Norman French. The Catholic Church had not yet clamped down on translations of religious works (this did not come until 1230) and it was still acceptable for religious works to be translated into the 'common tongue' provided that this was properly authorized. The Old Testament Book of Judges was translated from Latin into French for two leading Brothers of the Temple in England, Richard of Hastings and Osto of St Omer, during the third quarter of the twelfth century.[46] This described how the children of Israel defended the Promised Land, which had been won in the Book of Joshua. As the Templars' role was to defend the Holy Land, which had been won by the First Crusade, there was an obvious parallel. Such a translation could have been read aloud to the Templars at meals, as the Rule stated (section 288).

Other translations into Anglo-Norman French writings were produced by an unknown poet for Brother Henry d'Arcy, commander of Temple Bruer in Lincolnshire in 1161–74: these were a 'Lives of the Fathers', the deeds of early Christians; an account of the future coming of Antichrist; a version of the well-known account of St Paul's descent into Hell; and the Life of St Thaïs, the converted prostitute, a popular legend in the Middle Ages.[47] Some of these works had an obvious attraction for the Templars: St Thaïs had lived a sinful life before her conversion, just as many secular knights would have done before joining the Order of the Temple – at least according to section 49 of the Rule. The account of Antichrist stressed the importance of holding firm to the faith despite all temptations and persecutions and promised a great reward in Heaven to all who stayed faithful to Christ until the end.

The account of Antichrist was particularly important for the Templars. Some contemporaries interpreted the crusades and the recapture of the holy places in an eschatalogical context. They believed that they were part of the coming of Christ's kingdom. But first Antichrist must be defeated. Antichrist's coming had been foretold by the apostles (1 John 2: 18), and his coming would prove that the end of the world was nigh. Some Christian writers identified Mohammad with Antichrist.[48] Therefore the Templars, champions of Christendom against the Muslims, were in the front line of the war against Antichrist and needed to be well informed on the subject.

The writings produced for the Templars give us some idea of their faith: straightforward and simple, without deep theological questioning, like the faith of the secular knights. The Templars themselves wrote very little. The Rule gives the impression that they were devout Catholic Christians. Letters written from the East to the West asking for aid include many expressions of faith, but such letters would normally have been written by an official notary and do not reveal the Templars' own beliefs at first hand. Two Templar poets are known: Ricaut Bonomel, who composed a song lamenting Baibars's victories in 1265 and attacking the pope for diverting crusaders to Sicily; and Oliver, who wrote in around 1270 hoping that King James I of Aragon would come to aid the Holy Land. Ricaut Bonomel's lament that God seems to be supporting the Muslims rather than the Christians may seem overstated to anyone unaware of the situation in the East in 1265, but in the circumstances it was perfectly understandable. Both songs promoted the crusade and encouraged those who heard them to come to the aid of the Holy Land.[49]

Otherwise, there is little evidence of Templar writing. The first version of the *Itinerarium Peregrinorum*, an account of the Third Crusade, contains material that must have originated from the Templars, but the history itself was not written by a Templar.[50] The historical writer now known as the 'Templar of Tyre' was not a Templar at all: his modern nickname comes from the fact he had been secretary to Master William de Beaujeu. There has been some speculation that the Templars were involved in the development of the legend of the Holy Grail, but careful reading reveals that this could not have been the case. The concept of knighthood in the Grail legends is different from the Templar ideal: the Grail knights act alone, not as part of a community.[51]

The Templar emphasis on the community of Brothers acting together was probably the reason why no individual Templars were recognized by the Catholic Church as saints. Because the whole Order had to work together in Christ's service, the Order would have tried to discourage members from venerating individual Brothers. If individuals were singled out for veneration this would encourage Brothers to 'go it alone' in the search for martyrdom and glory, which would destroy the vital cooperation and discipline on the battlefield. Nevertheless, some Brothers who died fighting bravely against the Muslims were 'written up' as martyrs, and may have been specially remembered within the Order. Two of these are recorded in the first version of the *Itinerarium Peregrinorum*. At the battle of the Spring of the Cresson on 1 May 1187:

> A remarkable and memorable event occurred. A certain Templar – a knight by profession, of Touraine by nation, Jacquelin de Maillé by name – brought all the enemy assault on himself through his outstanding courage. While the rest of his fellow knights (estimated to number 500) had either been captured or

killed, he bore all the force of the battle alone and shone out as
a glorious champion for the law of his God. He was surrounded
by enemy troops and almost abandoned by human aid, but
when he saw so many thousands running towards him from all
directions he strengthened his resolve and courageously
undertook the battle, one man against all.

His commendable courage won him his enemies' approval.
Many were sorry for him and affectionately urged him to
surrender, but he ignored their urgings, for he was not afraid to
die for Christ. At long last, crushed rather than conquered by
spears, stones and lances, he sank to the ground and joyfully
passed to heaven with the martyr's crown, triumphant.

It was indeed a gentle death with no place for sorrow, when
one man's sword had constructed such a great crown for himself
from the crowd laid all around him. Death is sweet when the
victor lies encircled by the impious people he has slain with his
victorious right hand. And because it so happened that the
warrior had been riding a white horse and had had white armour
and weapons, the Muslims, who knew that St George had this
appearance in battle, boasted that they had killed the Knight of
Shining Armour, the protector of the Christians.[52]

The writer goes on to describe how local people took parts
of Brother Jacquelin's body as relics. The whole account is full
of references which we would associate with the Templars:
death as a glorious service for Christ, death as joy, non-
Christians as the enemy, and a reference to the Christians'
protector St George, one of the saints venerated by the Order.
It is likely that this account originated with the Templars.

A later account in the same chronicle of a Templar
martyrdom was also probably recounted by the Templars.
After the defeat of the forces of the Kingdom of Jerusalem at
Hattin on 4 July 1187, Saladin had all the Templars beheaded:

A certain Templar named Nicholas had been so successful in
persuading the rest to undergo death willingly that the others

struggled to go in front of him and he only just succeeded in obtaining the glory of martyrdom first – which was an honour he very much strove for. Nor was the miraculous power of divine mercy missing. A ray of celestial light shone down clearly on the bodies of the holy martyrs during the three following nights, while they were still lying unburied.[53]

Again, this account stresses the glory of death in Christ's name, and honours the Templar who tries to become a martyr. Self-sacrifice for God's glory may not appeal to many modern people, but it was the ideal which underpinned the knighthood of the Temple.

Away from the battle lines, the Templars lived much like other religious Orders, and played their role as a religious Order in society. The Rule of the Order did not require it to look after the poor and sick, yet the Brothers did give hospitality to travellers. They were responsible for some hospices in the West, and were involved in dispensing charity among outsiders, to both men and women.[54] Two stories were recounted by third parties during the trial proceedings about Templar priests using relics owned by the Order to cure men and women.[55] Like other new religious Orders of the twelfth and thirteenth centuries, particularly the Cistercians and Hospital of St John, the Templars had special privileges from the pope to protect them from the demands of bishops and secular lords and enable them to carry out their vocation more effectively (see figure 9). These were granted in a series of papal bulls (papal instructions were called 'bulls' after the papal seal or *bullum* which was attached to the parchment), issued from 1139 onwards. These privileges gave the Templars great freedom in their operations and helped them to attract and keep new members and attract associates and donations. Yet they also caused friction with the bishops. During the eleventh and twelfth century, prompted by the debates in the new universities such as Paris and Bologna, views of spirituality were changing.

Figure 9   Privileges given by the papacy to the Templars

1139: Innocent II: Omne Datum Optimum.

The Order may keep the booty it captures from the Muslims.

Donations to the Order are confirmed.

The Order's Rule of life under the Master is confirmed.

The Brothers may elect their Master without interference from anyone else.

The customs and observances of the Order cannot be infringed or changed except by the Master and with the consent of the wiser part of the Chapter of Brothers.

The Brothers should not give oaths of loyalty or homage or any oaths to anyone outside the Order.

No professed Brother may leave the Order to return to the secular world or join another religious Order.

They need not pay tithes (the tenth of produce due to the Church) on the produce of their own lands.

They may receive the right to collect tithes as a gift from laypeople or clergy, with the consent of the bishop or clergy concerned.

They may receive respectable clerks and priests who are ordained according to canon law (as far as they can tell) to serve the Order. They have to get the consent of the priests' bishops to do this. But if the bishop refuses, the pope will overrule him.

They can remove these priests if they disturb the peace of the Order or the house or are useless, with the consent of the wiser part of the Chapter.

These priests who stay a year and are approved of by the Brothers may take the profession of the Order, swearing to obey the Master, and remain in the Order. They will have the same support and clothes as the Brothers except for their priestly vestments. They are only responsible for 'care of souls' as far as the Order requests. They are not to be subject to anyone outside the Order (for example, the bishop).

The Order can have its clergy ordained by any bishop.

These clergy are not to preach for money, unless the Master makes arrangements for this.

The pope lays down the procedure for the admittance of priests to the Order.

The Brothers may build oratories (private chapels) wherever they live, and they can hear divine office there, and those who die as Brothers of the Order can be buried there.

Wherever the Brothers go, they may have their confessions heard by any Catholic priests, or receive unction or any sacrament.

These papal privileges and protection are extended to cover their household and servants.

1144: Celestine II: Milites Templi

The pope calls Brothers 'New Maccabees in the time of grace', referring to the warrior priests of the Jewish state in the second century BC.

The pope addresses the archbishops, bishops and other clergy. He describes the Templars defending pilgrims and storming the enemies of the Christians.

He urges the archbishops etc. to command their subjects to make a collection for the Templars. Whoever becomes a member of their confraternity will have one seventh of their penance remitted.

On death, members of the confraternity will have church burial unless they have been excommunicated by name.

When the Brothers come to receive the confraternity collection from a city or village that is under interdict, the churches are to be opened once a year and divine offices celebrated for that purpose only.

1145: Eugenius III: Milites Dei

To patriarchs, archbishops, bishops and other clergy. He promises them that he does not wish to damage their rights.

He has given the Templars permission to take on suitable priests to serve the spiritual needs of the Order. These priests are to be properly ordained and to have their bishop's permission to serve the Order.

The Brothers may take tithes and burital offerings in places where they have a house. They may build oratories for themselves and bury their Brothers and servants there when they die.

He asks the patriarchs, archbishops, and bishops to consecrate the Brothers' oratories and bless their cemeteries and permit their priests to work in peace.

Religious men could be regulars, following a religious rule (monks), or seculars, living in the ordinary world (archbishops, bishops and priests). From the time of the late Roman Empire it was believed that monks were the best Christians, and that those who wanted to follow the Christian life to its fullest should leave society and devote themselves to a life of prayer and contemplation. Because monks were the best Christians, they had the right to rule themselves and not to be interfered with by bishops. But from the mid-eleventh century, with the growth of interest in canon law (the law of the Church) these ideas were changing. Now many leading religious thinkers saw the concept of apostolic succession as more important. Christ had made the apostle Simon Peter the head of the Church, and Christ's authority had come down through the ages through Simon Peter and his successors as popes of Rome. The pope ordained the archbishops and archbishops ordained the bishops, while the bishops ordained the priests – so all authority within the Church could be traced back to the pope and thence back to Simon Peter and to Christ. Therefore, all clergy including monks should be under the authority of their bishop. The religious Orders who were exempt from the bishops' authority defied this concept and therefore came under heavy criticism from secular clergy such as William, archbishop of Tyre, John of Salisbury and Walter Map.

In 1179 at the Third Lateran Council the bishops accused the Templars and Hospitallers of not paying tithes even when they were due to do so; of having church services in towns that were under interdict and visiting churches that were under interdict more often than their privileges allowed, in order to collect more money; of allowing murderers and moneylenders and other lawbreakers to join their confraternity and be buried in Church ground even though Church law forbade it; and of flouting the authority of their bishops.[56] All these criticisms came as a result of the privileges granted by the papacy to enable them to carry out their vocation more efficiently. Quarrels between the Military Orders and the secular clergy continued throughout their history, and even when the Templars were dissolved in 1312 the bishops declared that they would not agree to the Hospitallers receiving the Templars' lands unless the pope first took away their privileges.

Nevertheless, on a day-to-day basis relations between the Templars and their bishops were usually good, and we even find the bishops giving donations to the Templars, ordaining the Templars' priests and staying at Templar houses when on their travels about their dioceses.[57] At a local level in western Christendom the Templars would mostly have been local people who were familiar with the local Church hierarchy and wanted to get on well with them. The close links between the Templars' commanderies in the West and the local bishops is illustrated by the fact that even the liturgies the Templars used in their chapels were the local diocesan liturgy, not a special Templar liturgy imposed from above.[58]

Some Templar churches were built to give a visual link to the East. Like the Hospital of St John and like many ex-crusaders, the Order built some of its churches with circular naves, recalling the circular-naved Church of the Holy Sepulchre (see plates 19–20). This fashion in ecclesiastical architecture was dying out by the late thirteenth century, when the Templars rebuilt their circular-naved church at Garway, in Herefordshire in the Welsh March, with a rectangular nave, while the Hospitallers did the same with their circular-naved church at Clerkenwell, north of London. Not all the churches were rebuilt and some of the round naves survive until the present day. It has been suggested that the rebuilding reflected the final loss of the Holy Land in 1291; there was no advantage in reminding outsiders that the Orders had failed in their primary purpose of defending the Holy Sepulchre.[59] Yet not all the Templars' and Hospitallers' churches had circular naves; for the most part they were built in the local style, even when the Order built from scratch (see, for example, plate 18). Clearly these Orders did not bring in their own architects and masons from outside when they wanted to build, but hired local workers on the spot. As with their liturgy, the Templars' buildings had a close tie to the locality.

How did the Templars' religious faith work itself out in practice? Was the average Templar particularly devout? It is clear that in the East the Templars' vocation was deeply felt and lived out by the Brothers in day-to-day experience. In the West, away from the frontiers of Christendom, the call to martyrdom and to self-sacrifice for Christ was less clearly relevant to everyday living. The trial proceedings indicate that some Brothers were appallingly ignorant about the basics of their religious life. For instance, many did not know that the cord they wore over their undershirt was supposed to symbolize chastity.[60] One thought that it was in case he was captured by the Saracens, when he would give it as his ransom.[61] Yet the majority of Brothers were well aware of its purpose and wore it with pride, and one Brother Humbert du Puy had even heard that a Brother Helias Aymery had fastened the cord so tightly around himself, in his zeal for chastity, that he was very badly hurt by it.[62]

Outsiders viewed the Order as pious, giving it extensive charitable donations. There were no complaints that the Brothers lacked piety. Outsiders certainly had plenty of opportunity to observe the Brothers' lives. During the trial proceedings in Cyprus, many of the lay witnesses said that they had seen the Brothers in church, showing great devotion during the services, and some had stayed at Templar houses. In 1251 Queen Margaret of France gave birth to a son, the count of Alençon, at the Templars' fortress of Castle Pilgrim, and Renaud de Vichiers, Master of the Temple, stood as godfather for the child despite the prohibition of this practice in the Rule.[63] So Templars' houses were not closed to outsiders, not even to women. Some Brothers kept up contact with their families, as their families provided the cord they had to wear around their waists. Brother Stephen of Troyes, who was interrogated at Poitiers in late June 1308, indicated that he had kept in contact with his mother, as he went to visit her after he left the Order of the Temple. On the way he was arrested by the Order and imprisoned for illegally abandoning the Order, but his mother ransomed him for 200 *livres* (pounds) on the condition he lived with her from then on.[64]

Before the trial of 1307–12, the Templars were never accused of heresy. Their devotion to St Euphemia underlines this, for Euphemia is regarded as having great power not only against pagans but also against heretics, following her miraculous condemnation of heresy during the Fourth Ecumenical Council of Chalcedon in 451.[65] The Templars' choice of Euphemia as a patron was very appropriate for a fanatically orthodox Christian religious Order that opposed non-Christians.

There is no evidence that the Templars were ever involved in heretical movements in Europe. Although the Templars held extensive territories in the south of France, where the Cathar heresy was widespread in the twelfth and thirteenth century, the Templars did not support the local nobility during the Albigensian Crusade. A local commentator, Bernard Sicart of Marvejols, criticized them for failing to help their former patrons. In fact the Templars accompanied the crusading army and sometimes lodged crusaders. They did not fight during the Albigensian Crusade, but this is not surprising, as their vocation did not commit them to fighting heretics and their resources were already widely stretched in the East.[66]

The Templars and Hospitallers were both accused of being too willing to make truces with the Muslims and trying to prolong the war in the East in order to collect more money. Matthew Paris, chronicler of St Albans Abbey, repeated these accusations, but in his account of the battle of Mansurah (February 1250) he added the Orders' response. This battle was a terrible defeat, but the Military Orders came out of it with a good reputation because they had advised Count Robert of Artois, commander of the vanguard, against attacking the enemy. Their advice had been ignored, and the battle was lost: clearly this was the count's fault, while the Orders were vindicated. Matthew imagined the argument before the attack, with Count Robert accusing the Military Orders of treachery. The Brothers reply:

> For what purpose, O noble Count, did we receive the religious habit? Surely not to overturn the Church of Christ and to lose our souls through plotting treachery? Far be it from us, far be it from us, no, far be it from every Christian![67]

This was the obvious answer to any accusation against the Orders' religious devotion. Why should anyone enter a religious Order with the intention of damning their souls to Hell? People entered a religious Order to save their souls in accordance with the teaching of the Christian Church. The Order of the Temple was regarded as a good Order in which to save one's soul and win a place in Heaven. At the start of the fourteenth century, in a new version of the epic Crusade Cycle, a poet described the epic hero Harpin de Bourges's reaction to the death of his wife:

> Count Harpin was very upset and troubled and so distressed at the death of his wife, and he hated the world so much, that he said to himself that he would never have another wife all the days of his life. Harpin the Redoubtable gave himself to the Temple; but this was not the end of his boldness. As long as he lived he brought grief on the Saracens and Slavs.[68]

Even after the loss of the kingdom of Jerusalem, the composer of a new version of a well-known epic could still depict the Order of the Temple as the best place for a doughty and pious knight to end his days.

6

MOST TRUSTWORTHY SERVANTS: IN THE SERVICE OF EUROPEAN KINGS

In his book on the trifles of courtiers, Walter Map remarked that even the pure and virtuous religious Order of Grandmont was attracting the attention of prominent people, and the Brothers were being called to royal councils and becoming involved in royal business.[1] For Walter, this showed the decline in the spirituality of a pious religious Order. Yet it was an inevitable development. As all authority was believed to come from God, all rulers wanted God's representatives to stand at their side and give approval to their government.

Since the beginnings of Christian government, rulers had associated themselves with religious people. During the period from the break-up of the Western Roman Empire to the eleventh century, monks and other religious men were particularly valued by rulers because they were educated and could be relied upon to act as honest, hardworking officials. Despite the efforts of reforming rulers such as the Emperor Charlemagne on the European Continent and King Alfred of

Wessex in England to set up schools and produce a more literate society, monks and clergy remained the backbone of secular administration – even the word for a cleric, *clericus*, became the standard word for a minor official who writes, 'clerk'. With the renaissance in culture and learning that began in the eleventh century and continued into the twelfth, this began to change: people outside the Church learnt to read and write, not only in their own language but also in Latin. Such people were called *literati*, 'literate'.

From the twelfth century onwards, the *literati* gradually took over royal government. Unlike monks, they were usually not from a noble background, and relied on the ruler for their promotion rather than on the power, influence and wealth of their own families. This made them reliable and loyal servants. They might be clergy in the lowest priestly orders, able to marry and hardly distinguishable from the non-clergy, the laity. Or they might simply be laity, from poorer knightly families or families from lower social classes. These people were unpopular with the old nobility, who saw that the *literati* were taking over royal government and winning power and wealth, while the nobility were steadily losing influence at court.

The Military Orders combined the best of all worlds for a ruler who wanted servants with the godly outlook and honesty of monks, the lack of worldly connections and self-interested loyalty of the new *literati*, and the military skills and traditional loyalty of the warrior class. All the Military Orders were much used by nobles, monarchs and the papacy in their governments. In return, they received donations and protection. The question remains as to whether the patronage of rulers cost the Orders more than it gave them.

Royal service
Because the Military Orders played such a prominent role in royal and papal service, this aspect of their history has been studied in detail by scholars.[2] Some of the Templars' services for the kings of Jerusalem and those of the Iberian Peninsula

and eastern Europe have already been described in Chapters 2 and 3. In these areas their service for rulers was primarily military, but in other parts of Europe – the British Isles, France, and Italy – it usually was not.

They were given positions of the utmost trust. From the time of Pope Alexander III onwards, a Templar and a Hospitaller routinely appeared as papal chamberlains, that is, attending on the pope in his own private chambers. This meant that they were constantly in his presence and able to speak to him privately, perhaps to obtain favours from him. They could also offer him support: when Pope Alexander III was struggling against the Emperor Frederick I Barbarossa (1155–90) and a succession of 'antipopes' or false popes appointed by the emperor, he could rely on the loyalty and the advice of Templars, Hospitallers and Cistercians. Hence it is not surprising that the pope did little to appease the Order's critics when the bishops at the Third Lateran Council in 1179 complained bitterly about the privileges of the Templars and Hospitallers, which enabled them to avoid the bishops' authority.

Templars appeared as papal messengers, treasurers and judge-delegates, as well as holding the office or marshal or porter at the papal court. Similar posts were held by the Hospitallers and the Teutonic Knights. The Templars' most famous services for rulers were financial. As the Order in the West had to raise cash and send it to the East, the Brothers had had to develop systems for handling large sums of cash. This expertise, added to the Order's charitable nature, made its Brothers an obvious choice as papal money carriers, as almoners (officials in charge of charitable donations to the poor), and as treasurers. In July 1220 a Templar and a Hospitaller carried Pope Honorius III's financial contribution to the Fifth Crusade out to Egypt; the pope entrusted it to these carriers, he said, as there was no one he could trust better.[3]

Secular rulers used the Templars in the same sorts of posts. William Marshal, earl of Pembroke, had a Templar as his almoner, one Brother Geoffrey.[4] In 1177 King Henry II of England chose Brother Roger the Templar as his almoner, and Templars continued to appear as royal almoners in England until 1255. Almoners could be expected to do more than distribute salt herring to the needy of London: during King John's war with his barons (1214–16) he gave his almoner, Brother Roger the Templar, responsibility for overseeing shipping and collecting freight duty. As almoner, Roger would have been used to dealing with money and handing out cash and goods, but the massive expansion of his responsibilities reflected the king's shortage of trustworthy servants during the war. From 1229 John's son Henry III had a particularly influential almoner, Brother Geoffrey the Templar (presumably not the same man as had worked for William Marshal), who became keeper of the wardrobe and thus controlled the king's personal treasury, and acted as a leading minister in the government. Matthew Paris blamed him for many of Henry's misdeeds and declared that he was finally sacked, but in fact Brother Geoffrey retired with honour in 1240. Kings of Scotland also had Templar almoners, as did kings of France. James II of Aragon had a Templar, Peter Peyronet, as almoner; he also acted as a crown agent.[5]

The Templars in particular also provided financial services for rulers. This could vary from making loans and looking after valuables to running the royal treasury, as in France. The Templars were not a bank in the modern sense of the word as their financial operations were merely a sideline, a result of their need to store and move large quantities of cash about Christendom. Money deposited with them was not pooled and reinvested, but remained in its owner's strongboxes within the Order's treasury, and could not be accessed without the owner's permission. In 1148, during the Second Crusade, both the Templars and the Hospitallers lent money to King Louis VII of France, without which (as he wrote to Abbot Suger, the regent in France) he could not have stayed so long in the East. In 1250, during Louis IX's crusade, the Templars allowed Louis to have the money he needed to ransom himself from the sultan of Egypt. The Treasurer initially refused the loan, but Jean de Joinville, who had come to borrow the money, threatened to smash open one of the strongboxes in the Templars' safe keeping and take the money he wanted from it. The Marshal of the Temple then stepped in and told the Treasurer to let Jean have the key. Strictly speaking the money should not have been loaned in such circumstances, but Joinville's threat of violence allowed the Order to bend the rules.[6]

A similar incident occurred in the Temple's headquarters in London in 1263, but this time without the Templars' connivance. King Henry III was in severe financial straits and his government was under threat from critics among the nobility. The annalist of Dunstable priory explains:

> The King came with the Queen [Eleanor of Provence] to the Tower of London on 26 May, while the Lord Edward [their eldest son, later Edward I] was staying at the Hospital [of St John] at Clerkenwell. All of them were short of money, and there was no one in London who would give them a penny on credit. So, since the Lord Edward did not like being in this embarassing position, on the feast of Saints Peter and Paul he assembled Robert Walrampnum and many others and went to the New Temple when the doors were closed. On his request, he was admitted, and he said that he wanted to see the jewels of the Queen, his mother. The custodian of the treasury was fetched, and the Lord Edward fraudulently entered the Temple's treasury with his men; whereupon they broke open the chests of certain persons there with iron hammers which they had brought with them, took much money to the value of a thousand pounds, and carried it away. When they heard about this crime, the citizens of London rose up against them and other members of the King's council who were staying in the city.[7]

The Templars had often lent King Henry III money, especially during the crisis years at the beginning of his reign;

but clearly they had refused to do so on this occasion and his 'bank raid' was the result. Edward's initial request to see his mother's jewels was perfectly reasonable, in that the jewels were kept in the New Temple for safe keeping; and the Templars, being unarmed, were unable to resist Edward and his men when they used force.

In 1232 the Order had been more successful in asserting its independence. King Henry had disgraced his former justiciar Hubert de Burgh and had confiscated all his property. According to Roger of Wendover, chronicler of St Albans Abbey, Henry heard that Hubert had a great deal of money deposited in the New Temple in London, and he summoned the Master of the Temple in England, demanding to know if this was so. The Master admitted that it was true, but he had no idea how much. The king insisted that the money be handed over to him, on the grounds that Hubert had embezzled it from the royal treasury, but the Brothers replied that they could not hand over any money deposited with them without the leave of the depositer. The king had to obtain permission from Hubert before the Templars would hand over the keys of his chests to the king.[8]

In England the royal treasury was part of the royal household, and run by royal officials; the New Temple merely provided additional safe deposit space. Although the Templars and Hospitallers were involved in the collection of the 'Saladin tithe' for the Third Crusade, they were not usually involved in royal financial administration. In France, the Templars took on the role of royal treasury. The Treasurer of the Paris Temple would also act as royal treasurer. The Order took in receipts of taxation and organized payment to royal officials, soldiers and so on. Not until 1295 did the king of France establish his own treasury at the Louvre, and even then he continued to use the Temple treasury. In 1303 some of the functions of the royal treasury were transferred back to the Temple. Clearly, the Order was essential to the efficient running of the French royal administration.[9]

As they did for the papacy, Templars regularly acted as messengers for kings and nobles. Like the friars in the thirteenth century and later, the Military Orders could be conveniently used for secret missions because they were inconspicuous. Templars and Hospitallers were always on the road, preaching and collecting alms from the faithful, and because they were religious men they were less likely than secular messengers to be stopped by an enemy and searched or even imprisoned. In 1170 one of Archbishop Thomas Becket's correspondents warned him that the Templars who brought him news were not simple and trustworthy religious men but were actually the agents of his enemy, King Henry II of England.[10]

Members of the Military Orders also gave advice to popes, kings and other rulers. The Templars had permanent representatives at the papal court from the 1230s, while the kings of England had since the twelfth century provided for the upkeep of a knight of the Order at their courts, with horses and servants. The Military Orders' advice would be particularly appropriate in holy war, so that we find Brothers of the Military Orders advising the kings of Jerusalem and the kings of Portugal and Aragon in their military strategies. Brothers of the Military Orders also acted in an advisory capacity during the Fourth Crusade, which did not actually reach the Holy Land but instead captured Constantinople. In June 1205, after the death of the first Latin emperor Baldwin of Flanders and the crowning of a second, his brother Henry, the new emperor Henry wrote to Pope Innocent III (1198–1216) explaining that the Templars and Hospitallers in his council agreed that the conquest of Constantinople by Latin Christians would produce unity in Christendom and help the war effort against the Muslims in the Holy Land.[11]

But Templars could also give advice in secular matters. King Henry II relied on the advice of Templars during his dispute with Thomas Becket, archbishop of Canterbury. King John of England (1199–1216) stated in his will that the Master of the

Temple in England, Brother Aimery de St Maur, was one of those whose advice he trusted and followed: high praise from this notoriously suspicious king.[12] King Louis IX of France made great use of the preceptors or commanders of the Temple in France and was so anxious to obtain the service of Brother Amaury de la Roche that he enlisted the help of Pope Urban IV to force the Order in the East to send Amaury to him. The Order at first refused, agreeing only after the pope had repeated his demand more strongly. Pope Urban declared that Louis wanted the commandery of France to be committed to a man whose sincerity of faith and probity he could trust, and that Louis believed Brother Amaury to be prudent and conspicuous for his wise advice. What was more, he was an old friend.[13] In 1266 Pope Clement IV moved Brother Amaury on: both he and Brother Philip d'Eglis of the Hospital were to be put at the disposal of Louis's brother Charles of Anjou, king of Naples, who required their service in Naples and Sicily to administer the houses of their Orders in that area. Charles also wanted their support in his wars against the supporters of the descendants of Frederick II of Hohenstaufen. In the following year, Clement authorized Brother Philip to take up arms against the enemies of Charles, but it is not clear whether the Templars were encouraged to do likewise. Brother Philip and his Hospitallers did take up arms and the Hospital's properties in Sicily suffered heavily as a result, but as the Templars did not suffer in the same way Brother Amaury must have managed to keep out of the war.[14]

Brother Amaury appeared again during Louis IX's second crusade, to Tunis, in which both he and Brother Philip d'Eglis took part. Brother Amaury acted as a commander, and was responsible for laying out ditches around the Christian camp and for overseeing those who guarded the diggers. He also took part in military action and was part of the king's council. Amaury advised that the Christian army needed larger forces before attacking the city of Tunis, and that King Louis should wait for the arrival of his brother, King Charles of Naples, who was late arriving. In the event, Charles did not arrive until Louis was on his deathbed.[15]

The services performed for the king of England by the Templars in Ireland are a particularly good illustration of the usefulness of the Order in an area where the king had few administrators whom he could trust. The Templars and the Hospitallers went to Ireland in the second half of the twelfth century with the Anglo-Norman, Welsh, Scottish and French colonists and invaders. They were given various donations of land and founded a number of commanderies.[16] The Military Orders first appear in the English royal administrative records for Ireland in September 1220 when Henry III's government instructed the justiciar (viceroy) of Ireland to deposit the proceeds of an 'aid' (a royal exaction) with the Templars and Hospitallers. The two Orders were then to send it to England, and would be held responsible for it.[17] This responsibility for the care of cash was the sort of duty the Orders regularly performed in England.

By 1234 the Templars' role had widened. In 1234 two Templars acted as intermediaries between the royal officials in Ireland and Richard Marshal, who was leading a rebellion. They persuaded Richard to come to a meeting, but the talks ended in battle, in which Richard was fatally wounded.[18] The Templars therefore failed as negotiators, but had shown themselves to be trustworthy royal servants. In the same year Henry III instructed the archbishop of Dublin, the justiciar of Ireland (Maurice fitzGerald) and the Master of the Knights Templar in Ireland that, every year, after the treasurer and barons of the exchequer had audited the accounts of Ireland, they were to go to the exchequer, view the accounts, and send a copy to the king.[19] Care of cash and acting as negotiators or ambassadors for a king were typical duties of Templars, and during the 1230s they were very much in favour with Henry III, perhaps because of the influence of Henry's almoner, adviser and official Brother Geoffrey the Templar. In 1236, however, the Master of the Temple in Ireland, Brother

Ralph of Southwark, abandoned the Order. Henry III wrote to the justiciar of Ireland ordering him to arrest Brother Ralph if he arrived in Ireland, and to receive Brother Roger le Waleis ('the Welshman') as the new Master.[20]

Brother Roger le Waleis appears in 1241 and 1242 with the archbishop of Dublin, the archdeacon of Dublin (who was royal treasurer) and Walerand of Wales auditing the accounts of the justiciar, Maurice fitzGerald, and in June 1243, 1244 and 1250 he was one of those auditing the treasurer's accounts. From this time the Master of the Temple in Ireland appeared sporadically auditing the treasurer's and justiciar's accounts: in 1253, 1270, 1278, 1280 and 1281. In 1301 the Templars were involved in the collection of 'the new custom duty of Waterford'.[21]

It is clear that the Templars were regarded as trustworthy, and particularly suited to holding responsibility in financial matters. However, they were not given as many responsibilities in Ireland as the Hospitallers were. Prominent Hospitallers in Ireland were given administrative posts, such as lieutenant justiciar. All the Cymro-Normans and Anglo-Normans holding land in Ireland were expected to give military service when necessary to defend the land, and all religious houses in Ireland had to be fortified against possible Irish attack. Of the two Military Orders in Ireland, however, it was the Prior of the Hospital in Ireland who was sometimes given military command.

As we have seen, the Templars did not usually take part in military operations against Christians, which were contrary to their vocation and absorbed resources which were needed in the East. In the Iberian Peninsula this sort of service was becoming increasingly difficult to avoid by the end of the thirteenth century.[22] The Military Orders were given a share of the lands conquered by the Fourth Crusade in 'Romania' (now Greece) in 1205–10, for which they were expected to give military service in the same way as secular landholders. It is not clear whether the Military Orders had played a military role in the conquest of Greece, or whether the gifts to them and to other religious Orders and the Church were a 'thank offering' for the conquest. In any case, many of the Templars' properties were taken back by the second generation of settlers, although they kept their properties in the Morea (Achaea).[23]

In 1298–9 King Edward I of England summoned the English Templars to join his army for his campaign in Scotland, and the Master in England, Brian le Jay, was killed at the Battle of Falkirk in 1298. In the fourteenth century the Hospital of St John would find it impossible to avoid this sort of service for the kings of England and France. King Edward I also demanded homage from the Masters of the Temple in England and Scotland, which the Order was not bound to pay according to the privileges it held from the pope. Again, the Hospital of St John would meet similar problems during the fourteenth century.[24] These developments reflect the growing power of 'national' monarchs by the late thirteenth century, which demanded that the supranational religious Orders place the interests of their 'natural' monarch above those of their Order.

Many members of the Military Orders were quite happy to put service to their king first, or to combine it with service to their Order. In 1163–4 Thierry Galeran, 'trusted friend' of King Louis VII of France, became a Templar. Thierry had been prominent in the king's service since at least 1140. As a Templar, he asked various favours of the king for the Order, which were granted.[25] In 1164 Brother Geoffrey Fulcher of the Order of the Temple wrote to Louis VII of France, addressing him as 'his dearest lord' and reporting that he had faithfully discharged a mission which Louis had given him when he left France for the East:

Don't think that the instructions which I rejoiced to receive from your mouth when I left you have slipped your servant's mind. For you said to me that I should greet the holy places on your behalf, and I should visit each of them and remember you there. I have not forgotten this. I have carried this ring which you sent me around the holy sites and placed it on each of the holy places in memory of you. I pray that you keep the ring safe in reverence of this.[26]

He enclosed the ring with the letter: Louis could keep it as a relic, a physical memento of the holy places. Even as a Templar official in the East, Geoffrey Fulcher remained the vassal and servant of his 'natural' sovereign, the king of France.

In short, the extensive services that the Templars performed for kings, in particular the kings of England and France, led to the Order becoming virtually an arm of the royal government. In 1244 Henry III of England made arrangements for the conferral of knighthood on Thomas of Curtun, a young man in his service who planned to join the Order of the Temple. Henry went to considerable expense in equipping Thomas, so it seems reasonable to assume that he expected Thomas to remain in his service even after he had joined the Templars.[27]

Donations to the Order

Rulers and popes not only demanded service, but also gave donations and assistance to the Military Orders. The primary motivation for a religious donation was the hope of receiving salvation.[28] Donations also brought social prestige; the fact that one could afford to make a donation showed one's wealth. In addition, donations gave the donor influence over the recipient. Gifts were essential to the Orders' survival, but also restricted them in their actions because they had to keep their donors happy in order to continue receiving their support. Because the Orders could not afford to offend their donors, they could not refuse the demands their donors made on them, even when these were a considerable drain on their resources and prompted criticism from others.

Papal support for the Templars stemmed from the Order's role in the defence of Christendom. Papal bulls compared the Templars to the Maccabees; the Templars were also *athletae Christi*, 'Christ's champions' (that is, fighting on Christ's behalf), and *pugiles Christi*, 'Christ's fighters'. The Templars showed Christ's love, for they were prepared to lay down their lives for their fellow-Christians. Successive popes confirmed the Order's ecclesiastical privileges and ordered the bishops to ensure that these were acknowledged. They tried to protect the Order from the casual violence endemic in society and gave the Brothers the right to defend themselves if attacked. They dealt with legal cases relating to the Order, and encouraged the Templars to continue in their fight against the enemies of Christendom.

The primary motivation for secular rulers giving to the Military Orders was the wish to support the defence of Christendom in the East. As the crusade was seen as the particular responsibility of all Christian kings, there was a great deal of moral pressure on them to support the Military Orders. For nobles, the crusade brought prestige and was an essential part of knighthood. If one could not go on crusade, one should give to a Military Order instead; if one could go on crusade, it was in one's interests to give to a Military Order, because the Order gave practical help to crusaders while they were in the East.

Reasons for preferring the Templars over another Military Order can only be guessed at. Family tradition was an important factor in religious donations: individuals kept up links with religious houses which were already connected to their family. Servants and vassals often gave to the same Order as their lord or employer. Some donors, particularly the poorer ones who were less able to travel, gave to the nearest attractive religious house. Sometimes family relationship or a personal friendship could be a factor. In the spring of 1137, Matilda of Boulogne, queen of England, gave Cressing in Essex to the Templars. Her uncles Godfrey of Bouillon and Baldwin of Edessa had been the first two Latin rulers of the kingdom of Jerusalem, while her father Eustace had been the closest heir to the kingdom on the death of Baldwin in 1118. Matilda had a strong dynastic interest in the kingdom of Jerusalem and wanted to support the religious Order that was helping to defend it. However, she did not give to the Hospital of St John. We can only speculate as to whether her family had other links with the Templars that led her to prefer the Templars over the Hospitallers: for instance, some of the early Templars, such as Godfrey of Saint Omer and Archembald of Saint Amand, came from the Low Countries and the area around Boulogne. Godfrey was a vassal of the counts of Boulogne.

Matilda later gave the Templars Witham in Essex and Cowley in Oxfordshire. All her donations were confirmed by her husband, King Stephen of England, who himself was the son of one of the leaders of the First Crusade.[29] Although Stephen's predecessor, Henry I of England, had given Hugh de Payns money in 1128 and had allowed him to collect donations in England, it was Matilda's generosity to the Order that laid the foundations of a long and close relationship between the Templars and the kings of England.

Donations from the kings of England varied. They preferred to give income and privileges rather than land. The Order was allowed to clear royal forest for agriculture, a practice that normally incurred a heavy fine. Henry II pardoned the Brothers for clearing extensive areas of royal forest:

Henry, by the grace of God king of England [etc.], greeting.

Know that I have conceded, and by this our charter confirmed, to the Brothers of the knighthood of the Temple at Jerusalem quittance of the assarts [clearances] of the lands listed below, viz: 2,000 acres of land in Wales at Garway [Herefordshire]; 40 acres in Shropshire at Botewood [a village which no longer exists]; 10 acres in Oxfordshire at Merton; 7 acres in Northamptonshire at Brandendene; 100 acres in Bedfordshire at Sharnbrook; and 7 acres in Huntingdonshire at Ogerston.

Therefore I wish and firmly command that the aforesaid Brothers of the knighthood of the Temple may have the aforesaid lands and hold them freely and quit of [all fines for] assarts. And I forbid that they be troubled or harassed over this, or that anyone should do them violence. Witness: Richard bishop of Winchester, etc.[30]

The pardon for the enormous clearances at Garway (plate 25) seems extraordinarily generous. Possibly Henry saw the Templars' presence at Garway as advantageous. Garway is in the Welsh March, an area administered by powerful nobles who did not always pay as much attention to royal authority as the king would have liked. The Templars, as faithful royal servants, would remind the local lords of royal authority, although as they were unarmed and the commandery at Garway was unfortified they could not actually enforce it.

The Templars held very little property in this part of Britain, where the Hospitallers were far better represented. They held a few other properties in Monmouthshire and Glamorgan. In the Gower, they held the church and manor of Llanmadoc, given to them by Countess Margaret of Warwick, lady of the Gower, in 1156. They also had a mill at the bridge of Pembroke Castle and the village of Templeton in Pembrokeshire.[31] This was all disputed territory, fought over by the Anglo-Norman marcher lords and the Welsh princes of Deheubarth. As in eastern Europe, giving disputed land to the Military Orders was a way of settling disputed frontiers while at the same time winning God's favour. But most such donations in south Wales and the Welsh March were given to the Hospitallers of St John, not the Templars. Possibly the Templars were seen as being too close to the king of England – and neither marcher lords nor Welsh princes wished to give the king of England more influence in the area than necessary.

Henry II also gave to the Templars one mark of silver each year from each county of England, and the same from each city, town and castle that rendered to the king more than 100 pounds each year. One of their tenants (called a *hospes*) in each borough was free from all royal exactions. The Order received fifty marks a year (£33) to maintain a knight in the Holy Land. Henry's gift of three carcasses of stags a year became ten carcasses under King John, specifically for the Order's provincial chapter at Pentecost. Only the gift of fifty marks a year was continued by Edward I of England.[32]

The Order also received various legal privileges, which meant that its tenants were partially exempt from royal jurisdiction. On 6 October 1189 Richard I gave the Templars extensive exemptions from royal jurisdiction and exactions.[33] These exemptions enabled the Order to engage in trade within England more easily and also carry their goods to port for export overseas. They did not have to pay traditional dues such shield tax, tallage and castle guard, which would have drained the resources needed for the defence of the Holy Land. They would not lose resources through having to wait for the king's judges when they needed to obtain justice, but could try thieves and lesser malefactors themselves. Only major crimes punishable by hanging or mutilation would still have to go to the king's courts.

During his crusade of 1189–92, Richard worked closely with the Templars, but this was not an equal relationship. While Richard valued the Templars' and Hospitallers' military advice, he was in command and their purpose (in his eyes) was to assist him. After his capture of the island of Cyprus, Richard sold the island to the Templars, who thus provided him with much-needed cash. Yet the Templars were unable to administer the island and tried to sell it back to Richard, who refused to return their money. He gave the island to Guy of Lusignan, who may have repaid the Templars, or given them extensive holdings in the island.[34] Richard also gave the Templars a new Master, Robert de Sablé or Sabloel, who had previously been one of his admirals and vassals. At around the same time, the Hospital of St John also elected an English Master, Garnier de Nablūs. According to some reports, Richard disguised himself as a Templar on his journey home from the East in autumn 1192, in order to avoid falling into the hands of his enemies – a scheme that failed. This story is probably not true, but Richard certainly had Templars in his entourage.[35]

The Templars' close relationship with the kings of England continued under King John and his son Henry III. The Templars' priests said masses for the soul of both kings, and in 1231 Henry III and his queen, Eleanor of Provence, promised that their bodies would be buried in the New Temple in London. This would mean that the New Temple became a royal mausoleum, and would receive extensive long-term financial support from the king's heirs. The Templars extended their church at the New Temple in anticipation, with a fine new rectangular nave in the latest architectural style (plate 21). But in 1246 Henry reversed his donation and decided that he and his queen would be buried in his own new foundation of Westminster Abbey. During the 1250s the Templars gradually declined in the royal favour; they were still a favoured Order, but they received fewer gifts and were not as close to the king as they had been. The royal almoner was no longer a Templar. The Hospitallers, on the other hand, continued to to be close to the monarch, and from 1273–80 the treasurer of England was a Hospitaller, Brother Joseph de Chauncey. But even the Hospitallers received favour, rather than gifts.[36]

Why did royal policy towards the Templars change? This is not an easy question to answer. It changed not only in England but also in Ireland, where the prior of the Hospital was given important administrative, financial and military responsibilities in the late thirteenth century while the Templars were asked only to audit the treasurer's accounts. It may be that by the second half of the thirteenth century the Hospitallers in the British Isles were attracting the sort of recruits who made good administrators, while the Templars were not: the Hospital's dual military–hospitaller vocation may have attracted more adaptable recruits than the Templars' all-military vocation. Perhaps the Hospitallers were more willing to be used as administrators while the Templars concentrated more single-mindedly on the defence of the Holy Land. It may be that as Henry III developed his own patterns of patronage, rebuilding Westminster Abbey and developing his own image as a pious ruler, he felt that he no longer needed to rely on his forefathers' patterns of patronage. It may be that he was not as interested in the crusade as his predecessors had been; although he took the cross three times, thereby undertaking to go on crusade, he never actually went.[37] It is also possible that after the retirement of Brother Geoffrey the Templar as almoner and keeper of the royal wardrobe Henry's personal link with the Templars had gone, and Henry no longer had a personal interest in the Order. It also appears that Henry began to regard the Military Orders as being as obstructive and difficult to work with as other religious Orders in England, and considered that they had already been given so much property and privileges that they undermined his royal authority. His financial problems certainly took their toll. The chronicler Matthew Paris depicted Henry criticizing the Hospitallers and Templars for having so many privileges and stating that he would take back what his predecessors had given them, because the Orders had become too proud. On this occasion Matthew took the side of the Military Orders against the king, depicting the Prior of the Hospital in England standing up to Henry and reminding him that he would only be king as long as he acted justly.[38]

Although the Templars were never so close to the king of England after 1240 as they had been earlier, they remained valued servants. Edward I expected the Master in England to do homage to him and to provide military service, as other religious Orders and lay lords did; the Templars were his loyal vassals. His son Edward II (1307–27) valued the Templars for their past and present service. When in November 1307 Pope Clement V ordered Edward II to have all the Templars arrested, Edward replied: 'The aforeseaid Master and Brothers have been constant in the purity of the Catholic faith and have been commended many times by us and all of our realm both for their way of life and for their customs. We cannot believe suspicions of this sort until we are given more evidence of them.' He begged the pope not to believe the lies that had been told about the Order.[39]

The changing relationship between the Templars and the kings of England was mirrored by developments in France. The Templars continued to serve the kings of France until the arrests of 1307, and supported Louis IX during both his crusades, as did the Hospitallers. However, although Philip II (1180–1223) had bequeathed 150,500 marks of silver to the Templars, Hospitallers and King John of the kingdom of Jerusalem in his will of September 1222, neither Louis IX nor his son Philip III made any bequests to the Templars or the Hospitallers in their wills. They concentrated instead on donations to more traditional monastic Orders such as the Cistercians, to new Orders such as the friars, to religious houses founded by the kings of France, such as La Victoire at Senlis (commemorating the victory at Bouvines in 1214), to lay Orders such as the beguines of Paris, and to hospitals and religious Orders set up to help the poor, poor ladies and orphans.[40]

The changing attitude of the kings of France towards the Military Orders reflected both the new religious climate of the thirteenth century and royal policy. Important reasons for donations to religious Orders were to gain influence and to win the support of that Order, but as political stability in western Christendom increased, so the social need for such donations was reduced. In the thirteenth century patterns of piety shifted from the institutional to the personal. Pious donors were now less likely to give to a large, institutionalized Order, and more likely to give to a local hospice where the local poor and sick were cared for, or to endow a chantry chapel for the benefit of their own soul alone. As a result, by the mid-thirteenth century donations to all religious Orders had declined.

Royal policy also reduced all donations to religious Orders during the thirteenth century. Legislation enacted by kings across Europe forbad donations in 'mortmain' – that is, to a religious institution – without royal licence. This was to prevent lands that owed dues to the king from passing into the hands of institutions that did not pay these dues, thereby causing royal revenues to be lost. In Sicily, Frederick II of Hohenstaufen set about recovering royal lands and rights in the 1220s.[41] We have already seen Henry III of England growing anxious about the threat posed to royal authority by religious Orders' privileges and possessions. His son Edward I passed the Statute of Mortmain in 1279: anyone wanting to make a donation to a religious Order must first apply for licence to do so. The king would then have an investigation made to discover whether his rights and interests would suffer any damage from the donation. Only if his interests would not be infringed could the donation go ahead. Edward also had extensive enquiries made throughout England into who held the various rights and privileges of the crown, and how they had come to pass to other persons. Those claiming possession of rights which ought to belong to the king had to produce the charter of donation, or at least have the support of the testimony of local jurors that they had possessed these rights from time out of mind.[42]

All these changes reduced the income enjoyed by all religious Orders by the early fourteenth century. They came at the same time as (and partly as a result of) inflation, which reduced the value of money rents and encouraged landlords to take land under cultivation themselves rather than renting it out to tenants – although this meant increased costs of cultivation. These changes caused particular problems for the Military Orders, whose expenses in the East were increasing as the level of donations in the West fell. They therefore had to go to greater lengths to exploit their lands and privileges in the West to the full in order to get the greatest possible income from them – but this led to criticism.

The Military Orders' association with popes and kings led them into a considerable amount of criticism, one way and the other. Their exemption from episcopal jurisdiction annoyed the bishops; their right to exempt their own tenants from some aspects of episcopal and royal jurisdiction caused even more annoyance. The Templars placed a cross on the house of their tenant in each royal borough who was free from royal exactions, and Templar associates living in their own houses placed crosses on their houses to show that they claimed exemption from episcopal jurisdiction. The Hospitallers, who had the same exemptions, did the same. During the trial of the Temple in England one of the charges that received particular attention from non-Templar witnesses was that the Templars denigrated the cross. 'Denigrating the cross' would have included misusing the cross by placing it on houses that were not entitled to display it.[43]

Matthew Paris's dislike of the Military Orders of the Temple and Hospital stemmed partly from their connection with King Henry III, whose policies Matthew disapproved of. In the same way, William of Tyre's and Walter Map's criticism of the Orders stemmed partly from the Orders' connection with the papacy and exemptions from the bishops' authority. As the Orders relied on these rulers for their continuing existence and protection, this was criticism they could hardly avoid.

However, the popes and monarchs also criticized the Military Orders for not carrying out their vocation or not serving them well. From the time of Alexander III onwards the papacy nagged the Brothers for abuses of their privileges. In 1207 Pope Innocent III reproved the Templars for abusing their privileges during interdicts. When all the churches were closed as spiritual punishment to a community, the Templars were allowed to hold services in their chapels, but they should not admit outsiders. Once a year they could also open churches that were under interdict in order to preach there and collect alms for the Holy Land. The problem was that they did admit outsiders to their chapels and opened churches more than once a year. They also allowed anyone to collect alms for them without checking their credentials, admitted all and sundry to their confraternity, including known criminals, murderers and adulterers, and they ignored the instructions of papal legates. Innocent was not singling out the Templars for criticism: he made similar complaints to the Hospitallers, and he also brought severe charges against the Cistercians. He wanted to reform these religious Orders because he was anxious to improve the spirituality of the Church, so that it would be able to fight heresy and recover the holy places.[44]

As the thirteenth century went on, popes became more concerned about the Military Orders' quarrels and dedication to the defence of the Holy Land. Gregory IX complained in March 1238 that he had heard that the Templars were not defending the pilgrim routes effectively (in fact there was a truce in operation at this time, which prevented the Templars from raiding against the Muslims). In 1278 Pope Nicholas III (1277–80) wrote to the Hospital, Temple and Teutonic Order. He said that they, before all other 'sons of light' (Christians), ought to be determined to clean the Holy Land of pollution (the Muslims) as they were specially assigned to the defence of the land. So that they would not be blamed for anything, he urged them to turn their attention to God and His land. If they did not, he would punish them. He must have been referring to the Military Orders' involvement in the various political disputes in the crusader states, but he was also ignoring the Orders' need for money and personnel to fight the Muslims. He himself concentrated on the political situation in Italy, and made no effort to send them aid. Unlike Gregory IX, who was genuinely concerned to promote the cause of the Latin Christians in the Holy Land, Nicholas III seems to have been more anxious to deflect criticism from himself.[45]

Henry III's reported complaints about the Templars' and Hospitallers' privileges echo the reported criticism by his uncle Richard I. Roger of Howden recorded that the famous preacher Fulk of Neuilly took Richard to task for his sins, and advised him to marry off his three daughters: pride, greed and sensuality (*luxuria*). Richard deftly picked up the allegory and turned it against the Church, retorting that he would marry pride to the Templars, greed to the Cistercians and sensuality to the bishops. In short, let the Church put its own house in order before criticizing him. As Richard valued the Templars during his crusade for their knighthood and military skills, it is interesting to find him here depicting them as members of the clergy – although the accusation of pride was particularly appropriate for knights.[46]

Criticism also arose when rulers were in conflict with one another. As faithful servants of the papacy, the king of France and the king of England, what were the Templars to do when these three quarrelled – as they did during the pontificate of Innocent III, for instance? The Brothers would choose which ruler should take precedence, but were then in danger of suffering repercussions from the others. Or they could try to serve all three and hope to preserve their official neutrality: this is what they did when Innocent III was in conflict with both King Philip II of France and King John of England. On an earlier occasion they had been less successful. In 1158 King Henry II of England and King Louis VII of France made an alliance whereby Louis's daughter Margaret, then still an infant, and Henry's eldest surviving son Henry, then aged three, were betrothed, to marry as soon as they were old enough. Margaret's dowry (the share of wealth she brought to the marriage) would be the Vexin, the disputed border lands between Henry's duchy of Normandy (for Henry was duke of Normandy as well as being king of England), and Louis's domains. As was usual, Margaret was sent to live with her future in-laws, but Louis was to keep the Vexin until the wedding took place. In 1160 the terms were renegotiated, and the castles were entrusted to the Templars, whom both parties regarded as neutral. However, later that year Henry had Margaret and young Henry married, and the Templars handed over the castles to him. Louis retaliated by driving the Templars in question out of France: they were Brothers Osto de St Omer, who had been the Master of the Temple in England, Richard of Hastings, who was at that time Master of the Temple in England, and Robert de Pirou, later commander of Temple Hirst in Yorkshire. Roger of Howden explains that they went to Henry, who welcomed them and rewarded them. In the records of Henry's reign, Brothers Osto and Richard frequently appear in the royal entourage. Although their Order was supposed to be neutral in disputes between Christian monarchs, their first loyalty was to their 'natural' king.[47]

Initially the papacy and monarchs had selected the Templars as trustworthy servants because of their piety and dedication to Christendom. Yet in papal and royal service the resources of their Order were distracted from the defence of Christendom; so, for example, the Templars in the East lost the service of the prudent and wise Amaury de la Roche. What is more, serving popes and kings involved the Order in political affairs, which brought the Brothers into disrepute – for instance, Matthew Paris's hatred of Brother Geoffrey the Templar, servant of King Henry III of England. And the more deeply involved the Templars were in papal and royal service, the more tarnished their pious and devoted image became. The Templars relied on papal and royal protection and patronage, which did much to give the Order its wealth and influence, but in the end would prove fatal to the Order.

7

COMMERCIAL AND ECONOMIC ACTIVITIES

In the mid-thirteenth century an English satirist, writing in Anglo-Norman French, set out to describe the whole of society in a work entitled 'Sur les états du monde' (on the classes of society). He considered the pope, the clergy, the peasantry, and finally the Military Orders of the Temple and Hospital. The clergy were guilty of greed, simony (buying Church appointments), nepotism (croneyism) and immorality. 'If they are saved, then I'm not lost!' declared the poet (lines 119–20). The Hospitallers were not interesting in hiring women's services, he claimed, as long as they had their horses. When he came to the Templars, however, he had only one thing to say.

> The Templars are most doughty men
> And they certainly know how to look after their own interests;
> But they are too fond of pennies.
> When prices are high
> They sell their wheat
> More willingly than they give it to their dependants.[1]

In short, the Templars were not interested in women, or in anything else apart from money.

Given the financial demands upon the Templars, it was hardly surprising that they were anxious to accumulate all possible funds. The previous chapter considered some of the particular problems facing the Order by the mid-thirteenth century: the decline in charitable donations and royal limitations on further donations. Yet commentators in the West and East considered that the Templars' and Hospitallers' concern about money was out of proportion to their needs. The Templars in particular were seen as not simply greedy but miserly.

It is no surprise, then, to find the Templars making money in many different areas. Much of their financial resources came from charitable donations, but the Order also generated much income for itself through independent economic and commercial activities, both in the East and in the West.

Wherever the Order produced grain from its fields it needed mills to grind it, but mills were also an important means of generating income. Since they were expensive to build and maintain, there were still relatively few mills in the twelfth century and those who owned them could charge highly for their use. In the twelfth century the majority were water-driven. The most notorious of the Templars' water-driven wheat mills was at Da'uk (plate 23) on the Nahr Kurdaneh (the River Belus), which flowed down from Recordane (Kurdaneh) to Acre. Upstream was a mill belonging to the Hospital. It used to be believed that the ruined mill in this area was the Hospital's mill, but, following archaeological survey work in summer 2000 by Idan Shaked of the Israel Antiquities Authority, it transpired that these ruins are the Templars' mill of Da'uk, while the Hospitallers' mill of Kurdaneh was about 380 metres upstream to the east.[2] These were large mills. As the land here is almost flat the mills had horizontal water wheels to make the best of the low head of water, but even then the Brothers had problems getting sufficient head of water to drive the wheels. From the first decades of the thirteenth century the two Orders were in constant dispute over the water supply to their mills.

The Templars used to close the sluices in the weir by their mill to build up a good head of water above the mill, but this flooded the Hospital's fields and stopped the Hospital's mill from operating. The Templars raised the banks on the Hospitallers' land to prevent the Hospital's fields from flooding when they closed their sluices, but the water still backed up against the Hospital's mill wheels. In retaliation, the Hospitallers would hold back the water so that the Templars' mill ran dry. Then, when a good head of water had built up, they would open their sluices, and the water would rush down the Templars' mill race and smash their wheels. The Hospitallers also complained that the Templars' weir prevented them from taking boats up and down the river to and from their mill. So they dismantled the Templars' weir to allow their boats through.

In 1235, following protracted legal actions, which had reached the papal court, an agreement was negotiated. To protect the Hospital's mill wheels from being stopped by the raised water level downstream, a mark was placed on the bottom side of the Hospital's mill, and the Templars were not allowed to raise the level of the water above that mark. In return, the Hospitallers were not to allow the water level to build up in their own millpond, damaging the Templars' mill wheels when it was released. The Hospitallers were to have two boats on the river, one above and one below the Templars' weir, and they were to unload their boats on one side of the weir and reload them on the other side. Neither Order should impede the boats on the river. This was not the end of the dispute, and another settlement had to be negotiated in 1262: the Templars had been obstructing the Hospitallers' boats and blocking the water course so that the river flooded – while the Hospitallers had been channelling off the water from the river. When the Hospitallers' mill had been out of action for a while, they had blocked off the channel of the river so that no water reached the Templars' mill.[3] This sorry saga illustrates the economic importance of mills to both Orders, but also the lack of respect that the personnel of each Order could show towards the other. It was this sort of petty incident that earned the two leading Military Orders a reputation for constant rivalry.

Because mills played such an important role in agriculture and were an excellent means of generating income, yet were expensive to maintain and operate, religious Orders were given many mills by their benefactors, as well as building their own. Not all water-mills were driven by rivers. Around the British coastline, with its large tidal ranges, many tidal mills were constructed during the Middle Ages. The millpond for these mills was filled by the tide as it came in, and then the head of tidal water in the pond was able to drive the mill for several hours. Tide millponds have to be very large and could cause a serious obstruction on a waterway. The Templars' tide mill on the River Fleet, near the New Temple on the River Thames just to the west of the city of London, was removed early in the fourteenth century for this reason. Temple Mill stood on the head of the tidal water on the River Lea to the north-east of the city of London. The Templars also owned a windmill at Dunwich in Suffolk, given to them by King Richard I of England.[4] It was not always economic for the Templars to operate mills themselves, and sometimes they rented them out to a third party, in return of payments of money or grain or other benefits in kind.

These mills ground grain produced both by the Order's tenants and by the Order itself. The Order's lands were cultivated in part directly by the Order (as *demense*) and partly let out to tenants. In areas where the Templars owned only a few small areas of land it was not administratively efficient to cultivate directly, and the Order preferred to let out the property. But even in such cases, in a period of inflation such as the late twelfth and early thirteenth century, when the value of rents fell rapidly, it could be more cost-effective to cultivate the land directly. In areas such as Essex where the Order held a single large area of land, direct cultivation was the more efficient option.

The barns for grain storage built by the Templars at their commandery at Cressing in Essex survive and have recently been restored (plate 24). These are not the only monastic barns surviving from the Middle Ages, but they are amongst the most impressive in Britain. The size of these barns is an indication that a large income was expected from the commandery, but in 1309 the total annual income was estimated at only £43 16s 9d, from which would be taken expenses of £14 14s, including the upkeep of three chaplains who said masses for the souls of donors, the supply of lamps and candles for the chapel, and the cost of bread and wheat, which was given in charity to the poor who came three days a week for alms.[5] What was left might have been enough to buy a horse (for instance), but not a particularly good one.

Apart from cultivating land that was already under the plough, all religious orders were involved in bringing new land into cultivation. They had the labour and the ready cash to do this. As a result they were often given marginal land by donors who could not afford to work it themselves, who hoped for some financial return from the land when it was cultivated – or at least an improvement in the local economic climate. Such donations to the Templars in the Iberian Peninsula and eastern and north-eastern Europe have been considered already. Some of this land was politically rather than agriculturally marginal. In Ireland the Templars received a number of donations from the new Cymro-Norman settlers in the late twelfth century, and while these were not on the frontier with the native Irish they can be seen as a sort of 'thank offering' for the success of the invasion and settlement from Britain, and marginal in the sense that the whole of Ireland was a new conquest. In south Wales it was mainly the Hospital of St John that benefited from this sort of donation, although the Templars' commandery at Garway in Herefordshire (plate 25) does fit the colonization pattern. This was land ripe for development, and the fact that the Templars cleared 2,000 acres of woodland indicates that they went about developing it with enthusiasm.

The Cistercians were the most famous recipients of marginal land, which they used to support huge flocks of sheep. The Templars generally brought in settlers to work the land. At Bruer in Lincolnshire (plate 26) they attracted tenants from the surrounding area and set up a new settlement. The fact that this no longer survives is a testament to the marginal nature of the land.[6] In the Iberian Peninsula they operated a far more extensive settlement policy. Here is a translation of a Templar charter issued in 1151 at Castelldans in Aragon to prospective settlers. The Templars granted the land to two individuals, who would then bring in other settlers.

In name of the supreme God who is triune and one, Amen. I, Peter de Cartila, and I, Frevol, and I, Aimery, and I, William de Tavernos, and all we Brothers together give our inheritance which we have in Castelldans, except our demense [the land farmed directly by the lord, and not let out to tenants] which we retain, to you Girbert and to you Bernad Ferrer; so that you may colonise it to the honour of God and the Temple, and such is the agreement between us and you that you, Girbert, may have and hold two *pareladas*[7] of land and a tower with the tithe and first-fruits[8] which you pay, and you, Bernad Ferrer, similarly two *pareladas* with your tower, paying tithe and first-fruits. We give and concede this to you and your sons and your posterity. But the other colonisers which you will cause to colonise the land to the honour of God and the Temple will pay us tithes and first-fruits and for each *parelada* they will pay each year one leg of pork worth twelve pence and four unleavened loaves and one day's work at sowing.[9]

Presumably these were favourable terms. Where land was not suitable for the plough it could be turned over to pasture. This is now the case at Garway, where flocks of sheep speckle the rolling green hills. The Templars had large flocks in Yorkshire, England, and also in the Iberian Peninsula. These were both important areas of wool production during the Middle Ages, but the Templars' production of wool was small in comparison with the Cistercians'.[10]

Religious Orders were also involved in industry: the extraction of coal and metal ores, the smelting of metals and manufacture. Evidence for this sort of operation in the Middle Ages is extremely localized, and operations depended on what was available or suitable in the locality. At Castle Pilgrim on the Palestinian coast, the Templars had a salting, where sea water was distilled to produce salt.[11] At the village of as-Sumairiya in the kingdom of Jerusalem there was a glass factory; the village belonged to the Templars in 1277.[12] In the West, where the Order was involved in wool production, an obvious industry was cloth manufacture. The process of fulling cloth was one of the first manufacturing processes to be mechanized; instead of cloth being washed and pounded by humans, this was done by huge wooden hammers powered by a water mill. The Templars had two fulling mills in 1185, one at their house at Newsam in Yorkshire and one at Barton on Windrush near Temple Guiting, Gloucestershire.[13] Like grain mills, industrial sites could be let out to third parties. In 1246 King Henry III of England gave the Templars two forges in Fleet Street, to the west of the city of London. As the Templars should have received 18d rent a year from these, the forges were obviously let out to tenants rather than being operated by the owner.[14]

In short, the Order produced whatever was most suitable for the locality. Just as its church services followed the practice of the local diocese, its church architecture followed the local style of architecture and many of its donors were drawn from the locality, so its production followed local practice. One would not think, visiting a commandery of the Order of the Temple in Europe, that this was an Order based in the Holy Land. One would simply assume that it was a local community of religious. This was why the Order sometimes built churches with circular naves or decorated the interior of its chapels with frescoes of its Brothers fighting in the East (see plates 5, 10, 19–20, 22): to remind the Brothers and outsiders of the Order's real vocation.

There were ways of making money other than agriculture and industry. The period from the early eleventh century to the early fourteenth century in Europe was a period of rapid economic and commercial growth. The population grew, new land was brought under cultivation, new towns and cities were founded, and there was much new building work within these new settlements. Trade and commerce expanded. This period of growth was caused by a variety of factors, including a period of warm, dry climate across Europe, increased political stability and an end to external invasions. The period of growth came to a close in the early fourteenth century, largely because of a change in the climate, which was becoming colder and wetter.[15] The cause of this climate change was a mystery to contemporaries, who either explained it as God's punishment for sinners (*peccatis exigentibus*) – which was also the standard reason given for the failure of crusades – or blamed it on the secret operations of hostile groups, such as the Jews, the lepers, heretics or witches.

During the period of good climate and economic and commercial growth the Templars rapidly expanded their economic and commercial operations to finance their military commitments in the East. The French historian Damien Carraz has recently reminded us that in most of Europe the Templars were an urban Order as much as a rural one.[16] They made money not only from farming, but also from rents and from commerce and trade. In 1301, for instance, one Lady Aveline of Provins gave the Order four rooms at Provins below 'the Cordeliers' and much other inherited property. She did this in return for the numerous favours that the Order had done her in the past, 'of her own good will, without force or wrangling and without constraint'.[17] Aveline's rooms would be let out, thereby raising revenue for the Order. Her charter does not state exactly what favours the Order had done for her; the most likely explanation is that the Order had lent her money.

All religious orders were used by lay people as a safe deposit for valuables, and were asked to lend money when lay people needed cash. The Templars in particular became well known for these sorts of financial services for the same reasons as they were used by kings as almoners, treasurers, and money carriers; the Order had developed systems for the collection, safe storage and transport of large sums of cash and other valuables in the West, for carrying to the East.[18] Merchants made much use of the New Temple in London and in Paris for depositing their valuables. The security of the Templars' systems was well known, and was taken for granted in the account in the Dunstable annals about the Lord Edward's 'bank raid' on the Temple, as well as Roger of Wendover's story about the Templars refusing to hand over Hubert de Burgh's money to the king.

There were remarkably few complaints about the Templars mishandling money deposited with them. The only specific criticism I have found is Jean de Joinville's bitter account of how the Templars 'mislaid' his wages of £360, which he had deposited with one Brother Stephen, the commander of the Templars' palace at Acre, soon after he arrived in the Holy Land in 1250. When Jean sent his representative to withdraw £40, the commander denied all knowledge of Jean and his money. Jean went to Brother Renaut de Vichiers, who had been Marshal when Louis IX was in prison in Egypt and who had allowed Jean to take the money needed for Louis's ransom. Thanks to Brother Renaut's compliance on that occasion, Louis had used his influence to encourage the Order to elect him as Master. Jean told Brother Renaut what had happened, but he refused to believe it:

When he heard this, he became very alarmed and said to me: 'Lord Joinville, I am very fond of you. But be certain that if you will not withdraw this claim, I will never have any more affection for you. For you wish to make people think that our Brothers are thieves.' And I said to him that, God willing, I would never withdraw my claim.[19]

Jean passed an anxious four days before the Master came to him 'all laughingly' and said that he had found Jean's money. The commander of the palace had been transferred, and Jean's money was returned to him. Although no other contemporary made such complaints, the repeated general accusation that the Templars were greedy may have been partly based on other such instances of mismanagement.

All religious orders lent money, but as Christians were not allowed to levy interest (this practice was called 'usury') they had to find other ways of covering the cost of the loan. There were various ways in which this could be done. Some Templar loans from southern France included a clause in the loan agreement that if the coin depreciated in value between the time of the loan and the repayment then the borrower must add a fixed sum to compensate the lender. As the fixed sum would remain the same however much the coin depreciated, it is likely that an interest charge lay buried in this fixed sum. Again, if land was given as the pledge for the debt it might be stipulated in the loan conditions that the produce from the land did not count towards the repayment of the loan.[20] Complaints of Templar greed could conceivably have sprung from such clauses, but the complainers did not specify loans as a particular cause of grief.

Among the privileges and exemptions that the Templars received from rulers were many rights connected with trade. For example, they were granted the right to hold weekly markets and annual fairs at many of their commanderies. They had royal permission to hold annual fairs at Witham in Essex and at Baldock in Hertfordshire; in 1212–13 King John conceded them the right of holding a market at their new town of 'Wulnesford' in the parish of Witham, and his son Henry III added an annual fair. In 1227 Henry III granted the right to hold a weekly market on Tuesdays at their town of Walshford in the parish of Ribston in Yorkshire, and to hold a yearly fair there, but in 1240 this was changed to Wetherby. Henry also changed the Templars' market at Temple Bruer, granted by Henry II, from a Thursday to a Wednesday, and granted the right to hold an annual fair.[21] These markets and fairs would form a focus for local trade, and bring much income to the Order both from dues paid by those taking part and also through boosting the local economy generally. The large number of markets and fairs granted to the Templars in England indicates that here at least trade was an important source of income for the Order.

The Templars' commercial privileges could sometimes cause disputes, as in the case of around the 1260s at Provins, in Champagne, France. The counts of Champagne had given the Templars rights to levy certain tolls on produce entering Provins. According to the merchants of the town, the Templars were exploiting these rights far beyond what was granted. The letter below was originally written in simple French; the tone throughout one of desperation.

> These are the complaints of the bourgeois of Provins about the treatment they have received from the Templars, contrary to the usages and customs of Provins. (Addressed to Theobald, Count of Champagne).
>
> Sir, we are showing you the wrongs that have been done to us as you are our earthly lord to whom we have recourse, for we have no recourse to anyone except to you. So, sir, we beg you for the sake of God that you help us so that we can live under your authority in the same way that we and ours have lived under your ancestors in the past.
>
> Sir, the freedoms of Provins are such that in exchange for a payment of 1d on Tuesdays when the market is at Provins the bourgeois are quit of paying toll on everything they buy and sell of anything to do with drapery in any place where they buy or sell in Provins.

Sir, we are accustomed and ought to have the right to weigh the wool; each person who can and wishes to, may weigh it in their house, and weigh it freely, without opposition. The weighers who weigh the wool are appointed by the bourgeois of Provins and are on oath; and if the bourgeois notice that the weighers are cheating they remove them and put in others.

Sir, what is more, in the three fairs which there are at Provins, that is to say the May fair, St Ayoul's fair and St Martin's fair, we are free of all tonnage [toll on weight of goods] for the first seven days of each of these fairs.

Sir, what is more, we have the following freedoms: if we have bought wool in some abbey, and it has been delivered to us and comes at our risk, we pay no toll. But we have been forced to pay, sir, so that we tell you that we have never since been able to get wool from the abbeys but they take it to Chalons and elsewhere, sir, and we have suffered great loss. The people in the abbeys tell us why: because when they sell their wool at Provins, wool which is still at their abbeys or still to be sheared, they shouldn't pay tonnage on it, or pesage, nor any other customs duty, and never have done, and for this reason they are taking their wool elsewhere, and have left the trade of Provins because they are being forced to pay pesage and tonnage.

Sir, we have complained several times about this, and Lord Lorant has been ordered to look into it, and we believe, sir, that the investigation was made, and if nothing was discovered, we beg you to command that it be made again. Sir, as it was your pleasure that we inform you, we wish to beg you [to do this] as you are our supreme lord, and we can have recourse to no one else but you.

Sir, we know truly that if you knew the great damage which you are suffering here from loss of rents, from your ovens, your mills, your fabric manufacturers and your other factories which you have at Provins, and the great damage which your bourgeois are suffering, which is also damage to you, for what your bourgeois have is also yours, and they cannot suffer damage without affecting you. Sir, even the wool which the merchants used to bring they now bring nothing, and the little which they do bring us is so expensive that we can't make any profit on it, so that the drapery industry in the town is in decline because of the lack of wool merchants coming from the abbeys, and they don't come because they can't enjoy the practices which they are used to.

Sir, we have held all the liberties which are recorded above from ancient times and enjoyed them in peace, and our lord your father, whom God absolve! confirmed them to us in his charter. Sir, for God's sake help us, because we have been suffering this on a daily basis for a good nine years or more before your people's very eyes and suffering losses in our businesses.[22]

In this instance, if the Templars' over-exploitation of their rights was damaging trade as much as the tradespeople of Provins claimed, the Templars were in fact damaging their own long-term interests. If the wool trade of Provins was destroyed, then the Templars would lose money. We may hope that the count of Champagne was able to persuade them of this, but regrettably we do not know the outcome of this complaint.

When the Templars had made their money in the West, they had to get it out to the East. There has been some debate among scholars as to whether any actual transfer of coin took place, but the current view is that coin was actually carried from the West to the East. This meant that the Templars needed ships (plate 27) to carry their coin, as well as agricultural produce, horses and personnel for the East. They also provided a secure carrying service for pilgrims – safer and cheaper than hiring a commercial carrier.[23] These would have been heavy transport vessels rather than warships. Much of the surviving evidence for Templar shipping comes from the relevant port records or royal records giving permission for the export of produce. At La Rochelle on the west coast of France during the twelfth century the Templars were given several vineyards and produced wine for their own consumption and for export;

although the cartulary of their house at La Rochelle is lost, the records of the port of La Rochelle show that the Templars were exporting wine by ship.[24] This was not a fleet in any modern sense. Again, these would have been transport vessels rather than warships, and the Templars probably hired them as they needed them, rather than buying their own.

The hierarchical statutes attached to the Templars' Rule, dating from the twelfth century before 1187, refer to the Order's ships at Acre (section 119), but do not state how many ships the Order owned. After 1312 the Hospital of St John was mainly involved in sea-based warfare and had an admiral in command of its marine operations, but only had four galleys (warships), with other vessels. It is unlikely that the Templars had any more galleys than the Hospitallers. The ships would have been very small by modern standards, too shallow in draught and sailing too low in the water to be able to withstand the heavy waves and winds of the open Atlantic, and suited for use only in the relatively shallow waters of the continental shelf. Nor could they carry enough water to be at sea for long periods.

Although navigation and shipping was improving rapidly from the twelfth century onwards, at this period European sailors could not venture far. Regular trading voyages to the Viking colonies on Greenland by British and Scandinavian merchants were made by 'island hopping' across the North Atlantic along a well-used route. In 1291 the Vivaldi Brothers of Genoa set out to sail down the African coast, but were never seen or heard of again. Still, developments in shipping continued, encouraged by hopes of finding new sources of trade and gold, as well as of converting pagans to Christ and winning honour and glory. By the 1330s the sailors of western Europe had ships that were able to sail out of the straits of Gibraltar, turn south and keep going with the currents and the wind. Only then were the Canary Islands rediscovered and mapped – they had been known to the classical world, but since lost sight of.[25] But these developments came too late to have involved the Templars; by the late thirteenth century they had no spare resources to use in Atlantic exploration, even if they had wished to do so, and by the 1330s the Order had been dissolved.

The earliest references to Templar ships outside the kingdom of Jerusalem come in the first decades of the thirteenth century, when they were operating at Constantinople and in the Bay of Biscay. In 1224 King Henry III of England hired a Templar ship, 'the Great Ship', and its captain, Brother Thomas of the Temple of Spain, for use in his wars in France. Henry later bought the ship from the Master of the Temple in Spain for 200 marks and kept it.[26] Presumably at that time the Templars in Spain had a few ships, if they could spare this one. However, as mentioned in Chapter 3, when the Templars of Aragon accompanied James I of Aragon as he set sail for the East, their ship's rudder broke, and they did not have a spare. This does not indicate great naval expertise or investment. When Berenguer of Cardona, Templar master of Aragon and Catalonia, set out in summer 1300 for a meeting with the Grand Master Jacques de Molay in Cyprus, he hired a merchant ship for the voyage, and another for the voyage home in spring 1301.[27] If one of the leading Templars in the Iberian Peninsula could not find a Templar ship for his transport, clearly the Order did not have many ships at its disposal.

Roger de Flor, who founded the notorious Catalan mercenary company that terrorized the Aegean in the early fourteenth century, began his career working on a Templar ship commanded by a Templar sergeant-Brother named Brother Vassayll of Marseille. When he was aged twenty the Master 'gave him the mantle', as Roger's biographer Ramon Muntaner put it, and made him a sergeant-Brother. A little while later the Templars acquired from the Genoese a great ship, 'the biggest made in those times', called the *Falcon*. Brother Roger was put in command. In this ship Roger made a lot of money for the Order – Ramon does not explain how, but presumably Roger was practising the same sort of licensed piracy against the

Muslims and those who traded with them as the Hospital of St John later practised in the Mediterranean. He also assisted in the evacuation of Acre in May 1291. In the aftermath of defeat, however, he was accused of keeping a great deal of money from the evacuation for himself. Ramon reports that 'the Master took from him all that he found on him, and later wanted to hang him'. Probably this was the judgement of the chapter: that Roger be stripped of his habit and hanged in punishment. When he heard of the judgement, Roger left the *Falcon* at Marseilles, borrowed money and bought his own ship, and went to offer his services to various secular rulers.[28]

The fact that the Templars' Spanish great ship also came equipped with its own captain, Brother Thomas, who remained with it after Henry III had bought it, indicates that this was the normal form of organization for the Templars' ships. Theoretically they belonged to the Order, but were run as individual units under Brothers who were experienced sailors. When they were not being used by the Order, for example for carrying pilgrims or produce, they engaged in privateering and other commercial enterprises. This was the normal method of organizing ships during the Middle Ages. Ships were owned and run by their captains, and hired by others as they were needed. Kings and others had no 'standing fleet' as such, as the timber ships were expensive to maintain and did not last for many years even if they were looked after.

Apart from terrorizing enemy shipping, the Templars' ships appear in the surviving records carrying pilgrims, grain, military personnel and equipment from the western Mediterranean to the East. Getting permission to sail from a western European port was not always a straightforward matter. There could be costly harbour dues to pay, and the local shippers resented the competition from outsiders. During times of war, rulers would normally close the ports and forbid all exports overseas, including those by the Templars to the East. The Templars would then have to negotiate to obtain permission to export their essential supplies.[29] The evidence indicates that the

Templars regularly shipped people, cash and produce from Marseilles from at least 1216. Brother Vassyll, who trained Brother Roger de Flor as a sailor, was from Marseilles. The Templars also shipped from Sicily and southern Italy, especially from the late 1260s when this area came under the control of Charles I of Anjou and his successors. This was the period when Brother Vassyll came to Brundisi and met the young Roger de Flor.

Ramon's account of Brother Roger's sudden departure from the Order of the Temple reminds us of the other side of the Templars' economic and commercial activities. The Order was dedicated to obtaining as much money as possible in the West in order to carry on the defence of the East. This sometimes meant causing offence and distress in the West as the Order strove to make the most of its exemptions and privileges. It also meant that the Order took a very harsh line against any Brother accused of embezzlement or wasting resources. Theft was punished by being expelled from the Order for ever.[30] Theft might include breaking a key or a lock, leaving the house and taking anything belonging to the Order (a few exceptions were specified) and misappropriation of property for any purpose. Brothers would lose their habit and be imprisoned in iron chains if they gave away the Order's property without permission, stole from people outside the house, or caused any loss to the Order, even for breaking a lock. Examples of causing loss to the Order included the case of a Brother throwing a mace after a bird and the mace falling into the river; a Brother who damaged a horse that had been entrusted to the Order's care when it was sick; a Brother who was trying out a sword (this usually involved hitting it on something hard, such as an anvil) and broke it; and a Brother who dropped a set of glass goblets and smashed one, then lost his temper and shouting: 'No thanks to God and His Mother for that' proceeded to smash the rest of the set.[31]

One of the reasons for the harshness of the Order's discipline was to impress upon outsiders that the Order was genuine in its determination to serve God and His Mother. In the examples cited above, it is striking that the Order punished only the Brother who had damaged an outsider by injuring their horse (his habit was taken from him), and excused the others. Yet because chapter proceedings could not be discussed with outsiders, outsiders would only know that one Brother had lost his habit and not about the others who had been excused.

Brothers who stole from, struck or otherwise harmed outsiders were very severely punished. Three Templars at Antioch who murdered some Christian merchants were sentenced to be whipped through Tripoli, Tyre and Acre, to restore public confidence in the Order's discipline. They were finally imprisoned in Castle Pilgrim, where they died.[32] Brother Gilbert of Ogerstan, who stole part of the Saladin tithe collected in England in 1188, was put in chains and disappeared into the Order's prison. Roger of Howden commented that no one knew what happened to him afterwards.[33] In 1301 Walter le Bachelor, Master of the Temple in Ireland, was accused of theft from the Order. As he had been a prominent figure in public life in Ireland this would have been a major scandal – but what followed made the scandal worse. He was stripped of his habit and imprisoned at the New Temple in London, where he died. Rumour said that he was starved to death. The Order would not even bury his body in its cemetery, on the grounds that he was excommunicate (formally cut off from the rest of Christianity) when he died.[34] Such harsh discipline should have impressed Christendom, but in fact it seems to have shocked contemporaries. The fate of Walter le Bachelor was one of the scandals brought against the Order in the British Isles during the trial of the Order. Master Gilbert of Bruer, a clerk who had been employed by the Templars, drew attention in his testimony to the Order's harsh dealings, observing that 'he has never regarded any of their dealings as suspect, except for the excessive punishment of their Brothers'.[35] At a period when religious belief was increasingly emphasizing the mercy of God, the humanity of Christ and the benign intervention of His

Mother, the Templars' harsh and apparently merciless discipline could have seemed to outsiders to be not only inhuman but even ungodly.

8

THE TRIAL OF THE TEMPLARS

After the loss of the Holy Land

The loss of Acre in May 1291 was a serious psychological blow to the Templars. The Order had lost its base in the Holy Land, most of its warriors and military equipment, and many valuable fortresses into which the Order had poured its resources for the past century and a half. The Templars' headquarters at Acre alone represented massive investment of money and labour, a testament to the military and political power of the Order in the East. Sited on the western point of the city on the approach to the harbour, its great walls towered over pilgrims arriving by ship from the West. The former secretary of Master William de Beaujeu described the complex as follows:

> the strongest part of the town, and it covered a great area by the sea, like a castle, for at the entrance there was a high, strong tower with a thick wall, twenty-eight feet thick, and on each corner of the tower was a turret, and on top of each of these

turrets was a lion *passant*, huge and gilded. The four lions and the gold and the labour cost 1,500 Saracen besants [the currency most used in the crusader states] and it was a very noble sight to see. There was another gate on the other corner towards the Pisa Road, with another tower, and close to this tower on the St Anne's Road was a noble palace which belonged to the Master. From there above the house of the nuns of St Anne was another high tower, where there were bells, and a very noble, tall church. There was another very old tower next to the sea, which Saladin had built a hundred years earlier, in which the Templars held their treasure. This was actually on the sea and the waves beat against it. There were other beautiful houses within the Temple, very noble, which I will not write about now.[1] *# p. 321*

Due to a fall in the land level and rise in the sea level since the fourteenth century, much of the site of the Templars' area at Acre is now under water, although there are some accessible remains being excavated.

The Order had also lost its leading military personnel in the fall of Acre. The Master, William de Beaujeu, was killed in the last battle. The Marshal, Peter de Sevrey, had commanded the final defence of the Templar's part of Acre, and had been executed by the Muslims when he went out to negotiate with the sultan under a promise of safe conduct. Most of the Brothers either died in the last battle or in the final defence of the Templars' fortress in Acre.

The surviving Templars were in a sorry state. They managed to evacuate some of their treasure from the treasury at Acre, while the precious possessions in their other surviving fortresses were safe, such as the relic of St Euphemia which had been at Castle Pilgrim. But they had lost everything else. Apparently the Brothers did not even send a letter to the West to inform their Brothers there of what had happened, indicating that the Order was in a state of near collapse. After the disasters of 1187, Grand Commander Terricus (Thierry) had written to the West to inform leading authorities of the situation in the

East; but in 1291, although the Master of the Hospital, John de Villiers, sent news to the Hospital in the West, nothing survives from the Templars. In May 1291 the remnant from Acre retreated first to their remaining castle of Sidon, where the Grand Commander, Thibaut Gaudini, was elected Master. After the evacuation of Sidon the convent retreated to Cyprus, where the Hospitallers had already set up their headquarters. Cyprus was conveniently situated for use as a bridgehead for attacks on the Syrian and Palestinian coastline, and could act as a mustering point for a new crusade. The Teutonic Order went to Venice, which is halfway between the Order's two crusading fronts: north-eastern Europe and the Holy Land.

The Military Orders could not afford to appear idle. As defenders of the Holy Land, they were first in line to be blamed for its loss. The popes were also anxious to appear to be doing something to recover the Holy Land: partly because they were genuinely concerned about it and partly to deflect criticism away from the papacy for its failure to send aid to the East and diverting would-be crusaders to Sicily. So the popes encouraged the Military Orders to remain active in the East – but now at sea, rather than on land.

In August 1291 Pope Nicholas IV called provincial councils to meet in February 1292 to consider how the Holy Land could be recovered. These were assemblies of clergy from each archbishopric. The pope suggested various points for discussion, including the question of whether the Military Orders should be unified. Given the power of papal suggestion, it is not surprising that every single provincial council declared that the Orders should indeed be unified and steps taken to ensure that they used their resources more efficiently. Yet nothing was done, as Pope Nicholas IV died in March 1292, before the conciliar decisions reached him.

Nicholas IV also ordered the Masters of the Temple and Hospital to build up a fleet, and in January 1292 he authorized them to use their ships to assist the Armenians. The 'Templar of Tyre', however, indicates that the Templars contributed only two ships to an expedition to help protect Cyprus against the Muslims. The Templars' military operations at sea were never large-scale, and apparently they never even established a formal title for the official in charge of naval operations.[2]

Thibaud Gaudini did not make a good impression on contemporaries, but he would have been an old man at the time of his election: he had been active in the Order since at least 1260. He died in 1291 or April 1292.[3] Jacques de Molay was elected in his place. Anxious to do something positive about the recovery of the Holy Land, in 1294 Jacques travelled to the West to see the pope, Boniface VIII (1294–1303), and discuss the possibilities for a new crusade. Boniface issued him with some privileges, to help raise money, and wrote to King Edward I in England asking him to allow the Order to export the supplies needed for Cyprus. Charles II of Naples (son of Charles I of Anjou) also allowed the export of materials to Cyprus. Jacques de Molay then went to France and England to try to raise support for a crusade. Yet neither monarch was able to commit himself to a crusade in the near future. Edward I of England, who had been on crusade before, had taken the cross again, intending to come out on crusade in 1294. But as Philip IV of France had invaded his territories in Aquitaine, Edward now had to make their defence a priority. Jacques de Molay returned to the East with promises and privileges, but no actual military aid and no hope of a crusade to follow.[4]

Meanwhile, Pope Boniface VIII was occupied with European affairs, especially in Sicily, where the attempts by Charles II of Anjou and his papal allies to recover the island had failed to dislodge the Aragonese ruler. After the revolt of the Sicilian Vespers in 1282 Sicily was ruled first by King Peter III of Aragon, then his second son James (later James II of Aragon), and then after 1295 by James's younger brother, Frederick. While the Aragonese were not the Sicilian rulers of papal choice it became clear that they could not be easily ejected, and they were clearly preferable to the Hohenstaufen whom Charles I of Anjou had originally displaced. A settlement was eventually concluded, the treaty of Caltabellotta (1302), which ended hostilities and laid down that Frederick would surrender Sicily to Charles II or his successor and be compensated with another kingdom such as Cyprus or Sardinia. The truce held, but the treaty was not put into effect.

The papacy had other problems in Italy. Boniface was a member of the Caetani family, and he favoured his relatives. The powerful Colonna family were rivals of the Caetani, and resented the pope's favouritism towards their enemies. The result was a war of arms and words between Boniface and the Colonna, including accusations that Boniface was a heretic and had had the previous pope, Celestine V (elected and resigned 1294), murdered.

Alongside Boniface's rivalry with his Italian political enemies he was involved in a quarrel with King Philip IV of France over the king's rights to tax the French clergy. By a bull of 1296, Boniface forbad secular rulers to tax the Church without his permission. Philip retaliated by forbidding the French clergy to send any money to Rome. Philip supported the Colonna in Italy against Boniface; Boniface refused to allow Philip to punish the bishop of Pamiers, who had been plotting against the king. The two sides waged a propaganda war against each other, but Philip's ministers were better at this than the pope. Boniface was accused of heresy, buying Church offices ('simony') and of not being a true pope because he had been elected by trickery; he had a private demon as an adviser, he had silver images of himself set up in churches, he was a sodomite; and he did not believe that the French had souls. The mastermind behind these accusations was Philip IV's new adviser, William de Nogaret.

Boniface was about to excommunicate Philip when William de Nogaret and Boniface's enemy Sciarra Colonna turned up at the papal court at Anagni with an army and arrested him. The pope was rescued by the citizens of the city, but shortly afterwards he died of shock.[5]

The crisis left the Church in Italy deeply divided. Boniface's successor, Benedict VIII (1303–4), tried to reconcile the parties, but lived for only eight months. Not until spring 1305 was the next pope elected, Bertrand de Got, archbishop of Bordeaux, who took the name Clement V (1305–14).[6] He was not related to any of the warring families of central Italy. As archbishop of Bordeaux his liege lord was the king of England, so that he was acceptable to the anti-French faction in the Church, yet he was a Frenchman, so Philip IV and his supporters would accept him. Clement was not a healthy man, and he inherited a papacy that had lost both prestige and power over the past decades through its involvement in factional infighting, its involvement in Sicily and its inability to assist the Latin Christians in the East. The political situation in Rome was so heated that Clement decided not to set up his court there. Philip IV offered him a refuge in France, which Clement accepted. In 1309 he established his court at Avignon – in France, but not in territory directly controlled by the king of France. There the papacy remained until 1378.

While the papacy was unable to help the refugees in the East, a hope of assistance for the recovery of the Holy Land had appeared in the person of the Mongol Ilkhan of Persia.[7] When the Mongols had initially erupted into eastern Europe in 1241 western Christendom had been terrified, but by 1280 leading churchmen regarded the Mongols as potential converts to Christianity and allies against the Muslims. The Mongol Ilkhans also regarded the Latin Christians as potential allies against the Mamluks of Egypt. In late 1299 the Ilkhan Ghazan of Persia – a recent convert to Islam – asked King Henry II of Cyprus and the Masters of the Hospital and Temple for their aid in his campaign against the Mamluks in Palestine. Over the next two years the Christian army attempted to cooperate with the Ilkhan's strategy, and although the two sides never succeeded in synchronizing their campaigns, the Templars were able to conquer Arwad Island (also known as Ruad island, formerly Arados: see plate 4), close to their former stronghold of Tortosa (Tartūs). In October 1302 the Mamluks attacked and sacked the island, killing or capturing the Templar garrison. The king of Cyprus and the Masters of the Orders assembled a relief force, but too late to save the island.

It has been suggested that the Templars were trying to set up a long-term base on Arwad with the intention of moving their headquarters there from Cyprus.[8] The problem was that Arwad is too small to be self-sufficient and was too close to the Mamluk-dominated coast for security. After the loss of Arwad, Jacques de Molay had no confidence in small advance expeditions, and concentrated on trying to raise a large crusade from the Order's base on Cyprus.

Cyprus was a more secure base than Arwad, but the Templars and Hospitallers could not mobilize resources there to support the large forces necessary for advances into the Holy Land. King Henry II's regime was on the defensive, not only because of the threat from Frederick of Sicily (due to receive Cyprus under the Treaty of Caltabellota) but also from his own brothers and vassals, who regarded him as an incompetent ruler. Henry was suspicious of the power and influence of the Military Orders, and restricted their operations on the island. The Templars had once briefly owned the island, and had extensive properties there. They were also allies of the king of Aragon, Frederick of Sicily's brother; and they were friendly with Charles II of Naples, who also had a claim to Cyprus. What if the Templars supported a take-over of Cyprus, to use it as the base for a new crusade? King Henry's suspicions were well-grounded: in 1306 the Templars and many Cypriot nobles supported his brother Amaury de Lusignan when the latter overthrew Henry and took over the government of Cyprus.[9]

Although little progress was made in organizing a crusade, various commentators in the West had drawn up tracts suggesting how the Holy Land could be recovered. Some had been prepared for the Second Council of Lyons of 1274, but more appeared after the loss of Acre in 1291. It is hard to say how serious these plans were, and some seem very impractical.

However, they gave the Military Orders an important role: the Orders were to lead the reconquest and were to be a standing army when the land was reconquered. To prevent rivalry between the Military Orders, most writers proposed that the Military Orders should be merged into one Order. The Master of this new Order would become king of the new kingdom of Jerusalem when it was conquered. Some writers suggested that this Master should be a king or a king's son from the West.[10]

In 1306 Pope Clement V called the Masters of the Temple and Hospital to his court at Poitiers in the kingdom of France to submit their own comments on the crusade and the suggestions that their Orders be unified. Jacques de Molay objected to the plans for unification. He said that the rivalry between the Orders had led to the Orders vying to do the best for Christendom – so it was beneficial. Unifying the Orders would cause resentment. As for the crusade, he did not trust small expeditions; he wanted one big campaign. Jacques knew that expeditions were doomed to failure unless substantial support from the West was guaranteed.

The comments of the Master of the Hospital, Fulk de Villaret, on the question of unification do not survive. His crusade proposal assumes that the Military Orders of the Hospital, Temple and the Teutonic Order will continue to operate as independent entities. Fulk planned a small expedition followed by a large one, a policy he then carried out. He put into train a small expedition to capture Rhodes, with Genoese support. This was successful, but the large expedition which he planned to follow never materialized.[11]

The aim to unify the Military Orders did not proceed as planned; in the event, the Orders combined when the Order of the Temple was dissolved and its properties given to the Hospital. Yet although these plans came to nothing, they show that western Christendom still viewed the Military Orders positively, even though they had failed to defend the Holy Land. Although the Orders needed a few reforms, they were not a hopeless case; they could still do great things for Christendom and fulfil their intended purpose. Even after 1291, they had their critics, as they had always done, but since 1250 there had actually been *less* criticism of their activities. This was because other religious orders, particularly the friars, were becoming far more unpopular than the Military Orders had ever been. In addition, because the situation in the East had seemed virtually hopeless since the 1250s, while exciting and alarming events were going on in Europe, many commentators wrote about events near to home and ignored what was going on in the East, so did not mention the Military Orders.

Although the Military Orders took their share of the blame for the loss of the city of Acre in 1291, they were not the only parties blamed; commentators also criticized the pope for failing to assist them, the king of Cyprus for ineffectual leadership, and the people of Acre for being sinners (this was a general accusation arising every time Christians were defeated by Muslims). Although the still positive roles given to the Military Orders in fictional literature were dictated largely by certain conventions, the Orders would not have appeared at all if writers and audiences did not have a good opinion of them. 'Templars' continued to appear in the versions of the Grail legend based on Wolfram von Eschenbach's *Parzival*: Wolfram wrote in the first decade of the thirteenth century, and his work was so popular that German authors continued to adapt and develop it throughout the Middle Ages. In Wolfram's version of the story, the Templars appeared as defenders of the Grail Castle and of the *Salva Terra*, the Holy Land where the Grail castle lies: showing that Wolfram's Grail Castle represents Jerusalem, the holy city guarded by the real Templars. Other Grail authors did not include the Templars, but Templars continued to be depicted in a favourable light in other fictional literature throughout the Middle Ages. In the late thirteenth century and early fourteenth century some commentators observed that the Templars 'used to be the best of all knights but have now declined', but their comments only show that although some contemporaries were disappointed in them, they still wanted to think well of them. In short, while a few writers complained that the Templars and other Military Orders had lost sight of their vocation, most commentators viewed them favourably.[12]

It thus came as a shock to almost everyone when on 13 October 1307 all the Templar Brothers in France were arrested on the orders of King Philip IV in surprise dawn raids. The Brothers were imprisoned and interrogated on a number of charges.[13]

The charges against the Templars

The Templars' innocence of the charges brought against them in 1307–8 (see figure 10) has been generally agreed since the work of the American historian Henry Charles Lea, published in 1889. Most historians now see the charges as an exercise in political propaganda, although in recent years a few have argued that there was some basis in the accusations.[14] The charges were carefully constructed. They all stemmed from popular myth about heretics and magicians, but some were also a malicious misinterpretation of the Order's actual practice.

The charges of irreligious kissing, adoring a cat, active homosexual practices, denying Christ, dishonouring the Mass, the involvement of the worshippers' everyday clothing in blasphemous worship, venerating an idol and excessive secrecy were all part and parcel of medieval beliefs about heretical religion. The members of the Waldensian movement were accused of being 'horrified at the Holy Cross' and worshipping a cat, while the Cathars were accused of denying the cross, worshipping a four-faced idol and wearing a cord as a symbol of their beliefs.[15]

Heresy can be defined as anything that does not conform to the accepted beliefs of society; in western Christendom in the Middle Ages it was any belief condemned by the Church. The actual beliefs of 'heretics' varied: the Waldensians were condemned for preaching without official Church authority, while the Cathars were dualists, believing that only spiritual things originated with God, while everything physical was created by

Figure 10   Summarized list of charges brought against the Templars

Errors of belief

The Templars denied Christ when they were received into the Order or soon after. They spat on the cross and defiled it.

They exchanged obscene kisses at their reception into the Order.

There were other dubious activities at their reception: they were made to swear that they would not leave the Order, receptions were held in secret, and sodomy was encouraged.

They had to swear not to reveal what was said at their reception.

They adored a cat.

They did not believe in the Mass or other sacraments of the Church. Their priests did not speak the words of consecration in the Mass (so donations for Masses to be said for a donor's soul would be wasted).

They were taught that the Master, Visitor and Commander (who were laity) could absolve them from sin – which only ordained priests could do.

They practised sodomy.

They venerated an idol, a bearded male head, and said that the head had great powers. Each of them wore around their waist a cord which had been wound around the head.

They were only allowed to confess their sins to a Brother of the Order.

They did not correct these errors, which were said to be 'of long and general observance', or 'ancient custom'.

Errors of practice

The Order did not make charitable gifts as it ought, nor was hospitality practised.

The Brothers did not reckon it a sin to acquire properties belonging to another by legal or illegal means.

They did not reckon it a sin to procure increase and profit for the Order in whatsoever way they could.

Perjury was not reckoned a sin if done to win gain for the Order.

Other suggestive evidence against the Order

The Brothers held chapters in secret, at night.

Many Brothers left the Order, 'because of the filth and errors of their Order'.

There was widespread scandal about these things.

This summary is based on the translation of the charges by Malcolm Barber, *The Trial of the Templars* (Cambridge, Cambridge University Press, 1978), pp. 248–52.

the devil. Devout Christians feared heresy because it was hidden (as no one can know for certain what another person believes) and because Christians believed that if heresy was not destroyed it would bring about the destruction of society. Either God would punish all Christians for not destroying the heretics, or the heretics themselves would destroy society directly, because they did not fear God and so did not respect the authorities whom God had approved. From the eleventh century onwards churchmen wrote of heresy as being a leprosy that was slowly destroying Christendom, or a cancer eating up Christendom from inside, or that heretics were locusts who devoured everything good in society, or scorpions who stung their victims unexpectedly and killed them. Fear of heresy in the Middle Ages was similar to the fear of communism in the United States in the 1950s or fear of satanism in Britain in the 1990s; often irrational and exaggerated, and resulting in the disgrace and misery of many completely innocent people who had been falsely accused.

Anxiety about heresy increased dramatically from the eleventh century onwards. Society was becoming more settled and wealthy, and literacy was spreading, so that the population as a whole became more ready and able to think for themselves and develop their own ideas about religion. The Church had not been able to meet the increased demands placed upon it by the increased population and growth of towns, so people turned elsewhere for spiritual support; and through the reform movement of the second half of the eleventh and first decades of the twelfth century the popes had encouraged the laity to question the lifestyle of its priests and to have higher expectations of how the clergy should live. In addition, the authorities of western Christendom were also more on the lookout for heresy. As governments became more organized and systems of administration developed, rulers became more determined to enforce single systems of belief.

Many pious people were accused of heresy; in fact some believed that the best way of identifying heretics was to look for extremely devout people. One mark of every heretic was their enthusiasm about their beliefs and their conviction that their beliefs alone were true. Several religious orders were accused of heresy. In 1238 Pope Gregory IX accused the Hospitallers of having heretics in their midst, and ordered them to reform themselves. At the Council of Vienne in 1312 the decree *Ad Nostrum* outlawed beliefs that were said to be held by the beguines and beghards, lay groups of woman and men who did not have a recognized rule and did not always live in organized houses. The Council considered condemning the beguines altogether, but decided to allow the organized houses to remain, provided that they were under proper ecclesiastical authority. Pope John XXII (1316–34) condemned the Spiritual Franciscans, a branch of the Franciscan Friars who tried to follow St Francis's original doctrine of absolute poverty. The problem was that these groups were defying norms of ecclesiastical authority, even though their actual beliefs were orthodox in other respects. Repression could be harsh, and some of the Spirituals who refused to agree to the pope's decision were burned at the stake.[16]

The Teutonic Order in Livonia was accused of heresy by its political enemies there in a series of appeals to the papacy in 1298, 1300 and 1305: the charges included attacking the Church, the burning of dead bodies (a pagan practice), and killing wounded Brothers. The Order defended itself and brought counter-charges, but the Order in Livonia was excommunicated and Pope Clement V ordered an investigation. However, the Order's allies were too powerful at the papal court for the case to proceed, and its enemies were too weak; eventually the charges were dropped.[17] All in all, there was nothing extraordinary about a religious order being accused of heresy.

Once a person had been accused of heresy, the charge could not be refuted unless it could be show that the person who had brought the charge was a personal enemy. It was very difficult to find anyone to defend heretics or to speak on their behalf because anyone defending them was likely to be accused of heresy themselves. It was the responsibility of the local bishop to investigate charges of heresy; he might appoint an investigator, but from the 1230s the pope also sometimes appointed investigators to seek out and deal with heresy in certain specific areas.[18]

Traditionally, the trial by ordeal had been used to find the truth in legal investigations, but because this always required the intervention of God (for example, if the accused was thrown into water they had to sink to prove their innocence) by the late twelfth century canon lawyers were becoming uneasy about using this method. At the Fourth Lateran Council of 1215 it was decided that the ordeal should no longer be used. Torture took the place of the ordeal in investigations; Pope Innocent IV licensed its use in heresy cases in 1252. It was not always used, however, since the threat of torture was often enough to gain the required confessions.[19]

Investigators assumed that that inflicting pain on a person would force them to tell the truth, unaware that it was more likely to force them to say what the investigator wanted them to say. Miscarriages of justice in Britain in the 1970s, such as the cases of the Guildford Four and the Birmingham Six, showed that it is not even necessary to use torture, but only to threaten violence and to use certain methods of interrogation, to persuade innocent people to confess to crimes as instructed.[20]

A person accused of heresy who confessed and repented would be given penance and absolved. A person accused of heresy who was believed guilty but who refused to confess was regarded as 'obdurate', stubbornly sticking to their crime, and worthy of punishment by death. As the Church was not supposed to shed blood, the heretic would be handed over to the secular authority to be punished. The traditional punishment for religious dissidents, going back beyond Roman law to the Middle Eastern Kingdoms of Old Testament times (see Daniel 3), was death by burning, a method of purification from evil.

Heretics who confessed and then went back on their confession were regarded as having returned to their guilt. They were handed over to the secular authorities and punished by burning at the stake. Heretics who confessed in part or who were suspected of not making a full repentance were sentenced to life imprisonment.[21]

Because it was almost impossible to escape from a charge of heresy once it had been made, a virtually certain means of ensuring the speedy fall of a political rival was to accuse him or her of heresy. Such charges increased during the thirteenth century, and the charges against the Templars obviously fit into this pattern.

On another level, the charges against the Templars echo medieval beliefs about magicians. Until the eleventh century the Church had not taken witchcraft and magic very seriously: once active paganism had died out in western Europe, witchcraft was viewed as little more than a collection of superstitious practices indulged in by deluded old women. It could be dangerous, but it was not a major threat to society as a whole. However, with the discovery of the scientific classical Greek and Arabic texts in the library of Toledo (captured by Alfonso VI of León-Castile in 1085), this attitude changed. For part and parcel with ancient science were magical texts, based on mathematics and the study of the stars and planets, and on the innate qualities of plants, stones and animals. They claimed to have been written by ancient philosophers, prophets, scientists, even gods, such as Hermes, Aristotle, Moses, Socrates, Plato, Ptolemy. They promised that through knowledge of heavens and the earth and correct application of that knowledge it was possible to control events to one's own will. This was clearly not mere superstition, but, it was believed, serious science. It deserved to be taken seriously; and so magic moved into the realm of the possible, the probable, and the extremely dangerous. Every king needed to know about it, and courtiers used it in an attempt to gain power and influence. But while magicians claimed to work only through the power and assistance of God, the Church as a whole was not so sure.

Magic, which involved controlling the spirits of the stars and other powers, could easily become demon-worship.[22]

Books of medieval magic and esoteric knowledge abound from the twelfth century onwards: books derived or claiming to derive from Persian and Greek astrological lore such as the *Cyranides* and the *Secreta Secretorum*, the mixed bag of astromagic, necromancy, spells and philosophy that makes up the *Picatrix* (translated from Arabic into Castilian Spanish for King Alfonso X, 'the wise', and then into Latin), magical texts such as the *Ars notoria*, which provides a set of magical pictures claiming to enable the lazy student to learn the seven liberal arts very quickly, and necromancer's handbooks. Such books would be kept secret, omitted from an owner's library catalogue, passed on quietly through networks of friends. They all emphasize the importance of secrecy, of keeping the book from the eyes of the uninitiated, of hard study and following a pious, austere lifestyle.

As the author of the *Picatrix* begins: 'To the praise and glory of the highest and omnipotent God whose quality it is to reveal to his predestined ones the secrets of the sciences' (*scientiorum*, which also means 'all forms of knowledge'). He explains: 'you should know that this secret which we intend to reveal in this book of ours cannot be acquired unless one first learns how to acquire it. And whoever intends to learn how to acquire it must study in the sciences and scrutinise them in proper order, because this secret cannot be gained except through wisdom and study in the sciences in the proper order. Moreover, there is great purity in this secret, which will be of great help to you.'[23] He then goes on to describe necromancy.

Secrecy, study and purity – all contained in a book! The charges against the Templars hinted that the Templars' Rule might be such a book. The Templars' operations in the East meant that they had been in frequent diplomatic contact with Muslims. Some Templars may have learned Arabic; the Order employed secretaries and also spies who knew Arabic. For educated Westerners, the obvious use for Arabic was for reading Arabic magic texts. Perhaps (they may have thought) the Templars' Rule was actually a translation of an Arabic magical text, as so many books of magic claimed to be. The fact that the Templars preferred outsiders not to read the Rule and actually stated in their statutes that it could be harmful if outsiders read it (section 326) tended to encourage such a belief. Yet some outsiders did read the Rule: one of the lay witnesses on Cyprus had read it and said that everything in it was good; Pope Clement V owned two copies, the Teutonic Order followed it, and various religious houses had copies of it. These outsiders knew that it was not a magical text. But for anyone not connected to the Order, the charges against the Templars hinted that the Order was actually involved in magical practices.

The charge that the Templars venerated a head also reinforced the charge of magic. Malcolm Barber has shown that the testimonies about this supposed head during the trial derive from medieval folklore. He has demonstrated that there is no evidence for the existence of a bearded head as described in the Templar trial proceedings.[24] It is true that those framing the charges against the Templars may have been thinking of a specific bearded head. Two masters of the Temple in Germany had Christ's head on their seals: Christ was the King of the Order, so it was reasonable for His head to appear on the seal. But elsewhere the Order used the image of the *agnus Dei*, the lamb of God, to represent Christ, and in all the rest of the surviving Templar iconography there are no bearded heads, of Christ or anyone else – unless the Templars were venerating their own bearded heads! The Hospitallers of St John, on the other hand, did venerate a bearded head, the head of St John the Baptist, which appears on seals of the Order in England. The head of St John the Baptist appears elsewhere in Hospitaller iconography in Britain, for example in the medieval painting of a bearded head now in the church at Templecombe in Somerset – Templecombe became a Hospitaller commandery after the dissolution of the Order of the Temple.[25] It is possible that this particular charge against the Templars was deliberately designed to confuse outsiders, who knew that the Hospitallers venerated a bearded head and could not always tell the Hospitallers and Templars apart from each other.

But the charge also recalls the magical texts of the period. In particular, *Picatrix* gives instructions as to how to use a severed human head for magical purposes. Again, there is an implication that the Templars were magicians.

The charge of venerating an idol that was said to have great powers also recalls the conventional picture of the Muslim in the western European writings of the twelfth, thirteenth and fourteenth centuries. Muslims were said to worship idols of Mohammad, Jupiter, Apollo and other gods. They were also said to blaspheme Christ, spit on the cross and dishonour it in other ways, as the Templars were accused of doing. For instance, Ambroise the trouvère and the author of the *Itinerarium Peregrinorum*, in their accounts of the siege of Acre of 1189–91, tell how a Muslim soldier stood on the walls of the city of Acre and beat a crucifix, waved it about 'with obscene movements, with filthy and sinful miming actions and blasphemously shouting impious words against our religion', and finally urinated on it. At that point one of the Christians shot him in the groin with a crossbow bolt, and he fell dead.[26]

So the Templars were being accused of behaving like Muslims; but stereotypical Muslims, not real Muslims. Real Muslims do not blaspheme Jesus Christ or His Mother the Virgin Mary, for in Islam Jesus is a great prophet, 'Isā, 'blessed be he!', and His Mother's virginity is accepted. Islam forbids the use of pictures of animals or people in worship, so the Muslims do not have idols. Thus the charges against the Templars do not indicate that the Templars had adopted Muslim practices, because the charges do not represent real Muslim practice. The Templars were being accused of becoming the stereotypical mythical Muslims of fiction.

Why should any group adopt a completely mythical set of practices, especially when they knew what the real Muslims did (because they had had frequent contact with them in the East) and they knew that according to Christian belief these mythical practices would lead to their damnation? As the Templars and Hospitallers were reported to have protested to Count Robert of Artois in 1250 at Mansurah, this was a ridiculous suggestion.[27]

The charge that that Templars were behaving like Muslims was irrational: if the Templars had become 'contaminated' with Muslim beliefs, they would have started acting like real Muslims, reading the Koran and praying to Allah rather than Christ; but they were not accused of doing this. They were accused of becoming 'fairy-tale' Muslims. As many magical texts had been composed by Muslims or translated into Arabic by Muslims, this accusation reinforced the charge that the Templars were magicians.

There were many known magicians operating during the Middle Ages, most of them either connected with a religious Order or in priestly Orders. Many rulers, including popes, employed magicians, but the only known Templar involvement in magic comes from after the dissolution of the Order, when an ex-Templar appears as one of the necromancers employed by a cardinal of the Church. As the Order had been dissolved, he was taking advantage of the new employment opportunity that had been thrust upon him; but as he failed to produce what his client wanted he does not seem to have been very successful in it.[28]

Medieval magic was a supremely literate science, contained in books that were usually in Latin, the language of literacy, designed to be read privately, not aloud. Some were in the vernacular, but Latin was more convenient for wide distribution and for keeping magical texts secret from outsiders. As we have seen, the Templars were not a literate Order. Very few of them could read Latin; books produced for Templars were written in the vernacular and were primarily intended to be read aloud to a group. Hence Templars would not have known anything about magic, let alone become involved in it.

The group most notorious for their involvement in magic during the Middle Ages was the secular priests. For a poor priest with an education and a low income, it would have been a great temptation to 'cash in' on his knowledge of Latin and make some money from his more gullible parishioners by performing simple magical tricks and producing 'magic potions'.

The other group with a particular interest in magic was the *literati*, the educated officials who provided the backbone of royal government. They might tinker with magic themselves. In 1315 Enguerrand of Marigny, former chamberlain and advisor of Philip IV of France, was hanged for using image magic against Philip's son and heir Louis X and Philip's nephew Charles of Valois.[29] The *literati* formed the social group which produced the ministers of Philip IV who brought the charges against the Templars. In short, the Templars were accused of the dubious activities that their accusers themselves actually practised in their spare time.

Attacks on political rivals on the basis of a charge of magic increased from the mid-thirteenth century onwards, in the same way as politically inspired charges of heresy. Typically, the charge of heresy and magic would be combined together, for magic was regarded as part of heresy. The charges of magic were more likely to be credible than charges of heresy, as most courtiers would at some time or other have been involved in magic, even if only in having their horoscope cast.

At the beginning of the fourteenth century, Walter Langton, bishop of Lichfield and treasurer of King Edward I, was accused by one John Lovetot of various crimes, including doing homage to the devil. The grounds for John Lovetot's accusations were personal grievances. This accusation did not go far because the king was not willing to support it, but it illustrates how it was becoming routine to accuse political opponents of blasphemy and the like, simply as part and parcel of a legal case.[30] In the notorious Kilkenny witchcraft trial of 1324, during which one of the defendants was burned at the stake as a witch, the original charges were brought so as to obtain a share in a disputed inheritance.[31] During the reign of Philip IV of France and his sons, political accusations of this sort were brought against Pope Boniface VIII, Bishop Guichard of Troyes and Enguerrand de Marigny.[32]

In short, the charges brought against the Templars accused them of heresy and magic, which was normal for political trials of the period. If the charges came to a trial, normal rules for heresy trials would apply: the Brothers would have little hope of clearing their names, and their only practical option would be to confess quickly in order to save their lives. In France this was exactly what happened.

As the charges against the Templars had no basis in previous criticism, and were clearly standard accusations, why did anyone believe them? The answer to this is twofold. First, hardly anyone outside the domains of the king of France did believe them. Second, within the kingdom of France the charges were carefully grounded in the actual activities of the Templars.

The charge that the Templars venerated a head was true, since the Templars did venerate the heads of at least two female martyrs, St Euphemia and one of St Ursula's maidens: the former in the East and the latter at Paris. These relics were well known, often seen and fully accounted for. The veneration of saints' relics was a standard part of orthodox Roman Catholic practice, and all religious Orders venerated relics. But the Order was not being accused of venerating the head of St Euphemia, for this was not a crime. The charges mixed the known Templar veneration for the relics of saints with the known Hospitaller veneration for the bearded head of St John the Baptist and produced the mysterious 'Templar head' that so baffled contemporaries and has misled many commentators since. In so doing, whoever formulated the charge was also mocking the cult of relics, which was coming under criticism from educated people.[33] As the Templars were devoted to the cult of relics, and took great pride in their devotion, presumably whoever formulated the charge saw their devotion as foolish and grounded in ignorance.

The charge that the Templars did not honour the Mass hit the Order at a sensitive point. The Order relied for much of its income and its patrons' support on its priests performing Mass for the souls of donors and their families. The Templars were proud of their service for God in their chapels: Jacques de Molay declared to the papal commissioners in 1308 that he did not know of any Order that had better or more beautiful ornamentation and relics and everything necessary for divine worship or whose priests and clerics performed the divine service better. One of the lay witnesses on Cyprus, Parseval de Mar, agreed with him: the Templars' chapels were better decorated than those of any other religious Order.[34] Yet the charges, which completely denied all that the Templars were most proud of in their service for God, claimed that the Templars had not upheld Christendom against the Muslims, but had adopted Muslim beliefs and practices. Their beautiful chapels, devoted divine service and well-cared for relics were a sham.

The charges also made fun of the Brothers. They were known for their ignorance of theology. Some would not have known the difference between the chaplain absolving them from sins against God and the Master absolving them from faults against the Rule. The charge that they were taught that the Master, Visitor and Commander could absolve them from sin, which was theologically unsound, reflects the Brothers' ignorance. The charge that they venerated a bearded head mocked their beards. The charge that they were told at their reception that they could indulge in sodomy poked fun at the Brothers' chastity. Careful reading of the trial records reveals that the Brothers were actually told that if there was a shortage of beds – for instance, when they were travelling on the road – they might have to sleep two to a bed.[35]

Finally, did Jacques de Molay have a pet cat? It is impossible to know how far the charges against the Templars reflect personal situations at that time. The Brothers were baffled by the accusation that they adored a cat. Some did say that they had seen cats come in to reception ceremonies or to chapter meetings at various times: sometimes a white cat, sometimes black or brown. The Templars' commanderies were agricultural concerns with large barns where food was stored, so the commandery cat(s) would have been important members of the community, with the task of keeping down rats and mice in the barns. It is true that the charge of adoring a cat was a standard charge against heretics, but it would be interesting to know if it also reflected a particular situation within the Order at the time of the trial.[36]

In short, the charges were ingeniously devised to make the most of the Templars' weak points and undermine their strongest points, so it was impossible for them to escape. Who, then, devised the charges?

The original charges of 1307 were framed by one Esquiu de Floyran of Béziers, co-prior of Montfaucon. In January 1308 he wrote to James II of Aragon in jubilant mood, informing James that his accusations against the Templars, which James had refused to believe, had been taken seriously by Philip IV of France. Esquiu had made four accusations: the Templars denied Christ at their reception and spat on the cross, they were told at their reception that they could have sex with each other because they could not have sex with women, they kissed their receptor on the base of the spine, the navel and the mouth, and they worshipped an idol. According to Esquiu, when James had originally dismissed Esquiu's stories he had told him that if he could prove them, he would give him 3,000 *livres* (pounds). Esquiu reckoned that the Templar confessions under torture in France in late 1307 constituted proof, and was writing to claim his money.[37]

Esquiu's original accusations fitted the pattern of accusations of devil-worship brought against leading political figures of this period such as Pope Boniface VIII and Walter Langton. Like these, his accusations were presumably promoted by a personal grievance that had no obvious connection with the accusations. Just as Edward I of England dismissed the charges against Walter Langton, so James II had dismissed the charges against the Templars. The fact that Philip IV and his ministers took them seriously indicates that they had their own motives for attacking the Templars. Scholars believe that the final 'worked up' version of the charges against the Templars was devised by William de Nogaret, who masterminded Philip IV's attack on Pope Boniface VIII, and went on to use similar charges against Bishop Guichard of Troyes. Nogaret knew how to frame the charges to the best effect.[38]

In the nineteenth century the French scholar Jules Michelet suggested that the charges involving the denial of Christ and other abuses during the reception of Brothers to the Order actually referred to an obedience test. Michelet and later scholars surmised that the Brothers were told to deny Christ either in commemoration of Simon Peter's denial of Christ, or to ensure that they would obey every command they were given, or because if they were captured by the Muslims they would be put under pressure to deny Christ, so the performance at their reception was to prepare them for this.[39]

This last theory is based on the testimonies of two Templars during the trial. But it does not stand up to examination. If the Templars wanted to test new Brothers' obedience, they could easily have found a difficult test that did not involve denying the very purpose of the Order – the service of Christ. Again, if the Brothers were commemorating Simon Peter's denial of Christ, this should have been generally known in the Order – but it was not.

If the Templars wanted to establish whether Brothers could stand up to Muslim pressure to deny Christ, then surely applicants would not have been admitted to the Order if they agreed to deny Christ. Yet those Brothers who confessed to this charge implied that it made no difference whether they denied Christ or refused to deny. In fact, they seemed completely bewildered as to why they should have been asked to deny. If there had been any truth in the charge, there must have been some reasoning behind this denial; and if there had been some reasoning behind it, at least one of the officials who had admitted Brothers to the Order should have known what it was. But although a few witnesses in France offered explanations, no two explanations agreed; and no one tried to defend this supposed practice. Outside the areas under the direct control of the king of France or his relations and where no torture was used, hardly anyone confessed to anything. Brother Imbert or Himbert Blanc, Commander of the Auvergne, was in England at the time of the arrests and gave his testimony without the assistance of torture. Back in France, many Brothers of the Temple said that they had been admitted to the Order by Imbert and that he had insisted that they deny Christ, and so on. Imbert could easily have saved himself by explaining the reasoning behind this procedure, if any existed. But he denied that he had ever admitted anyone to the Order except by the proper procedures laid down in the Order's regulations. His refusal to admit to any of the abuses that his Brothers in France had wished on him meant that he was labelled as a non-confessed heretic and sentenced to lifetime imprisonment.[40] The obvious conclusion is that he was telling the truth: there were no abuses, and he had never received any Brother except by the proper procedures.

It must be said that no real effort was made during the trial of the Templars to discover the truth behind the charges, or the true situation in the Order. The purpose of a heresy trial was to prove the charges of heresy, not to find out the truth. So only the Brothers of the Order were arrested: the nuns of Mühlen and any other Templar Sisters, associates of the Order living within the Order's houses, and servants were not. It is true that the charges only affected the Brothers, but the Sisters, associates and servants would have known what was going on in the Order's houses and could have given testimony. The fact that only a few servants of the Order were interrogated indicates that the investigators did not want their testimony, as if they did not believe that it would support the charges.

Some non-Templars gave evidence during the trial. On Cyprus, third-party evidence was heard at length and was virtually unanimous: the charges were absolutely false. In France a few non-Templars gave evidence, some in favour of the Order and some against. In England, Scotland and Ireland, where the Brothers refused to confess to anything, a good deal of third-party evidence was heard, as the inquisitors tried to prove the Templars' guilt through their public reputation. In England this produced some extraordinary stories reminiscent of twentieth-century gothic horror movies and/or the sort of bawdy humour represented by the British *Carry On* films of the 1950s to 1970s. Such evidence is fascinating evidence for the tradition of English horror and English humour, but was not very helpful in convicting the Templars: stories were vague, without names or dates, and the people actually involved in the stories were never called to corroborate them. One friar told a story about some Templars who were staying with 'a certain matron' – a mature, married woman – in York. She came to take one Templar's dirty clothes for washing, and found that he had hidden his underpants in the latrine. Pulling them out, she found a cross on them.[41] The story was told to demonstrate that the Templars dishonoured the cross by putting it on their underclothes; cynics might add that as Templars were notorious for putting their cross on everything else they owned (to show that it was exempt from paying tithes and certain secular dues) why not their underwear as well? But the woman in question never appeared to confirm the tale.

One lady, however, did appear to give evidence, Agnes *Cocacota* or *Louekete*, who claimed to be friendly with one of the Brothers' servants. According to Brother John de Bercia of the Friars Minor, Agnes had been told by the 'valet' or serving lad of the commander of the Templars' house in London about someone who had surreptitiously entered one of the Templars' secret chapter meetings. The investigators managed to find

Agnes and get her own version of events. She said that she had been told by one Robert, the 'valet' of Brother John de Moun, then commander of the New Temple in London, about how one Walter, a servant of the Order, had managed to overhear a chapter meeting. Agnes had also told Brother John de Bercia that the Templars sexually abused each other.[42] Where was Walter? Why was Robert the valet not called to give evidence? – presumably because the whole story was a fabrication.

The course of the trial

The charges, then, were false. Yet all but four of the 138 Templars in Paris who were arrested on 13 October 1307 and interrogated, confessed to some or all of the charges.[43] The reason for this was explained by a contemporary writer:

> They were arrested without warning, suddenly, without right, and without any judgement being made against them. They were shamefully and dishonourably incarcerated with destructive rage, afflicted with taunts, the gravest threats, and various sorts of torture, compelled to die or produce absurd lies which they knew nothing about, wrongly given into the hands of their enemies, who force them through those torments to read out a foul, filthy and lying list which cannot be conceived by human ears and should not enter the human heart. But when the brothers refuse to produce these lies, although they know absolutely nothing about them, the torments of the attendants who press them daily force them to speak the lies, saying that they must recite them before the Jacobins [the Dominican friars who interrogated them] and assert that they are true if they wish to preserve their lives and obtain the king's plentiful grace.[44]

According to this anonymous friend of the Order, writing in Paris in early 1308, thirty-six Brothers in Paris had died under torture rather than confess, while many others elsewhere in France had also died. He declared that these Brothers were martyrs and now had their reward in Heaven. But the

Dominican friars and others involved in the interrogation refused to listen to the Brothers' insistence that all the charges were false, and continued to torture them until either they confessed or died.

What is more, if they do not say these things, not only before but even after torture they are always held in dark prison cells, with only the bread of sorrow and the water of affliction, in winter time with the pressing cold, lying with sighs and grief on the ground, without straw or coverings. In the middle of the night, to increase their terror, now one and now another are taken from cell to cell. Those whom the investigators have killed in torture they secretly bury in the stable or in the garden, out of fear that such horrible and savage deeds should reach the royal ears, since they have told and tell the king that the aforesaid brothers did not confess their crimes by violence but of their own accord.

Anyone who is defeated by the tortures and produces the lies which the attendants and Jacobins want, although they ought to be punished for lying even though they did not want to lie, is raised up to chambers where they are happily provided with everything they need, so that they will keep up the lie. They are continually warned with threats, or with rough or flattering words. What is more, a certain monk – or more truly a demoniac – ceaselessly runs through the chambers at any hour, day and night, tempting the Brothers and extending warnings of what will happen to them. And if he discovers that anyone has repented of the said lies, he sends them straight back to the aforesaid afflictions and penuries.

What more is there to say? In short, I say that human tongue cannot express the punishments, afflictions, miseries, taunts, and dire kinds of tortures which have been suffered by the said innocents in the space of three months since the day of their arrest, because by day and night constant sobs and sighs have not ceased in their cells, nor have cries and gnashing of teeth ceased in their tortures. Is it amazing if they say what the torturer wants, since truth kills them and lies liberate them from death?[45]

This writer makes the significant point that the king did not know what was happening to the Templars: the interrogators told him that they had confessed of their own accord, which was giving Philip a false impression of the Order's guilt. Scholars are divided over whether Philip believed the charges himself. This writer indicates that he did, but that he was deliberately misled by his advisors.

On Thursday 27 November 1309, Ponzard de Gizy, commander of Payns, was questioned by the papal commissioners. Ponzard described his experiences after the arrests:

He was asked whether he had ever been tortured, and he replied that he had, three months before his confession made in the presence of the lord bishop of Paris: his hands tied behind his back so tightly that the blood ran down to his fingernails, in a certain pit in which he could only take one step; protesting and saying that if he was put to the torture again he would deny everything that he had said now and say whatever he was told to say. For a short time he had been prepared to have his head cut off, or to suffer fire or boiling for the honour of the said Order, but now that he had suffered imprisonment for the past two years he was not able to bear such long tortures as he had already been in.

. . . And because the same Brother Ponzard said that he was afraid that his imprisonment would be made worse because he had put himself forward to defend the said Order, he begged that they would make sure that it did not get worse because of what he had said, and the said lords commissioner said to the said provost of Poitou and John of Gamville that they should not harm him in any way because he had put himself forward to defend the aforesaid Order. They replied that they would not harm him any more because of this.[46]

So the Templars in France confessed because of torture and fear of torture, and knowing that the moment that they confessed – even though the confession was a lie – the agony would stop and they would be well cared for. They were also afraid to go back on their confessions because they feared that the torture would begin again.

Pope Clement V was furious that Philip had arrested the Templars without consulting him. Only the pope had the authority to order the arrest of a religious Order. He claimed that he had known about the rumours against the Order and had been planning an investigation, but as he had not yet done anything it is uncertain what steps he had planned to take. In any case, on 22 November 1307 he sent out letters to the kings of Catholic Christendom telling them to arrest and interrogate the Templars.

None of the kings of western Christendom was in a position to refuse to obey the pope or to oppose Philip IV of France. The king of Naples was Charles II, a first cousin once removed of Philip IV, and ready to fall into line with his wishes. The kings of Aragon and England were enemies of the king of France, did not trust his motives in the arrests, made considerable use of the Templars in their own administration, and refused to comply. But these monarchs could not defy Philip IV and the pope completely. Edward I of England, crusader and patron of the Templars, had died on 7 July 1307 and his son and heir Edward II had many problems of his own: lack of money, a war in Scotland, and barons who wanted a share of royal wealth and authority. James II of Aragon was a great king, but he also had his own problems with his nobles and feared French military might on his northern frontier.

Germany was fragmented with no ruler in overall control. Sicily was ruled by Frederick of Aragon, younger brother of James II of Aragon, who had no interest in arresting the Templars, but was not strong enough to defy the pope. The ruler of Cyprus was the usurper Amaury de Lusignan. He did not want to arrest the Templars, because they were his supporters; at the same time, he could not afford to anger the pope, because his political position was weak. He tried to arrest the Templars, but they refused to be arrested. A short conflict in May 1308 was followed by the Templars' surrender. They were confined to their estates, but were not in heavy imprisonment.[47] The trial itself did not begin until May 1310 or 1311.

Pope Clement V demanded that the case in France be turned over to the Church authorities. At this point, Jacques de Molay and the other high dignitaries of the Order in France revoked their confessions, saying that they had confessed out of fear of being tortured. Clement was not convinced that the Order was guilty, and in February 1308 he suspended the trial.

Philip began to mobilize what we now call 'popular opinion' against the Order, just as he had done against Pope Boniface VIII. He argued that it had been his duty to arrest the Templars.[48] He addressed seven questions to the doctors (learned scholars) of the University of Paris on the legitimacy of his action. These included: could the lay ruler act alone when heresy was clear? As the Order had been proven guilty, could he have the right to arrest them? Wasn't the Order really an order of knights, not of monks – so under the authority of the king, not of the Church?[49] The doctors replied on 25 March 1308. They stated that the Order was a religious Order and so not under the king's jurisdiction. But because of the Templars' confessions, they said, there was a strong suspicion that all the members of the Order were heretics or guilty of heresy. This was not very satisfactory for Philip IV, but apparently he regarded it as enough to justify his action.

The historian Sophia Menache has argued that Philip IV largely succeeded in convincing his own subjects in the early stages of the trial of the Templars that the Order was guilty, although the nobility and the bishops were not fully convinced. Outside France, however, Philip was not successful.[50] Yet the trial could not be stopped while Philip wanted it to continue, because the Templars in France had confessed to the charges – despite the fact that the confessions were produced by torture.

In early May 1308 Philip called the representatives of the three estates of his kingdom – the clergy, nobles and bourgeois – to a *parlement* at Tours. Representatives went with the king to Pope Clement V at Poitiers to put pressure on him to continue the trial, but the pope stood firm. In June 1308 King Philip allowed the pope to hear the testimonies of seventy-two Templars, while in August at Chinon three cardinals heard the confessions of the leading Templars then in France. These hearings seem to have convinced Clement to continue the trial.

The Vatican archivist Barbara Frale, who discovered the document with the full record of these testimonies, has argued that the pope decided that 'the strange profession ceremony was simply an entrance ritual' and forgave the Templars. In fact, the pope made no reference to entrance rituals, but declared that the Templars had confessed 'horrible and dishonourable things'. As they were repentant, they had been absolved, but they would still have to perform penance – on 18 March 1314 they were condemned to lifetime imprisonment. Far from dismissing the charges, the pope issued a series of bulls setting out the procedure for the trial to continue under the supervision of the bishops. He also called a Church Council to meet at Vienne in southern France in 1310 to decide the fate of the Order.[51]

The second wave of investigations, supervised by the bishops, began in 1309. The pope also set up a papal commission to look into whether the Order as a whole was guilty; this first met in November 1309. Yet the Templars were very unwilling to defend the Order for the reasons that Ponzard de Gizy stated: they were afraid that their conditions of imprisonment would be made worse, or that they would be bullied in other ways. Jacques de Molay finally agreed to defend the Order, but stated that he needed legal advisors because he did not have enough legal knowledge to defend it by himself; and he needed to have documents translated into French, as he could not read Latin. Then he went back on his undertaking and said that he would only give his testimony before the pope.

It is possible that his jailers had put pressure on him to dissuade him from defending his Order.[52]

In February 1310 fifteen Brothers came forward who were prepared to defend the Order. Others joined them, until at last over 600 Brothers had agreed to defend the Order. However, most of these had previously confessed to the charges they were now about to deny, and were therefore relapsed heretics. The punishment for relapsed heretics was burning at the stake. On 12 May 1310 Philip of Marigny, archbishop of Sens, brother of Philip IV's counsellor Enguerrand of Marigny, had fifty-four Brothers of the Temple who had agreed to defend their Order burned as relapsed heretics. The Templars continued to declare their innocence as they burned and the people watching were both impressed and surprised. Elsewhere in France, other Templars who had undertaken to defend the Order were burned, and this effectively ended the defence.[53]

The leading Brothers in the movement to defend the Order were priest-Brothers Renaud or Reginald de Provins and Peter de Bologna, who had had some legal training. In December 1310 they abandoned their defence, and Peter disappeared – their jailers claimed that he had escaped. Modern historians have assumed that Peter was probably murdered by his jailers, but recently the Italian scholar Elena Bellomo has established that Peter de Bologna returned to Bologna, where he died in 1329.[54]

The papal commission wound up on 26 May 1311 and its findings went to the Council of Vienne, which had been postponed by Clement and finally opened on 16 October 1311. Most of those present at the council wanted to hear the Order's case properly. But Clement was afraid of Philip IV of France, who would not allow the Order to be acquitted. A group of Templars who appeared at the council to defend the Order was arrested. Philip IV called the representatives of the three estates of France to a *parlement* at Lyons in March 1312, and on 20 March he entered Vienne with his army. On 22 March the pope issued a bull, *Vox in Excelso*, in which he stated that although the Order of the Temple had not been proven guilty, it had been so defamed that it could not continue. He therefore dissolved the Order, 'not by way of judgement but as a provision and an apostolic decision': a politician's way of saying that the Order was not guilty but that he had no choice in the matter. This bull was read to the council on 3 April: a clerk then rose and forbad anyone to speak, on pain of excommunication. The delegates at the Council, many of whom did not believe that the Templars were guilty, were furious: they had expected to be able to debate the case, and yet no debate was allowed. Philip IV and his army would not have permitted it.[55]

On 6 May 1312 Clement V declared by papal bull that the Brothers of the Temple who had been recognized to be innocent, or who had confessed and been reconciled to the Church, would receive a pension and could live in the Order's former houses or in a monastery. Their monastic vows were still valid, and they were not allowed to go back to their secular lives. Those Brothers who were known to be guilty but who had not confessed, or those who had relapsed, would be tried.

This last category included four of the chief officers of the Order in France, then in prison in Paris: the Grand Master Jacques de Molay, the Commander of Normandy Geoffrey de Charney, the Commander of Aquitaine and Poitou Geoffrey de Gonneville, and the Commander of the Île de la France and Visitor Hugh Pairaud. (The Commander of the Auvergne was in England.) In late December 1313 the pope set up a commission to judge them. Jacques de Molay tried to defend the Order, and was amazed to hear the final judgement on 18 March 1314: the four were condemned to eternal imprisonment as relapsed heretics. Jacques de Molay and Geoffrey de Charney protested loudly, and were condemned to burn as obdurate heretics that evening.

The chronicle attributed to the contemporary commentator Geoffrey of Paris gives a description of the Grand Master's death. Written shortly after the events described, he claims to have seen what he describes, although in fact his account is not completely accurate because he does not mention Geoffrey de

Charney. Instead he describes 'two brothers' who were there with the Grand Master. In any case, his description must reflect the stories in circulation in Paris at the time of writing: around 1316, two years after the Grand Master's death and the deaths of both Philip IV and Clement V. The extract begins as Jacques de Molay has been brought to the island where he is to be burned.

The Master contradicted the cardinal, and said to him that he believed in Our Lord and that there was no more loyal and better Christian than he was; and if there happened to be any evil Brother in the Order, that could well be the case, for he had often heard that there are evil people everywhere. But he did not know anything in the Order which did not originate in good faith and in the Christian law. He would not abandon his Order, but would suffer death there for God's sake, and for justice and for right. No one present was so hard-hearted that they did not cross themselves many times [for pity] when they heard him speak about his Order like this.

Seeing the fire ready, the Master took off his clothes. I say what I saw: he stood there in just his shirt, happily and in good spirits. He did not tremble, no matter how they dragged and prodded at him. They took hold of him to tie him to the stake; he agreed to this, happy and rejoicing. They tied his hands with a cord, but first he said to them: 'Sirs, at least, let me join my hands together for a little while and make my prayer to God, for now is the time and the season to pray. I see here my judgement, the place where I must die a short time hence; God knows that my death is wrong and a sin. So in a short time evil things will befall those who have condemned us to death; God will avenge our death.'

'Sirs,' he said, 'you should know, without any argument, that all those who have acted against us will suffer for what they have done to us. I wish to die in this belief. See here my faith: and I beg you to turn my face towards the church of Our Lady, from whom Our Lord was born.'

His request was met. He died like this, and met his death so
sweetly that everyone was amazed.

The writer ends his account in a bewildered tone: 'There is
great debate in the world over this, but I don't know what to
say to you about it. Some speak out of jealousy, others otherwise; I don't know who is telling the truth and who is lying.'
He concludes: 'You can fool the Church, but you can't fool
God. I won't say any more – draw your own conclusions.'[56]

With even his own supporters uncertain as to whether the
Templars were actually guilty, Philip IV of France had hardly
won his case. It was a strange heresy in which not a single
person who confessed to it was prepared to defend its beliefs,
and many preferred to die rather than admit that they had
believed any of it. Yet throughout the course of the trial in
France it was clear that Philip was determined to convict the
Templars by any means, and the question remains as to why he
was so determined to do so.[57]

Malcolm Barber has drawn attention to Philip's severe
financial difficulties, and the way in which every individual or
group who stood in the way of his financial policy or whose
demise could assist his financial situation was charged with
heresy and brought down, such as the Jews and the Templars.
For the most part, contemporaries outside France and countries
under French influence were convinced that Philip attacked the
Templars in order to get their wealth. Certainly the Templars
possessed a great deal of land, although they were always short
of ready cash.

Some scholars have argued that because Philip IV was a very
pious man he would not have attacked the Templars if they had
not been guilty of heresy. Yet even the most devout king can
commit crimes against the Church in the name of piety: Henry
VIII of England, who split the English Church from the
Roman Catholic Church, was a very pious man who wrote
books on theology and a tract condemning the work of the
Church reformer Martin Luther.

It is true that Philip IV was devout, and came from a long line of pious rulers. His grandfather, Louis IX, was canonized (recognised as a saint) in 1295, during Philip IV's reign. The kings of France depicted themselves and had been depicted as the 'most Christian king' since the twelfth century, but Philip and his ministers laid special emphasis upon this aspect of his kingship.[58] As the most Christian king, it was his duty to destroy all unbelievers (for instance, by driving the Jews out of France in 1306) and to root out heresy wherever it might be found.

Philip IV's regime was constantly under threat: from the king of England, Edward I, in Aquitaine, and in the fact that Edward had led a crusade while Philip had not; from the kings of Aragon and their brothers in Sicily, and on his southern frontier; in Flanders, where his army was heavily defeated by the Flemish infantry at Courtrai in 1302; from the pope, in the person of Boniface VIII, denying the king the right to tax his own clergy. This was also a time when the whole of western European society felt itself to be under threat. Western Christendom had lost the Holy Land; the climate was deteriorating, and harvests were failing; people wondered whether God was angry with them, whether evil magic was at work, or whether certain groups were out to destroy society.[59] Against this atmosphere of fear and uncertainty, the king must prove that he was indeed the most Christian king and able to deal with such dangers. So it is not surprising that Philip and his ministers reacted violently against any hint of heresy. We might even suspect that they used any excuse to attack vulnerable persons on charges of heresy, in order to reinforce the king's image as 'the most Christian king'.

Such an attack was made against Marguerite Porete, a laywoman from north-eastern France who wrote a book in French called *The Mirror of Simple Souls*. Even though three religious authorities had approved it, in 1306 the bishop of Cambrai, Guy de Colmieu, condemned the book as heretical and burned it, ordering Marguerite to stop spreading her ideas and writings. Marguerite, believing that Christ had authorized her work, continued to circulate her book among the laity. She was arrested by the next bishop of Cambrai, Philip of Marigny (later archbishop of Sens, the same who had fifty-four Templars burned as relapsed heretics in May 1310), and by late 1308 she was in custody in Paris, under investigation for heresy. The Dominican William of Paris, inquisitor, was in charge of her case; at the same time he was also in charge of the investigation against the Templars. Marguerite firmly denied that she was a heretic, but her book was condemned as heretical. In May 1310 she was condemned as a relapsed heretic, handed over to the secular authorities and burned at the stake with her book on 1 June 1310.

Her book continued to circulate and was translated into several European languages: Latin, Italian, Middle English. Many manuscripts of these translations survive, indicating that it was widely read. In 1927 it was published with the 'ut imprimatur', which meant that it had been approved by the Roman Catholic Church as reading material for good Catholics. No one realized that it had been burnt as heretical in 1310 until in 1946 Romana Guarnieri demonstrated that it was in fact Marguerite's book. The work is now attracting much favourable attention from scholars, and several modern translations have appeared.[60]

In short, Marguerite's book was not heretical, but Philip IV's regime interpreted it as such. Marguerite – a laywoman without powerful friends – was an easy target for a king who needed to keep proving himself 'the most Christian king' by destroying heresy. The king whose administration burned an unimportant woman for writing a good Catholic book, arrested Pope Boniface VIII for insisting on his supremacy over the Church and Bishop Guichard of Troyes on trumped-up charges, would not have held back from arresting a religious Order, if it was in his interests to do so.

Philip's most obvious interest in the Templars was their lands, because land equalled wealth and Philip needed money badly. But contemporaries also saw another motive. There was more to Philip's view of himself as 'most Christian king' than simply keeping the Church in France clear of heresy. He also wanted to launch a new crusade. James II of Aragon's reaction to Philip's arrest of the Templars was that this was part of a plot by Philip to take over the crusade.[61] He and his ministers had heard reports that Philip wanted to use the Templars' possessions to form a new Military Order which would then go to recover the Holy Land. This would be under his command, or the command of one of his sons. James's fear was that in this way the numerous important fortresses held by the Templars in Aragon would fall into French hands. He initially opposed the abolition of the Order, but when he saw it could not be saved he was determined to secure its property for himself. He agreed finally to the Hospital receiving the Templars' possessions in Aragon itself only on condition that the Templars' and Hospitallers' fortresses in Valencia, a frontier zone, were given to a new Military Order, which would be under his own control.

From the safe distance of seven centuries James's fears might seem ridiculous, but he knew Philip IV better than we do. Philip IV was heir to a long tradition of crusading by the French kings. His grandfather Louis IX had led two crusades; Philip had led none. What was more reasonable than that he should make plans to take over the greatest Military Order and lead it to victory?

The trial of the Temple can also be seen as a result of Philip's feud with the papacy. By destroying a religious Order that had been one of the exempt orders of the Catholic Church, under the direct jurisdiction of the papacy, the French king demonstrated that the papacy was no longer independent but controlled by the French king.

Other motives were suggested by contemporaries: some said that Jacques de Molay and Philip IV had quarrelled over money.[62] The charges against the Templars may also reflect the scorn which Philip IV's ministers felt for the old-fashioned, under-educated Templars who were still performing so many duties in royal finance – the trial was a rather violent way of getting rid of the 'old regime'.

Clearly, the Order of the Temple was vulnerable to attack; it had failed in its basic vocation, the defence of the Holy Land. The other politically inspired witchcraft and heresy trials of this period show that many people were prepared to use accusations of witchcraft and heresy to destroy a potential rival or get rich. All three leading Military Orders came under attack to some extent. The Temple was the most vulnerable, in that it had been the most prominent in the defence of the Holy Land. The simplest explanation for Philip IV's attack on the Templars is that he wanted their wealth. Yet other motivations – his piety, the crusade, the papacy and his ministers' dislike of the 'old regime' – worked together to encourage him to take Esquiu de Floyran's accusations seriously in 1307.

Outside France, the trial went rather differently.[63] In England, Edward II did not believe the charges, but in late December 1307 was forced to agree to the arrest of the Templars because he needed papal support for his war in Scotland, and he was about to marry Philip IV's daughter, Isabelle. Initially the Templars were treated well, no torture was used and no Templars confessed. The investigators of heresy, sent by the pope from France, put pressure on Edward to allow them to use torture in order to force the Brothers to confess, but even when Edward finally agreed in December 1309, no one was prepared to torture them. At last, at the end of June 1311, with the encouragement of torture three Templars imprisoned in London confessed to some of the charges. In the diocese of York no torture was used and no Brothers confessed. All the Templars in Britain were allowed to swear off or abjure all heresy, and were sent to monasteries to do penance for the sins they might have committed.[64]

In Germany the archbishop of Magdeburg was hostile to the Templars and besieged one of their castles, but the bishop of Halberstadt, an ally of the Order, excommunicated him and the

Templars escaped. At Mainz in May 1310 a group of armed Templars burst into the provincial council declaring themselves ready to defend the Order, and the nobles who had accompanied them stood up for the Brothers' innocence. The Templars were set free. In the Mark of Brandenburg, the margrave took over the Templars' property but let the commanders remain in office as his officials.[65]

In Italy, procedures varied from place to place. In the kingdom of Naples, torture was used – King Charles II was related to Philip IV of France – and some Brothers confessed. The archbishop of Ravenna was favourable to the Order, did not use torture, and declared the Brothers innocent. In Venice the state ran the investigation and the Templars were not even arrested. In Florence, where torture was allegedly not used, six out of thirteen Brothers made confessions and the other seven did not.[66]

In Aragon the Templars took refuge in their castles, appealed to the king and pope and declared their innocence. James II besieged and captured the castles (plates 7–9) and imprisoned the Templars. Some torture was used, but none of the Brothers confessed to the charges. In 1312 the Church council of Tarragona released them all and gave them pensions.[67]

In Castile, the Templars initially resisted arrest, and maintained their innocence with such success that a Church Council at Salamanca in October 1310 declared them innocent of all the charges. It is not clear what became of the Templars after this; they may have entered other religious houses.[68] Clive Porro has shown that in Portugal, no trial took place. In August 1307 King Dinis brought a legal case against the Templars in Portugal to recover from them properties which his ancestors had allowed them to hold in return for serving the king. Unlike the king of France, King Dinis was able to take over Templar property and establish his control over the Order without resorting to charges of heresy. He later used the Templars' former properties to set up a new Military Order in Portugal, the Order of Christ.[69]

Most of the leading officials of the Templars and the central convent were still on Cyprus. If the ruler of Cyprus had supported the Order, it would have been difficult for the pope to dissolve it. However, the trial in Cyprus was interrupted in June 1310, when the usurper Amaury was murdered by one of his household knights. King Henry II returned to power and put the Templars into close imprisonment in Famagusta – not so much on papal orders as because the Templars had assisted Amaury. In 1311 the king uncovered an alleged conspiracy to take over the kingdom from him, give the crown to Amaury's eldest son, release Amaury's supporters and put Brother Aimo of Oiselay, marshal of the Temple, in control of the government. King Henry exiled some of the plotters and sentenced the four ringleaders to death by drowning. Brother Aimo, many other Templars and other leading opponents of Henry were imprisoned in Kyrenia Castle, where they died in 1316 or 1317.[70] Although the trial of the Order gave Henry an excuse to destroy the Order, he would probably have destroyed it in any case, as a dangerous political rival.

It is not known what became of the Templars in the Morea (Achaea, Greece), Croatia, Hungary, Austria, Bohemia and Poland.

The aftermath of the trial

After announcing the dissolution of the Order of the Temple, on 2 May 1312 in the bull *Ad Providum* Clement V gave the Templars' possessions to the Order of the Hospital – with the exception of those in the Iberian Peninsula. The Hospital was to compensate Philip for his expenses in arresting and interrogating the Templars.

Philip IV was probably not happy with this decision, which also met with a howl of protest from the Council of Vienne. The representatives accused the Hospital of evil deeds (*mali*) and vices (*vizi*), and of spending their wealth on fair halls and palaces rather than on the war against the infidel. The Aragonese representatives said that the Hospital was guilty of fraud and had no intention of carrying on a crusade in the East but only wanted to capture the island of Rhodes, which was a Greek island and therefore Christian already.

On 6 May the Council issued many ordinances concerning the Hospital: all its privileges were suspended except its exemption from the jurisdiction of the bishops, and the Order was to send all its knights to the East, leaving only a few Brothers to administer its lands in the West. Chapels and parish churches in the West were to be handed over to the local bishops. Only when it had done this could the Hospital of St John receive the Templars' lands. Philip IV agreed to this decision.

But none of this reform took place. Philip IV and Clement V died in 1314, before anything had been done to reform the Hospital. When the next pope, John XXII, was elected in 1316, he set about reforming the Hospital's financial situation, but did nothing about the complaints against the Order in 1312.[71]

John tried to ensure that all the Templars' properties outside the Iberian Peninsula passed to the Hospital (see for example plates 28 and 29). In Cyprus, this had already been done: in November 1312 the Hospitallers received not only the Templars' lands but also their treasury, including their relics, which they took to Rhodes. The Templars' central archive was left on Cyprus, where it probably remained until the loss of the island to the Ottoman Turks in 1571. The Templars' relics, however, went with the Hospital to Malta in 1530, and remained until the Order was evicted from Malta by Napoleon in 1798, when they were either looted by Napoleon's soldiers or abandoned by the Brothers.

Elsewhere, the transfer of property to the Hospital was patchy. In England the Templars' properties had been seized by King Edward II or by the noble families who had originally given them to the Temple. Edward used the lands to reward his friends and to finance his Scottish campaigns, and was reluctant to hand them over to the Hospital. The legal disputes dragged on for years: in England, some lands were never handed over;

in Germany, some passed to the Hospital but many returned to the families of the original donors.[72]

John XXII also settled the problem of the Templars' properties in the Iberian Peninsula. In 1317 he approved the creation of two new Military Orders: in Portugal, the Order of Christ, which would receive the Templars' lands there, and in Valencia in the kingdom of Aragon, the Order of Montesa, which would receive both the Templars' and the Hospitallers' lands. In compensation, the Hospitallers would receive the former Templar lands in the rest of the kingdom of Aragon. Both Portugal and Valencia were frontier areas where a Military Order could still play an active role against the Muslims. Neither of these new Orders, however, were replacements for the Order of the Temple. Although they were religious Orders, they were also royal orders, and their function was to serve their respective kings as well as serving God.

The Order of Montesa was actually set up in July 1319, when James II of Aragon ceded the Order the castle of Montesa. Other properties were also given to it. The Order had some initial difficulties: there was disagreement over which properties it owned, and the first Master, Brother Guillem de Eril, fell ill and died a few months after his election. However, the Order survived and went on to perform loyal service for the king. It was involved in the conquest of Sardinia; it supported the king during civil wars. The Order of Christ in Portugal, set up by King Dinis in 1319, performed the same sorts of roles (plate 30). It was also involved in the exploration and missionary activities of Portuguese princes and explorers from the fifteenth century. Prince Henry 'the Navigator' became administrator of the Order in 1420 and used the Order and its revenues in his exploration and colonization policies, which he depicted as crusading and missionary operations. In 1455 Pope Nicholas V (1447–55) granted it power, dominion and spiritual jurisdiction over all overseas lands from Cape Bojador, all through Guinea and the southern coast of Africa to the Indies: the East Indies were meant, but this would later be interpreted as the West

Indies. The explorer Vasco da Gama was a member of the Order of Christ.[73]

The Order of the Temple was not destroyed because it had outlived its purpose, because it was corrupt, or because it was in decline. The loss of Acre in 1291 had been a heavy blow, but the Templars were rebuilding and realigning their Order. Like the Hospitallers, they were beginning to develop naval operations, while Jacques de Molay was busy campaigning for a new crusade, which was why he was in France in 1307. Jacques was convinced that only a large military expedition led by the kings and high nobility of Europe had any chance of making significant military gains in the East, and he would settle for nothing less. By supporting the overthrow of King Henry II of Cyprus in 1306 the Order also had a ruler in Cyprus (Amaury de Lusignan) who would support it, and a strategically placed island to use as a base. As ever, the Order put its trust in kings and princes. If these had supported it as Jacques de Molay hoped, the Order could have survived and continued its military activity in the East, as the Hospital of St John did. But in the West these kings and princes were either unable to save it (as in England and Aragon) or decided that more could be gained by attacking the Order than by supporting it (in France); and in Cyprus, the murder of Amaury de Lusignan left the Order without a protector and open to the wrath of the returning King Henry II.

The Order's central convent on Cyprus was destroyed by King Henry in 1310 in retaliation for the Order's support for Amaury. The Order could not continue to operate without its chief officials. Trial or no trial, once Henry II of Cyprus had destroyed its centre of operations, the Order would have ceased to exist in the East whatever was happening in Europe. In a sense, the trial of the Templars was a sideshow. It was the Templars' involvement in the political affairs of Cyprus in the early fourteenth century that directly brought about the destruction of the Order.

The Hospital of St John, in contrast, struck out on its own. Fulk de Villaret, Grand Master of the Hospital, settled for a small campaign to capture Rhodes, where his Order could continue its existence away from the political upheavals of Cyprus. He convinced Pope Clement V to give his Order the Templars' lands, and he managed to survive the Council of Vienne's attempts to reform his Order. Fulk's schemes were less ambitious, but they relied less on the help of kings and princes, of great political powers who had their own agendas. The Templars had always been close to kings. It was the king of Jerusalem, Baldwin II, who had given the first 'poor knights of Christ of Jerusalem' his palace and made them the knights of the Temple. It was also the kings of Christendom who brought about the Order's end.

9

CONCLUSION:
THE TEMPLAR MYTH

The impact of the trial of the Templars varied from area to area. In the Mark of Brandenburg, where no Templars were arrested, people would not have noticed any changes. In areas where the Templars were arrested, lands were taken into royal custody and pensioners and other creditors went unpaid, outsiders would certainly have noticed the upheaval. Some Templars were unaccounted for: in Germany and eastern Europe many were not arrested, and their later history is unknown. Some of their lands passed to the Hospital of St John; some did not. In France, any Templar who escaped custody was hunted down and imprisoned; in England, the sheriff of York was in no hurry to lock up the Templars.[1] As it was regarded as dishonourable for a knight to run away, most Templars did not try to flee. Yet Brother Bernard des Fons fled to Tunis and became ambassador for the Muslim ruler of Tunis; there may have been others who acted similarly.[2]

Some Templars remained in Muslim prisons in the East, captured either during the final fall of Acre or on Arwad. The German priest Ludolf of Sudheim met two such ex-Templar prisoners during his pilgrimage to the East in around 1340.[3] Others lived on in religious houses in the West, supported by a daily pension.[4] A few took up new career opportunities, such as the would-be Templar necromancer mentioned in the previous chapter. All in all, the end of the Order of the Temple was rather untidy.

Contemporary views of the downfall of the Order varied according to their geographical location: those within lands controlled by the king of France or his relatives or in their service supported the trial; others condemned it.[5] Opinions did not soften with time, and late in the fourteenth century the St Alban's chronicler Thomas of Walsingham was still condemning the trial.[6] Templar properties continued to be called 'the Temple' long after they had passed to the Hospital of St John.[7] The Flemish continued to refer to the Templars as 'white Templars' and the Hospitallers as 'Black Templars', on the basis of their knights' mantles.[8] Writers of fictional literature were confused as to the relationship between the two orders: Joanot Martorell, writing his great novel *Tirant lo Blanc* in the 1460s, stated that the Hospital of St John was founded after the Order of the Temple had been destroyed by the Muslims, and that the Hospital had rebuilt the Temple of Solomon on Rhodes.[9]

The Templars continued to appear in fictional literature throughout the Middle Ages, although usually in peaceful roles rather than fighting the Muslims; perhaps because audiences were not absolutely sure what the Templars' role in the Holy Land had been. They continued to appear as defenders of the Grail Castle in German works written in the tradition of Wolfram von Eschenbach's *Parzival*, but not in other Grail romances.[10] Their image in fictional literature was almost invariably good; they were holy men, dedicated to God's service.

There were obvious moral lessons to draw from the downfall of the Templars: fortune rules all in this world, how quickly the great can fall from favour, how the poor knights of Christ became rich and proud and so they met their downfall. Commentators were not slow to make such points. In fact, it is only human nature to try to come up with some reasonable explanation for the Templars' sudden and unexpected downfall at a time when they were still an active and pious religious Order. Historians from the Middle Ages to the present day have developed a 'model' of the rise and fall of the Templars: the pure ideals of the first knights became contaminated as the Order grew rich and involved in politics; the Order became corrupt and greedy and increasingly unpopular, and meanwhile the West lost interest in the Crusades; so when Philip IV of France attacked the Order for its money, no one defended it and the Order fell. Because this provides an attractively simple explanation for the otherwise unjust and inexplicable fall of the Order, this 'model' has gained wide acceptance, despite the fact that it is false.

The modern image of the Templars as magicians with secret esoteric knowledge of the divine is rather different from the devout but uneducated warriors who have been the subject of this book. Scholars such as Malcolm Barber, Peter Partner and John Walker have traced the development of this 'post-Templar history' in depth, while others such as Sharan Newman and Evelyn Lord have produced accessible surveys of the modern myths for non-experts.[11] Their researches indicate that there were no accusations of magic against the Templars until the work of Henry Cornelius Agrippa in the sixteenth century, which mentioned the Templars in passing as a group destroyed after being accused of witchcraft.[12] Scholars in general ignored such views. For example, Thomas Fuller, in his *Historie of the Holy Warre* (1639), made no reference to magic in his account of the Templars' trial, concluding: 'They are conceived in generall to be guiltlesse and innocent from those damnable sinnes wherewith they were charged,' and 'the chief cause of their ruine was their extraordinary wealth.'[13] It was not until the mid-eighteenth century, with the rise of secret societies such as the Freemasons, that the Templars came to the attention of the educated, upper middle-class layman as an example of a secret society that had been destroyed because of its esoteric knowledge. Initially the Freemasons claimed no link with the Templars: it was the German Masons who in the 1760s introduced the idea that the Templars must have had secret wisdom and magical powers, which they had learned while they held the so-called Temple of Solomon in Jerusalem. This wisdom and power, they claimed, had been handed on down a secret line of succession to the present-day Masons.[14]

Such 'medieval mystery' fitted well with the growing Romantic movement of the period.[15] Short-lived 'Templar' orders were set up in France and England.[16] Writers of fiction developed the concept of the Templars as an institution with secret purposes. The most famous of these was Walter Scott (1771–1832), whose negative depictions of Templars in *Ivanhoe* (1819) and *The Talisman* (1825) are still influential. Scott used the modern myth of the Templars as a secret society combined with the traditional 'model' of the gradual corruption of the Templars to create threatening yet fascinating villains. The negative image of the Templars in *The Talisman*, which is set during the Third Crusade, reappears in modern films based on this crusade, most recently *Kingdom of Heaven* (2005). Another sinister depiction appeared in George Macdonald's gothic novel *Phantastes* (1858), where the hero, transferred to 'fairyland', comes across a mysteriously rectangular woodland clearing, walled with yew trees, in which stand 'three ranks of men, in white robes, standing silent and solemn, each with a sword by his side, although the rest of his costume and bearing was more priestly than soldierly'. The author calls this area a 'temple'. At one end is a platform, on which is a throne on which a 'majestic-looking figure' sits, which turns out to be a wooden idol. A youth and a girl are led up to the platform and sent through a door; we assume that they are going to some happy mystery, but then discover that they have been killed. The hero destroys the idol, which turns out to contain a huge beast that devoured the young people offered to it; the hero kills the beast, but is himself killed by the sword-wielding white-clad priests. The word 'Templar' is never mentioned, but the parallels with the Templars and the charges against them are clear: white-clad knights who are also religious, operating in a temple, worshipping an idol which destroys its young initiates.[17]

The evil atmosphere around these 'Templars' was echoed half a century later in M. J. James's short story 'Oh Whistle, and I'll Come to You, My Lad' (1904), where a bronze whistle found in the ruins of one of the Templars' circular chapels summons a ghostly creature which tries to destroy the whistler. The original purpose of such a whistle remains unclear, but the reader is left with the impression that the Templars were a dubious organization: 'you never knew what they might not have been up to'.[18]

For James, as for Scott and Macdonald, the primary purpose of his writing was to entertain. However, some writers of the eighteenth and nineteenth centuries developed the myth of the Templars as a sinister secret society for political or religious reasons, even fabricating physical evidence in order to 'prove' their arguments. Such writers were following the example of those who had contrived the original charges against the Templars: projecting their own fantasies and obsessions on to their victims. For example, in 1796 Charles Louis Cadet de Cassicour portrayed the Templars as part of a secret conspiracy which was behind the French Revolution and the execution of King Louis XVI, in revenge for the death of Jacques de Molay in 1314.[19] In 1818 Joseph von Hammer Purgstall published a book entitled *The Mystery of Baphomet Revealed* that linked the Templars to the Gnostics, a religious movement of the early Christian era, condemned by pagans and Christians alike for their alleged sexual depravity. Hammer argued that the Templars were Gnostics and the 'Templars' head' was a Gnostic idol called Baphomet. In fact 'Baphomet' is simply the Old French word for the name Mohammad and the Gnostics did not have idols, because they did not worship anything with a physical form. They believed that the physical world is an invention of evil, while God is incorporeal and belongs to the realm of light, beyond the spheres of physical existence. Gnostic religion was a long way from the beliefs of the Templars, who were orthodox Catholics. Peter Partner has concluded that Hammer attacked the 'Templar masons' in order to discredit the Freemasons.[20]

Hammer's vein of pseudo-history won a large following and underlies the modern mythical Templars. He also linked his mythical Templars to the legend of the Holy Grail, arguing that the Grail legend itself represented Gnostic mysteries. The fact that Wolfram von Eschenbach put 'Templars' into his Grail story encouraged Hammer and his successors to believe that the Templars (whom they did not understand) must be deeply connected with the Grail legend (which they did not understand either). The Templars appear by name only in Wolfram's version of the story and its sequels, but their absence elsewhere only encouraged scholars to search for hidden Templar influence in all the Grail romances.[21]

Yet the medieval stories of the Holy Grail have no direct connection with the Templars. Like the Order of the Temple, such stories catered for knights, being written for knights and sometimes by knights; and like the Order, they set out the way in which knights could reach God. However, unlike the Order of the Temple, the Grail stories depicted knights finding God by themselves, through their own personal quest, with little help from priests or the institution of the Church. In contrast, Templars had to commit themselves to a religious Order and vow to obey a superior without question, live without sexual intercourse and without personal wealth, and very probably die in action against the Muslims. The Grail stories allowed knights to find God without having to sacrifice their independence of action, obey anyone or give up their wealth. In addition, Muslims could also find the Holy Grail; they had to convert to Christianity before they could see it, but they could be much more successful in the search for the Grail than many Christians. This did not fit the Templars' ideal of fighting and killing Muslims as enemies of Christ.

Since the latter part of the nineteenth century, the supposed Templar involvement in the Grail legends has reinforced the supposed Templar connection with secret societies and esoteric knowledge.[22] However, this 'Templar myth' did not enter mainstream culture until 1983, with the publication of *The Holy Blood and the Holy Grail*, by Michael Baigent, Richard Leigh and Henry Lincoln. This bestselling book stimulated wide interest in the Templars. Many 'discoveries' about the Templars have followed, many of which are little more than fantasy, with less basis in actual historical events than most historical novels.[23]

Yet the Templars have not always had a negative or occult image in modern times. In the mid-nineteenth-century United States several temperance fraternities took the title 'Good Templars'. They named themselves after the medieval Knights Templar partly because of the play on words between 'temperance' and 'Templar', perhaps partly because of a myth that the original Templars drank sour milk, and also because they were fighting 'a great crusade' against 'this terrible vice' of alcohol.[24] In 1851, in Utica, New York State, an 'Independent Order of Good Templars' was set up, which grew to become a world-wide organization, the International Order of Good Templars or IOGT. Urging absolute abstinence from alcohol, the Order also campaigned for prohibition, strove to provide social facilities that served only non-alcoholic beverages, promoted education and self-help, and supported decent working conditions for working people. It had its own youth organization and produced its own newspapers and books. Its institutions included fine regalia, impressive titles, secret passwords and ceremonies that 'cannot be divulged to the uninitiated'. The majority of its members were drawn from the skilled working and lower middle classes.[25]

Unlike the original medieval Order of the Temple, women were admitted as members from early in the Good Templars' history, and played a significant role in the organization. Women rarely held the highest offices in the Order, but often held the offices of Vice Templar and superintendent of Juvenile Templars – the support roles that were socially acceptable for women. Even these restricted roles allowed the women who held them more freedom than was then usual in western society – Jessie Forsyth, a leading campaigner within the Good Templars from 1872 to 1937, relished her opportunities to travel and meet people in the United States, Europe and Australia.[26] The Good Templars were less successful in promoting racial equality within the Order, leading to a temporary schism in 1876: the British Good Templars broke away in protest at the refusal of the Good Templars of the southern Unites States to allow racially mixed lodges.[27]

At the beginning of the twenty-first century, the IOGT is still active around the globe, campaigning against the use of alcohol and other drugs, equality for all, peace, justice and education.[28] It remains an example of a modern 'Templar' organization not associated with the occult or esoteric knowledge. Another Templar group with a positive message, also founded in around 1850, was the German Templar movement, set up by a Lutheran pastor and dedicated to 'the spiritual and economic development of the Holy Land'. The society was so named because 'each member of the Society was to be a "stone" in the spiritual Temple of Jerusalem'. The society was intended to show that 'a reasonable economic standard could be attained by adherence to religious principles in religious life'.[29]

The German Templars founded a number of communities in Palestine, which was then under Ottoman rule, and lived peacefully and prosperously until the First World War, when Britain first occupied Palestine. Some of the German Templars emigrated to Australia, but the Palestinian settlements of

Sarona, Waldheim and Wilhelma survived until the British mandate in Palestine ended after the Second World War. In 1947 the British High Commissioner of Palestine, having decided that the German Templars' property did not constitute 'enemy property' – as the organization had had no relations with the Nazis – was anxious to arrange its sale and allow the remaining German Templars to join their co-religionists in Australia. The German Templars were in danger from zealots in Palestine – two had been killed when one of their settlements was attacked – and the Australian government was willing to allow them entry to Australia if they could finance themselves. Some of the property was sold in spring 1948, but the new state of Israel refused to release the proceeds. Eventually the German Templars successfully emigrated to Australia and the United States, but the dispute over who owed them what dragged on for many years, not being resolved until the 1960s.[30] The modern 'Temple Society' in Australia does not now claim any link with the medieval Knights Templar, and uses the spelling 'Templer' to refer to its members.[31]

Some Templar appearances in literature since the mid-nineteenth century have mirrored these positive images of the Order. Edgar Wallace (1875–1932), thriller-writer supreme, was a member of a temperance society in his youth and made the occasional reference to the 'Good Templars' in his works. In *Angel Esquire* (1908) we meet an inspector of police who is a past Chief Templar; *The Hand of Power* (1927) refers to them alongside other fraternities: 'these societies . . . Good Templars and Buffaloes and Sons of the Phoenix, and knights of the Round Table'; while *White Face* (1930) features a conscientious, if unimaginative, policeman who is a member of the local 'Good Templar' lodge and dreams of becoming Chief Templar.[32] We are left with the impression that the Good Templars are a worthy part of modern society.

Jerome K. Jerome, in his *Three Men in a Boat, to say Nothing of the Dog* (1889), mentioned the Templars only in passing in his description of Bisham Abbey, 'whose stone walls have rung to the shouts of the Knights Templars', before going on to describe a ghost story of the seventeenth century.[33] For Jerome, the Templars were not associated with ghosts but were a positive part of England's past. The image of the Templars is darker in John Meade Falkner's *The Nebuly Coat* (1903), in which the heir to the Blandamer estates makes a vow 'as faithfully as ever taken by a Templar' to serve his family interests.[34] In the event, he murders twice and sacrifices his own life in this cause. The central image of the story is of a great church undergoing restoration, which has stood firm for so many centuries but is no longer able to carry the burden of its own weight: a literal case of decline and fall.

Perhaps the most poignant of these depictions of the Templars as a positive and integral part of England's past appears in Rudyard Kipling's story 'They' (1904), which describes enduring love and the pain of loss.[35] The narrator, returning to southern England from the United States, becomes lost as he drives through the rolling hills of the Downs. He passes a Norman church, a Roman road, 'an old smithy that cries aloud how it had once been a hall of the Knights Templar' and finally comes to a Tudor hall, where dwell a blind, childless woman, and the ghosts of children. Our narrator realizes the truth of the place when the ghost of his own dead child kisses his hand. Here the Templars form part of the enduring network of the past which is for ever lost to us but in which our lives are based and from which they draw meaning. The ghosts are affectionate and loving, far from the menacing spirit of M. R. James's 'Oh, Whistle'.

A positive image of the Templars is also echoed in Leslie Charteris's adventure stories of Simon Templar, 'The Saint', a sort of proto-James Bond figure who works outside the law against international criminal conspiracies, and protects the innocent and vulnerable. Although the connection with the medieval Templars is seldom made explicit, Charteris explicitly draws a parallel with the (supposed) ideals of medieval chivalry. In the first story, *Knight Templar* (1930), the hero is described as living in 'a world of flamboyant colours and magnificently medieval delights', and compared to a series of medieval heroes: 'It was Gawain before the Grail, it was Bayard on the bridge of Garigliano, it was Roland at the gates of Spain.'[36] In *The Saint Overboard* (1936), he is 'the perfect gentle knight, dying to save a lady's honour'.[37] In *Vendetta for the Saint* (1964), the hero's connection with the Templars is articulated in a discussion about the origins of the Mafia:

> 'Right up to the unification of Italy, the Mafia were usually on the side of the oppressed. Only after that it turned to extortion and murder.'
>
> 'I seem to have heard that something like that happened to the original Knights Templar,' said the Saint reflectively. 'But aside from that, I don't see why you should connect them with me.'[38]

Later, in discussion with the Sicilian heroine of the story, the Saint describes the Knights Templar as 'a dubiously noble band not unknown in these parts' and claims a connection with them.[39] As he adds that he cannot prove that he is actually descended from them, the connection must be that he is on the side of the oppressed, although readers of *The Saint* will know that he is also sometimes involved in extortion and murder – of criminals. Charteris's swashbuckling hero was far from the austere, hard-working Good Templars and German Templars of the mid-nineteenth century, but nevertheless played a positive – if underground – role in society.

The Templars of fiction have taken many forms over the past two hundred years, from sinister villains to chivalrous defenders of the oppressed. Today, several modern institutions exist which carry the name 'Templar'. Some of these new 'Orders of the Temple' carry out charitable work, like the 'Good Templars' of the temperance movement; others have a religious aspect and offer their members spiritual insights. Still others are a cover for criminal activities. These new 'Templar'

Orders are themselves now the subject of scholarly study. It is a strange tribute to the enduring appeal of this ordinary religious order – in existence for less than two centuries, and last seen nearly seven hundred years ago – that not only the original Order but also the myth of the Order and the 'false' modern Orders that bear its name have become part of serious history.

NOTES

Notes to the Introduction

1. Jonathan Riley-Smith, *Hospitallers: the History of the Order of St. John* (London and Rio Grande, OH: Hambledon Press, 1999), p. 54.
2. Anne Gilmour-Bryson, *The Trial of the Templars in the Papal State and in the Abruzzi* (Vatican City: Biblioteca Apostolica Vaticana, 1982), pp. 38, 142, 184; *International Mobility in the Military Orders (Twelfth to Fifteenth Centuries): Travelling on Christ's Business*, ed. Jochen Burgtorf and Helen Nicholson (Cardiff: University of Wales Press, 2006), p. 203.
3. Helen Nicholson, *The Knights Hospitaller* (Woodbridge: Boydell, 2001), pp. 46–53, esp. p. 52; Norman Housley, *The Later Crusades, 1274–1580: From Lyons to Alcazar* (Oxford: Oxford University Press, 1992), p. 221.
4. Matthew Paris, *Chronica majora*, ed. H. R. Luard, RS 57, 7 vols (London: Longman, 1872–83), vol. 3, p. 177.
5. For a fuller discussion of medieval use of torture and modern studies on its effects, see Helen Nicholson, *The Knights Templar on Trial* (Stroud: The History Press, 2009), ch. 1.
6. *Le Procès des Templiers d'Auvergne, 1309–1311: Edition de l'interrogatoire de juin 1309*, ed. Roger Sève and Anne-Marie Chagny-Sève (Paris: Éditions de C.T.H.S., 1986), pp. 54–5.
7. On this see Malcolm Barber, *The Trial of the Templars*, 2nd edn (Cambridge: Cambridge University Press, 2006), pp. 217–58

(evidence from outside France), pp. 294–311 (modern scholars); Peter Partner, *The Murdered Magicians: The Templars and Their Myth* (Oxford: Oxford University Press, 1981), pp. 153–5: rev. edn, *The Knights Templar and their Myth* (Rochester, VT: Destiny Books, 1990), pp. 80–1; Alan Forey, *The Military Orders From the Twelfth to the Early Fourteenth Centuries* (Basingstoke: Macmillan, 1992), pp. 231–33.

8. Anne Gilmour-Bryson, 'The London Templar Trial Testimony: "Truth", Myth or Fable?' in *A World Explored: Essays in Honour of Laurie Gardiner*, ed. Anne Gilmour-Bryson (Parkville, Victoria: University of Melbourne History Dept., 1993), pp. 44–61; Nicholson, *Knights Templar on Trial*, ch. 4.

9. Recent publications include: *Excavations at a Templar Preceptory: South Witham, Lincolnshire 1965–67*, ed. Philip Mayes (Leeds: Society for Medieval Archaeology, 2002); Christopher Gerrard, *Paisaje y señorío: la Casa Conventual de Ambel (Zaragoza): arqueología, arquitectura e historia de las Órdenes Militares del Temple y del Hospital* (Zaragoza: Institución Fernando el Católico, 2003); idem, 'Opposing Identity: Muslims, Christians and the Military Orders in Rural Aragon', *Medieval Archaeology*, 43 (1999), 143–60; Adrian J. Boas, *Archaeology of the Military Orders: A Survey of the Urban Centres, Rural Settlement and Castles of the Military Orders in the Latin East (c.1120–1291)* (London and New York: Routledge, 2006).

10. Ronald Decker, Thierry Depaulis and Michael Dummett, *A Wicked Pack of Cards: The Origin of the Occult Tarot* (London: Duckworth Press, 1996), p. ix. The 'occult tarot' did not appear until the eighteenth century, four hundred years after the demise of the Templars.

11. James Given, 'Chasing Phantoms: Philip IV and the Fantastic', in *Heresy and the Persecuting Society in the Middle Ages: Essays on the Work of R.I. Moore*, ed. Michael Frassetto (Leiden: Brill, 2006), pp. 271–89; and see the articles in *The Debate on the Trial of the Templars*, ed. Jochen Burgtorf, Paul Crawford and Helen J. Nicholson (Aldershot, Hants and Burlington, VT: Ashgate, forthcoming).

12. On this coup and its aftermath see Peter W. Edbury, *The Kingdom of Cyprus and the Crusades, 1191–1374* (Cambridge: Cambridge University Press, 1991), pp. 107–17, 121, note 76, 125–31.

13. Marie Luise Bulst-Thiele, *Sacrae domus militiae Templi*

Hierosolymitani magistri: Untersuchungen zur Geschichte des Templerordens 1118/9–1314 (Göttingen: Vandenhoeck & Ruprecht, 1974), p. 377.

14. Michael Schüpferling, *Der Tempelherren-orden in Deutschland. Dissertation zur Erlangung der Doktorwürde* (Bamberg: Dr J. Kirsch, 1915), 33–4, note 4; Anthony Luttrell and Helen J. Nicholson, 'Introduction' in *Hospitaller Women in the Middle Ages*, ed. A. Luttrell and H. J. Nicholson (Aldershot, Hants and Burlington, VT: Ashgate, 2006), p. 26.

15. *Papsttum und Untergang des Templerordens*, ed. Heinrich Finke, 2 vols (Münster: Aschendorff, 1907), vol. 2, pp. 226–7, no. 121.

16. *The Knights Hospitallers in England: Being the Report of Prior Philip de Thame to the General Master Elyan de Villanova for AD 1338*, ed. Lambert B. Larking and John M. Kemble, Camden Society first series no. 65 (1857), p. 129. On the modern myth that the Templars fled to Scotland see Evelyn Lord, *The Knights Templar in Britain* (London: Longman, 2002), p. 154; Sharan Newman, *The Real History Behind the Templars* (New York: Berkley Books, 2007), p. 394.

17. Bulst-Thiele, *Sacrae domus*; Alain Demurger, *Vie et mort de l'ordre du Temple, 1120–1314* (Paris: Seuil, 1985, 1989, 1993, etc.); Alain Demurger, *Les templiers: une chevalerie chre´tienne au moyen âge* (Paris: Seuil, 2005); Forey, *The Military Orders*; Malcolm Barber, *The New Knighthood: A History of the Order of the Temple* (Cambridge, Cambridge University Press, 1994).

Notes to Chapter 1: The Origins of the Order of the Temple

1. On the First Crusade and those who took part, see Jonathan Riley-Smith, *The First Crusade and the Idea of Crusading* (London: Athlone Press, 1986); idem, *The First Crusaders, 1095–1131* (Cambridge: Cambridge University Press, 1997); John France, *Victory in the East: A Military History of the First Crusade* (Cambridge: Cambridge University Press, 1994).

2. On the situation in the Middle East when the Christians arrived in the 1090s see Carole Hillenbrand, 'The First Crusade: the Muslim Perspective', in *The First Crusade: Origins and Impact*, ed. Jonathan Phillips (Manchester: Manchester University Press, 1997), pp. 130–42; Carole Hillenbrand, *The Crusades: Islamic Perspectives* (Edinburgh: Edinburgh University Press, 1998); Bernard Hamilton, *The Latin Church in the Crusader States: The Secular Church*

(London: Variorum, 1980), pp. 159–211.

3. The author has confirmed with her own eyes that it is still possible to glimpse the golden Dome of the Rock from the roof of the church at Montjoie. Good eyesight or spectacles are required.

4. Ivo, bishop of Chartres, 'Epistolae', no. 245 in *PL*, vol. 162, cols 251–3. On Hugh see Malcolm Barber, 'The Origins of the Order of the Temple', *Studia Monastica*, 12 (1970), 219–40; reprinted in his *Crusaders and Heretics, 12th–14th Centuries* (Aldershot: Variorum, 1995), article 1; Demurger, *Vie et mort de l'ordre du Temple*, pp. 22–7; Simonetta Cerrini, 'Le fondateur de l'ordre du Temple à ses frères: Hugues de Payns et le Sermo Christi militibus', in *Dei gesta per Francos: Études sur les croisades dédiées à Jean Richard – Crusade Studies in Honour of Jean Richard*, ed. Michel Balard, Benjamin Z. Kedar and Jonathan Riley-Smith (Aldershot: Ashgate, 2001), pp. 99–110.

5. On knightly confraternities see Alan Forey, 'The Emergence of the Military Order in the Twelfth Century', *Journal of Ecclesiastical History*, 36 (1985), 175–95: here 189; reprinted in his *Military Orders and Crusades* (Aldershot: Variorum, 1994), article 1. For one particular confraternity see Marcus Bull, 'The Confraternity of La Sauve-Majeure: a Foreshadowing of the Military Order?', in *MO*, 1, pp. 313–19. On specifically knightly piety, see Maurice Keen, *Chivalry* (New Haven and London: Yale University Press, 1984), pp. 51–63.

6. This was the conclusion of Rudolf Hiestand, 'Kardinalbischof Matthäus von Albano, das Konzil von Troyes und die Entstehung des Templerordens', *Zeitschrift für Kirchengeschichte*, 99 (1988), 295–325; agreed by Barber, *The New Knighthood*, pp. 9–10; Demurger, *Vie et mort de l'ordre du Temple*, p. 24.

7. For the French and Latin text of the Rule see *Règle*, here sections 7 and 8. A new edition is in preparation by Simonetta Cerrini. For a translation of the French text, see J. M. Upton-Ward, *The Rule of the Templars: The French Text of the Rule of the Order of the Temple* (Woodbridge: Boydell and Brewer, 1992).

8. Guillaume de Tyr, *Chronique*, ed. R. B. C. Huygens, Corpus Christianorum, Continuatio Mediaeualis, 63, 63A (Turnholt: Brepols, 1986), vol. 1, pp. 553–4, Bk 1, ch. 7.

9. Simon de St Bertin, 'Gesta abbatum Sancti Bertini Sithensium', ed. O. Holder-Egger, in *MGH SS*, vol. 13, p. 649.

10. *The Ecclesiastical History of Orderic Vitalis*, ed. and trans. Marjorie Chibnall, 6 vols (Oxford: Oxford University Press, 1969–80), vol. 6, pp. 308–10, Bk 12, ch. 29.

11. Bernard of Clairvaux, 'Liber ad milites Templi de laude novae militiae', in *Opera*, ed. Jean Leclercq and H. M. Rohais, 8 vols (Rome, Editiones Cistercienses, 1957–77), vol. 3, pp. 205–39. There is a translation: 'In Praise of the New Knighthood', trans. Conrad Greenia, in *The Works of Bernard of Clairvaux*, vol. 7: *Treatises III*, (Kalamazoo, MI: Cistercian Publications, 1977), pp. 127–67. See also Forey, 'Literacy and Learning', p. 195; *Procès*, vol. 1, p. 389; Simonetta Cerrini, 'A New Edition of the Latin and French Rule of the Temple', in *MO*, 2, pp. 207–15: here pp. 208–11.

12. Barber, *New Knighthood*, pp. 44–9; William J. Purkis, *Crusading Spirituality in the Holy Land and Iberia, c.1095–c.1187* (Woodbridge: Boydell and Brewer, 2008), pp. 101–11.

13. Otto of Freising, 'Chronicon', ed. R. Wilmans, *MGH SS*, vol. 20, pp. 252–3; Anselm, Bishop of Havelberg, 'Dialogi' or 'Anticimenon', written for Pope Eugenius III, in *PL*, vol. 188, col. 1156; 'Ex Ricardi Pictaviensis chronica', ed. G. Waitz, *MGH SS*, vol. 26, p. 80. On Anselm, see Lawrence F. Barmann, 'Reform Ideology in the *Dialogi* of Anselm of Havelberg', *Church History*, 30 (1961), 374–95; Pegatha Taylor, 'Moral Agency in Crusade and Colonization: Anselm of Havelberg and the Wendish Crusade', *International History Review*, 22 (2000), 757–84; Jay T. Lees, *Anselm of Havelberg: Deeds into Words in the Twelfth Century* (Leiden: Brill, 1998).

14. *Règle*, sections 5–6.

15. Cerrini, 'A New Edition', pp. 208–11; Eric Christiansen, *The Northern Crusades: The Baltic and the Catholic Frontier, 1100–1525* (Basingstoke: Macmillan, 1980), pp. 74–5; 2nd edn (London: Penguin, 1997), pp. 77, 78; Innocent III, 'Registers', in *PL*, vols 214–16, here vol. 216, cols 325–6, year 13, no. 141. The trial of the Templars in Cyprus is translated in *The Trial of the Templars in Cyprus: A Complete English Edition*, trans. Anne Gilmour-Bryson (Leiden: Brill, 1998), here p. 72.

16. Letter printed by Bulst-Thiele, *Sacrae domus*, pp. 360–2.

17. *Procès*, vol. 1, pp. 603, 613, 615, vol. 2, pp. 228, 232; Oxford, Bodleian Library, MS Bodley 454, fols 24v, 25v, 34r.

18. *Der Untergang des Templerordens mit urkundlichen und kritischen Beiträgen*, ed. Konrad Schottmüller, 2 vols (Berlin, 1887, repr. Vaduz,

Liechtenstein: Sändig Reprint, 1991), vol. 2, p. 67; MS Bodley 454, fol. 120r.

19. Bernard of Clairvaux, 'Epistolae', in *PL*, vol. 182, cols 493–4: letter 277. Translated in *The Letters of Bernard of Clairvaux*, ed. Bruno Scott James (Stroud: Sutton, 1998), letter 410.

20. Walter Map, *De nugis curialium*, ed. and trans. M. R. James, C. N. L. Brooke and R. A. B. Mynors (Oxford: Oxford University Press, 1983), p. 54.

21. *Chronique d'Ernoul et de Bernard le trésorier*, ed. L. de Mas Latrie, SHF (Paris: J. Renouard, 1871), pp. 7–8.

22. For this, see Anthony Luttrell, 'The Earliest Templars', in *Autour de la première croisade. Actes du colloque de la Society for the Study of the Crusades and the Latin East: Clermont-Ferrand, 22–25 juin 1995*, ed. Michel Balard (Paris: Publications de la Sorbonne, 1996), pp. 193–202. On the Hospitallers, see Jonathan Riley-Smith, *The Knights of St John in Jerusalem and Cyprus: c.1050–1310* (London: Macmillan, 1967). See also Cristina Dondi, *The Liturgy of the Canons Regular of the Holy Sepulchre of Jerusalem: A Study and a Catalogue of the Manuscript Sources* (Turnhout: Brepols, 2004).

23. For the dates and the success of their mission see Barber, *New Knighthood*, pp. 12–14.

24. *CT*, no. 31.

25. Georges Duby, *The Three Orders: Feudal Society Imagined*, trans. Arthur Goldhammer, foreword by Thomas N. Bisson (Chicago: University of Chicago Press, 1980).

26. *Règle*, section 2.

27. *CT*, no. 4.

28. Barber, 'The Origins of the Order of the Temple', 227.

29. *Papsturkunden für Templer und Johanniter, Archivberichte und Texte*, ed. Rudolf Hiestand, Abhandungen der Akademie der Wissenschaften in Göttingen, phil.-hist. Klasse, dritte Folge, no. 77 (Göttingen: Vandenhoeck and Ruprecht, 1972), no. 3.

30. *Lettres des Premiers Chartreux*, 1: *S. Bruno, Guigues, S. Anthelme*, ed. 'A Carthusian', Sources Chrétiennes, 88 (Paris: Cerf, 1962), no. 2, pp. 154–61.

31. Letter composed by Nicholas de Clairvaux for Brother Gauchier to a certain Knight of the Temple on spiritual friendship, in Nicholas de Clairvaux, 'Epistolae', *PL*, vol. 196, cols 1616–17.

32. *The Letters of Peter the Venerable*, ed. Giles Constable, 2 vols

(Cambridge, MA: Harvard University Press, 1967), vol. 1, pp. 407–9: no. 172. Here p. 407.

33. *Letters of Peter the Venerable*, vol. 1, pp. 410–13: no. 173. Here p. 411.

34. Isaac de Stella, 'Sermones', no. 48: *PL*, vol. 194, cols 1853–56A: here 1854 BC. For a new translation, see Dániel Deme, *The Selected Works of Isaac of Stella: A Cistercian Voice from the Twelfth Century* (Aldershot and Burlington, VT: Ashgate, 2007), p. 133. On Isaac see also Benjamin Z. Kedar, *Crusade and Mission: European Approaches Toward the Muslims* (Princeton: Princeton University Press, 1984), pp. 104–6.

35. John of Salisbury, *Policraticus*, ed. C. C. I. Webb (Oxford: Clarendon Press, 1909), vol. 2, pp. 193, lines 4–5, Bk 7, ch. 21.

36. Walter Map, *De nugis*, pp. 59–67.

37. *Augustine: Political Writings*, trans. Michael W. Tkacz and Douglas Kries, intro. E. L. Fortin (Indianapolis: Hackett, 1994), pp. 219–220, 221–9.

38. Jean Flori, *Idéologie du Glaive: Préhistoire de la chevalerie* (Geneva: Droz, 1983); John Gilchrist, 'The Papacy and War against "the Saracens"', in *International History Review*, 10 (1988), 174–97; Ian Robinson, 'Gregory VII and the Soldiers of Christ', *History*, 58 (1973), 169–92.

39. Cerrini, 'Le fondateur de l'ordre du Temple à ses frères'; Dominic Selwood, '*Quid autem dubitaverunt*: the Saint, the Sinner, the Temple and a Possible Chronology', in *Autour de la première croisade*, ed. Balard, pp. 221–30. For the text, see: Jean Leclercq, 'Un document sur les débuts des Templiers', *Revue de l'histoire ecclesiastique*, 52 (1957), 86–9; Ch. Schlafert, 'Lettre inédite de Hugues de Saint-Victor aux Chevaliers du Temple', *Revue d'ascetique et de mystique*, 34 (1958), 275–99.

40. *La Chanson de Roland*, ed. F. Whitehead (Oxford: Blackwell, 1942), lines 1877–82.

41. *Les deux rédactions en vers du moniage Guillaume, chansons de geste du XIIe siècle*, ed. W. Cloetta, vol. 1, SATF (Paris: Firmin Didot, 1906), laisses 9, 14.

42. Matthew Paris, *Historia Anglorum, sive… Historia minor, item… Abbreviatio chronicorum Angliae*, ed. Frederic Madden, RS 44, 3 vols (London: Longman, 1866–69), vol. 1, p. 223.

Notes to Chapter 2: The Latin East

1. Jacquemart Giélée, *Renart le nouvel*, ed. H. Roussel, SATF (Paris: A. & J. Picard, 1961), lines 7555–79.

2. *Chronique d'Ernoul*, p. 161 (1187); *Die Register Innocenz' III*, ed. Othmar Hageneder and Anton Haidacher, 2 vols in 4 (Graz and Cologne: Verlag der Österreichischen Akademie der Wissenschaften, 1964–68; Rome and Vienna: Verlag der Österreichischen Akademie der Wissenschaften, 1979–83), vol. 3, no. 247 (1199); Innocent III, 'Registers', *PL*, vol. 216 col. 56, year 12, no. 45 (1209); 'Annals of Burton' in *Annales monastici*, ed. H. R. Luard, RS 36 (5 vols, London, Longman, 1864–69), vol. 1, p. 494 (1260); Ch. Kohler and Ch. V. Langlois, 'Lettres inédits concernant les croisades (1275–1307)', *Bibliothèque de l'école des chartes*, 52 (1891), 45–63, no. I.

3. For this, see my *Love, War and the Grail: Templars, Hospitallers and Teutonic Knights in Medieval Epic and Romance, 1150–1500* (Leiden: Brill, 2001), pp. 105–47.

4. Alan Forey, 'The Militarisation of the Hospital of St John', *Studia Monastica*, 26 (1984), 75–89; repr. in his *Military Orders and Crusades* (Aldershot: Ashgate, 1994), ix; Rudolf Hiestand, 'Die Anfänge der Johanniter', *Die geistlichen Ritterordern Europas*, ed. Josef Fleckenstein and Manfred Hellmann, Vorträge und Forschungen 26 (Sigmaringen: Jan Thorbecke Verlag, 1980), pp. 31–80; Luis García Guijarro Ramos, 'La militarización de la Orden del Hospital: líneas para un debate,' in *Ordens Militares: Guerra, Religião, Podar et Cultura – Actas do III Encontra sobre Ordens Militares*, 2 (Lisbon: Edições Colibri, 1999), pp. 293–302; WT, vol. 2, p. 661; Bk 14, ch. 22.

5. See Forey, *The Military Orders*, pp. 19–23.

6. Ibid., pp. 68–9, 79. For the Military Orders' military activities in the East see also Alan Demurger, 'Templiers et Hospitaliers dans les combats de Terre Sainte', in *Le combatant au moyen âge*, Société des Historiens Médiévistes de l'Enseignement Supérieur Public (Paris: SHMES, 1991), pp. 77–96.

7. 'Imād al-Dīn al-Isfahānī, *Conquête de la Syrie et de la Palestine par Saladin (al-Fath al-qussî fî l-fath al-qudsî)*, trans. Henri Massé (Paris: Paul Geuthner, 1972), pp. 30, 36, 41, 141–2.

8. A. W. Lawrence, 'The Castle of Baghras', pp. 34–84, and J. S. C. Riley-Smith, 'The Templars and the Teutonic Knights in Cilician Armenia', pp. 92–117, in *The Cilician Kingdom of Armenia*, ed. T. S. R. Boase (Edinburgh: Scottish Academic Press, 1978).

9. Denys Pringle, 'Templar Castles Between Jaffa and Jerusalem', *MO*, 2, pp. 89–109: here pp. 94–5.

10. WT, vol. 2, pp. 775–6, Bk 17, ch. 12; 2, pp. 659–61, Bk 14, ch. 22; 2, pp. 706–9, Bk 15, chs 24–5.

11. Jonathan Riley-Smith, 'The Templars and the Castle of Tortosa in Syria: An Unknown Document Concerning the Acquisition of the Fortress', *English Historical Review*, 84 (1969), 278–88.

12. On Safed, see Hugh Kennedy, *Crusader Castles* (Cambridge: Cambridge University Press, 1994), pp. 128–9; Denys Pringle, 'Reconstructing the Castle of Safad', *Palestine Exploration Quarterly*, 117 (1985), 139–48; Peter Jackson, 'The Crusades of 1239–41 and their Aftermath', *Bulletin of the School of Oriental and African Studies*, 50 (1987), 32–60: here 42; for the 'De constructione' see R. B. C. Huygens, 'Un nouveau texte du traité "De constructione castri Saphet"', *Studi Medievali*, 4.1 (1965), 355–87; Kennedy, *Crusader Castles*, pp. 190–8. On Baibars see Peter Thorau, *The Lion of Egypt: Sultan Baybars I*, trans. Peter M. Holt (London and New York: Longman, 1992).

13. The situation is set out by Hans Eberhard Mayer, *The Crusades*, trans. John Gillingham, 2nd edn (Oxford: Oxford University Press, 1988), pp. 278–9.

14. WT, vol. 2, pp. 996–8, 1000–1003; Bk 21, chs 25 (26), 27 (28)–29 (30); *Chronique d'Ernoul*, pp. 51–4.

15. Oliver the schoolmaster of Cologne, 'Letters', in *Die Schriften des Kölner Domscholasters, späteren Bischofs von Paderborn und Kardinelbischofs von S. Sabina, Oliverus,* ed. H. Hoogeweg, BLVS 202 (Tübingen: Litterar. Verein, 1894), pp. 290–1, 'Historia Damiatina', in ibid., p. 207; 'Annales Coloniensies maximi', ed. Karl Pertz, *MGH SS*, vol. 17, p. 832; Roger of Wendover, *Flores historiarum*, ed. Henry G. Hewlett, RS 84, 3 vols (London: Longman, 1886–89), vol. 2, pp. 206–7; *Lettres de Jacques de Vitry (1160/1170–1240), éveque de Saint-Jean d'Acre*, ed. R. B. C. Huygens (Leiden: Brill, 1960), no. 3, p. 99; Jacques de Vitry, *Lettres de la cinquième croisade* (Turnhout: Brepols, 1998), p. 82, no. 3, lines 47–53; Kennedy, *Crusader Castles*, pp. 124–5.

16. Arguing that the military orders developed the concentric castle plan to meet their military and religious needs: Joan Fuguet Sans, 'Els Castells Tempers de Gardeny i Miravet i el seu paper innovador en la Poliorcètica i l'Arquitectura Catalanes del Segle XII', *Acta historica et*

archælogica mediævalia, 13 (1992), 353–74; idem, 'L'architecture militaire des commanderies templières de la couronne d'Aragon', in *La commanderie: institution des ordres militaires dans l'Occident mé diéval*, ed. Anthony Luttrell and Léon Pressouyre (Paris: Comité des travaux historiques et scientifiques, 2002), pp. 187–217, here p. 216; discussion and dismissal of the theory: Boas, *Archaeology of the Military Orders*, p. 279; Richard P. Harper and Denys Pringle, *Belmont Castle: the Excavation of a Crusader Stronghold in the Kingdom of Jerusalem* (Oxford: Oxford University Press, 2000), pp. 213, 215; arguing that the concentric design developed in response to Muslim siege techniques: Ronnie Ellenblum, 'Frankish and Muslim Siege Warfare and the Construction of Frankish Concentric Castles', in *Dei Gesta Per Francos, études sur les croisades dédiées à Jean Richard; Crusade Studies in Honour of Jean Richard*, ed. Michel Balard, Benjamin Z. Kedar and Jonathan Riley-Smith (Aldershot: Ashgate, 2001), pp. 187–98.

17. Forey, *The Military Orders*, p. 69.

18. *Chronique d'Ernoul*, p. 149; *La continuation de Guillaume de Tyr (1184–97)*, ed. M. R. Morgan (Paris: Paul Geuthner, 1982), pp. 40–1, section 27: this is translated in Peter Edbury, *The Conquest of Jerusalem and the Third Crusade: Sources in Translation* (Aldershot: Scolar, 1986). For the Spring of the Cresson see Denys Pringle, 'The Spring of the Cresson in Crusading History', in *Dei gesta per Francos*, ed. Balard *et al.*, pp. 231–40.

19. 'Imād al-Dīn, pp. 142–4.

20. WT, vol. 2, p. 879, Bk 19, ch. 11; Joseph Delaville le Roulx, 'Un nouveau manuscrit de la règle du Temple', *Annuaire-Bulletin de la Société de l'Histoire de France*, 26 (1889), 185–214, here 209–11; J. M. Upton-Ward, 'The Surrender of Gaston and the Rule of the Templars', in *MO*, 1, pp. 179–88.

21. 'Continuatio Praemonstratensis', ed. D.L. Bethmann, *MGH SS*, vol. 6, pp. 455–6; Guy of Bazoches, 'Cronosgraphia', Bibliothèque nationale, Paris, MS lat. 4998, fol. 63r. I am indebted to Professor Benjamin Kedar for supplying me with a copy of Guy's manuscript. Guy's account is also quoted by Aubrey des Trois Fontaines, ed. P. Scheffer-Boichorst, *MGH SS*, vol. 23, p. 846; see also Baldwin of Ninove, 'Chronicon', ed. O. Holder-Egger, *MGH SS*, vol. 25, p. 534. For the Muslim sources see: Isma'īl Abu'l-Fidā, *al-Mukhtasar fī akhbār al-bashar*, in 'Resumé de l'histoire des Croisades tiré des

annales d'Abu'l-Feda', *RHC Or*, vol. 1, pp. 30–1; Ibn al-Athir, in 'Extrait du Kamel-Altevarykh', *RHC Or*, vol. 1, p. 495; *An Arab-Syrian Gentleman and Warrior in the Period of the Crusades: Memoirs of Usāmah ibn Munqidh*, trans Philip K. Hitti (New York, 1929; repr. Princeton: Princeton University Press, 1987), pp. 44–54.

22. WT, vol. 2, pp. 822–3, Bk 18, ch. 9; Walter Map, *De nugis*, pp. 62–6.

23. Pope Hadrian IV, 'Lettres', *RHGF*, vol. 15, p. 682.

24. WT, vol. 2, pp. 682–4, Bk 15, ch. 6; Barber, *New Knighthood*, p. 35.

25. Matthew Paris, *Chronica majora*, vol. 3, pp. 404–6; *Historia Anglorum*, vol. 2, p. 399; *Abbreviatio*, vol. 3, p. 274; cf. Barber, *New Knighthood*, p. 232.

26. It may have been this incident that led to Stephen de Sissy falling into disfavour in 1262 with Pope Urban IV, formerly patriarch of Jerusalem, although this is not clear. Stephen was dismissed from office and had to do penance, but was later restored to office in the Order and was commander of Apulia and Sicily in the early 1270s: Bulst-Thiele, *Sacrae domus*, pp. 240–5; Barber, *New Knighthood*, p. 158; Jochen Burgtorf, *The Central Convent of Hospitallers and Templars: History, Organization, and Personnel (1099/1120–1310)* (Leiden: Brill, 2008), p. 659.

27. WT, vol. 2, p. 1008; Bk 22, ch. 2.

28. AbūShamah, 'Le Livre des deux jardins', *RHC Or*, vols 4–5, here vol. 4, p. 185; Robert of Torigny, *Chronicle*, in *Chronicles of the Reign of Stephen, Henry II and Richard I*, ed. R. Howlett, RS 82, 4 vols (London: Longman, 1884–89), vol. 4, p. 288. For later versions of this story see *Chronique d'Ernoul*, pp. 255–6; *Continuation de Guillaume de Tyr*, pp. 58–9, section 46, p. 86, section 75. See also Peter W. Edbury, 'The Lyons *Eracles* and the Old French Continuations of William of Tyre', in *Montjoie: Studies in Crusade History in Honour of Hans Eberhard Mayer*, ed. Benjamin Z. Kedar, Jonathan Riley-Smith and Rudolf Hiestand (Aldershot: Ashgate, 1997), pp. 139–53; Helen Nicholson, *Templars, Hospitallers and Teutonic Knights: Images of the Military Orders, 1128–1291* (Leicester: Leicester University Press, 1993), pp. 83–4.

29. 'Theoderich's description of the Holy Places', trans. Aubrey Stewart, PPTS 5 (London, 1891), pp. 45–9, 59, 60, 64, chs 28, 29, 30, 39, 40, 44; Theodoricus, *Libellus de locis sanctis*, ed. M. L. and W. Bulst (Heidelberg: Winter, 1976), pp. 35–7, 43, 44, 46; *Jerusalem Pilgrimage, 1099–1185*, ed. and trans. John Wilkinson with Joyce Hill and W. F.

Ryan, Hakluyt Society, 2nd series, 167 (1988), pp. 303–5, 310–12.

30. Einar Joranson, 'The Palestine pilgrimage of Henry the Lion', in *Medieval and Historiographical Essays in Honor of James Westfall Thompson*, ed. James Lea Cate and Eugene N. Anderson (Chicago: Chicago University Press, 1938; repr. Port Washington, NY: Kennikat Press, 1966), pp. 146–225.

31. WT, vol. 2, pp. 873–4; Bk 19, ch. 8.

32. For Baldwin IV see now Bernard Hamilton, *The Leper King and his Heirs: Baldwin IV and the Crusader Kingdom of Jerusalem* (Cambridge: Cambridge University Press, 2000); see also Bernard Hamilton, 'The Elephant of Christ: Reynald of Châtillon', in *Religious Motivation: Biographical and Sociological Problems for the Church Historian*, ed. Derek Baker, *Studies in Church History*, 15 (1978), pp. 97–108: here p. 100 and note 24; WT, vol. 2, pp. 979–96, Bk 21, chs 13 (14)–24 (25); Abū al-Fidā, 'Annals', in *RHC Or*, vol. 1, p. 48; Ralph of Diss, 'Ymagines historiarum', in *The Historical Works of Master Ralph of Diceto*, ed. William Stubbs, RS 68, 2 vols (London: Longman, 1876), vol. 1, pp. 423–4.

33. Roger of Howden, *Gesta Henrici Secundi*, ed. William Stubbs, RS 49, 2 vols (London: Longman, 1867), vol. 1, pp. 130–1 and note 10; Roger of Howden, *Chronica*, ed. William Stubbs, RS 51, 4 vols (London: Longman, 1868–71), vol. 2, pp. 131–2. For earlier versions of the myth of the enchanted gold see, for instance, Gregory of Tours, *Histoire des Francs*, ed. Henri Omont and Gaston Collon, 2 vols (Paris: Alphonse Picard et fils, 1886–93), vol. 1, pp. 133–4, Bk 4, ch. 42: trans. Lewis Thorpe as *The History of the Franks* (Harmondsworth: Penguin, 1974), p. 238; 'Math, son of Mathonwy', in *The Mabinogion*, trans. Jeffrey Gantz (Harmondsworth: Penguin, 1976), p. 101. For the Muslims and bad coin, see: Leslie Brubaker and John Haldon, *Byzantium in the Iconoclast Era (ca 680–850): the Sources: An Annotated Survey* (Aldershot: Ashgate, 2001), p. 304, citing A. Müller, ed., *Ibn abī Usaibiʿa, kitāb ʿuyūn al-anbāʾ, fī tabaqāt al-atibbā (The Book of Sources of Information about the Categories of Doctors)*, 3 vols (Cairo and Königsberg. 1882–4), vol. 1, p. 313; *The Life of Alonso de Contreras, Knight of the Military Order of St John, Native of Madrid, written by Himself (1582 to 1633)*, trans. Catherine Alison Phillips, intro. David Hannay (London: Jonathan Cape, 1926), p. 60.

34. Ralph of Diss, 'Ymagines historiarum', pp. 423–4.

35. *Itinerarium peregrinorum et gesta regis Ricardi*, ed. William Stubbs, vol. 2 of his *Chronicles and Memorials of the Reign of Richard I*, RS 38 (London: Longman, 1864), Bk 4, ch. 17, p. 261; corresponding passage in Ambroise, *Estoire de la guerre sainte*, ed. Gaston Paris (Paris: Imprimerie nationale, 1897), lines 6122–210; new edn: *The History of the Holy War: Ambroise's Estoire de la guerre sainte*, ed. Marianne Ailes and Malcolm Barber, trans. Marianne Ailes (Woodbridge: Boydell Press, 2003), lines 6148–57; *Chronicle of the Third Crusade*, trans. Helen Nicholson (Aldershot: Ashgate, 1997), p. 246.

36. Benjamin Z. Kedar, 'The *Tractatus de locis et statu sancte terrae ierosolimitanae*', in *The Crusades and Their Sources: Essays Presented to Bernard Hamilton*, ed. John France and William G. Zajac (Aldershot: Ashgate, 1998), pp. 111–33: here pp. 127–8. There is also a translation in *Anonymous Pilgrim V.2* in *Anonymous Pilgrims I–VIII (11th and 12th Centuries)*, trans Aubrey Stewart, PPTS 6 (London, 1894), pp. 29–30.

37. Oliver, 'Historia Damiatina', pp. 209–11.

38. *Continuation de Guillaume de Tyr*, p. 39, section 25; *RHC Historiens Occidentaux*, vol. 2, p. 40. For the date of the *Continuation*, see Edbury, 'The Lyons *Eracles* and the Old French Continuations of William of Tyre'. The Continuation indicates that the Templar Marshal was Jacquelin de Maillé, but Burgtorf has shown that in fact it was Robert Fraisnel: *Central Convent*, p. 576. On Gerald de Ridefort see now Malcolm Barber, 'The reputation of Gerard of Ridefort', in *MO*, 4.

39. *Règle*, sections 148–68, 172; and see Matthew Bennett, '*La règle du Temple* as a Military Manual or How to Deliver a Cavalry Charge', in *Studies in Medieval History presented to R. Allen Brown*, ed. Christopher Harper-Bill *et al.* (Woodbridge: Boydell and Brewer, 1989), repr. in *The Rule of the Templars*, trans. Upton-Ward, pp. 175–88.

40. See, for instance, *Itinerarium peregrinorum et gesta regis Ricardi*, Bk 4, ch. 30, pp. 291–2; corresponding passage in Ambroise, *Estoire*, lines 7233–366; new edn: lines 7221–96; *Chronicle of the Third Crusade*, pp. 269–70.

41. Odo: *RRH*, nos 465, 487, pp. 122, 128; Gerard: *RRH*, nos 587, 588, pp. 156–7.

42. Helen Nicholson, 'Before William of Tyre: European Reports of the

Military Orders' Deeds in the East, 1150–1185', in *MO*, 2, pp. 111–18: here 116.

43. *Chronique d'Ernoul*, pp. 158–61; *La continuation de Guillaume de Tyr*, pp. 43–6, sections 30–34: this is translated in Edbury, *The Conquest of Jerusalem*. For the sources which accuse Raymond of Tripoli of treachery, see Guy of Bazoches, 'Cronosgraphia', fol. 63v.; William of Newburgh, 'Historia rerum anglicanum', in *Chronicles of the Reigns of Stephen, Henry II and Richard I*, ed. R. Howlett, vol. 1, p. 258; Roger of Howden, *Gesta*, vol. 2, p. 11; Roger of Howden, *Chronica*, vol. 2, pp. 319–20; Ambroise, *Estoire*, lines 2447–9, 2512–21; new edn: lines 2443–50, 2507–16; *Itinerarium peregrinorum et gesta regis Ricardi*, Bk 1, ch. 5, pp. 13–14; translated in *Chronicle of the Third Crusade*, pp. 31–32, and note 26.

44. E.g., 'Fragmentum de captione Damiatae', in *Quinti belli sacri scriptores minores*, ed. Reinhold Röhricht, Société de l'orient latin, no. 162 (Geneva: J.-G. Fick, 1879), pp. 185, 188, 198; *MGH Epistolae III: epistoli saeculi XIII e regestis pontificum Romanorum selecti*, ed. G. H. Pertz and Karl Rodenburg, 3 vols (Berlin: Weidmann, 1883–94), vol. 1, no. 80, p. 60; Oliver, 'Historia Damiatina', pp. 176, 215; 'Letters', pp. 291–2.

45. For the Templars during the Third Crusade see especially *Itinerarium peregrinorum et gesta regis Ricardi*, Bk 4, chs 10–24, pp. 250–82; corresponding passage in Ambroise, *Estoire*, new edn: lines 5856–7, 5942–5; *Chronicle of the Third Crusade*, pp. 237–62. For the Fifth Crusade, see Oliver, 'Historia Damiatina', pp. 271–4. For Frederick's crusade see 'Eracles', p. 373.

46. *Itinerarium peregrinorum et gesta regis Ricardi*, Bk 6, chs 1–2, 7, pp. 381–2, 393–4; corresponding passage in Ambroise, *Estoire*, new edn: lines 10171–2, 10185–7; *Chronicle of the Third Crusade*, pp. 336–7, 344–5; cf. Roger of Howden, *Chronica*, vol. 3, p. 183; Ralph of Coggeshall, *Chronicon anglicanum*, ed. J. Stevenson, RS 66 (London: Longman, 1875), pp. 38–9.

47. Barber, *New Knighthood*, pp. 149–50; see also Matthew Paris, *Chronica majora*, vol. 5, pp. 148–54; 'Du bon William Longespee', ed. Simon Lloyd, in 'William Longespee II: The Making of an English Crusading Hero', *Nottingham Medieval Studies*, 35 (1991), 41–70 and 36 (1992), 79–125; 'Rothelin', *RHC Occ*, 2, pp. 604–6; *Récits d'un Ménestrel de Reims du treizième siècle*, ed. N. de Wailly, SHF (Paris: Librairie Renouard, 1876), pp. 196–8, sections 381–3; Jean de Joinville,

La vie de Saint Louis: le témoignage de Jehan, seigneur de Joinville.
Text du XIVe siècle, ed. Noël Lynn Corbett (Sherbrooke: Quebec,
Naaman, 1977), p. 127, sections 218–19. There is a translation in
Joinville and Villehardouin, *Chronicles of the Crusades*, trans. M. R.
B. Shaw (Harmondsworth: Penguin, 1963), pp. 218–19.

48. *Itinerarium peregrinorum et gesta regis Ricardi*, Bk 3, ch. 7, p. 218;
corresponding passage in Ambroise, *Estoire*, lines 4741–808;
Chronicle of the Third Crusade, p. 209; Oliver, 'Historia Damiatina',
pp. 181, 194; 'Fragmentum de captione Damiatae', pp. 177–8.

49. Joinville, *La vie de Saint Louis*, pp. 161–3, sections 381–5.

50. 'Imād al-Dīn, p. 329; contrast Joinville, *La vie de Saint Louis*, p. 190,
sections 511–14, where the Templars' readiness to conduct
negotiations with the sultan of Damascus alarmed Louis.

51. Peter Edbury, 'The Templars in Cyprus', in *MO*, 1, pp. 189–95: here
p. 189–90.

52. Odo of Deuil, *De profectione Ludovici VII in orientem*, ed. Virginia
G. Berry (New York: W. W. Norton, 1948), p. 124–8, 134.

53. Alan Forey, 'The Failure of the Siege of Damascus', *Journal of
Medieval History*, 10 (1984), 13–24.

54. WT, vol. 2, pp. 768–6, Bk 17, ch. 7. For the crusade see Giles
Constable, 'The Second Crusade as seen by Contemporaries',
Traditio, 9 (1953), 213–79.

55. 'Annales Casinenses', ed. G. H. Pertz, *MGH SS*, vol. 19, p. 310;
'Annales Colonienses maximi', ed. K. Pertz, *MGH SS*, vol. 17, p. 761;
Gerhoh of Reichersberg, writing in 1160–62, 'De investigatione
Antichristi', ed. E. Sackur, *MGH Libelli de lite*, vol. 3, p. 377.

56. 'Casus monasterii Petrihusensis', ed. O. Abel and L. Weiland, *MGH
SS*, vol. 20, p. 674.

57. John of Salisbury, *Historia Pontificalis*, ed. Marjorie Chibnall
(Edinburgh: Nelson, 1956), p. 55; John of Würzburg, 'Descriptio
Terrae Sanctae' in *PL*, vol. 155, col. 1087; 'Annales Herbipolenses',
ed. G. H. Pertz, *MGH SS*, vol. 16, p. 7.

58. Gerhoh of Reichersberg, 'De investigatione', p. 377: Michael the
Syrian, *Le chronique de Michel le Syrien, patriarche Jacobite
d'Antioche, 1166–1199*, ed. J. B. Chabot, 4 vols (Paris: 1899–1910;
reprinted Brussels: Culture et Civilisation, 1963), vol. 3, p. 276; *The
Chronography of Gregory Abū'l Faraj (1225–86), the son of Aaron,
the Hebrew physician, commonly known as Bar Hebraeus, being the
first part of his history of the world*, ed. E. A. W. Budge, 2 vols

(London: 1932, repr. Amsterdam: APA, 1976), vol. 1, p. 274.

59. Ralph of Coggeshall, *Chronicon*, p. 12

60. Gervase of Canterbury, *Historical Works*, ed. William Stubbs, RS 73, 2 vols (London: Longman, 1879–90), vol. 1, pp. 137–8.

61. *Chronique d'Ernoul*, pp. 12–13; Albert Milioli, 'Liber de temporibus et aetatibus et cronica imperatorum', ed. O. Holder-Egger, *MGH SS*, vol. 31, pp. 639–40.

62. *Itinerarium peregrinorum et gesta regis Ricardi*, Bk 5, ch. 6, pp. 316–17; see also the corresponding passage in Ambroise, *Estoire*, lines 7967–8096; *Chronicle of the Third Crusade*, pp. 288–9.

63. 'Sigebert auctarium Aquicinense', ed. D. L. C. Bethmann, *MGH SS*, vol. 6, p. 396; 'Sigebert auctarium Affligemiense', ed. D. L. C. Bethmann, *MGH SS*, vol. 6, p. 401.

64. WT, vol. 2, pp. 1001–2, Bk 21, ch. 28 (29); *Libellus de expugnatione Terrae Sanctae per Saladinum*, in Ralph of Coggeshall, *Chronicon anglicanum*, pp. 209–66: here 211–16; *Itinerarium peregrinorum et gesta regis Ricardi*, Bk 1, chs. 2, 29, pp. 7–9, 70; *Das Itinerarium Peregrinorum. Eine zeitgenössische englische Chronik zum dritten Kreuzzug in ursprünglicher Gestalt*, ed. Hans Eberhard Mayer, (Stuttgart: Anton Hiersemann, 1962), p. 248 line 6 – p. 249 line 20, p. 313 line 31 – p. 314 line 3; *Chronicle of the Third Crusade*, p. 79.

65. Nigel Wireker, *Speculum stultorum*, ed. John H. Mozeley and Robert R. Raymo (Berkeley and Los Angeles: University of California Press, 1960), lines 2051–68: here 2059–68; Guiot de Provins, 'La Bible', in *Les œuvres de Guiot de Provins, poète lyrique et satirique*, ed. John Orr (Manchester: Manchester University Press, 1915), lines 1695–739: here lines 1785–8. For praise, see the analysis in my *Love, War and the Grail*, especially pp. 49–57; Jacques de Vitry, 'Sermones', in *Analecta novissima spicilegii solesmensis: altera continuatio* 2, *Tusculana*, ed. J. B. Pitra (Paris: Roger et Chernowitz, 1888), Sermon 38, p. 420.

66. Otto of St Blasien, 'Continuatio Sanblasiana', ed. R. Wilmans, *MGH SS*, vol. 20, p. 327.

67. Annals of Burton, pp. 491–5.

68. Matthew Paris, *Chronica majora*, vol. 4, pp. 288–343; Jackson, 'The Crusades of 1239–41 and their Aftermath'; Marie Luise Bulst-Thiele, 'Zur Geschichte der Ritterorden und des Königsreichs Jerusalem im 13 Jahrhundert bis zur Schlacht bei la Forbie am 17 Okt 1244', *Deutsches Archiv für Erforschung des Mittelalters*, 22 (1966), 197–226;

Joshua Prawer, 'Military Orders and Crusader Politics in the Second Half of the XIIIth century', in *Die geistlichen Ritterorden Europas*, ed. Fleckenstein and Hellmann, pp. 217–29.

69. *An Arab-Syrian Gentleman and Warrior*, pp. 163–4, 53.

70. WT, vol. 2, pp. 953–5; Bk 20, chs 29–30; Friedrich Lundgreen, *Wilhelm von Tyrus und der Templerorden* (Berlin: Emil Emering, 1911), p. 150.

71. Jacques de Vitry, 'Historia orientalis', in *Gesta Dei per Francos*, ed. J. Bongars, 3 vols (Hanover: typis Wechelianis apud heredes L. Aubrii, 1611), vol. 1, part 2, p. 1063, Bk 3, ch. 14.

72. On this see my *Templars, Hospitallers*, p. 130 and notes 9, 10 and 11.

73. On this see my 'Knights and Lovers: the Military Orders in the Romantic Literature of the Thirteenth Century', in *MO*, 1, pp. 340–45: here 342; and see my *Love, War and the Grail*, p. 46.

74. Guy of Bazoches, 'Cronosgraphia', fol. 63v.; William of Newburgh, 'Historia rerum anglicanum', vol. 1, p. 258; Roger of Howden, *Gesta*, vol. 2, p. 11; Roger of Howden, *Chronica*, vol. 2, pp. 319–20; Ambroise, *Estoire*, lines 2447–9, 2512–21; *Itinerarium peregrinorum et gesta regis Ricardi*, Bk 1, ch. 5, pp. 13–14; translated in *Chronicle of the Third Crusade*, pp. 31–32, and note 26.

75. T. S. R. Boase, 'The History of the Kingdom', in his *The Cilician Kingdom of Armenia*, pp. 1–33; Riley-Smith, 'The Templars and Teutonic Knights in Cilician Armenia', in ibid., pp. 92–117.

76. *Chronique d'Ernoul*, p. 462.

77. Peter Jackson, 'The Crisis in the Holy Land in 1260', *English Historical Review*, 95 (1980), 481–513; Peter Jackson, 'The End of Hohenstaufen Rule in Syria', *Bulletin of the Institute of Historical Research*, 59 (1986), 20–36; Peter M. Holt, 'Mamluk–Frankish Diplomatic Relations in the Reign of Baybars (685–76/1260–77)', *Nottingham Medieval Studies*, 32 (1988), 180–98; Peter W. Edbury, 'The Disputed Regency of the Kingdom of Jerusalem, 1264–6 and 1268', *Camden Miscellany*, 27 (Camden 4th series, 22, 1979), 1–47; reprinted in his *Kingdoms of the Crusaders* (Aldershot, Ashgate, 1999), V.

78. 'Eracles', p. 474; Bulst-Thiele, *Sacrae domus*, pp. 263–6.

79. Ch. Kohler and Ch. V. Langlois, 'Lettres inédits concernant les croisades (1275–1307)', *Bibliothèque de l'école des chartes*, 52 (1891), 45–63: here pp. 55ff.; *RRH*, no. 1404, p. 364.

80. Bulst-Thiele, *Sacrae domus*, pp. 267–71; L. de Mas Latrie, *Histoire de*

l'Île de Chypre sous le règne des princes de la maison de Lusignan, 3 vols (Paris: Imprimerie impériale, 1852–61), vol. 3, pp. 662–8; Hamilton, *Latin Church in the Crusader States*, pp. 237–40.

81. Translated from the edition by Antoine de Bastard, 'La colère et la douleur d'un templier en Terre Sainte: *<Ir'e dolors s'es dins mon cor asseza>*', *Revue des langues romaines*, 81 (1974), 333–73: here 357, lines 33–44.

82. Nicholson, *Templars, Hospitallers*, p. 127.

83. 'Cronica S. Petri Erfordiensis moderna', ed. O. Holder-Egger, *MGH SS*, vol. 30, pp. 424–5.

84. For the loss of Acre and its aftermath see Silvia Schein, *Fideles Crucis: The Papacy, the West, and the Recovery of the Holy Land, 1274–1314* (Oxford: Oxford University Press, 1991), esp. pp. 74–6, 114–28.

85. On this see Peter W. Edbury and John Rowe, *William of Tyre: Historian of the Latin East* (Cambridge: Cambridge University Press, 1988), pp. 61–5, 123–7, 163–4; R. H. C. Davis, 'William of Tyre', in *Relations between East and West in the Middle Ages*, ed. Derek Baker (Edinburgh: Edinburgh University Press, 1987), pp. 64–76.

Notes to Chapter 3: Holy War in the Iberian Peninsula and in Eastern Europe

1. On what follows see Angus Mackay, *Spain in the Middle Ages: From Frontier to Empire, 1000–1500* (Basingstoke: Macmillan, 1977); Alan Forey, 'The Military Orders and the Spanish Reconquest in the Twelfth and Thirteenth Centuries', *Traditio*, 40 (1984), 197–234; reprinted in his *Military Orders and Crusades*, article V; Alan Forey, *The Templars in the Corona de Aragón* (London: Oxford University Press, 1973); Joan Fuguet and Carme Plaza, *Los Templarios en la Península Ibérica* (Barcelona: ElCobre, 2005).

2. Marcus Bull, *Knightly Piety and the Lay Response to the First Crusade* (Oxford: Oxford University Press, 1993), pp. 72–8, argues that this letter may not be connected with the Barbastro campaign and that historians have misinterpreted it.

3. For the above three paragraphs see Henry Livermore, *A History of Portugal* (Cambridge: Cambridge University Press, 1947), pp. 62, 74–81, 85, 97–9, 108, 113, 132; Fuguet and Plaza, *Los Templarios*, pp. 190–5; Forey, *The Military Orders*, p. 23; Barber, *New Knighthood*, pp. 32–4; Forey, 'Military Orders and Spanish Reconquest', 199; *CT*, nos 10, 11, 381, and see also nos 19, 24, 363.

4. Forey, *Templars in the Corona de Aragón*, pp. 9–17; Forey, *The Military Orders*, p. 23; *CT*, nos 33, 38, 47, 72, 145, 314.

5. Luttrell, 'Earliest Templars'; Anthony Luttrell, 'The Earliest Hospitallers', in *Montjoie*, ed. Kedar *et al.*, pp. 37–54; Kaspar Elm, 'Kanoniker und Ritter vom Heiligen Grab. Ein Beitrag zur Entstehung und Frühgeschichte der palästinensischen Ritterorden', in his *Umbilicus Mundi: Beiträge zur Geschichte Jerusalems, der Kreuzzüge, des Kapitels vom Hlg. Grab in Jerusalem und der Ritterorden* (Bruges: Sint Kruis, 1998), pp. 63–105; reprinted from *Die geistlichen Ritterorden Europas*, ed. Fleckenstein and Hellmann, pp. 141–69.

6. Elena Lourie, 'The Confraternity of Belchite, the Ribat and the Temple', *Viator*, 13 (1982), 159–76, reprinted in her *Crusade and Colonisation* (Aldershot: Variorum, 1990). For the opposing arguments see Forey, 'Emergence of the Military Order', and Bull, 'The Confraternity of La Sauve-Majeure'. For an overview see Barber, *New Knighthood*, pp. 26–32.

7. *CT*, 314; Forey, *Templars in the Corona de Aragón*, pp. 21–3.

8. Forey, *Templars in the Corona de Aragón*, pp. 26–31.

9. Forey, *Templars in the Corona de Aragón*, pp. 31–3; Jaume I, *Crònica o llibre dels faits*, ed. Ferran Soldevila (Barcelona: Editions 62, 1988), chs 95–7; trans. as *The Chronicle of James I of Aragon*, trans John Forster, 2 vols (London: Chapman and Hall, 1883), chs 95–7, vol. 1, pp. 183–7; see now the new translation, Damian Smith and Helena Buffery, *The Book of Deeds of James I of Aragon: A Translation of the Medieval Catalan* (Aldershot: Ashgate, 2003), pp. 114–16.

10. *Chronicle of James I*, ch. 117, pp. 210–11; *Book of Deeds*, pp. 129–30.

11. *Chronicle of James I*, chs 487–9, pp. 603–4; *Book of Deeds*, pp. 339–41.

12. *Chronicle of James I*, ch. 95, pp. 183–4; *Book of Deeds*, p. 114.

13. *Chronicle of James I*, ch. 165, pp. 266–7; *Book of Deeds*, pp. 161–2.

14. Forey, *Templars in the Corona de Aragón*, p. 140.

15. *CH*, no. 4007. For the Temple and Hospital helping Peter III's defence against the crusaders in 1285 see Bernat Desclot, *Crònica*, ed. Miquel Coll I Alentorn (Barcelona: Editorial Barcino, 1949), chapter 19; translated as Bernat Desclot, *Chronicle of the Reign of King Pedro III of Aragon, AD 1276–1285*, ed. F.L. Critchlow (Princeton: Princeton University Press, 1928), p. 139. See also Forey, *Templars in the Corona de Aragón*, pp. 134–41.

16. Madrid, Biblioteca del Monasterio de El Escorial, ms. T.I.6, Libro de los juegos de Ajedrez, Dados y Tablos, escrito por orden de Alfonso X, fol. 25.

17. Constable, 'Second Crusade as seen by Contemporaries', 233; Livermore, *History of Portugal*, pp. 113–14.

18. Desclot, *Chronicle*, ch. 134, pp. 200–1.

19. For the plans of 1274 see Jacques de Molay's comments in *Le Dossier de l'affaire des Templiers*, ed. Georges Lizerand (Paris: Librairie Ancienne Honoré Champion, 1923), pp. 2–5. For James II and the Templars, see: Luis García-Guijarro Ramos, 'The Extinction of the Order of the Temple in the Kingdom of Valencia and Early Montesa, 1307–1330: A Case of Transition from Universalist to Territorialized Military Orders', in *The Debate on the Trial of the Templars*, ed. Burgtorf, Crawford and Nicholson (forthcoming).

20. On the Teutonic Knights see Eric Christiansen, *The Northern Crusades* (Basingstoke: Macmillan, 1980; new edn Harmondsworth: Penguin, 1997); William Urban, *The Teutonic Knights: a Military History* (London: Greenhill, 2003).

21. For donations to the Templars in Germany see Bulst-Thiele, *Sacrae domus*, pp. 211, 74; Schüpferling, *Der Tempelherren-orden in Deutschland*, esp. pp. 240–1.

22. Libor Jan and Vít Jesenský, 'Hospitaller and Templar Commanderies in Bohemia and Moravia: their Structure and Architectural Forms', in *MO*, 2, pp. 235–49: here 238–43; Libor Jan, 'Böhmische und mährische Adelige als Förderer und Mitglieder der Geistlichen Ritterorden', in *The Crusades and the Military Orders: Expanding the Frontiers of Medieval Latin Christianity*, ed. József Laszlovszky and Zsolt Hunyadi (Budapest: Central European University Press, 2001), pp. 303–17.

23. For my information on the Templars in Hungary I am indebted to Zsolt Hunyadi, Balázs Stossek, and Lelja Dobronić. See Lelja Dobronić, *Viteški redovi Templarii i Ivanovci u Hrvatsjoi* (Zagreb: Krscanska sadasnjost, 1984); Balázs Stossek, 'Maisons et possessions des Templiers en Hongrie', and Zsolt Hunyadi, 'The Knights of St John in the Medieval Kingdom of Hungary: Houses, Personnel, and a Particular Activity up to c.1400', in *The Crusades and the Military Orders*, ed. Laszlovszky and Hunyadi, pp. 245–51, 253–68.

24. 'Ex Thomas historia pontificum Salonitanorum et Spalatinorum', ed. L. von Heineman, *MGH SS*, vol. 29, pp. 577, 578, 587; Thomas

archidiaconi Spalatensis, *Historia Salonitanorum atque Spalatinorum pontificum*, ed. Olga Perić, ed. and trans. Damir Karbić, Mirjana Matijević Sokol and James Ross Sweeney (Budapest and New York: Central European University Press, 2006), pp. 148–9, 264–7, 160–3. On the events of 1241 see Peter Jackson, 'The Crusade Against the Mongols (1241)', *Journal of Ecclesiastical History*, 42 (1991), 1–18; Bulst-Thiele, *Sacrae domus*, p. 213.

25. 'Ex historiae regum Franciae continuatione Parisiensi', ed. O. Holder-Egger, *MGH SS*, vol. 26, pp. 604–5. A league is two and a half miles, or four kilometres.

26. Bulst-Thiele, *Sacrae domus*, p. 212.

27. Walter Kuhn, 'Kirchliche Siedlung als Grenzschutz 1200 bis 1250 (am Beispiel des mittleren Oderraumes)', *Ostdeutsche Wissenschaft: Jahrbuch des Ostdeutschen Kulturrates*, 9 (1962), 6–55: here 18; Karl Borchardt, 'The Hospitallers in Pomerania: Between the Priories of Bohemia and *Alamania*', in *MO*, 2, pp. 295–306: here 300.

28. Maria Starnawska, 'Crusade Orders on Polish Lands during the Middle Ages. Adaptation in a Peripheral Environment', *Quaestiones Medii Aevi Novi*, 2 (1997), 121–42: here 129; Schüpferling, *Der Tempelherren-orden in Deutschland*, p. 241; Barber, *New Knighthood*, 249.

29. On this see Kuhn, 'Kirchliche Siedlung', 12–15, 21, 28–9; Nicholson, *Templars, Hospitallers*, p. 52.

30. Helmut Lüpke, *Untersuchungen zur Geschichte des Templerordens im Gebiet der norostdeutschen Kolonisation. Inaugural Dissertation zur Erlangung der Doktorwürde genehmigt von der Philosophischen Fakultät der Friedrich-Wilhelms-Universität zu Berlin* (Bernburg, 1933), pp. 12–15; idem, 'Das Land Tempelburg. Ein historische-geographische Untersuchung', *Baltische Studien*, 35 (1933), 43–97; Kuhn, 'Kirchliche Siedlung', 30–32.

31. *Acta sanctorum quotquot toto orbe coluntur: vel a catholicis scriptoribus celebrantur quæ ex latinis & græcis, aliarumque gentium antiquis monumentis*, ed. Joannes Bollandus and Godefridus Henschenius, 2nd edn, ed. Joanne Carnandet, 70 vols and supplement (Brussels, Paris and Rome, 1863ff.), October VIII, p. 232E.

32. Boleslaw B. Szczesniak, *The Knights Hospitallers in Poland and Lithuania* (The Hague and Paris: Mouton, 1969), pp. 15–16.

33. Kuhn, 'Kirchliche Siedlung', pp. 46–54.

34. For the Templars and Łuków see Walter Kuhn, 'Ritterorden als

Grenzhüter des Abendlandes gegen das östliche Heidentum', *Ostdeutsche Wissenschaft*, 6 (1959), 7–70, here 42–52; Starnawska, 'Crusade Orders'.

Notes to Chapter 4: The Organization and Government of the Order

1. Charles Tipton, 'The 1330 General Chapter of the Knights Hospitaller at Montpellier', *Traditio*, 24 (1968), 293–308.

2. Jochen Burgtorf, *The Central Convent of the Hospitallers and Templars: History, Organization, and Personnel (1099/1120–1310)* (Leiden: Brill, 2008), p. 3.

3. *Règle*, sections 198–223.

4. On the Master's role and authority see Barber, *New Knighthood*, pp. 187–8; see also Burgtorf, *Central Convent*, pp. 240–6.

5. I am grateful to Jochen Burgtorf for information on the location of Templar general chapters. See now Burgtorf, *Central Convent*, p. 52 and note 208, pp. 183–6, 191–2.

6. *Règle*, sections 88, 93, 562, 569, 585, 606, 616, 634; and see *The Rule of the Templars*, trans. Upton-Ward, p. 142, note 546.2.

7. Burgtorf, *Central Convent*, pp. 113–14, 183–6. On the proceedings of Hospitaller general chapters see Riley-Smith, *Knights of St John*, pp. 286–90; Tipton, '1330 Chapter General of the Knights Hospitallers at Montpellier'; Jürgen Sarnowsky, 'The Oligarchy at Work. The Chapters General of the Hospitallers in the XVth Century (1421–1522)', in *Autour de la première croisade*, ed. Balard, pp. 267–76. On the Templars' general chapter laying down regulations, see *Procès des Templiers d'Auvergne*, p. 120; MS Bodley 454, fols 64v, 65r, 65v, 66r.

8. Burgtorf, *Central Convent*, pp. 406–24; Bulst-Thiele, *Sacrae domus*, pp. 81–2 (Philip de Milly joined the Order in 1164–5 and became Master in 1169), pp. 125–6 on Robert de Sablé.

9. Édouard Rey, 'Geoffroy Fulcher, grand-commandeur du Temple 1151–1170', *Revue de Champagne et de Brie*, year 19, 2nd series 6 (1894), 259–69; see also Barber, *New Knighthood*, pp. 189–90; Burgtorf, *Central Convent*, pp. 48–9, 532–4.

10. For the Orders' officials see *Règle*, sections 99–137, 169–79, 190–221; Jochen Burgtorf, 'Leadership Structures in the Orders of the Hospital and Temple (Twelfth to Early Fourteenth Century) – Select Aspects', in: *The Crusades and the Military Orders*, ed. Laszlovszky and Hunyadi, pp. 379–94; Jochen Burgtorf, 'Wind Beneath the Wings:

Subordinate Headquarters Officials in the Hospital and Temple from the Twelfth to the Early Fourteenth Centuries', in *MO*, 2, pp. 217–24; Burgtorf, *Central Convent*, pp. 179–338, esp. 179, 248, 252–5.

11. 'Chronique d'Amadi' in *Chroniques d'Amadi et de Strambaldi*, ed. R. de Mas Latrie, 2 vols (Paris, 1891–3), vol. 1, p. 360; Burgtorf, Central Convent, pp. 310–11.

12. Burgtorf, *Central Convent*, p. 329; for the Hospital of St James of Andravida, transferred to the Templars by Pope Innocent IV, see *Les registres d'Innocent IV*, ed. Élie Berger, BEFAR, 4 vols (Paris: E. Thorin, 1884–1921), no. 2869, vol. 1, p. 429; confirmed around 1250 by William de Villehardouin: *Livre de la conqueste de la princée du l'Amorée. Chronique de la Morée (1204–1305)*, ed. Jean Longnon (Paris: Renouard, 1909) p. 212; *Crusaders as conquerors: the Chronicle of the Morea*, trans. Harold E. Lurier (New York and London: Columbia University Press, 1964) p. 290; *The Templars: Selected Sources*, ed. and trans. Malcolm Barber and Keith Bate (Manchester: Manchester University Press, 2002), pp. 199–200 ('hostel' at the commandery of Corval in Normandy); see also Malcolm Barber, 'The Charitable and Medical Activities of the Hospitallers and Templars', in *A History of Pastoral Care*, ed. Gillian R. Evans (London: Cassell, 2000), pp. 148–68: here pp. 156–7, 165–6; for a different view see Alan Forey, 'The Charitable Activities of the Templars', *Viator*, 34 (2003), 109–41: here 125–36, 138–40; for further discussion, see 'Relations between Houses of the Order of the Temple in Britain and their Local Communities, as indicated during the Trial of the Templars, 1307–12', in *Knighthoods of Christ: Essays on the History of the Crusades and the Knights Templar*, ed. Norman Housley (Aldershot, Hants. and Burlington, VT: Ashgate, 2007), pp. 195–207: here pp. 196–8.

13. *Untergang des Templerordens,* ed. Schottmüller, vol. 2, pp. 176, 191, 263, 323; *Trial of the Templars in Cyprus*, pp. 93, 116, 213, 288. For 'prior' as the title of a priest in charge of a parish on Cyprus, see Jean Richard, *Chypre sous les Lusignans. Documents chypriotes des archives du Vatican (XIVe et XVe siècles)* (Paris: P. Geuthner, 1962), p. 93 and note 8. See also Burgtorf, *Central Convent*, pp. 336–8.

14. Forey, *The Military Orders*, p. 149; Bulst-Thiele, *Sacrae domus*, p. 211.

15. Forey, *The Military Orders*, p. 155.

16. For the seals of the Order of the Temple, see Forey, *Templars in the Corona de Aragón*, pp. 453–4 and notes 4 and 5; he also cites J.

Menéndez Pidal, *Catálogo de sellos españoles de la edad medía: Archivo Histórico Nacional: sección sigilografía* (Madrid, 1929), p. 182. See also Paul de Saint-Hilaire, *Les Sceaux des Templiers et leurs symboles* (Puiseaux: Pardès, 1991): but some of Saint-Hilaire's references are incorrect, and he includes the seal of Thierry de Nussa (p. 100), who was actually prior of the Hospital in England, not a Templar. See also Bulst-Thiele, *Sacrae domus*, pp. 369–79, 415–19. For the Hospital of St John, see E. J. King, *The Seals of the Order of St John of Jerusalem* (London: Methuen, 1932).

17. Helen Nicholson, 'The Military Orders and the Kings of England in the Twelfth and Thirteenth Centuries', in *From Clermont to Jerusalem: The Crusades and Crusader Societies, 1095–1500*, ed. Alan V. Murray (Turnhout: Brepols, 1998), pp. 203–18: here 208.

18. Victor Carrière, *Histoire et Cartulaire des Templiers de Provins* (Paris: Champion, 1919), no. 11, p. 49. For another grant of serfs, which the serfs confirmed, see *The Templars: Selected Sources*, ed. Barber and Bate, pp. 172–4.

19. On laundresses, see: P.J. Goldberg, *Women, Work and Lifecycle in a Medieval Economy: Women in York and Yorkshire c.1300–1520* (Oxford: Oxford University Press, 1992), p. 135; P. J. Goldberg, 'Women's work, women's role in the late medieval north', in *Profit, Piety and the Professions*, ed. M. A. Hicks (Gloucester: Alan Sutton, 1990), pp. 34–50, here 47; Henrietta Leyser, *Medieval Women: A Social History of Women in England 450–1500* (London: Weidenfeld and Nicolson, 1995), p. 151. On dairymaids, see below.

20. Historical archdiocescan archive of Tarragona, Cartulari A-B, fol. 177r: printed by Francesco Tommasi, 'Uomini e donne negli ordini militari di Terrasanta: Per il problema delle case doppie e miste negli ordini giovannita, templare e teutonico (secc. XII–XIV), in *Doppelkloster und andere Formen der symbiose mannlicher und weiblicher Religiosen in Mittelalter*, ed. Kaspar Elm and Michel Parisse, *Berliner historische Studien* 28 (1992), 177–202, here 201. I am informed by Professor Juan Fuguet Sans that the word 'preceptrix' is written out in full in the charter and that the reading is absolutely clear. I am very grateful to him for clarifying this point.

21. On the architecture of the Templars' commanderies see Roberta Gilchrist, *Contemplation and Action: The Other Monasticism* (London: Leicester University Press, 1995), pp. 69–105; Pál Ritoók, 'The Architecture of the Knights Templars in England', in *MO*, 1,

pp. 167–78; Jan and Jesenský, 'Hospitaller and Templar Commanderies' and the works to which these refer.

22. See Thomas Bérard's letter to Amadeus in the 'Annals of Burton', ed. Luard, giving the Order's church plate as its most valuable possession, pp. 491–5; see also James de Molay's evidence to the papal commissioners, 28 November 1309, in *Dossier de l'affaire des Templiers*, ed. Lizerand, p. 166; Eileen Gooder, *Temple Balsall: The Warwickshire preceptory of the Templars and their Fate* (Chichester: Phillimore, 1995), pp. 71–2; Sebastián Salvadó, 'Icons, Crosses and the Liturgical Objects of Templar Chapels in the Crown of Aragon', in *The Debate on the Trial of the Templars*, ed. Burgtorf, Crawford and Nicholson.

23. William Rees, 'The Templar Manor of Llanmadoc', *Bulletin of the Board of Celtic Studies*, 13, part III (1949), 144–5.

24. Pictures printed in my *Knights Templar: A New History*, pp. 48, 127.

25. Burgtorf, 'Leadership Structures', pp. 385–6. On proportions of sergeants to knights in the Order see Alan Forey, 'Recruitment to the Military Orders (Twelfth to Fourteenth Centuries)', *Viator*, 17 (1986), 139–71: here 144–5; reprinted in his *Military Orders and Crusades*, article 2.

26. A useful summary of the development of knighthood in England, for example, can be found in Peter Coss, *The Knight in Medieval England, 1000–1400* (Stroud: Alan Sutton, 1993), pp. 1–99.

27. A good example of this is 'The Childhood of Vivien': *Les enfances Vivien*, ed. Magali Rouguier (Geneva: Droz, 1997), from line 531.

28. Malcolm Barber, 'The Social Context of the Templars', *Transactions of the Royal Historical Society*, 34 (1984), 27–46, and reprinted in his *Crusaders and Heretics*, VIII; Keen, *Chivalry*, pp. 44–63; Nicholson, *Love, War and the Grail*, pp. 5–7, 204–19, 222–6.

29. Nicholson, *Templars, Hospitallers*, pp. 29–30, 43, 48, 50, 71–4.

30. *Règle*, section 586.

31. Dieter Wojtecki, *Studien zur Personengeschichte des Deutschen Ordens im 13 Jahrhundert*, Quellen und Studien zur Geschichte des östlichen Europas, ed. Manfred Hellmann, 3 (Wiesbaden: F. Steiner, 1971), pp. 78–80, 88–91; Forey, 'Recruitment'.

32. Jacques de Vitry, Sermon 37, p. 410.

33. Jacques de Vitry, Sermon 37, p. 407; *Dossier de l'affaire des Templiers*, ed. Lizerand, pp. 160–2.

34. *Règle*, sections 17, 68.

35. *Règle*, section 56 of the Latin Rule, and see sections 70–2 of the French Rule.

36. María Echániz Sans, *Las Mujeres de la Orden Militar de Santiago en la Edad Media* (Salamanca: Junta de Castilla y León, 1992); Constance H. Berman, 'Were There Twelfth Century Cistercian Nuns?' *Church History*, 68 (1999), 824–64; Sally Thompson, 'The Problem of the Cistercian Nuns in the Twelfth and Early Thirteenth Centuries', in *Medieval Women*, ed. Derek Baker, *Studies in Church History: Subsidia*, 1 (1978), pp. 227–52; John B. Freed, 'Urban Development and the "cura monialium" in Thirteenth-Century Germany', *Viator*, 3 (1972), 311–26; Carol Neel, 'The Origins of the Beguines', *Signs: Journal of Women in Culture and Society*, 14 (1989), 321–41. On the Teutonic Order, see: *Die Statuten des Deutschen Ordens nach den ältesten Handschriften*, ed. Max Perlbach (Halle a. S.: M. Niemayer, 1890), p. 52, no. 31; see also pp. 131, 132. Udo Arnold, 'Die Frau im Deutschen Orden', in *Stationen Einer Hochschullaufbahn: Festschrift für Annette Kuhn zum 65. Geburtstag*, ed. Udo Arnold, Peter Meyers and Uta C. Schmidt (Dortmund: Edition Ebersbach, 1999), pp. 261–76, here pp. 254–5. I am indebted to Dr Karl Borchardt for providing me with a copy of this article. See also Johannes Adriaan Mol, *De Friese Huizen van de Duitse Order: Nes, Steenkerk en Schoten en hun plaats in het middeleeuse Friese kloosterlandscap* (Ljouwert: Fryske Akademy, 1991), pp. 68–76. I am very grateful to Dr Mol for providing me with a copy of the forthcoming German translation of his book.

37. Charter printed by Schüpferling, *Der Tempelherren-orden in Deutschland*, pp. 33–4, note 4; Tommasi, 'Uomini e donne negli ordini militari', 195 note 76, citing *Lettres communes des papes d'Avignon…Jean XXII (1316–1334)*, no. 18845. See also Luttrell and Nicholson, 'Introduction', in Luttrell and Nicholson, *Hospitaller Women*, p. 26. I am very grateful to Markus Menzendorff for his work in locating the site of Mühlen in modern Osthofen; apparently nothing remains of the nunnery today.

38. Schüpferling, *Der Tempelherren-orden in Deutschland*, pp. 61–2.

39. *Règle*, 68, section 69 (section 55 of the Latin Rule).

40. For examples see Forey, 'Women and the Military Orders in the Twelfth and Thirteenth Centuries', *Studia monastica*, 29 (1987), 63–92: here 65–6; reprinted in his *Military Orders and Crusades*, article 4 and in *Hospitaller Women*, ed. Luttrell and Nicholson, p. 46–7;

Barber, *New Knighthood*, pp. 261–2 and note 120; Tommasi, 'Uomini e donne negli ordini militari', 183–4, translated as 'Men and Women of the Hospitaller, Templar and Teutonic Orders: Twelfth to Fourteenth Centuries', in *Hospitaller Women*, ed. Luttrell and Nicholson, pp. 71–88, here 73–4.

41. *Procès*, vol. 1, pp. 591–4.

42. Gisli H. Gudjonsson, *The Psychology of Interrogations, Confessions and Testimony* (New York: Wiley, 1992), esp. pp. 205–59.

43. Tommasi, 'Uomine e donne negli ordini militari', 201–2 (here 201), with commentary at pp. 200–1.

44. Charter printed in 'Documents relatifs aux croisades', in *Le Chevalier au Cygne et Godefroid de Bouillon, poëme historique publié pour la première fois avec de nouvelles recherches sur les légendes qui ont rapport à la Belgique, un travail et des documents sur les croisades*, ed. Le Baron de Reiffenberg, 3 vols (Brussels: M. Hayez, 1846–54), vol. 1 p. 429, no. 9.

45. For the standard definition see: Riley-Smith, *Knights of St John*, pp. 242–6 (here for the Hospital, but these are standard terms). See also Elisabeth Magnou, 'Oblature, classe chevaleresque et servage dans les maisons méridonales du Temple au XII siècle', *Annales du Midi*, 73 (1961), 377–97; María Echániz Sans, *Las Mujeres de la Orden Militar de Santiago*, p. 53. Dominic Selwood argues, and I agree, that the 'rigid classification system adopted' here 'imposes order on to what was, by its nature, flexible, and obscures the individual nature of the arrangements': *Knights of the Cloister: Templars and Hospitallers in Central-Southern Occitania 1100–1300* (Woodbridge: Boydell and Brewer, 1999), pp. 117–22, here note 148. This problem is also discussed by Tommasi, 'Men and Women', pp. 79–81. See now Jochen G. Schenk, 'Forms of lay association with the Order of the Temple', *Journal of Medieval History*, 34 (2008), 79–103; Damien Carraz, 'L'affiliation des laics aux commanderies templières et hospitalières de la basse vallée du Rhône (XIIe–XIIIe siècles)', in *Religiones militares: Contributi alla storia degli Ordini religioso-militari nel medioevo*, ed. Anthony Luttrell and Francesco Tommasi (Città di Castello: Selecta Editrice, 2008), pp. 171–90.

46. The evidence is laid out by Forey, 'Women and the Military Orders', 66 and note 17.

47. Between 1189 and 1193 one Joanna, wife of Richard, a knight of Chalfield in Wiltshire, resolved 'to subject herself through the grace

of God to the Rule of the Temple' in her old age: *Records of the Templars in England in the twelfth century: the inquest of 1185 with illustrative charters and documents*, ed. Beatrice A. Lees (London: Oxford University Press, 1935), p. 210.

48. For a confraternity in a traditional religious house see Giles Constable, 'The *Liber Memorialis* of Remiremont', *Speculum*, 47 (1972), 261–77; Hiro Tsurushima, 'The confraternity of Rochester Cathedral Priory about 1100', *Anglo-Norman Studies*, 14 (1992), 313–37. I am indebted to Dr Bill Aird for these references.

49. H. von Hammerstein, 'Der Besitz der Tempelherren in Lotharingen', *Jahrbuch des Gesellschaft für lotharingische Geschichte und Altertumskunde*, 7 part 1 (1895), 1–29, here p. 19, no. 38.

50. Alan Forey, 'Novitiate and Instruction in the Military Orders in the Twelfth and Thirteenth Centuries', *Speculum*, 61 (1986), 1–17; reprinted in his *Military Orders and Crusades*, article 3.

51. *Règle*, sections 657–86.

52. Nicholson, *Knights Templar on Trial*, pp. 171–3; for specific points see MS Bodley 454, fols 143r, 145r, 146r, 147v, 149r (receptions in Ireland); Barber, *New Knighthood*, p. 303 (France); Barber, *Trial of the Templars*, 2nd edn, p. 70 (Germany); Keen, *Chivalry*, pp. 65, 79.

53. For Brothers buying their own cords see *Procès*, vol. 1, pp. 340, 442, 478, 544, vol. 2, p. 475; for their families (especially their own sisters) supplying them, see ibid., vol. 1, pp. 299–300, 314, 352; for the girlfriend, see ibid., vol. 1, p. 294.

54. *Records of the Templars*, pp. 56–7; *Dossier de l'affaire des Templiers*, ed. Lizerand, p. 54: '*A la daerie a trois baasses*'. For Baugy see also Forey, 'Women and the Military Orders', 69; reprinted in *Hospitaller Women*, ed. Luttrell and Nicholson, p. 49. For Corval see *The Templars: Selected Sources*, ed. Barber and Bate, pp. 199–200.

55. Alan Forey, 'Provision for the Aged in Templar Commanderies', in *La Commanderie: Institution des ordres militaires dans l'Occident médiéval*, ed. Anthony Luttrell and Léon Pressouyre (Paris: Comité des travaux historiques et scientifiques, 2002), pp. 178–83.

56. *Les contes moralisés de Nicole Bozon, Frère Mineur*, ed. Lucy Toulmin Smith and Paul Meyer, SATF (Paris: Firmin Didot, 1998), pp. 181–2.

Notes to Chapter 5: Religious Life

1. *Règle*, section 385; see also sections 225, 326, 418, 550; for the Hospital see *CH*, nos. 2213.82, 2186. The problems in keeping events

in a monastery secret are well illustrated by the fire at Bury St Edmunds Abbey in 1198: although the monks went to enormous lengths to cover up all signs of the fire, the pilgrims who arrived the following morning had already heard about it: Jocelin of Brakelond, *Chronicle of the Abbey of Bury St Edmunds*, trans. Diana Greenway and Jane Sayers (Oxford: Oxford University Press, 1989), p. 96.

2. 'Nouveau manuscrit de la règle du Temple', p. 196, section 7.

3. *Règle*, sections 236, 452, 594, 625.

4. *Papsttum*, vol. 2, p. 330: Brother John de Villiers.

5. *Procès*, vol. 1, pp. 76, 259, 326; *Papsttum*, vol. 2, p. 337.

6. *Untergang des Templerordens*, ed. Schottmüller, vol. 2, p. 390.

7. Helen Nicholson, 'Knights and Lovers: the Military Orders in the Romantic Literature of the Thirteenth Century', in *MO*, 1, pp. 340–5; idem, *Love, War and the Grail*, pp. 43, 45–57, 63; Peter Linehan, *The Ladies of Zamora* (Manchester: Manchester University Press, 1997); *CH*, no. 2186; 'De Frere Denise', in *Nouveau recueil complet des fabliaux*, ed. Willem Noomen, vol. 4 (Assen and Maastricht: Van Gorcum, 1991), no. 56, pp. 1–23; Christiansen, *The Northern Crusades* (1980), pp. 84–5; new edn (1997), p. 88; Anthony Luttrell, 'Gli Ospitalieri di San Giovanni di Gerusalemme dal continente alle isole', in *Acri 1291: La Fine della Presenza degli Ordini Militari in Terra Sancta e I Nuovi Orientamenti nel XIV secolo*, ed. Francesco Tommasi (Perugia: Quattroemne, 1996), pp. 75–91, here p. 83; repr. in his *The Hospitaller State on Rhodes and its Western Provinces, 1306–1462* (Aldershot: Ashgate, 1999), article 2; Anthony Luttrell, 'Hospitaller Life in Aragon', in *God and Man in Medieval Spain. Essays in Honour of J. R. L. Highfield*, ed. D. W. Lomax and D. Mackenzie (Warminster: Aris and Phillips, 1989), pp. 97–115, here p. 111; reprinted in his *Hospitallers of Rhodes and their Mediterranean World* (Aldershot: Variorum, 1992), article 15.

8. *Règle*, section 573. This was referred to as the only known case by some witnesses during the trial: *Procès*, vol. 1, pp. 196, 386–7.

9. Barber, 'The Trial of the Templars revisited', *MO*, 2, pp. 329–42, here p. 338, note 35, citing: *Procès*, vol. 2, pp. 290, 294: the first case in question was aimed against the Master of the Order, and may reflect this Brother's resentment of the leadership of the Order rather than actual events; the second recounted vague activities by two named Brothers 'on a certain night'. See also Anne Gilmour-Bryson, 'A Look

Through the Keyhole: Templars in Italy from the Trial Testimony', *MO*, 3, pp. 123–30; MS Bodley 454 fol. 150r. For a full discussion see Anne Gilmour-Bryson, 'Sodomy and the Knights Templar', *Journal of the History of Sexuality*, 7 (1996), 151–83. For the three confessions which appear most likely to be genuine see *Procès*, vol. 2, p. 286; *Procès des Templiers d'Auvergne*, pp. 148, 215.

10. For the Benedictines and Cistercians as active homosexuals see John of Salisbury, *Policraticus*, vol. 2, p. 199, Bk 7, ch. 21, 695 c–d, and note on line 21: he is considering the alms-collecting activities of the Cistercians and Cluniacs. See also Walter Map, *De nugis*, p. 80, on Cistercian monks having sex with boys; for sodomy at the Benedictine abbey of Bury St Edmunds see P. L. Heywroth, 'Jocelin of Brakelond, Abbot Samson, and the case of William the Sacrist', in *Middle English Studies Presented to Norman Davis in Honour of his Seventieth Birthday*, ed. Douglas Gray and E. G. Stanley (Oxford: Clarendon Press, 1983), pp. 175–94. For the susceptibility of monks to good-looking young men see, for example, the experiences of Saint Euphrosine, disguised as a man: 'La vie de Sainte Euphrosine', ed. Raymond T. Hill, *Romanic Review*, 10 (1919), 159–69, 191–32, here pp. 205–6, lines 564–83. There is an extensive bibliography on the subject in V. A. Kolve, 'Ganymede/*Son of Getron*: Medieval Monasticism and the Drama of Same-Sex Desire', *Speculum*, 73 (1998), 1014–67.

11. Barber, *New Knighthood*, pp. 215–16; Peter W. Edbury, *John of Ibelin and the Kingdom of Jerusalem* (Woodbridge: Boydell and Brewer, 1997), pp. 39–40, 50–1, 64.

12. For instance, for masses said for King John of England, see *Register of Walter Gray, Lord Archbishop of York*, ed. James Raine, Surtees Society, 56 (Durham, 1872), p. 24, no. 115; for masses said for King Henry III of England, see *Calendar of the Charter Rolls preserved in the Public Record Office, 1226–1516*, 6 vols (London: HMSO, 1903–27), 1226–57, p. 135; for the lamp at Metz, see Chapter 4, p. 146, above. For Sandford and Cowley, see *The Sandford Cartulary*, ed. Agnes M. Leys, 2 vols, Oxfordshire Record Society, 19, 22 (1938–1940), vol. 1, pp. 56–9, 61–2, 86, 90–1, 105, nos. 74–6, 81, 120, 125, 146. For Templar chapels see also Chapter 4, p. 135, above.

13. *Trial of the Templars in Cyprus*, pp. 55–74, 409–36.

14. *Procès*, vol. 1, pp. 120–4.

15. *Caesarii Heisterbachensis monachi Cisterciensis Dialogus miraculorum*,

ed. Joseph Strange, 2 vols (Cologne, Bonn and Brussels: H. Lempertz, 1851), vol. 2, p. 119.

16. Jacques de Vitry, 'Sermones', Sermon 37, pp. 412–13, Sermon 38, p. 420.

17. Walter Map, *De nugis*, pp. 374–6, 58–60.

18. For early donation charters to Mary see *CT*, nos. 43, 95, 119, 120, 124, 125, 139, etc.

19. *Cartulaire de la commanderie de Richerenches de l'ordre du Temple (1136–1214)*, ed. le Marquis de Ripert-Monclar (Avignon, 1907), pp. 70, 71, 183, 184, 202, nos. 67, 69, 206–7, 227; *Les registres de Nicholas IV*, ed. Ernest Langlois, BEFAR (Paris, 1905), no. 897. For the situation in central-southern Occitania, see Selwood, *Knights of the Cloister*, p. 210: 'The Temple dedicated all its churches to the Blessed Virgin'.

20. *Règle*, sections 675–7, 685; and see *Procès*, vol. 1, p. 558, vol. 2, p.173.

21. 'Lamentacio quedam pro Templariis', ed. C.R. Cheney, in his 'The Downfall of the Templars and a Letter in their Defence', in idem, *Medieval Texts and Studies* (Oxford: Clarendon Press, 1973), pp. 314–27: here p. 326. This was previously published in *Medieval Miscellany Presented to Eugène Vinaver*, ed. F. Whitehead, A. H. Diverres and F. H. Sutcliffe (Manchester: Manchester University Press, 1965).

22. For Mary's upbringing in the temple, see the 'Protoevangelium of James', *New Testament Apocrypha*, revised edn, ed. Wilhelm Schneemelcher, English trans. ed. R. McL. Wilson, 2 vols (Louisville, KT and Cambridge: James Clarke, 1991), vol. 1, pp. 429–30; this was made known to Christians in western Europe through the Latin Gospel of 'pseudo-Matthew', ibid., pp. 422–4, 457–8; from which it passed into the Golden Legend in the account 'De annunciatione dominica': no. 51, trans. as 'The annunciation', in Jacobus de Voragine, *The Golden Legend: Readings on the Saints*, trans. William Granger Ryan, 2 vols (Princeton: Princeton University Press, 1993), vol. 1, p. 197. For the legend that Mary was given prior warning of the annunciation while she was living in the temple, see 'The Questions of Bartholomew', *New Testament Apocrypha*, vol. 1, pp. 544–5. For the Annunciation according to the *Chanson de Jérusalem*, see: *The Old French Crusade Cycle*, vol. 6: *La Chanson de Jérusalem*, ed. Nigel Thorpe (Tuscaloosa: University of Alabama Press, 1991), line 7681.

23. *Procès*, vol. 1, p. 419; *Untergang des Templerordens*, ed. Schottmüller,

vol. 2, p. 65; MS Bodley 454, fol. 106r; 'Deminutio laboris examinantium processus contra ordinem Templi in Anglia, quasi per modum rubricarum', in *Untergang des Templerordens*, ed. Schottmüller, vol. 2, pp. 78–102, at p. 93; *Annales Londonienses*, ed. William Stubbs, in *Chronicles of the Reigns of Edward 1 and Edward II*, RS 76, 2 vols (London: Longman, 1882), vol. 1, pp. 180–98: here p. 195.

24. 'Philippi descriptio Terrae Sanctae', in W. A. Neumann, 'Drei mittelalterliche Pilgerschriften III', *Oesterreichische Vierteljahresshrift für katholische Theologie*, 11 (1872), 76, note.

25. See the accounts of these miracles by Thietmar and Guy of Chat, edited by P. Devos, 'Les premières versions occidental de la légende de Saïdnaia', *Analecta Bollandiana*, 65 (1947), 255–6, 258, 273. On Saïdnaia see Bernard Hamilton, 'Our Lady of Saidnaiya: an Orthodox Shrine Revered by Muslims and Knights Templar at the Time of the Crusades', in *The Holy Land, Holy Lands, and Christian History: Studies in Church History*, 36 (2001).

26. Caroline Walker Bynum, 'And Woman His Humanity', in her *Fragmentation and Redemption: Essays on Gender and the Human Body in Medieval Religion* (New York: Zone Books, 1992), pp. 151–79: here 152–3; and see her footnote in ibid., p. 357, no. 5.

27. On 'feminine' virtues and their application to men and especially male religious, see Caroline Walker Bynum, *Jesus as Mother: Studies in the Spirituality of the High Middle Ages* (Berkeley: University of California Press, 1982), pp. 128, 138, 259–62; Bynum, *Fragmentation*, pp. 35–7, 108–9, 156, 165–6, 171, 175–9, 218; Joan Ferrante, *Woman as Image in Medieval Literature: From the Twelfth Century to Dante* (New York: Columbia University Press, 1975, repr. Durham, NC: Labyrinth Press, 1985), pp. 45, 69, 107, 127.

28. *Perceforest: Deuxième Partie*, ed. Gilles Roussineau, vol. 2 (Geneva: Droz, 2001), p. 255. For the most recent study, see Silvia Huot, *Postcolonial Fictions in the 'Roman De Perceforest': Cultural Identities and Hybridities* (Cambridge: D. S. Brewer, 2007). For Ninianne see *Lancelot do Lac: The Non-Cyclic Old French Prose Romance*, ed. Elspeth Kennedy, 2 vols (Oxford: Clarendon Press, 1980), vol. 1, pp. 141–7; *Lancelot, roman en prose du XIIIe siècle*, ed. Alexandre Micha. 9 vols (Geneva: Droz, 1978–83), vol. 7, pp. 245–58, section XXIa, parts 7–22. For Perceval's sister, see *La Queste del Saint Graal, roman du XIIIe siècle*, ed. Albert Pauphilet (Paris: Champion, 1980), pp.

201–10, 226–8: or see the translation by Pauline Matarasso (Harmondsworth: Penguin, 1969).

29. For what follows see also my 'The Head of St Euphemia: Templar Devotion to Female Saints', in *Gendering the Crusades*, ed. Susan B. Edgington and Sarah Lambert (Cardiff: University of Wales Press, 2001), pp. 108–20.

30. For a summary of the medieval Catholic attitude towards saints' relics, see Bernard Hamilton, *Religion in the Medieval West* (London: Edward Arnold, 1986), pp. 126–8. For the importance of relics to religious institutions see, for example, Patrick J. Geary, *Furta sacra: Thefts of Relics in the Central Middle Ages* (Princeton: Princeton University Press, 1978); Debra J. Birch, 'Selling the Saints: Competition among Pilgrimage Centres in the Twelfth Century', *Medieval History*, 2.2 (1992), 20–34; Patrick J. Geary, *Living with the Dead in the Middle Ages* (Ithaca: Cornell University Press, 1994), pp. 163–76, 194–218.

31. 'Philippi descriptio', 76; new edition: Frater Philippus de Busseriis, 'Liber peregrinationum, 1285–1291', in *Itinera Hierosolymitana crucesignatorum (saec. XII–XIII)*, ed. S de Sandoli, Studium Biblicum Franciscum: collection maior 24, 4 vols (Jerusalem: Franciscan Print Press, 1978–1984), vol. 4, p. 246, ch. 56.

32. *Procès*, vol. 1, pp. 143–4.

33. Peter von Dusberg, *Chronik des Preussenlandes*, ed. Klaus Scholz and Dieter Wojtecki (Darmstadt: Wissenschaftliche Buchgesellschaft, 1984), pp. 138–40, section 36.

34. *Procès*, vol. 1, pp. 143–4; *Untergang des Templerordens*, ed. Schottmüller, vol. 2, pp. 136, 209, 210, 215; *Trial of the Templars in Cyprus*, pp. 140, 141, 149. *Procès*, vol. 1, p. 419 simply refers to the 'relics' of St Euphemia.

35. Francesco Tommasi, 'I Templari e il culto delle reliquie', in *I Templari: mito e storia. Atti del convegno internazionale di studi alla magione Templare di Poggibonsi-Siena*, ed. Giovanni Minnucci and Franca Sardi (Singalunga-Siena: Casa Editrice A. G. Viti-Riccucci, 1989), pp. 191–210, here p. 209; *Acta sanctorum*, Sept. V (16 September), p. 262.

36. *Untergang des Templerordens*, ed. Schottmüller, vol. 2, pp. 209, 210, 215, and see also p. 129; *Procès*, vol. 2, pp. 240, 249; *Papsttum*, vol. 2, p. 355; see also the testimonies of a series of Templars who had heard since their arrest vague reports of an idol held overseas: *Procès des Templiers d'Auvergne*, pp. 115, 123, 126, 132, 134, 137, 140, 148, 151,

153, 162–3, 164, 166, 169, 178, 182, 185, 188, 194–6, 199, 207–9, 211, 213, 215, 217. On the supposed cult of the Templars' head see Malcolm Barber, 'The Templars and the Turin Shroud', *Catholic Historical Review*, 68 (1982), 206–25, here 214–22; reprinted in Barber, *Crusaders and Heretics*, article 6; see also Barber, *New Knighthood*, pp. 306–7, for a summary of his arguments.

37. *Procès*, vol. 1, p. 419; see also the Templar depositions in *Procès des Templiers d'Auvergne*, pp. 115, 123, 132, 140, 148, 151, 162, 169, 185, 194, 207, where these Brothers stated that they had heard that their cords had touched the mysterious idol overseas.

38. *Procès*, vol. 1, pp. 257, 502, vol. 2, pp. 192, 364, 367; see also vol. 1, p. 399; *Untergang des Templerordens*, ed. Schottmüller, vol. 2, p. 59, may refer to a chapter meeting at Paris; ibid., vol. 2, p. 19 refers vaguely to a 'holy head' which this Brother had heard of; ibid., vol. 2, p. 30, describes a model of a head sitting on the altar, as was normal for reliquaries; ibid., vol. 2, p. 50, describes a white head and again could be a garbled description of a silver reliquary; in *Papsttum*, vol. 2, p. 335, Brother Stephen of Troyes stated that he saw a head at the Paris chapter, but said that it was the head of Hugh de Payns.

39. *Procès*, vol. 2, p. 218.

40. *Procès*, vol. 1, p. 502.

41. 'Et erat ibi quedam cedula consuta in qua erat scriptum caput LVIIIm': *Procès*, vol. 2, p. 218.

42. Tommasi, 'I Templari e il culto', p. 207.

43. The seals show a knight on horseback carrying a shield with a cross motif: this may be St George. See Forey, *Templars in the Corona de Aragón*, p. 453 and notes 4 and 5, and citing Menéndez Pidal, *Catálogo de sellos españoles de la edad média*, p. 182; see also Paul de Saint-Hilaire, *Les Sceaux des Templiers*, pp. 95, 115; and see the seal of Roustan de Comps, at Marseilles, Archives Départementales des Bouches-du-Rhône, la cour des Comptes de Provence, B319 and printed in my *Knights Templar: A New History*, p. 150. For Safed see Denys Pringle, 'Reconstructing the castle of Safad', *Palestine Exploration Quarterly*, 117 (1985), 139–48: here p. 148, quoting Ibn al-Fūrat, *Ayyubids, Mamluks and Crusaders. Selections from the Tārīk al-Duwal wa'l-Mulūk of Ibn al-Fūrat*, text and trans. U. and M. C. Lyons, introduction by Jonathan Riley-Smith, 2 vols (Cambridge: Heffer, 1971), vol. 2, p. 105; for Cressac see Paul Deschamps and Marc Thibaut, *La Peinture murale en France: le haut moyen âge et l'époque*

romane (Paris: Plon, 1951), pp. 132–6; for anecdotes involving the Order and St George see *Das Itinerarium Peregrinorum*, ed. Mayer, p. 249; *Itinerarium peregrinorum et gesta regis Ricardi*, Bk 1, ch. 2, p. 7; *Quinti belli sacri scriptores minores*, pp. 99–100, 130–1, 157; for the prayer see *Procès*, vol. 1, pp. 120–4. For other evidence of Templar veneration of St George see Barber, *New Knighthood*, pp. 202, 271.

44. Jocelin of Brakelond, *Chronicle*, especially p. 104; see also Jane Sayers, 'Violence in the Medieval Cloister', *Journal of Ecclesiastical History*, 41 (1990), 533–42.

45. Alan Forey, 'Literacy and Learning in the Military Orders during the Twelfth and Thirteenth Centuries', *MO*, 2, pp. 185–206: here p. 206.

46. *Le livre des Juges. Les cinq textes de la version française faite au XII siècle pour les chevaliers du Temple*, ed. le Marquis d'Albon (Lyons: Société des bibliophiles Lyonnois, 1913).

47. Paul Meyer, 'Notice sur le manuscrit Fr. 24862 de la Bibliothèque nationale contenant divers ouvrages composés ou écrits en Angleterre', *Notices et extraits des manuscrits de la Bibliothèque nationale et autres bibliothèques publiés par l'Académie des inscriptions et de belles-lettres*, 35 (1896), 131–68; R. C. D. Perman, 'Henri d'Arci: the Shorter Works', in *Studies in Medieval French Presented to Alfred Ewert in Honour of his Seventieth Birthday*, ed. E.A. Francis (Oxford: Clarendon Press, 1961), pp. 279–321; 'The Vision of St Paul', trans. in *The Templars: Selected Sources*, ed. Barber and Bate, pp. 111–15; see also Dominica Legge, *Anglo-Norman Literature and its Background* (Oxford: Clarendon Press, 1963), pp. 191–2.

48. On the eschatalogical context of the Crusades see especially Norman Cohn, *The Pursuit of the Millenium: Revolutionary Millenarians and Mystical Anarchists of the Middle Ages* (London: Secker and Warburg, 1957, and later editions), pp. 61–76. On Antichrist and the Muslims see also John V. Tolan, 'Muslims as Pagan Idolators in Chronicles of the First Crusade', in *Western Views of Islam in Medieval and Early Modern Europe: Perception of Other*, ed. David R. Blanks and Michael Frassetto (New York: St Martin's Press, 1999), pp. 97–117. I am grateful to John Tolan for sending me a copy of his article.

49. For Ricaut Bonomel see Antoine de Bastard, 'La colère et la douleur d'un templier en Terre Sainte', 333–73; translated in *The Templars: Selected Sources*, ed. Barber and Bate, pp. 232–4; for Brother Oliver the Templar, 'Estat aurai lonc temps en pessamen', see *Choix des*

poésies originales des troubadours, ed. M. Raynouard, 6 vols (Paris: F. Didot, 1816–21), vol. 5, p. 272.

50. Hannes Möhring, 'Eine Chronik aus der Zeit des dritten Kreuzzuges: das sogennante *Itinerarium Peregrinorum* I', *Innsbrucker Historische Studien*, 5 (1982), 149–62; *Chronicle of the Third Crusade*, pp. 7–9.

51. Nicholson, *Love, War and the Grail*, pp. 102–83.

52. Taken from my translation in *Chronicle of the Third Crusade*, pp. 25–5, Bk 1, ch. 2.

53. Ibid., p. 34, Bk 1, ch. 5.

54. *Untergang des Templerordens*, ed. Schottmüller, vol. 2, p. 134 (Brindisi proceedings), 259, 265, 273, 292, 333, 336, 337, 340, 391, 392 (Cyprus proceedings); on hospices, see note 12 on Chapter 4, above.

55. *Untergang des Templerordens*, ed. Schottmüller, vol. 2, pp. 392–3; *Procès*, vol. 1, p. 647.

56. *CH*, no. 560.

57. Nicholson, *Templars, Hospitallers*, pp. 53, 153 nn. 121–7.

58. Cristina Dondi, 'Manoscritti liturgici dei templari e degli ospedalieri: le nuove prospettive aperte dal sacramentario templare di Modena (Biblioteca Capitolare O. II. 13)', in *I Templari, la guerra e la santità*, ed. Simonetta Cerrini (Rimini: Il Cerchio, 2000), pp. 85–131; Cristina Dondi, *The Liturgy of the Canons Regular of the Holy Sepulchre of Jerusalem: a Study and a Catalogue of the Manuscript Sources* (Turnhout: Brepols, 2004), p. 41.

59. Gilchrist, *Contemplation and Action*, p. 94. Apart from the round-naved churches she mentions, the Templars had round-naved churches at their houses in Paris and Prague, and a circular chapel at Castle Pilgrim ('Atlīt).

60. For instance, *Procès*, vol. 1, pp. 299–300, 314, 318, 323, 594; *Procès des Templiers d'Auvergne*, pp. 116, 120, 123, 129, 132, 137, 140, 148, 151, 153, 162, 166, 169, 177, 182, 185, 194, 196, 202, 209, 211, 213, 215, 217, 219.

61. *Procès*, vol. 1, p. 219.

62. *Procès*, vol. 1, p. 267.

63. On Cypriot witnesses see note 11, above. Joinville, *La vie de Saint Louis*, p. 190, section 514; see also Barber, *New Knighthood*, p. 214, and see p. 372, note 117; for the rule against being godfather, see *Règle*, section 72.

64. *Papsttum*, vol. 2, p. 336.

65. Nicholson, 'The Head of St Euphemia', pp. 108–20. For my

information on the cult of St Euphemia in the Greek Orthodox Church today I am indebted to the research of Dr Judith Upton-Ward of Fatih University, Istanbul. See also St Euphemia's entry in the *Acta Sanctorum*, Sept V (16 September).

66. Nicholson, *Templars, Hospitallers*, pp. 71, 77; Selwood, *Knights of the Cloister*, pp. 43–7.

67. Matthew Paris, *Chronica majora*, vol. 5, pp. 149–50.

68. *Old French Crusade Cycle, VIII: The London-Turin Version*, ed. Peter R. Grillo (Tuscaloosa, AL: University of Alabama Press, 1994), lines 13442–8; and see my *Love, War and the Grail*, p. 45 and pp. 43–64 for the literary context.

Notes to Chapter 6: Most Trustworthy Servants

1. Walter Map, *De nugis*, p. 114.

2. See, for instance, Marie Luise Bulst-Thiele, 'Templer in königlichen und päpstlichen Diensten', in *Festscrift Percy Ernst Schramm*, ed. Peter Classen and Peter Scheibert, 2 vols (Wiesbaden: F. Steiner, 1964), vol. 1, pp. 289–308; Léopold Delisle, 'Mémoire sur les opérations financières des Templiers', *Mémoires de l'Institut National de France, Académie des Inscriptions et Belles-Lettres*, 33, 2 (1889); Alain Demurger, 'Trésor des Templiers, trésor du roi. Mise au point sur les opérations financières des Templiers', *Pouvoir et Gestion: cinquièmes rencontres, 29 et 30 novembre 1996* (Toulouse: Presses de l'Université des sciences sociales de Toulouse, 1996), pp. 73–85; Thomas W. Parker, *The Knights Templars in England* (Turson: University of Arizona Press, 1963); Jules Piquet, *Des banquiers au moyen âge: Les Templiers. Étude sur leur opérations financières* (Paris: Hachette, 1939); Agnes Sandys, 'The Financial and Administrative Importance of the London Temple in the Thirteenth Century', in *Essays in Medieval History presented to Thomas Frederick Tout*, ed. A. G. Little and F. M. Powicke (Manchester: Manchester University Press, 1925), pp. 147–62; Nicholson, *Templars, Hospitallers*, pp. 15–34; Nicholson, 'The Military Orders and the Kings of England'; Clarence Perkins, 'The Knights Templars in the British Isles', *English Historical Review*, 25 (1910), 209–30; see also *Records of the Templars*, p. lviii. The information which follows is drawn from these sources. See now also Ignacio de la Torre, 'The London and Paris Temples: a Comparative Analysis of their Financial Services for the Kings during the 13th Century', in *MO*, 4.

3. *Monumenta Germaniae Historica Epistolae saeculi XIII e regestis pontificum Romanorum selecti*, ed. G. H. Pertz and K. Rodenburg, 3 vols (Berlin, 1883–94), vol. 1, p. 90, no. 124.

4. *L'histoire de Guillaume le Maréchal, comte de Striguil et de Pembroke*, ed. Paul Meyer, SHF, 3 vols (Paris: Renouard, 1891–1901), lines 18317–20; new edn: *History of William Marshal*, 3 vols, ed. A. J. Holden, trans. S. Gregory, historical notes by David Crouch, Anglo-Norman Text Society (London: Birkbeck College, 2002–6).

5. See the material in note 2 above, and Robert I. Burns, *The Crusader Kingdom of Valencia: Reconstruction on a Thirteenth Century Frontier*, 2 vols (Cambridge, MA: Harvard University Press, 1967), vol. 1, p. 194.

6. Barber, *New Knighthood*, pp. 67–9, 153–4.

7. Dunstable Annals, in *Annales monastici*, vol. 3, p. 222.

8. Roger of Wendover, *Flores historiarum*, ed. Henry R. Hewlett, RS 84, 3 vols (London: Longman, 1886–9), vol. 3, p. 41; Matthew Paris, *Chronica majora*, vol. 3, pp. 232–3.

9. For a summary see Barber, *New Knighthood*, pp. 296–7.

10. Thomas of Canterbury, 'Epistolae', in *RHGF*, vol. 16, pp. 430–2, no. 274.

11. Innocent III, 'Registres', *PL*, vol. 215, col. 708, year 8, no. 131.

12. *Foedera, conventions, litterae et cuiuscumque generis acta publica inter reges Angliae et alios quosvis imperatores...* , ed. Thomas Rymer and Robert Sanderson, revised by Adam Clark, Frederick Holbrooke and John Caley, 4 vols in 7 parts (London: George Eyre and Andrew Strahan, 1816–69), vol. 1, p. 144.

13. *Les registres d'Urbain IV (1261–1264)*, ed. Jean Guiraud, BEFAR (Paris, 1900–29), nos. 760, 765, 771; Burgtorf, *Central Convent*, pp. 425, 445, 471.

14. *CH*, nos. 3221, 3228; Nicholson, *Templars, Hospitallers*, pp. 32–3; Burgtorf, *Central Convent*, pp. 425, 470–1.

15. 'Chronique de Primat, traduite par Jean du Vignay', in *RHGF*, vol. 23, pp. 50–51, 54–5; Burgtorf, *Central Convent*, p. 473.

16. The standard work on the Templars in Ireland remains Herbert Wood, 'The Templars in Ireland', *Proceedings of the Royal Irish Academy*, 26, section C, no. 14 (July, 1907), 327–77; the standard work on the Hospitallers is Caesar Litton Falkiner, 'The Hospital of St John of Jerusalem in Ireland', *Proceedings of the Royal Irish Academy*, 26C, no. 12 (March, 1907), 275–317. For donations to the Templars see:

Aubrey Gwynn and R. N. Hadcock, *Medieval Religious Houses in Ireland* (London: Longman, 1970), pp. 329–31, 342; *Calendar of Documents Relating to Ireland, preserved in Her Majesty's Public Record Office, London*, ed. H. S. Sweetman, 5 vols (London: HMSO, 1875–86), henceforth cited as *CDRI*, vol. 1, p. 13, no. 83; W. E. Wightman, *The Lacy Family in England and Normandy, 1066–1194* (Oxford: Oxford University Press, 1966), pp. 82, 189, 207. See now also Helen Nicholson, 'Serving King and Crusade: The Military Orders in Royal Service in Ireland, 1220–1400', in *The Experience of Crusading*, vol. 1: *Western Approaches*, ed. Marcus Bull and Norman Housley (Cambridge: Cambridge University Press, 2003), pp. 233–52.

17. *CDRI*, vol. 1, pp. 147–8, no. 966.

18. Roger of Wendover, *Flores historiarum*, vol. 2, pp. 80–83; Matthew Paris, *Chronica majora*, vol. 3, pp. 274–6.

19. *CDRI*, vol. 1, pp. 320–21, nos. 2157, 2161.

20. *CDRI*, vol. 1, p. 336, no. 2264.

21. *CDRI*, vol. 1, p. 381, no. 2556, pp. 391–2, no. 2623, p. 403, no. 2703, p. 458, no. 3071; *CDRI*, vol. 2, p. 36, no. 238, p. 40, no. 266; *CDRI*, vol. 3, p. 143, no. 881, pp. 282–3, nos 1485, 1489, p. 345, no. 1678, p. 397, no. 1846; *CDRI*, vol. 4, p. 376, no. 825.

22. On this subject see Alan Forey, 'The Military Orders and Holy War against Christians in the thirteenth century', *English Historical Review*, 104 (1989), 1–24: repr. in his *Military Orders and Crusades*, article 7.

23. Peter Lock, 'The Military Orders in Mainland Greece', in *MO*, 1, pp. 333–9.

24. On Falkirk and Edward I see Parker, *The Knights Templars in England*, p. 48; on the Hospital see Simon Phillips, *The Prior of the Knights Hospitaller in Late Medieval England* (Woodbridge: Boydell and Brewer, 2009), pp. 45–58.

25. *Études sur les actes de Louis VII*, ed. Achille Luchaire (Paris: A. Picard, 1885), pp. 254–5, no. 485, pp. 259–60, no. 504, pp. 291–2, no. 608, p. 305, no. 652. For Thierry before he became a Templar, see nos 50, 54, 55, 57, 200, 270, 277, 278, 279, 286, 289, 296, 303, 339, 340. See also *Records of the Templars*, p. 214; letters of Suger, abbot of St Denis, in *RHGF*, vol. 15, p. 524, no. 109.

26. *RHGF*, vol. 16, p. 38, no. 124; *RRH*, no. 398.

27. *Close Rolls of the Reign of Henry III Preserved in the Public Record*

Office (London: HMSO, 1902–1975), 1242–1247, p. 311.

28. On lay patrons and religious Orders in general see, for instance, C. B. Bouchard, *Sword, Miter and Cloister: Nobility and the Church in Burgundy, 980–1198* (Ithaca and London: Cornell University Press, 1987); Emma Mason, 'Timeo Barones et Dona Ferentes', in *Religious Motivation: Biographical and Sociological Problems for the Church Historian*, ed. Derek Baker, *Studies in Church History*, 15 (1978), pp. 61–75.

29. *Regesta regum Anglo-Normannorum 1066–1154*, vol. 3: *1135–1154*, ed. H. W. C. Davis, H. A. Cronne and R. H. C. Davis (Oxford: Clarendon Press, 1968), pp. 310–14, nos 843–53; *Records of the Templars*, pp. xxxix–xl.

30. *Records of the Templars*, pp. 142–3.

31. William Rees, *History of the Order of St John of Jerusalem in Wales and on the Welsh Border, including an Account of the Templars* (Cardiff: Western Mail and Echo, 1947), pp. 31–2, 51–3.

32. *Records of the Templars*, pp. 140–42; Perkins, 'Knights Templars in the British Isles', 216; Nicholson, 'Military Orders and Kings of England', pp. 207–9. A mark is two-thirds of a pound.

33. *Records of the Templars*, pp. 139–40.

34. Peter W. Edbury, 'The Templars in Cyprus', *MO*, 1, pp. 189–95: here pp. 189–91.

35. Bulst-Thiele, *Sacrae domus*, p. 125; *Chronique d'Ernoul*, pp. 296–7; Ralph of Coggeshall, *Chronicon*, p. 54.

36. Nicholson, 'Military Orders and Kings of England', pp. 205–9.

37. Alan Forey, 'The Crusading Vows of the English King Henry III', *Durham University Journal*, 65 (1973), 229–47; reprinted in his *Military Orders and Crusades*, article 13. For the crusading policy of the English monarchy see also Simon Lloyd, *English Society and the Crusade, 1216–1307* (Oxford: Oxford University Press, 1988); Christopher Tyerman, *England and the Crusades, 1095–1588* (Chicago and London: Chicago University Press, 1988).

38. Matthew Paris, *Chronica majora*, vol. 5, p. 339.

39. *Foedera*, ed. Rymer and Sanderson, vol. 2.1, p. 20.

40. *Recueil des actes de Philippe Auguste, roi de France*, vol. 4: *Années du règne XXXVII à XLIV (1er novembre 1215–14 juillet 1223)*, ed. Charles Samaran and Michel Nortier (Paris: Imprimerie nationale, 1979), pp. 471–72; *Layettes du trésor des chartes*, ed. Alexandre Teulet et al., 5 vols (Paris: Archives nationales, 1863–1909), vol. 4, p. 419, no.

5638; *Spicilegium sive collectio veterum aliquot scriptorum qui in Galliae Bibliothecis delituerant*, ed. Luke d'Achery, vol. 3 (Paris: Montalant, 1723; repr. Farnborough: Gregg Press, 1967–68), pp. 691–2.

41. *Historia diplomatica Fridericii Secundi*, ed. J. L. A. Huillard-Bréholles, 6 vols in 11 (Paris: Henri Plon, 1852–61, repr. Turin, 1963), vol. 4.1, pp. 227–9.

42. For a summary see Maurice Powicke, *The Thirteenth Century, 1216–1307*, 2nd edn (Oxford: Oxford University Press, 1962), pp. 325, 358, 376–7.

43. 'Deminutio laboris examinantium processus', pp. 81–3.

44. On this see Nicholson, *Templars, Hospitallers*, pp. 29–31; Innocent III, 'Registres', *PL*, vol. 215, cols 1217–18, year 10, no. 121.

45. *Les registres de Grégoire IX*, ed. Lucien Auvray, BEFAR, 2 vols (Paris: E. de Boccard, 1896–1907), no. 4129; *Les registres de Nicolas III (1277–1280)*, ed. J. Gay and Suzanne Vitte, BEFAR (Paris: E. de Boccard, 1898–1938), no. 167; *CH*, no. 3674.

46. Roger of Howden, *Chronica*, vol. 4, pp. 76–7.

47. W. L. Warren, *Henry II* (London: Methuen, 1973), pp. 72, 88, 90; Roger of Howden, *Chronica*, vol. 1, p. 218; *Records of the Templars*, pp. li–liv and note on p. lii, 273.

Notes to Chapter 7: Commercial and Economic Activities

1. 'Sur les états du monde', *Anglo-Norman Political Songs*, ed. Isabel S. T. Aspin, Anglo-Norman Texts, 11 (Oxford: Blackwell, 1953), p. 123, verse 24.

2. This report is based on information supplied to me by Idan Shaked in a communication of 14 November 2000. I am extremely grateful to him for this information. See his article in Hebrew, 'Identifying the Medieval Flour Mills at Doq and Recordane', in *Cathedra*, 98 (2000), 61–72. I am also very grateful to Professor Denys Pringle for drawing my attention to Idan Shaked's work.

3. *CH*, nos. 2117, 3045; Riley-Smith, *Knights of St John*, p. 446; Denys Pringle, *Secular Buildings in the Crusader Kingdom of Jerusalem: An Archaeological Gazetteer* (Cambridge: Cambridge University Press, 1997), p. 47, no. 85, and pp. 62–4, no. 133.

4. Geoffrey Day, *Tide Mills in England and Wales* (Woodbridge: Friends of Woodbridge Tide Mill, 1994), pp. 10–11, 20; Richard Holt, *The Mills of Medieval England* (Oxford: Blackwell, 1988), p. 173; *Records*

of the Templars, pp. xxii, 135, 449.

5. P. M. Ryan, 'Cressing Temple: Its History from Documentary Sources', in *Cressing Temple: A Templar and Hospitaller Manor in Essex*, ed. D. D. Andrews (Chelmsford: Essex County Council Planning, 1993), pp. 11–24; see also Tim Robey, 'The Archaeology of Cressing Temple' in ibid., pp. 37–50; and for other medieval barns see Dave Stenning, 'The Cressing Barns and the Early Development of Barns in South-East England', in ibid., pp. 51–75.

6. *Records of the Templars*, pp. clxxxii–clxxxiv.

7. An area of land that could be ploughed by a yoke of oxen in a day. In theory, the equivalent of the English acre.

8. A due paid to the Church from the harvest.

9. Forey, *The Templars in the Corona de Aragón*, pp. 368–9; for other examples of settlement charters see *The Templars: Selected Sources*, ed. and trans. Malcolm Barber and Keith Bate (Manchester: Manchester University Press, 2002), pp. 170–2.

10. T. N. Bisson, 'Credit, Prices and Agrarian Production in Catalonia: a Templar Account (1180–1188)', in *Order and Innovation in the Middle Ages*, ed. W. C. Jordan *et al.* (Princeton: Princeton University Press, 1976); for wool production in Normandy, see *The Templars: Selected Sources*, ed. Barber and Bate, pp. 191, 195, 197, 198; for England, see Nicholson, *Knights Templar on Trial*, pp. 77–9

11. Pringle, *Secular Buildings*, p. 24, no. 22, p. 26, no. 28.

12. Pringle, *Secular Buildings*, p. 96, no. 208.

13. Holt, *Mills*, p. 153.

14. *Records of the Templars*, pp. 167–8.

15. In the winter of 1309–10, the River Thames froze, which was hitherto unheard-of: *Chronicles of the Reigns of Edward I and Edward II*, vol. 1: *Annales Londonienses and Annales Paulini*, ed. William Stubbs, RS 76 (London: Longman, 1882), p. 158.

16. Damien Carraz, *L'Ordre du Temple dans la basse vallée du Rhône (1124–1312): Ordres militaires, croisades de sociétés méridionales* (Lyons: Presses universitaires, 2005), pp. 256–83.

17. Victor Carrière, *L'histoire et cartulaire des Templiers de Provins* (Paris: Champion, 1919), no. 160, pp. 168–71.

18. On the Templars' financial operations, see, for instance: Delisle, 'Mémoire sur les opérations financières des Templiers'; Demurger, 'Trésor des Templiers, trésor du roi'; D. M. Metcalf, 'The Templars as Bankers and Monetary Transfers between East and West in the

Twelfth Century', in *Coinage in the Latin East: The Fourth Oxford Symposium on Coinage and Monetary History*, ed. Peter W. Edbury and D. M. Metcalf, British Archaeological Reports, International Series, 77 (1980), 1–17; Piquet, *Des banquiers au moyen âge: Les Templiers*; Sandys, 'The Financial and Administrative Importance of the London Temple'; Parker, *The Knights Templars in England*; Clarence Perkins, 'The Knights Templars in the British Isles', *English Historical Review*, 25 (1910), 209–30.

19. Joinville, *La vie de Saint Louis*, pp. 168–9. See also the translation by M. R. B. Shaw, Joinville and Villehardouin, *Chronicles of the Crusades*, p. 267.

20. See, for instance, Templar loans in *Les plus anciennes chartes en langue Provençale*, ed. Clovis Brunel, 2 vols (Paris: A. Picard, 1926–52), nos 103, 125; MS Bodley 454, fol. 154r.

21. *Rotuli chartarum in Turri Londinensi asservati*, ed. Thomas Duffus Hardy, vol. 1.1 (London: Eyre and Spottiswoode, 1837), pp. 2b, 3, 188; *Calendar of the Charter Rolls Preserved in the Public Record Office*, vol. 1 (London: HMSO, 1903), pp. 5, 8, 22, 255; *Records of the Templars*, p. 254.

22. Carrière, *L'histoire et cartulaire des Templiers de Provins*, pp. 152–4, no. 148.

23. On all of this see Malcolm Barber, 'Supplying the Crusader States: the Role of the Templars', in *The Horns of Hattin*, ed. Benjamin Z. Kedar (Jerusalem: Yad Izak Ben-Zvi and Aldershot: Variorum, 1992), pp. 314–26; reprinted in his *Crusaders and Heretics*, article 12; Metcalf, 'The Templars as Bankers'.

24. Jean-Claude Bonnin, 'Les Templiers et la mer, l'exemple de La Rochelle,' *La Commanderie*, ed. Luttrell and Pressouyre, pp. 307–15.

25. On naval exploration in this period see Felipe Fernández-Armesto, *Before Columbus: Exploration and Colonisation from the Mediterranean to the Atlantic, 1229–1492* (Basingstoke: Macmillan, 1987), esp. pp. 152–3. See also J. R. S. Phillips, *The Medieval Expansion of Europe* (Oxford: Oxford University Press, 1988, 1998), parts II and III; and on Greenland Kirsten A. Seaver, *The Frozen Echo: Greenland and the Exploration of North America, ca. 1000–1500* (Stanford, CA: Stanford University Press, 1996).

26. Barber, 'Supplying the Crusader States', p. 324; Nicholson, 'Military Orders and the Kings of England', pp. 212–14.

27. Alain Demurger, 'Between Barcelona and Cyprus: The Travels of

Berenguer of Cardona, Templar Master of Aragon and Catalonia (1300–1), in *International Mobility in the Military Order, Twelfth to Fifteenth Centuries: Travelling on Christ's Business*, ed. Jochen Burgtorf and Helen J. Nicholson (Cardiff: University of Wales Press, 2006), pp. 65–74.

28. Ramon Muntaner, *Chronicle*, ch. 194. There are various editions of the chronicle. One of the most recent is Ramon Muntaner, *Crònica*, ed. Marina Gustà, 3rd edn (Barcelona: Edicions 62, 1989). For an English translation, see Lady Goodenough, *Chronicle of Muntaner*, vol. 2, Hakluyt Society 2nd series, 50 (1920), pp. 466–9.

29. The evidence is most conveniently set out and summarized by Barber, 'Supplying the Crusader States', pp. 324–6.

30. *Règle*, section 423.

31. *Règle*, sections 598, 600, 604–9. The Brother in section 608 shouted '*Mau gre en eust Dieu et sa mere*'.

32. *Règle*, sections 553–4.

33. Roger of Howden, *Gesta*, vol. 2, pp. 47–8; Roger of Howden, *Chronica*, vol. 2, p. 354.

34. Wood, 'Templars in Ireland', 333.

35. MS Bodley 454, fol. 60r.

Notes to Chapter 8: The Trial of the Templars

1. 'Le Templier de Tyr', in *Les gestes des Chyprois, recueil de chroniques françaises écrites en orient en XIII et XIV siècles*, ed. G. Raynaud, Société de l'orient latin (Paris, 1887; repr. Osnabrück, 1968), p. 253; new edn: *Cronica del Templare di Tiro*, ed. L. Minervina (Naples: Liguori, 2000), pp. 220, 222. For another translation, see: Paul Crawford, *The 'Templar of Tyre': Part III of the 'Deeds of the Cypriots'* (Aldershot: Ashgate, 2003), p. 114.

2. Burgtorf, *Central Convent*, p. 145; Crawford, *The 'Templar of Tyre'*, section 537, p. 131; Silvia Schein, 'The Templars: the Regular Army of the Holy Land and the Spearhead of the Army of its Reconquest', in *I Templari: mito e storia*, ed. Minnucci and Sardi, pp. 15–25, here p. 22.

3. Bulst Thiele, *Sacrae domus*, pp. 291–4; Anthony Luttrell, 'The Election of the Templar Master Jacques de Molay', in *Debate on the Trial of the Templars*, ed. Burgtorf, Crawford and Nicholson.

4. On Jacques of Molay see Bulst Thiele, *Sacrae domus*, pp. 294–359; Alain Demurger, *The Last Templar: The Tragedy of Jacques de Molay*,

last Grand Master of the Temple, trans. Antonia Nevill (London: Profile, 2005); Malcolm Barber, *New Knighthood*, pp. 290–5

5. Norman Cohn, *Europe's Inner Demons: The Demonization of Christians in Medieval Christendom* (London: Chatto and Heinemann, 1975; London: Pimlico, 1993), pp. 118–23; Elizabeth Hallam, *Capetian France, 987–1328* (London: Longman, 1980), pp. 313–17; Malcolm Barber, *The Two Cities: Medieval Europe 1050–1320* (London: Routledge, 1992), pp. 114–16.

6. On Clement see Sophia Menache, *Pope Clement V* (Cambridge: Cambridge University Press, 1998).

7. Silvia Schein, '*Gesta Dei per Mongolos* 1300. The Genesis of a Non-Event', *English Historical Review*, 94 (1979), 805–19.

8. For discussion of this question, see Paul Crawford, 'Imagination and the Templars: The Development of the Order-State in the early fourteenth Century', *ΕΠΕΤΗΡΙΔΑ* (Epeterida), 30 (2004), 113–21.

9. On the situation in Cyprus see Edbury, *Cyprus and the Crusades*, pp. 107–17 and p. 121, note 76.

10. Alan Forey, 'The Military Orders in the Crusading Proposals of the Late Thirteenth and Early Fourteenth Centuries', *Traditio*, 36 (1980), 317–45 and in his *Military Orders and Crusades*, article 8; Antony Leopold, *How to Recover the Holy Land: the Crusade Proposals of the Late Thirteenth and Early Fourteenth Centuries* (Aldershot: Ashgate, 2000); Silvia Schein, *Fideles crucis: The Papacy, the West, and the Recovery of the Holy Land* (Oxford: Oxford University Press, 1991); Schein, 'The Templars: the Regular Army of the Holy Land'; Silvia Schein, 'The Future Regnum Hierusalem: A Chapter in Medieval State Planning', *Journal of Medieval History*, 10 (1984), 95–105.

11. Jacques's comments were written in Latin. They are printed with a French translation in *Dossier de l'affaire des Templiers*, pp. 2–15 and translated in *The Templars: Selected Sources*, ed. Barber and Bate, pp. 234–8; for his crusade plan see ibid., pp. 105–9. Fulk's plan is translated by Norman Housley, *Documents on the Later Crusades, 1274–1580* (Basingstoke: Macmillan, 1996), pp. 40–7. See also Alain Demurger, 'Les ordres militaires et la croisade au début du XIVe siècle: Quelques remarques sur les traités de croisade de Jacques de Molay et de Foulques de Villaret', in *Dei gesta per Francos*, ed. Balard et al., pp. 117–28.

12. Schein, *Fideles crucis*, pp. 112–39; Nicholson, *Templars, Hospitallers*, pp. 71–4; Nicholson, *Love, War and the Grail*, pp. 78–87, 106–7.

13. For the course of the trial see: Barber, *Trial of the Templars*; Demurger, *Vie et mort de l'ordre du Temple*, pp. 289–352; Marie Luise Bulst-Thiele, 'Der Prozess gegen den Templerorden', in *Die geistlichen Ritterorden Europas*, ed. Fleckenstein and Hellmann, pp. 375–402.

14. Henry Charles Lea, *A History of the Inquisition in the Middle Ages*, 3 vols (New York: Macmillan, 1887–9 and reprints), vol. 3, esp. p. 334. See also: Kaspar Elm, 'Der Templerprozess, 1307–1312', reprinted in his *Umbilicus Mundi*, pp. 507–27: here p. 509. See also: Malcolm Barber, 'Propaganda in the Middle Ages: the Charges Against the Templars', *Nottingham Medieval Studies*, 17 (1973), pp. 42–57; Malcolm Barber, 'The Trial of the Templars Revisited', in *MO*, 2, pp. 329–42. For the debate over the basis of the charges see the survey by Barber, *Trial of the Templars*, pp. 68, 69–72, 120, 133–7, 143–7, 150–1, 155, 160–1, 184, 192–6, 283; pp. 296–304, especially p. 304. For individual views on both sides see Elena Bellomo, *The Templar Order in North-west Italy (1142–c.1330)* (Leiden: Brill, 2008), p. 201; Jonathan Riley-Smith, 'Were the Templars Guilty?', in *The Medieval Crusade*, ed. Susan J. Ridyard (Woodbridge: Boydell, 2004), pp. 107–24 (discussed by Barber, *Trial of the Templars*, pp. 307–8); Demurger, *Les Templiers*, pp. 489–94; Arnaud de la Croix, *L'Ordre du Temple et le reniement du Christ* (Paris: Editions du Rocher, 2004); Barbara Frale, 'The Chinon Chart: Papal absolution to the last Templar, Master Jacques de Molay', *Journal of Medieval History*, 30 (2004), 109–34.

15. Barber, 'Propaganda in the Middle Ages', here 57; Edward Peters, *Heresy and Authority in Medieval Europe: Documents in Translation* (London: Scolar, 1980), no. 27, p. 162; no. 22A, p. 134; Barber, *Trial of the Templars*, pp. 204–5, 209, 213; Bernard Gui, *The Inquisitor's Guide: a Medieval Manual on Heretics*, trans. and ed. Janet Shirley (Welwyn Garden City: Ravenhall, 2006), p. 57.

16. See Malcolm Lambert, *Medieval Heresy: Popular Movements from the Gregorian Reform to the Reformation*, 2nd edn (Oxford: Blackwells, 1992), here pp. 186–8, 208–12. On Gregory IX's accusation against the Hospital see *CH*, no. 2186.

17. Norman Housley, *The Avignon Papacy and the Crusades, 1305–1378* (Oxford: Oxford University Press, 1986), pp. 267–71.

18. H. A. Kelly, 'Inquision and the Prosecution of Heresy: Misconceptions and Abuses', *Church History*, 58 (1989), 439–51; Richard Kieckhefer, 'The Office of Inquisition and Medieval Heresy:

the Transition from Personal to Institutional Jurisdiction', *Journal of Ecclesiastical History*, 46 (1995), 36–61.

19. Edward Peters, *Torture* (Oxford: Blackwell, 1985), pp. 50, 57–8, 65–6.

20. For research in this area see Gisli H. Gudjonsson, *The Psychology of Interrogations, Confessions and Testimony* (New York: Wiley, 1992), esp. pp. 205–59.

21. Bernard Hamilton, *The Albigensian Crusade*, Historical Association Pamphlet, G. 85 (London: Historical Association, 1974), pp. 25–7.

22. For the rise of medieval magic, its role in society and its persecution see: Cohn, *Europe's Inner Demons*; Richard Kieckhefer, *Magic in the Middle Ages* (Cambridge: Cambridge University Press, 1989). For some medieval magical texts and studies on these see *Picatrix: The Latin Version of the Ghāyat Al-Hakīm*, ed. David Pingree (London: Warburg Institute, 1986); *Textes latins et vieux français relatifs aux Cyranides*, ed. Louis Delatte (Liège and Paris, 1942); Richard Kieckhefer, *Forbidden Rites: A Necromancer's Manual of the Fifteenth Century* (Stroud: Sutton Publishing, 1997); *Conjuring Spirits: Texts and Traditions of Medieval Ritual Magic*, ed. Claire Fanger (Stroud: Sutton Publishing, 1998).

23. *Picatrix*, pp. 1, 4.

24. Barber, 'Propaganda', 51–4; Malcolm Barber, 'The Templars and the Turin Shroud', *Catholic Historical Review*, 68 (1982), 206–25: reprinted in Barber, *Crusaders and Heretics*, article 6.

25. Gilchrist, *Contemplation and Action*, pp. 95–6; Jonathan Riley-Smith, *Hospitallers: The History of the Order of St John* (London and Rio Grande, OH: Hambledon Press, 1999), p. 53.

26. Ambroise, *Estoire*, lines 3701–30; new edn, lines 3696–722; *Chronicle of the Third Crusade*, Bk 1, ch. 56, pp. 110–11. See also Tolan, 'Muslims as Pagan Idolators'; C. Meredith Jones, 'The Conventional Saracen of the *Chanson de Geste*', *Speculum*, 17 (1942), 201–25; Matthew Bennet, 'First Crusaders' Images of Muslims: the Influence of Vernacular Poetry?' *Forum for Modern Language Studies*, 22.2 (1986), 101–22.

27. Matthew Paris, *Chronica majora*, vol. 5, pp. 149–50.

28. See Kieckhefer, *Forbidden Rites*, p. 187.

29. Richard Kieckhefer, *European Witch Trials: Their Foundations in Popular and Learned Culture, 1300–1500* (Berkeley and Los Angeles: University of California Press, 1976), pp. 12, 109.

30. A. Beardwood, 'The Trial of Walter Langton, Bishop of Lichfield', *Transactions of the American Philosophical Society*, New Series, 54 part 3 (Philadelphia, 1964), pp. 7–8; Kieckhefer, *European Witch Trials*, pp. 13, 108.

31. A. Neary, 'The Origins and Character of the Kilkenny Witchcraft Case of 1324', *Proceedings of the Royal Irish Academy Section C*, 83 (1983), 333–50; Kieckhefer, *European Witch Trials*, pp. 13–14, 111.

32. Cohn, *Europe's Inner Demons*, pp. 118–30; Kieckhefer, *European Witch Trials*, p. 12.

33. Patrick Geary has pointed out that from the eleventh century onwards cults shifted from veneration of a body to a statue or picture or to the consecrated host, and that piety was moving away from localized cults focused on a local saint's relics towards 'a wider and more individualistic form of veneration': Geary, *Living with the Dead*, pp. 175–6. The implication in the accusations against the Templars that it is idolatrous to venerate a saint's skull certainly seems to reflect such a shift in piety. For discussion of the role of the *literati* in the accusations see Barber, 'Trial of the Templars Revisited', pp. 340–2.

34. Jacques de Molay's evidence to the papal commissioners, 28 November 1309, in *Dossier de l'affaire des Templiers*, p. 166; see also Thomas Bérard's letter to Amadeus in the Annals of Burton, giving the Order's church plate as its most valuable possession: pp. 491–5; *Untergang des Templerordens*, ed. Schottmüller, vol. 2, p. 160; *Trial of the Templars on Cyprus*, p. 67.

35. Gilmour-Bryson, 'Sodomy and the Knights Templar', 179, 180; *Procès*, vol. 1, pp. 242, 250, 317, 333, 345–6, 354, 567, vol. 2, p. 178.

36. For some of the cats mentioned during the trial see *Papsttum*, vol. 2, pp. 344 (brown cat), 345, 347 (black cat), 349 (brown cat), 350, 351 (white cat), 352–5, 357 (black cat), 361, 362 (black cat). This is one set of confessions from the Vatican archives. Only one cat turns up in the Auvergne trial depositions, walking into a chapter meeting: *Procès des Templiers d'Auvergne*, p. 56 and no. 11. The editor remarks that this was 'a stray, no doubt'.

37. *Papsttum*, vol. 2, pp. 83–5, no. 57; trans. in *The Templars: Selected Sources*, ed. Barber and Bate, pp. 256–7. On Esquiu de Floyran, also known as Esquieu de Floyrac, see David Bryson, 'Three "Traitors" of the Temple: was their Truth the whole Truth?', in *The Debate on the Trial of the Templars*, ed. Burgtorf, Crawford and Nicholson.

38. Cohn, *Europe's Inner Demons*, pp. 123–30; Barber, 'The Trial of the Templars Revisited', 339–40.

39. For discussion of these and similar theories see Partner, *Knights Templar and their Myth*, pp. 68–9, 153–5; Forey, *The Military Orders*, pp. 231–3; Barber, *Trial of the Templars*, pp. 304–8.

40. *Procès des Templiers d'Auvergne*, pp. 89, 245–63; *Papsttum*, vol. 2, p. 74, no. 50.

41. *Untergang des Templerordens*, ed. Schottmüller, vol. 2, pp. 81–3.

42. Ibid., pp. 83, 90, and note 1; MS Bodley 454, fols 98r–v. For the various records of the trial in the British Isles see Nicholson, *Knights Templar on Trial*, pp. 14, 94–5,175–6, 183–4; on Agnes, see pp. 117–18. For the texts, see my new edition, *The Trial of the Templars in the British Isles* (Aldershot: Ashgate, forthcoming).

43. On the trial in France see Demurger, *Vie et mort de l'ordre du Temple*, pp. 298–322; Barber, *Trial of the Templars*; William Chester Jordan, *Unceasing Strife, Unending Fear: Jacques de Thérines and the Freedom of the Church in the Age of the Last Capetians* (Princeton: Princeton University Press, 2005), pp. 22–32.

44. C. R. Cheney, 'The Downfall of the Templars and a Letter in their Defence', p. 323.

45. Ibid., pp. 323–5.

46. *Dossier de l'affaire des Templiers*, pp. 154–63; for another translation, this time of the whole testimony, see *The Templars: Selected Sources*, ed. Barber and Bate, pp. 289–92.

47. Peter Edbury, *The Kingdom of Cyprus and the Crusades, 1191–1374* (Cambridge: Cambridge University Press, 1991), p. 121.

48. Malcolm Barber, 'The World Picture of Philip the Fair', *Journal of Medieval History*, 8 (1982), 13–27; reprinted in his *Crusaders and Heretics*, VII.

49. For Philip's questions to the University see Paul F. Crawford, 'The University of Paris and the Trial of the Templars', in *MO*, 3, pp. 115–22.

50. Sophia Menache, 'Contemporary Attitudes Concerning the Templars' Affair: Propaganda's Fiasco?', *Journal of Medieval History*, 8 (1982), 135–47.

51. Barber, *Trial of the Templars*, pp. 116–26; Menache, *Clement V*, p. 224–5; Frale, 'The Chinon Chart' 127.

52. Barber, *Trial of the Templars*, pp. 126–49: on Molay, see pp. 143–5, 147–9.

53. Barber, *Trial of the Templars*, pp. 149–52, 175–82.

54. Barber, *Trial of the Templars*, pp. 146, 150–63, 173, 182; Elena Bellomo, *The Templar Order in North-west Italy (1142–c.1330)* (Leiden: Brill, 2008), pp. 206–7.

55. On the Council of Vienne and its aftermath, see Menache, *Clement V*, pp. 235–9; Barber, *Trial of the Templars*, pp. 259–70; Jordan, *Unceasing Strife, Unending Fear*, pp. 40–55.

56. *La chronique métrique attribuée à Geffroy de Paris*, ed. Armel Diverrès (Paris: Société d'Édition Les Belles Lettres, 1956), lines 5691–5740, 5758–62, 5767–70.

57. For a survey of possible motivations for Philip IV, see Barber, *New Knighthood*, pp. 295–301; Barber, 'Trial of the Templars Revisited'; Forey, *The Military Orders*, pp. 235–9. See also Ignacio de la Torre, 'The Monetary Fluctuations that Seriously Damaged Philip IV's Kingdom, and Their Relevance to the Arrest of the Templars', in *Debate on the Trial of the Templars*, ed. Burgtorf, Crawford and Nicholson; Alain Provost, 'On the Margin of the Templars' Trial: the Case of Bishop Guichard of Troyes', in ibid.; Bernard Schotte, 'Fighting the King of France: Templars and Hospitallers in the Flemish Rebellion of 1302', in ibid.; James Given, 'Chasing Phantoms: Philip IV and the Fantastic', in *Heresy and the Persecuting Society in the Middle Ages: Essays on the Work of R.I. Moore*, ed. Michael Frassetto (Leiden: Brill, 2006).

58. Schein, *Fideles crucis*, p. 145 and note 10.

59. See, for instance, Malcolm Barber, 'Lepers, Jews and Moslems: the Plot to Overthrow Christendom in 1321', *History*, 66 (1981), 1–17; repr. in his *Crusaders and Heretics*, article 4; see also his 'The Pastoureaux of 1320', *Journal of Ecclesiastical History*, 32 (1981), 143–66, repr. in his *Crusaders and Heretics*, article 5.

60. Robert Lerner, *The Heresy of the Free Spirit in the Later Middle Ages* (Notre Dame and London: Notre Dame University Press, 1972), pp. 71–8. For the text, see Marguerite Porete, *Le Mirouer des simples ames*, ed. Romana Guarnieri, Corpus Christianorum Continuatio Medievalis, 69 (Turnholt: Brepols, 1986). Translations of Marguerite's work into English include: Marguerite Porete, *The Mirror of Simple Souls*, trans. Ellen L. Babinsky (New York: Paulist Press, 1993); trans. Charles Crawford with intro. by Anne L. Barstow (New York: Crossroad, 1990); and trans. Edmund Colledge, J. C. Marler and Judith Grant (Notre Dame and London: Notre Dame University

Press, 1999). For studies, see also, for instance: Lambert, *Medieval Heresy*, pp. 181–8, esp. p. 184; Robert Lerner, 'The Angel of Philadelphia in the reign of Philip the Fair: the Case of Guiard de Cressonart,' in *Order and Innovation in the Middle Ages: Essays in Honour of Joseph R. Strayer*, ed. William Jordan et al. (Princeton: Princeton University Press, 1976); Michael G. Sargent, 'The Annihilation of Marguerite Porete', *Viator*, 28 (1997), 253–79; Jordan, *Unceasing Strife, Unending Fear*, pp. 32–6.

61. *Papsttum*, vol. 2, pp. 89–90, no. 60, p. 51, no. 34, pp. 116–19, no. 75.

62. For this see Barber, *New Knighthood*, p. 289.

63. What follows is based mainly on Bulst-Thiele, 'Das Prozess'.

64. Clarence Perkins, 'The Trial of the Knights Templars in England', *English Historical Review*, 24 (1909), 432–47; Nicholson, *Knights Templar on Trial*.

65. Barber, *Trial of the Templars*, pp. 250–2.

66. Barber, *Trial of the Templars*, pp. 241–50; Elena Bellomo, 'Rinaldo da Concorezzo, Archbishop of Ravenna, and the Trial of the Templars in North Italy', in *The Debate on the Trial of the Templars*, ed. Burgtorf, Crawford and Nicholson.

67. Alan Forey, *The Fall of the Templars in the Crown of Aragon* (Aldershot: Ashgate, 2001).

68. Philippe Josserand, *Église et pouvoir dans la Péninsule Ibérique: les orders militaries dans le royaume de Castile (1252–1369)* (Madrid: Casa de Velázquez, 2004), pp. 50–60.

69. Clive Porro, 'Reassessing the Dissolution of the Templars: King Dinis and their Suppression in Portugal', in *The Debate on the Trial of the Templars*, ed. Burgtorf, Crawford and Nicholson (forthcomng).

70. Edbury, *Kingdom of Cyprus*, pp. 125, 129–30, 136; *Chronique d'Amadi*, pp. 360, 392, 395, 397–8. On the trial of the Templars in Cyprus see also *Trial of the Templars in Cyprus*; Barber, *Trial of the Templars*, pp. 252–8; Bulst-Thiele, 'Das Prozess', p. 393.

71. Anthony Luttrell, 'Gli Ospitalieri e l'eredità dei Templari, 1305–1378', in *I Templari: Mito e Storia*, ed. Minnucci and Sardi, pp. 67–86; repr. in his *The Hospitallers of Rhodes and their Mediterranean World*, article 3: summarized by Barber in *New Knighthood*, p. 309.

72. Clarence Perkins, 'The Wealth of the Templars in England and the Disposition of it after their dissolution', *American Historical Review*, 15 (1910), 252–63; Schüpferling, *Der Tempelherren-orden in Deutschland*, pp. 240–1.

73. Luis García-Guijarro Ramos, 'Los Origenes de la Orden de Montesa', in *Las Órdenes Militares en el Mediterráneo Occidental (s.XII–XVIII)* (Madrid: Casa de Velázquez, 1989), pp. 69–83; E. Guinot Rodríguez, 'La Fundación de la Orden Militar de Santa María de Montesa', *Saitabi*, 35 (1985), 75–86. I am indebted to Professor Luis García-Guijarro Ramos for providing me with copies of these articles. For information on the Order of Christ in English, see, for example, P. E. Russell, 'Prince Henry the Navigator', *Diamente*, 11 (1960), 3–30, here 13, 14, 16, 21: repr. in his *Portugal, Spain and the African Atlantic, 1343–1490: Chivalry and Crusade from John of Gaunt to Henry the Navigator* (Aldershot: Variorum, 1995), article 11; idem, 'Prince Henry and the Necessary End', *Studies in the Portuguese Discoveries I. Proceedings of the First Colloquium of the Centre for the Study of the Portuguese Discoveries*, ed. T. F. Earle and S. Parkinson (Warminster: Aris and Phillips Ltd., 1992), pp. 1–15, here 4, 6; reprinted in his his *Portugal, Spain and the African Atlantic*, article 17; Paula Pinto Costa and António Pestana de Vasconcelos, 'Christ, Santiago and Avis: an Approach to the Rules of the Portuguese Military Orders in the Late Middle Ages', *MO*, 2, pp. 251–7, here p. 257. See also Fernández-Armesto, *Before Columbus*, p. 187.

Notes to Chapter 9: Conclusion

1. Edward II complained to the sheriff of York, 4 January 1311, that Templars were still wandering freely: *Foedera*, ed. Rymer and Sanderson, vol. 2.1, p. 125.
2. *Papsttum*, vol. 2, pp. 226–7, no. 121.
3. Barber, *New Knighthood*, p. 1.
4. Rosalind Hill, 'Fourpenny retirement: the Yorkshire Templars in the fourteenth century', in *The Church and Wealth*, ed. W. J. Sheils and Diane Wood, *Studies in Church History*, 24 (1987), pp. 123–8.
5. For a study see Ansgar Konrad Wildermann, *Die Beurteilung des Templerprozesses bis zum 17. Jahrhundert* (Freiburg: Universität Freiburg, 1971); and see Menache, 'Contemporary Attitudes'.
6. *Chronica monasterii S. Albani. Thomas Walsingham, quondam monachi S. Albani, Historia anglicana*, ed. Henry Thomas Riley, RS 28, 2 vols (London: Longman, 1863–4), vol. 1, p. 127.
7. Nicholson, *Love, War and the Grail*, pp. 231–2; Selwood, *Knights of the Cloister*, p. 5 and note 13.

8. Bernard Schotte, 'Fighting the King of France: Templars and Hospitallers in the Flemish rebellion of 1302', in *Debate on the Trial of the Templars (1307–2007)*, ed. Burgtorf, Crawford and Nicholson (forthcoming).

9. Joanot Martorell, Martí Joan de Galba, *Tirant lo Blanc*, ed. Marti de Riquer and Maria Josepa Gallofré, 2nd edn, 2 vols (Barcelona: Edicions 62, 1985), ch. 98, vol. 1, pp. 159–60. For an English translation, see David H. Rosenthal, *Tirant lo Blanc* (London: Macmillan, 1984).

10. Nicholson, *Love, War and the Grail*, pp. 102–83.

11. Barber, *New Knighthood*, pp. 314–34; Barber, 'The Templars and the Turin Shroud'; Partner, *Knights Templar and their Myth*; John Walker, 'The Templars are Everywhere': An Examination of the Myths behind Templar Survival after 1307', in *Debate on the Trial of the Templars (1307–2007)*, ed. Burgtorf, Crawford and Nicholson (forthcoming); Sharan Newman, *The Real History Behind the Templars* (New York: Berkley, 2007); Evelyn Lord, *The Knights Templar in Britain* (Harlow: Longman, 2002), pp. 207–23; Evelyn Lord, *The Templar's Curse* (Harlow: Longman, 2007), pp. 157–77.

12. Partner, *Knights Templar and their Myth*, pp. 91–4.

13. Thomas Fuller, *The Historie of the Holy Warre* (Cambridge: Thomas Buck, 1639), Bk 5, ch. 3, p. 233.

14. Partner, *Knights Templar and their Myth*, pp. 110–34.

15. For images of the Templars in the Romantic movement of the eighteenth and nineteenth centuries, see Partner, *Knights Templar and their Myth*, pp. 156–68; Barber, *New Knighthood*, pp. 323–30.

16. Partner, *Knights Templar and their Myth*, pp. 110–36, 145–9; Elizabeth Siberry, 'Victorian Perceptions of the Military Orders', in *MO*, 1, pp. 365–72: here pp. 366–8.

17. George Macdonald, *Phantastes and Lilith*, ed. C. S. Lewis (London: Victor Gollanz, 1962), pp. 173–5.

18. M. J. James, 'Oh Whistle, and I'll Come to You, My Lad', in *Casting the Runes and Other Ghost Stories*, ed. Michael Cox (Oxford: Oxford University Press, 1987), pp. 57–77, quotation at p. 70.

19. Barber, *New Knighthood*, p. 318.

20. Partner, *Knights Templar and their Myth*, pp. 140–52. On Gnosticism and pagan and Christian reactions to it, see Hans Jones, *The Gnostic Religion: The Message of the Alien God and the Beginnings of Christianity*, 2nd edn (Boston: Beacon Press, 1963), pp. 253–4, 262–5, 266–83.

21. Partner, *Knights Templar and their Myth*, p. 141. For the legends of the Holy Grail see my *Love, War and the Grail*, pp. 102–83.

22. Partner, *Murdered Magicians*, pp. 170–2.

23. For further discussion, see the works in note 11 to this chapter.

24. Joseph H. Brown, *A Romantic Crusade: Being Interesting Sidelights in the History of the International Order of Good Templars in England* (Birmingham: Templar Printing Works, 1951), p. 7; quotations from Louisa May Alcott, *Jack and Jill* (Boston, MA: Roberts Bros, 1893; repr. Cleveland and New York: World Publishing Company, 1948), ch. 19, p. 267.

25. The Good Templars' working-class self-help ethos is set out clearly by William Hargreaves, *The Lost and Found! Or Who is the Heir?* (New York: National Temperance Society, 1901); see also David M. Fahey, *The Collected Writings of Jessie Forsyth, 1847–1937: The Good Templars and Temperance Reform on Three Continents* (Lampeter: Edwin Mellen Press, 1988), pp. 11–14; for the quotation see Alcott, *Jack and Jill*, ch. 19, p. 266.

26. For the first women members of the Order see Isaac Newton Pierce and Silvanus Phillips Thompson, *History of the Independent Order of Good Templars* (Birmingham: Grand Lodge of England, 1873), pp. 16–17. See Fahey, *Collected Writings of Jessie Forsyth*, pp. 7–8, 28–9, 55–7; see also Mrs M'Kinnon, quoted by T. Honeyman, *Good Templary in Scotland: its Work and Workers, 1869–1894* (Glasgow: Grand Lodge of Scotland, 1894), p. 11.

27. Fahey, *Collected Writings of Jessie Forsyth*, p. 24; cf. Brown, *A Romantic Crusade*, p. 7 (the British view); John B. Collings, *A Concise History of Good Templary in England, 1868–1895* (Birmingham: Grand Lodge Offices, n.d. [1895]), p. 6.

28. As stated on the organization's website, http://www.iogt.org/index.asp

29. London, The National Archives (TNA): Public Record Office, T 220/1165 (Israel Custodian of Enemy Property: German Templar affairs, 1947–48), pp. 151–2.

30. TNA, T 220/1165, pp. 28, 41, 59–61, 90, 91,141, 192; TNA, T 220/1169, pp. 30, 49, 60–3, etc. See also Roger Wettenhall, 'The Templars and Australia: Crusading Orders and a Statutory Authority', *Australian Studies*, 16 (2001), 131–50, here 143–5: my thanks to Dr Bill Jones for drawing this last to my attention.

31. Wettenhall, 'Templars and Australia', 147.

32. Margaret Lane, *Edgar Wallace: The Biography of a Phenomenon* (London: William Heinemann, 1939), pp. 38–9, 41–2, 47–50, 53; Edgar Wallace, *Angel Esquire* (London: Arrowsmith, 1908; repr. Oxford: Tallis, 1966), ch. 3, p. 21; idem, *The Hand of Power* (London: John Long, 1927), ch. 8, p. 40; idem, *White Face* (London: Hodder and Stoughton, 1930, rev. edn, 1966), ch. 5, p. 38, ch. 6, p. 40.

33. Jerome K. Jerome, *Three Men in a Boat, to Say Nothing of the Dog!* (London: Dent, 1889; repr. Harmondsworth: Penguin, 1963), ch. 13, p. 120.

34. John Meade Falkner, *The Nebuly Coat* (London: Edward Arnold, 1903; repr. Oxford: Oxford University Press, 1988), p. 354.

35. Rudyard Kipling, 'They', published in his *Traffics and Discoveries* (London, 1904); repr. *Great Tales of Terror and the Supernatural*, ed. Herbert A. Wise and Phyllis Fraser (London: Hammond and Hammond, 1957, 5th edn 1966), here p. 567.

36. Leslie Charteris, *Knight Templar* (London: Hodder and Stoughton, 1930; repr as *The Avenging Saint*, 1960), ch. 9.1, p. 110.

37. Leslie Charteris, *The Saint Overboard* (London: Hodder and Stoughton, 1936), ch. 7, p. 182.

38. Leslie Charteris, *Vendetta for the Saint* (London: Hodder and Stoughton, 1964), ch. 2.4, p. 48.

39. Ibid., ch. 4, p. 76.

FURTHER READING

Full details of the sources used for this book can be found in the notes. The following list concentrates on works in English.

General

Barber, Malcolm, *The Trial of the Templars*, 2nd edn (Cambridge: Cambridge University Press, 2006).

——, *The New Knighthood: A History of the Order of the Temple* (Cambridge: Cambridge University Press, 1994).

——, *Crusaders and Heretics, 12th–14th Centuries* (Aldershot: Variorum, 1995).

Burgtorf, Jochen, *The Central Convent of Hospitallers and Templars: History, Organization, and Personnel (1099/1120– 1310)* (Leiden: Brill, 2008).

Demurger, Alain, *Les Templiers: une chevalerie chrétienne au moyen âge* (Paris: Seuil, 2005).

Forey, Alan J., *The Military Orders from the Twelfth to the Early Fourteenth Centuries* (Basingstoke: Macmillan, 1992).

——, *Military Orders and Crusades* (Aldershot: Variorum, 1994).

Nicholson, Helen, *Templars, Hospitallers and Teutonic Knights: Images of the Military Orders, 1128–1291* (Leicester: Leicester University Press, 1993).

——, *Love, War and the Grail: Templars, Hospitallers and Teutonic*

Knights in Medieval Epic and Romance, 1150–1500 (Leiden: Brill, 2000).

Partner, Peter, *The Knights Templar and their Myth* (Rochester, VT: Destiny Books, 1990).

The Templars in the Latin East

Boas, Adrian J., *Archaeology of the Military Orders: A Survey of the Urban Centres, Rural Settlement and Castles of the Military Orders in the Latin East (c.1120–1291)* (London: Routledge, 2006).

Boase, T. S. R., *The Cilician Kingdom of Armenia* (Edinburgh: Scottish Academic Press, 1978).

Johns, C. N., *Pilgrim's Castle ('Atlit), David's Tower (Jerusalem) and Qal'at ar-Rabal ('Ajlun)*, ed. Denys Pringle (Aldershot: Ashgate, 1997).

Kennedy, Hugh, *Crusader Castles* (Cambridge: Cambridge University Press, 1994).

Marshall, Christopher, *Warfare in the Latin East, 1192–1291* (Cambridge: Cambridge University Press, 1992).

Smail, R. C., *Crusading Warfare, 1097–1193*, 2nd edn with a new bibliographical introduction by Christopher Marshall (Cambridge: Cambridge University Press, 1995).

The Templars in the West

Bellomo, Elena, *The Templar Order in North-west Italy (1142-c.1330)* (Leiden: Brill, 2008).

Forey, Alan J., *The Templars in the Corona de Aragón* (London: Oxford University Press, 1973).

——, *The Fall of the Templars in the Crown of Aragon* (Aldershot: Ashgate, 2001).

Gooder, Eileen A., *Temple Balsall: The Warwickshire Preceptory of the Templars and their Fate* (Chichester: Phillimore, 1995).

Selwood, Dominic, *Knights of the Cloister: Templars and Hospitallers in Central-Southern Occitania c.1100-c.1300* (Boydell: Woodbridge, 1999).

Major primary sources translated into English

Chronicle of the Third Crusade: A Translation of the Itinerarium peregrinorum et gesta regis Ricardi, trans. Helen Nicholson (Aldershot: Ashgate, 1997).

Crusader Syria in the Thirteenth Century: The Rothelin Continuation of the History of William of Tyre with part of the Eracles or Acre Text, trans. Janet Shirley (Aldershot: Ashgate, 1999).

The Conquest of Jerusalem and the Third Crusade: Sources in Translation, trans. Peter W. Edbury (Aldershot: Ashgate, 1996).

Jean de Joinville, in Joinville and Villehardouin, *Chronicles of the Crusades*, trans. M. R. B. Shaw (Harmondsworth: Penguin, 1963).

Jerusalem Pilgrimage 1099–1185, ed. John Wilkinson, J. Hill and W. F. Ryan, Hakluyt Society 2nd series, 167 (1988).

Matthew Paris, *Matthew Paris's English history, from the year 1235 to 1273*, translated from the Latin by J. A. Giles, 3 vols (London: G. Bell, 1889–93) – a translation of the *Chronica majora* from 1235 to the end, and the continuation.

——, *The Flowers of History, especially such as relate to the affairs of Britain. From the beginning of the world to the year 1307: collected by Matthew of Westminster*, translated from the original by C. D. Yonge, 2 vols (London: Henry G. Bohn, 1853) – a translation of Matthew Paris's *Flores historiarum* and its sequels.

Odo of Deuil, *De profectione Ludovici VII in orientem: The Journey of Louis VII to the East*, ed. and trans. Virginia G. Berry (New York: W.W. Norton, 1965).

Oliver of Paderborn, 'The capture of Damietta', in *Christian Society and the Crusaders, 1198–1229: Sources in Translation, Including 'The capture of Damietta' by Oliver of Paderborn*, trans. John J. Gavigan, ed. Edward Peters (Philadelphia: University of Pennsylvania Press, 1971).

Roger of Wendover, *Flowers of History: Comprising the History of England ... Formerly ascribed to Matthew Paris*, trans. from the Latin by J. A. Giles, 2 vols (London: Bohn, 1849) – a translation of Roger of Wendover's *Flores historiarum*.

The Rule of the Templars: The French Text of the Rule of the Order of the Temple, trans. J. M. Upton-Ward (Woodbridge: Boydell and Brewer, 1992).

The 'Templar of Tyre': Part III of the 'Deeds of the Cypriots', trans. Paul Crawford (Aldershot: Ashgate, 2003).

The Trial of the Templars in Cyprus: A Complete English Edition, trans. Anne Gilmour-Bryson (Leiden: Brill, 1998).

Usāmah ibn Munqidh, 'Memoirs', in *An Arab-Syrian Gentleman and Warrior in the Period of the Crusades: Memoirs of Usāmah ibn-*

Munqidh, trans. Philip K. Hitti (repr. Princeton: Princeton University Press, 1987).

Walter Map, *De nugis curialium*, ed. and trans. M. R. James, C. N. L. Brooke and R. A. B. Mynors (Oxford: Oxford University Press, 1983).

William, Archbishop of Tyre, *A History of Deeds Done Beyond the Sea*, trans. E. A. Babcock and A. C. Krey, 2 vols (repr. New York: Octagon Books, 1976).

Collections of essays on Crusades and Military Orders

Autour de la première croisade. Actes du colloque de la Society for the Study of the Crusades and the Latin East: Clermont-Ferrand, 22–25 juin 1995, ed. Michel Balard (Paris: Publications de la Sorbonne, 1996).

Dei gesta per Francos: Études sur les croisades dédiées à Jean Richard – Crusade Studies in Honour of Jean Richard, ed. Michel Balard, Benjamin Z. Kedar and Jonathan Riley-Smith (Aldershot: Ashgate, 2001).

The Horns of Hattin, ed. Benjamin Z. Kedar (Jerusalem: Yad Izhak Ben-Zvi, and London: Variorum, 1992).

International Mobility in the Military Orders (Twelfth to Fifteenth Centuries): Travelling on Christ's Business, ed. Jochen Burgtorf and Helen Nicholson (Cardiff: University of Wales Press, 2006).

The Military Orders: Fighting for the Faith and Caring for the Sick, ed. Malcolm Barber (Aldershot: Ashgate, 1994).

The Military Orders. Vol. 2: *Welfare and Warfare*, ed. Helen Nicholson (Aldershot: Ashgate, 1998).

The Military Orders. Vol. 3: *History and Heritage*, ed. Victor Mallia-Milanes (Aldershot: Ashgate, 2008).

The Military Orders. Vol. 4: *On Land and by Sea*, ed. Judi Upton-Ward (Aldershot: Ashgate, 2008)

The Second Crusade and the Cistercians, ed. Michael Gervers (New York: St Martin's Press, 1992).

INDEX

Note: page numbers in *italic* refer to illustrations or examples. Where more than one page number is listed against a heading, page numbers in **bold** indicate significant treatment of a subject. Some subheadings have been placed in chronological order.

The following abbreviations have been used:

Abp. – archbishop; Bp. – bishop; Ct. – count; K. – king; M. – Master; Q. – queen; W–wife